THE BURROWS-WHEELER TRANSFORM:
Data Compression, Suffix Arrays, and Pattern Matching

T0138061

THE BURROWS-WHEELER TRANSFORM:
Data Compression, Suffix Arrays, and Pattern Matching

Donald Adjeroh
West Virginia University

Tim Bell
University of Canterbury

Amar Mukherjee
University of Central Florida

 Springer

Donald Adjeroh
West Virginia University
Morgantown, WV 26506
USA
adjeroh@csee.wvu.edu

Amar Mukherjee
University of Central Florida
Orlando, FL 32816-2362
USA
amar@eecs.ucf.edu

Tim Bell
University of Canterbury
Christchurch
New Zealand
tim.bell@canterbury.ac.nz

The Burrows-Wheeler Transform: Data Compression, Suffix Arrays, and Pattern Matching
Donald Adjeroh, Tim Bell, and Amar Mukherjee

ISBN-13: 978-1-4419-4628-7   e-ISBN-13: 978-0-387-78909-5

Printed on acid-free paper.

9 8 7 6 5 4 3 2 1

springer.com

Preface

The Burrows-Wheeler Transform is one of the best lossless compression methods available. It is an intriguing — even puzzling — approach to squeezing redundancy out of data, it has an interesting history, and it has applications well beyond its original purpose as a compression method. It is a relatively late addition to the compression canon, and hence our motivation to write this book, looking at the method in detail, bringing together the threads that led to its discovery and development, and speculating on what future ideas might grow out of it.

The book is aimed at a wide audience, ranging from those interested in learning a little more than the short descriptions of the BWT given in standard texts, through to those whose research is building on what we know about compression and pattern matching. The first few chapters are a careful description suitable for readers with an elementary computer science background (and these chapters have been used in undergraduate courses), but later chapters collect a wide range of detailed developments, some of which are built on advanced concepts from a range of computer science topics (for example, some of the advanced material has been used in a graduate computer science course in string algorithms). Some of the later explanations require some mathematical sophistication, but most should be accessible to those with a broad background in computer science.

We have aimed to provide a detailed introduction to the current state of knowledge about the Burrows-Wheeler Transform. This ranges from explanations and examples of how the transform works, through analyzing the theoretical performance of the transform from various view points, to considering issues relevant to implementing it on "real" systems. Each chapter (except the last one) contains a "further reading" section to guide the reader around the large collection of literature that has explored the BWT in detail, and Appendix B points to ongoing research.

An important theme in this book is pattern matching and text indexing using the BWT. Because the transformed text contains a sorted version of the original text, it has considerable potential to help with locating patterns, and we look in detail at a number of variations that have been proposed and evaluated.

The BWT literature uses a variety of notation for the various structures used in the transform. Where possible we have tried to use standard notation, but unfortunately some key notations conflict with those used in the standard pattern matching literature, and so we have chosen to coin some new notations to avoid having the same notation with two meanings, at times in the same paragraph! Appendix A gives a summary of the notation used to avoid any confusion.

The BWT continues to be actively researched, and this book is merely a milestone in its history. Appendix B gives links to web sites that will be worth watching for future developments of the BWT and related systems.

We are also aware that despite some excellent help with checking this book, it will contain errors and require updates. An errata site is available at http://www.cosc.canterbury.ac.nz/tim.bell/bwt/. We welcome feedback on the book, and this can be sent to the authors via the contact details on this web site.

Acknowledgements

Many people have contributed to this book either directly or indirectly.

We have to first acknowledge the late David Wheeler, who conceived the idea on which this entire book is based. In researching the background of the BWT it has been inspiring to discover the role that this modest individual has played in making and influencing the history of computing in many areas, not just in data compression. Michael Burrows played an important role in developing and publishing the transform, and we have been very fortunate to receive valuable input from him while writing this book, including his insight into implementing the BWT on current and upcoming computer technology. We have also appreciated discussions with Dr. Joyce Wheeler, David Wheeler's wife, who has been able to help us with details of the history relating to the development of the transform. The photo of David Wheeler in Figure 1.3 was taken by Chris Hadley (University of Cambridge Computer Laboratory), and kindly supplied by Joyce Wheeler.

We also particularly wish to thank Peter Fenwick, who has been heavily involved in this book from the early stages of planning through to the final stages of checking. He has been a fount of wisdom, insight and information stemming from his long history of work on the Burrows-Wheeler Transform.

Our students who have worked with us on the BWT have our sincere thanks for a lot of detailed work and many useful discussions. We are particularly grateful to Andrew Firth, who performed an extensive comparison of BWT-based searching methods. Much of Chapter 7 draws on this work, and we are grateful for his permission to use it. Jie Lin, Fei Nan, Matt Powell, Ravi Vijaya Satya, Tao Tao, Nan Zhang and Yong Zhang have also contributed a number of ideas that appear in this text. A preliminary version of some chapters in this book have been used in a graduate course on string algorithms, and we are grateful to the students for their comments and suggestions.

We have been fortunate to have many members of the BWT research community assist with advice and helping check parts of the book, particularly Paolo Ferragina, Craig Nevill-Manning, Giovanni Manzini, Alistair Moffat, Bill Smyth, Rossano Venturini, and Ian Witten. We also thank Ziya Arnavut, Mitsuharu Arimura and Kunihiko Sadakane, for providing us requested copies of their papers.

Many other people have contributed to practical aspects of this work: Jay Holland has lent us his sharp eye to assist with proof-reading — we appreciate his careful checking, and any errors are likely to have been introduced after he checked the text! Isaac Freeman has worked extensively on drawing and editing the figures for us; Julie Faris has helped with administrative aspects, Denise Tjon Ket Tjong with computer system support and help with technical issues, and Stacey Mickelbart has provided technical writing assistance. Amy Brais, our editor at Springer, has been most supportive in guiding us through the process of putting the book together.

Our respective universities, West Virginia University, the University of Canterbury, and the University of Central Florida have been very supportive of this project. Some of this work has been done while traveling, and we particularly acknowledge the Huazhong University of Science and Technology in Wuhan, China, which provided an excellent environment for writing.

The support from National Science Foundation grants (9977336, 0207819, 0312724, 0228370, 0312484) on data compression and compressed-domain pattern matching helped develop our interest in the Burrows-Wheeler Transform. A DOE CAREER grant (DE-FG02-02ER25541) provided support for studying the use of the BWT in biological sequence analysis. The NSF grant on "U.S., New Zealand and Australia Collaboration on Research on Data Compression" (0331188, 0331896) brought the authors of this book together in New Zealand to conceive and brainstorm this book.

The people who have made the greatest contribution, of course, are our families, who have released us for many long hours to write, re-write and fine tune this book. We are grateful to our wives, Leonie, Judith and Pampa, and other family members (some of whom have supported us for decades, and others who are only just about to learn what it means to have an academic for a parent), for their love and moral support throughout the project: Donald-Patrick (who was born during the writing of the book), Elise-Cindel, Andrew, Michael, Paula, Mita, Cecilia, Don and Nuella.

Morgantown, West Virginia
Christchurch, New Zealand
Orlando, Florida

Don Adjeroh
Tim Bell
Amar Mukherjee

Contents

1 Introduction 1
  1.1 An example of a Burrows-Wheeler Transform 3
  1.2 Genesis of the Burrows-Wheeler Transform 5
  1.3 Transformation 8
  1.4 Permutation 11
  1.5 Recency 12
  1.6 Pattern matching 13
  1.7 Organization of this book 14
  1.8 Further reading 16

2 How the Burrows-Wheeler Transform works 19
  2.1 The forward Burrows-Wheeler Transform 19
  2.2 The reverse Burrows-Wheeler Transform 23
  2.3 Special cases 29
  2.4 Further reading 31

3 Coders for the Burrows-Wheeler Transform 33
  3.1 Entropy coding 33
  3.2 Run-length and arithmetic coder 38
  3.3 Move-to-front lists 39
  3.4 Frequency counting methods 42
  3.5 Inversion Frequencies (IF) 43
  3.6 Distance coding 44
  3.7 Wavelet trees 45
  3.8 Other permutations 46
  3.9 Block size 47
  3.10 Further reading 48

4 Suffix trees and suffix arrays 51
  4.1 Suffix Trees 51
      4.1.1 Basic notations and definitions 52

4.1.2   Construction of a suffix tree 54
4.1.3   Ukkonen's suffix tree algorithm 57
4.1.4   From implicit suffix tree to true suffix tree 64
4.1.5   Farach's recursive construction 66
4.1.6   Generalized suffix trees 73
4.1.7   Implementation issues 74
4.2   Suffix arrays 75
4.2.1   Traditional string sorting 76
4.2.2   Suffix arrays via suffix trees 78
4.2.3   Manber-Myers suffix sorting algorithm 78
4.2.4   Linear-time direct suffix sorting 81
4.3   Space issues in suffix trees and suffix arrays 85
4.4   Further reading 88

5   **Analysis of the Burrows-Wheeler Transform** 91
5.1   The BWT, suffix trees and suffix arrays 93
5.2   Computational complexity 95
5.2.1   BWT first stage — the transform 95
5.2.2   BWT second stage — coding the transformed text..... 95
5.3   BWT context clustering property 97
5.3.1   Context trees 97
5.3.2   Estimation using context trees 100
5.3.3   BWT and context trees 103
5.4   Analysis of BWT output 104
5.4.1   Theoretical distribution of BWT output 104
5.4.2   Empirical distribution of BWT output 105
5.5   Analysis of BWT compression performance 119
5.5.1   Definitions and notation 120
5.5.2   Performance using recency ranking 123
5.5.3   Performance without LGT 129
5.5.4   Performance using piecewise constant parameters 132
5.5.5   Performance on general sources via empirical entropy .. 133
5.6   Relationship with other compression schemes 135
5.6.1   Context-based schemes 135
5.6.2   Symbol ranking schemes 148
5.7   Further reading 149

6   **Variants of the Burrows-Wheeler Transform** 153
6.1   The sort transform 154
6.1.1   Forward sort transform 154
6.1.2   Inverse sort transform 155
6.1.3   Performance of the sort transform 159
6.2   Lexical permutation sorting 163
6.2.1   Sorting permutations 164
6.2.2   Lexical permutation sorting algorithm 167

6.3 The extended BWT 168
     6.3.1 Sort order between strings 168
     6.3.2 Performing the extended BWT 169
     6.3.3 Inverting the transform 170
6.4 Sort-based context similarity measurement.................. 173
     6.4.1 Context similarity measurement and ranking.......... 173
     6.4.2 The prefix list data structure 175
     6.4.3 Relationship with the Burrows-Wheeler Transform..... 178
     6.4.4 Performance of the prefix list 180
6.5 Word-based compression 180
     6.5.1 General word-based compression 181
     6.5.2 Word-based Burrows-Wheeler Transform 183
6.6 Further reading 185

7 **Exact and approximate pattern matching**.................. 187
7.1 Exact pattern matching algorithms 188
     7.1.1 Brute force matching 189
     7.1.2 The Knuth-Morris-Pratt Algorithm 190
     7.1.3 The Boyer-Moore algorithm 195
     7.1.4 The Karp-Rabin algorithm 197
     7.1.5 The shift-and method 199
     7.1.6 Multiple pattern matching......................... 200
     7.1.7 Pattern matching with don't-care characters 204
7.2 Pattern matching using the Burrows-Wheeler Transform 207
     7.2.1 Boyer-Moore pattern matching using the BWT........ 209
     7.2.2 BWT-based exact pattern matching with binary search 209
     7.2.3 BWT-based exact pattern matching with suffix arrays . 214
     7.2.4 Pattern matching using the FM-index............... 215
     7.2.5 Algorithm improvements with overwritten arrays 220
7.3 Performance of BWT-based exact pattern matching.......... 221
     7.3.1 Compression performance 222
     7.3.2 Search performance............................... 224
     7.3.3 Array construction speeds 231
     7.3.4 Comparison with LZ-based compressed-domain
            pattern matching................................. 232
7.4 Approximate pattern matching 233
     7.4.1 Edit distance: dynamic programming formulation...... 234
     7.4.2 Edit graphs...................................... 236
     7.4.3 Local similarity 237
     7.4.4 The longest common subsequence problem............ 239
     7.4.5 String matching with k differences 244
     7.4.6 The k-mismatch problem using the BWT............ 247
     7.4.7 k-approximate matching using the BWT 253
7.5 Hardware algorithms for pattern matching................. 255
     7.5.1 An equivalent hardware algorithm 256

7.5.2   A brief review of other hardware algorithms 258
7.6   Conclusion 259
7.7   Further reading 260

8   Other applications of the Burrows-Wheeler Transform 265
8.1   Compressed suffix trees and compressed suffix arrays 266
      8.1.1   Compressed suffix trees 267
      8.1.2   Compressed suffix arrays 270
8.2   Compressed full-text indexing 275
      8.2.1   Full-text indexing using CSTs and CSAs 276
      8.2.2   Searching on compressed suffix trees 277
      8.2.3   Searching on compressed suffix arrays. 278
8.3   Bioinformatics and computational biology 278
      8.3.1   DNA sequence compression 279
      8.3.2   Analysis of repetition structures 280
      8.3.3   Whole-genome comparisons 281
      8.3.4   Genome annotation 282
      8.3.5   Distance measure between sequences and phylogeny ... 283
8.4   Test data compression 284
      8.4.1   Nature of test data 285
      8.4.2   BWT-based test data compression 286
8.5   Image compression, computer vision and machine translation . 287
      8.5.1   Image compression 287
      8.5.2   Shape matching 292
      8.5.3   Machine translation 294
8.6   Joint source-channel coding 296
      8.6.1   General source coding via channel coding............ 297
      8.6.2   BWT-based joint source-channel coding 298
8.7   Prediction and entropy estimation 299
8.8   Further reading 301

9   Conclusion 305

A   Notation 309

B   Ongoing work on the Burrows-Wheeler Transform 313
B.1   BWT-related web sites 313
B.2   Ph.D. theses relating to the Burrows-Wheeler Transform 314

References 317

Index 341

1

Introduction

The greatest masterpiece in literature is only a dictionary out of order.
Jean Cocteau

Here is a two word phrase in which the characters have been rearranged:
atd nrsoocimpsea. Can you work out what the two words are that contain
all these characters (including the space)? They could be comedian pastors,
but they aren't. Nor are they darpa economists, massacred potion, maniac
doorsteps or even scooped martians.

This puzzle is an example of the Burrows-Wheeler Transform (BWT),
which uses the intriguing idea of muddling (we prefer to call it permuting) the
letters in a document to make it easier to find a compact representation and to
perform other kinds of processing. What is amazing about the BWT is that
although there are 2,615,348,735,999 different ways to unmuddle the above
characters into possible anagrams, the Burrows-Wheeler Transform makes it
very easy to find the unique correct permutation very quickly.

The main point of permuting a text using the BWT is not to make it difficult to read, but to make it easy to compress. For example, for the following
line from Hamlet's famous soliloquy:

"To be or not to be: that is the question, whether tis nobler in the
mind to suffer the slings and arrows of outrageous fortune."

we get the transformed text:

"sdoosrtesrsefeeoe:nsrrtdn,r h onnhbhhbglfhuhnofu antttttw mltt bs
ioaiui Tttn i fne r eoeetraoguiwi e ao es e. urqstoo o"

Notice that many characters in the transformed text appear in runs, or very close to previous occurrences. For longer texts this is even more noticeable; here is a typical excerpt from a Burrows-Wheeler Transform of all of Shakespeare's Hamlet:

```
nnnnnnnnnnnnnnnnnnntnnnnnnnhnnngnnnnnnnnjnnnnnhdnnng
nnnnonnNnnnhhNnnnnnnnnntnnhnnnnnnnnnnnnnnnNnndnnnhnn
nnnNnnnnnnnnnnnnnnnnnnnnnonntnnNNnnnnnnnndngnnnnnnn
nnnnnnnNnnnnnnnngnnnnnnnnnnnnnnnnnnngnnnnnnnnonnnnnn
nnnNNnlnnnhnnnnnnnnnnntdbdnnrrmnnmnmnnnuoccpppppppdnr
rDolBbbdddodbbBddbbddbdBdbbdbdDddddBbbbbdDbubbdbdbB
```

This clustering of characters makes compression very easy. One simplistic way to code it would be to replace repeated characters with a number that says how many times it is repeated; for example, the first line above could be coded as:

```
19nt7nh3ng8nj5nhd3ng
```

In practice BWT coders use more sophisticated representations that take advantage of the mixture of frequently occurring characters (for example, the first four lines in the above example contain only 8 different characters, almost all of which are "n", "N", "h" or "g"). The point is that the transform makes the encoding task a lot simpler, and importantly, can give compression that is comparable with the very best lossless compression methods. Furthermore, it is generally faster than methods that give a similar amount of compression.

It has transpired that the BWT is useful for a lot more than compression because it contains an implicit sorted index of the input string. In this book we will review many of its other uses, especially for pattern-matching and full-text indexing, which leads to applications ranging from bioinformatics to machine translation.

The Burrows-Wheeler Transform method is often referred to as "block sorting", because it takes a *block* of text and permutes it. The main disadvantage of the block-wise approach is that it cannot process text character by character; it must read in a block (typically tens of kilobytes) and then compress it. This is not a limitation for most purposes, but it does rule out some applications that need to process data on-the-fly as it arrives. Another important point is that the text can be *sorted*; throughout this book we assume a unique ordering on the characters or symbols that are in the text so that substrings can be compared by the sorting algorithms. Most implementations work with a character set such as ASCII or 8-bit bytes, for which comparisons are trivial, but we shall see later that variations are possible where we take a more sophisticated approach to the ordering.

1.1 An example of a Burrows-Wheeler Transform

In this section we will give a simple example of how a text is transformed and reconstructed using the BWT. The method described here is for clarity of explanation, and in later chapters we will look at equivalent approaches that are a lot faster and simpler to implement, so don't be put off if it seems to be resource-hungry.

We will use a rather short block of text in this example: "aardvark$". The dollar sign is a sentinel, or end of string character, that we've added to simplify the explanation.

To generate the BWT, we list all nine rotations of the nine-character string, as shown in Figure 1.1a; that is, for every position in the string, we create a string of nine characters, wrapping around to the beginning if it runs off the end. The list is then sorted into lexical (dictionary) order (Figure 1.1b) (in this case we've assumed that $ comes at the start of the lexical ordering). The transform is now complete, and the last column (i.e. last character of each row from top to bottom) is the output (Figure 1.1c).

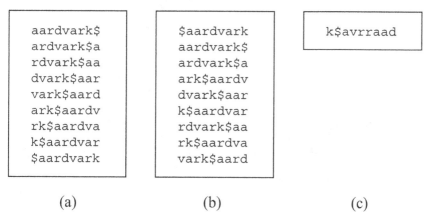

```
aardvark$          $aardvark          k$avrraad
ardvark$a          aardvark$
rdvark$aa          ardvark$a
dvark$aar          ark$aardv
vark$aard          dvark$aar
ark$aardv          k$aardvar
rk$aardva          rdvark$aa
k$aardvar          rk$aardva
$aardvark          vark$aard

   (a)                (b)                (c)
```

Fig. 1.1. Burrows-Wheeler Transform of the string "aardvark$": (a) all rotations of the text are listed; (b) the list is sorted; (c) the last column is extracted as the BWT

The transform is that simple; in fact, in practice it is even simpler, as the substrings are never created, but are simply stored as references to positions in the original string. The size of the transformed text is identical to the original, and contains exactly the same characters but in a different order. This might seem to have achieved nothing, but as we shall see, it makes the text much easier to compress because it has drawn together characters that occur in related contexts — that is, characters that precede the same substrings.

It might seem that decoding the transformed text would be very difficult; after all, how do you "unmuddle" a list when there is an exponential number of ways to do it? The amazing thing about the BWT is that the reverse transform not only exists, but it can be done efficiently. A key observation is that we can reconstruct the list in Figure 1.1b, one column at a time. Figure 1.2a reproduces the list that we wish to construct, with the columns labeled. Traditionally we use F and L to label the first and last columns respectively; the others have been numbered for reference.

$F2345678L$
$aardvark
aardvark$
ardvark$a
ark$aardv
dvark$aar
k$aardvar
rdvark$aa
rk$aardva
vark$aard

(a)

$F2345678L$	
	k
	$
	a
	v
	r
	r
	a
	a
	d

(b)

$F2345678L$	
$	k
a	$
a	a
a	v
d	r
k	r
r	a
r	a
v	d

(c)

LF		F2
k$		$a
$a		aa
aa		ar
va	sort	ar
rd		dv
rk		k$
ar		rd
ar		rk
dv		va

(d)   (e)

$F2345678L$	
$a	k
aa	$
ar	a
ar	v
dv	r
k$	r
rd	a
rk	a
va	d

(f)

$F2345678L$	
$aa	k
aar	$
ard	a
ark	v
dva	r
k$a	r
rdv	a
rk$	a
var	d

(g)

Fig. 1.2. Decoding the BWT: (a) the encoding information that we are trying to reconstruct; (b) the transformed BWT text in column L; (c) adding column F; (d) using L and F to extract all pairs of characters; (e) sorting the pairs; (f) adding the sorted pairs to the reconstruction; (g) adding sorted triples to the reconstruction

Column L is what the encoder sent to the decoder, so the reconstruction can start by filling column L (Figure 1.2b). Now observe that column F is simply all of the characters in the text in lexical order. Since the transformed text contains all of the characters, we can reproduce column F simply by sorting column L (Figure 1.2c).

Our next observation is that because of the wrap-around from the rotations used to generate the substrings, for a particular row, the character in column L must be followed by the one in column F in the original string. Thus we can find all pairs of characters in the original string by taking pairs from the last and then first columns (Figure 1.2d). If we sort these pairs (Figure 1.2e), they will give us the pairs in column 1 (F) and 2, and we now know three of the columns (Figure 1.2f).

Applying the wrap-around principle again, we can find all triples in the original text, sort them, and add them to the list (Figure 1.2g). We continue doing this until the whole list has been reproduced, giving us the information that the encoder had (Figure 1.2a). At this point it is trivial to read off the original string; we can take any row, and starting after the end-of-file symbol, read the characters, wrapping around at the end of the row.

This may seem like a lot of work to do the decoding. In practice most of the process just described is unnecessary and decoding can be done in $O(n)$ time by creating an auxiliary array that enables us to navigate around the transformed text. This is covered in detail in Chapter 2, but in the meantime, we will observe that the relationships just described mean that we can easily match the characters in columns L and F.

The transform that we have just described doesn't change the size of the file that has been transformed. However, when it is done to large files, we shall see that it makes the file a lot easier to compress because we end up with a very obvious clustering of characters.

1.2 Genesis of the Burrows-Wheeler Transform

The Burrows-Wheeler Transform is one of the most effective text compression methods to come out of the 20th century, yet its intriguing method of compression and its unusual history have meant that it was almost overlooked!

Data compression has turned out to be fundamental to getting things done on digital devices. Without MP3 files we couldn't download music or carry lots of songs in portable devices; without JPEG files digital cameras would only take a few shots before filling up and photos on web pages would take forever to load; and without the MPEG standard DVDs would only hold a few minutes of movies and the phrase "viral video" would never have been coined.

In this book we focus on *lossless* methods, which are able to decompress a file to exactly the same as it was before being compressed. However, many *lossy* methods (which are typically used for sound and images) rely on lossless methods in their final stage.

Compression on computers spans the second half of the 20th century. Shannon's ground-breaking paper on information theory is generally regarded as the foundation of compression systems (Shannon, 1948). The paper included a proposed coding method that has come to be known as Shannon-Fano coding, which was one of the earliest methods used to take advantage of some characters being more likely than others. Shannon-Fano coding is suboptimal, and it was one of Fano's students, David Huffman, who in 1952 published his well-known algorithm (Huffman, 1952), which became a stock technique and is still used today as a part of many kinds of compression system, including general-purpose lossless methods and systems for compressing audio and images. The next major improvements in compression performance came in the late 1970s, when Ziv and Lempel published the "LZ" methods which are still widely used in formats such as GIF and PNG images, as well as the ZIP and GZIP utilities (Ziv and Lempel, 1977, 1978). The LZ family of methods became popular because it gave excellent compression and yet was practical to run on computers at the time. By the time the 1980s arrived, Rissanen and Langdon (1979) had published a significant improvement on Huffman coding, called "Arithmetic Coding"[1]. This opened up a new way of looking at compression, and became the basis of a new wave of compression methods in the mid 1980s that used sophisticated models of text to achieve a new level of compression by "predicting" what the next character would be. At the time these methods were too resource intensive to be used as a utility, but they provided a new benchmark for compression performance. Of particular note was the PPM method, developed by Cleary and Witten (1984), and several subsequent variations that set new records for the amount of compression that could be achieved.

Arguably the last 20th century breakthrough in general purpose lossless compression methods was Burrows and Wheeler's enigmatic transform, the BWT. David Wheeler had come up with the transform as early as 1978, but it wasn't until 1994 that, with the help of Mike Burrows, the idea was turned into a practical data compression method, which was then published in a Digital Systems Research Center (Palo Alto) research report (Burrows and Wheeler, 1994). Their "block-sorting code", also dubbed the "Burrows-Wheeler Transform", left compression practitioners scratching their heads, as it involved rearranging the characters in a text before encoding, and then magically arranging them back in their original order in the decoder. The fact that the original can be re-created at all is somewhat astonishing, and their early work took some time to receive the recognition it deserved. Within a couple of years several authors and programmers had picked up the idea, apparently mainly through publications by Peter Fenwick (Fenwick, 1995b,c,

---

[1] Peter Elias had come up with the idea some time earlier, but apart from a brief mention in Abrahamson's 1963 book *Information Theory and Coding*, it did not get published as a feasible coding method until Rissanen and Langdon's paper appeared.

1996a,b) which led to Julian Seward's BZIP implementation. Around the same time there was a writeup by Mark Nelson in *Dr Dobb's Journal* (Nelson, 1996), and the BWT also appeared through informal channels such as on-line discussion groups.

Burrows and Wheeler have other significant achievements in the field of computing. David Wheeler (1927–2004) had a distinguished career, having worked on several early computers, including EDSAC which, in 1949, became the first stored program computer to be completed. Wheeler invented a method of calling closed subroutines which led to having a library of carefully tested subroutines, a concept that has been crucial for breaking down complexity in computer programming. Together with Maurice Wilkes and Stanley Gill, in 1951 he published the first book on digital computer programming[2]. He also did important work in cryptography, including the "Tiny Encryption Algorithm" (TEA), an encryption system that could be written in just eight lines of code, which made a mockery of US regulations that controlled the export of encryption algorithms — this one was small enough to memorize! Wheeler also designed and commissioned the first version of the Cambridge Ring, an experimental local network system based on a ring topology.

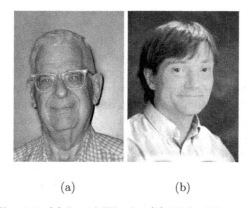

(a)   (b)

Fig. 1.3. (a) David Wheeler (b) Michael Burrows

His work on compression developed during his time as a research consultant at Bell Labs (Murray Hill, N.J.) in 1978 and 1983. He retired in 1994 (the same year that the seminal BWT paper was released). His distinctions include being a Fellow of the Royal Society (1981), and a Fellow of the ACM (1994).

Michael Burrows also has a high profile outside his contribution to the BWT. He is one of the main people who developed the AltaVista search

---

[2] *The Preparation of Programs for an Electronic Digital Computer*, published by Addison-Wesley Press, Cambridge.

engine in 1995, which represented the state of the art prior to the arrival of Google's search engine. He later worked for Microsoft, and in 2007 is a senior researcher working at Google on their distributed infrastructure. Burrows had been supervised by Wheeler in the mid-1980s doing a PhD at Cambridge, and then went to work at Digital in the US. Wheeler had invented the transform in the 1970s, but it wasn't until he visited Digital in Palo Alto and then worked remotely with Burrows by email in 1990 that it was finally written up as a compression method.

In the late 1990s BWT was still regarded as being too slow for many applications, but its compression performance became well understood. Wheeler's "bred" (block reduce) and "bexp" (block expand) programs provided a publicly available implementation of the BWT method that proved the concept, but it was Julian Seward's efficient implementation as a general purpose utility called BZIP in 1996 that established BWT as something that had practical utility. A new version of Seward's utility called BZIP2 is now widely used because on today's hardware it can compress large files at speeds that are quite acceptable for interaction, to a smaller size than other widely used general purpose methods. For example, the 4 Mbyte file "bible.txt" from the Canterbury corpus can be compressed by BZIP2 in about 2 seconds on a 2.4 GHz computer, and decompressed in about 1 second. The GZIP utility compresses about three times as fast (and decompresses an order of magnitude faster), but the GZIP file is 40% larger than the BZIP2 one. Interestingly, BZIP2 combines one of the most recent compression breakthroughs (BWT) with one of the first (Huffman coding).

By the late 1990s researchers began to realize that the BWT approach might be useful for more than just compressing text. Because the BWT happens to "sort" the text into alphabetical order, the permuted text has the added benefit of acting as a kind of dictionary for the original text. Traditionally an index and the compressed text would be stored separately, even though they contain effectively the same information. In this light, the BWT is an intermediate representation that is halfway between a text and an index; the original text can be reconstructed efficiently from it, yet sorted lists like the one shown in Figure 1.1b are ripe for binary searching, giving very fast searching for arbitrary fragments in the text.

In this book we explore this intriguing view of a transformed file as both the text and an index, and look at applications that exploit this. But first let's take a look at some key ideas behind the BWT: transformation, permutation, and recency.

1.3 Transformation

Suppose you had to calculate, in Roman numerals, the sum MCMXCIX + I. Perhaps you know a method for adding Roman numerals, but chances are that you would have transformed the problem into a more familiar notation: 1999

+ 1. The sum is now easily calculated, and the answer in Roman numerals is obtained by a reverse transform, as shown in Figure 1.4.

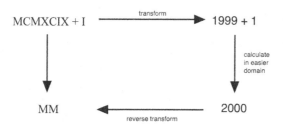

Fig. 1.4. Calculating MCMXCIX + I using a transform

Different representations have different strengths; Roman numerals might not seem that easy to work with, but they look impressive, and some say that they are used to show the dates in movie and TV credits to make it difficult for a casual viewer to determine how old the film is.

Transformations have long been put to more practical uses in engineering, to convert a representation to a "space" in which it is easier to work with. One of the best known is the Fourier transform, which converts a signal into the sum of a set of sine waves. In this format, it is easy to perform operations such as boosting the bass in an audio signal (just increase the amplitude of the low frequency sine waves), or to find areas in an image with a lot of detail (look for high frequency sine waves with a high amplitude).

Transformations related to the Fourier transform, especially the Discrete Cosine Transform (DCT), have long been used in lossy compression methods for audio and image compression, such as MP3 and JPEG. Viewing a signal as a sum of cosine waves makes it easy to compress because it is possible to decrease the level of detail stored, especially for components that are difficult to hear or see — in fact, some frequencies could even be eliminated. The information is also easy to decompress, as it is simply the sum of the frequency components.

Transforms open up new ways to manipulate and store data, in the same way as the language one is using can affect the way that we understand our world (the Sapir–Whorf hypothesis). Or more bluntly, when the only tool that you have is a hammer, every problem looks like a nail. A transformation gives us a new tool to solve a problem, a new language to describe what we can do with the data.

Generally a transform doesn't change the amount of data used to represent a signal; it just gives us a new way of looking at it. Here, any compression happens after the transformation, and is done either by exploiting patterns exposed by the transformation, or by using a less accurate representation for components in a way that is not likely to be perceived by a human.

The Burrows-Wheeler Transform was a breakthrough because it provided a reversible transformation for text that made it significantly easier to compress. There are many other reversible transformations that could be applied to a text — for example, the characters could be stored backwards, or the first two letters after each space could be transposed — but these don't help us to compress the text. The power of the BWT is that it pulls together related characters, in the same way that a Fourier transform separates out high-frequency components from low-frequency ones.

For example, Figure 1.5 shows a segment of a BWT-sorted file for Shakespeare's Hamlet. It is sorted into lexical order, starting at the first (F) column. Because each row of the table is generated by wrapping around the original text, the last (L) column is actually the character that comes *before* the one in the F column. So from the figure we can see that "ot " is normally preceded by n, but occasionally by h, g or j. It now becomes clear why we get so much repetition in the transformed file; the characters are clustered according to what words or phrases they are likely to precede — u is likely to precede estion, m or w are likely to precede ent, and so on. Some characters are very predictable — osencrantz and Guildenstern is always preceded by an R, while others are less so — est occurs in Hamlet preceded by every letter of the alphabet except a, o, q, v, x, y and z.

F	... L
ot look upon his like again. ...	n
ot look upon me; Lest with th ...	n
ot love on the wing,-- As I p ...	h
ot love your father; But that ...	n
ot made them well, they imita ...	n
ot madness That I have utter' ...	n
ot me'? Ros. To think, my lor ...	n
ot me; no, nor woman neither, ...	n
ot me? Ham. No, by the rood, ...	g
ot mend his pace with beating ...	n
ot mine own. Besides, to be d ...	n
ot mine. Ham. No, nor mine no ...	n
ot mock me, fellow-student. I ...	n
ot monstrous that this player ...	n
ot more like. Ham. But where ...	n
ot more native to the heart, ...	n
ot more ugly to the thing tha ...	n
ot more, my lord. Ham. Is not ...	j
ot move thus. Oph. You must s ...	n
ot much approve me.--Well, si ...	n

Fig. 1.5. Part of the BWT sorted list for Shakespeare's Hamlet

1.4 Permutation

Permutations are rearrangements of the order of symbols, such as the rearrangement of letters in anagrams which we have already mentioned (for example "eleven plus two" is an anagram of "twelve plus one"). Traditionally permutations don't allow the repetition of a symbol — in fact, a mathematical permutation is a subset of symbols taken from a set of distinct symbols. In the context of this book we are interested in rearrangements of a string that can contain duplicate characters.

If duplicates are not allowed then the number of permutations of n symbols is simply $n!$, the factorial of n. For example, the 6 characters abcdef can be arranged $6! = 720$ ways. Allowing duplicates reduces the number of permutations; in the extreme, a string such as aaaaaa which contains only one distinct character has only one permutation. In general, if we have n characters in the text, with one character occurring n_1 times, another n_2 times and so on, then the number of permutations possible is $\frac{n!}{n_1!n_2!...n_k!}$. Hence for our opening example, atd nrsoocimpsea, we have $n = 16$, three of the n_i values are 2 (for a, s and o), and the rest are 1, giving us $\frac{16!}{2.2.2}$ =2,615,348,736,000 possible permutations (including the unpermuted text itself). The number of permutations for a text will generally exhibit a combinatorial explosion of possibilities, which makes the existence of the reverse BWT all the more surprising.

Permutations have been a staple method for encryption, and are featured in the widely used "Advanced Encryption Standard" (AES), and its 1976 predecessor, the "Data Encryption Standard" (DES). In encryption, the function of permutation is to remove any clues that might be obtained by the juxtaposition of characters. It is somewhat ironic that the Burrows-Wheeler Transform, which also permutes the text, has almost the opposite purpose, as it highlights the regularities of adjacent characters. It may even be that one of the reasons that the BWT was initially viewed with some suspicion is that the main application of permutations in coding up to that time had been to make it impossible to reverse the coding. The connection with encryption is intriguing because Burrows also developed the "Tiny Encryption Algorithm" (TEA) mentioned earlier, which is based on a similar structure to DES and AES.

Two special cases of a permutation arise in the process of performing the Burrows-Wheeler Transform. One is the *circular shift* permutation, which can be seen in the rows of Figure 1.1a, where all of the characters are moved one position to the left, and the first character moves to the last position. A text of n characters usually has n circular shift permutations, although if the text is entirely composed of repeated substrings (such as blahblahblah) then some of the n circular shifts will produce the same string. This situation is very unlikely to occur in practice (the most likely case being a file containing only a single character repeated many times), but it is a case which causes unusual behavior for the BWT.

The other kind of permutation that arises in the BWT is one found in the *columns* of a sorted list such as the one in Figure 1.1b. Each column is also a permutation of the input text, with the first one containing all identical characters grouped together. This column is the result of sorting the input characters, and indeed sorting is a special case of permutation. The last column is the output of the transform, and is the one permutation of the text that we are the most interested in. The BWT uses this particular permutation which is dictated by the sort order, but later we will look at methods that use slightly different permutations based on different ways of comparing substrings of the text.

Finally, a trivial permutation which comes up when discussing the Burrows-Wheeler Transform is the reverse of the input string. The simplest implementation of the BWT will output the file in reverse order, although this is easily avoided by reversing the input when it is read into memory before encoding, or reversing the output from the decoder. In general reversing a string does not affect compression performance, but in some practical situations it can. This is discussed in Section 2.2.

1.5 Recency

In the physical world, it's often efficient to keep recently used documents, equipment or other resources nearby on the basis that the most recently used items are the most likely to be used again. Of course, one can argue the opposite: if something has been used a lot recently then perhaps we will be finished with it soon! In practice the recency effect is a safe observation to take advantage of, and the output of the Burrows-Wheeler Transform very much amplifies any recency effects in the text by bringing together characters that have occurred in related contexts.

The traditional use of the recency effect on computers is the LRU (least recently used) mechanism for caching: when data needs to be displaced from high-speed memory, we generally favor discarding the data that has been used furthest in the past. The extreme form of a recency mechanism is the stack, which allows access to only the *most* recently used item. While this might seem limiting, the stack is a very powerful construct, especially for the complex task of parsing recursively structured input such as programming languages; and of course, the stack is fundamental to most programming language implementations for allowing recursive function invocations.

There are various ways to take advantage of the recency effect of the BWT output, and these are discussed in detail in Chapter 3. The original BWT paper used a "move-to-front" (MTF) system where the shortest codes are allocated to the characters at the "front" of a list. When a character is to be coded, its position in the list is transmitted and then it is moved to the front of the list, thereby demoting all the other characters that were ahead of it in the list. Variations of this approach have been used very successfully with the BWT.

To implement the MTF system, the compression of the BWT output could be done by simply storing how many different characters have been encountered since the previous occurrence of the current character. For example, if the text abbc has just been decoded then if a 2 is received next it would represent an a (because you would need to skip two *different* characters to get to the previous a), while a b would be coded as a 1, and c as a 0. Very small numbers will be common in the output from the MTF system, and these numbers are then represented by codes that use fewer bits for smaller numbers, and more bits for the larger ones.

An alternative approach which has found favor in recent years for compressing the BWT output avoids using the move-to-front strategy to capture the recency effect; we simply use a conventional coder (adaptive Huffman or arithmetic coding) and bias the probabilities to favor recent occurrences of characters. Since the coders work with estimated probabilities, we just need a system that estimates high probabilities for characters that have occurred a lot recently, since the coder will use shorter codes for the high probability events. This is done by having recent occurrences of a character contribute significantly more to its estimated probability than past ones by reducing the weight of "old" characters. For the BWT this bias for recency has to be very strong, as repeated characters can occur in relatively small clusters. This will be discussed in more detail in Section 3.2.

1.6 Pattern matching

Compression and pattern matching are closely related. One way of looking at a compression method is that it simply looks for patterns, and takes advantage of them to remove repetition. For example, Ziv-Lempel methods search previous sections of a text for matches; if Shakespeare's "Hamlet" is being compressed[3], and the next string to be encoded is the 18th occurrence of the string "noble", the system will search to find that the string occurred 1366 characters earlier, and can replace it with a reference that points back 1366 characters, and gives the length of the match (5 characters). In other compression methods the pattern is a *context* that is being searched for, to make predictions based on what has happened in past occurrences of the context — for example, a compression system might want to know what character is most likely to come after "noble", and could find this out by locating all previous occurrences of "noble" which will reveal that 16 of the 17 previous occurrences were followed by a space, and one was followed by an "r".

Because the compression process involves pattern matching, it makes sense to try to harness all the searching done during compression if a user wants

---

[3] There are several versions of Hamlet available; these statistics are for a particular version from Project Gutenberg.

to search for a key in the compressed text. This means that we might be able to search a compressed document without decompressing it, which is "compressed-domain searching". Simplistically, one might compress the search key, and try to find the encoded key in the compressed file. Unfortunately this is unlikely to work in practice because the encoding of a substring can depend on other text surrounding it, although a number of algorithms have been developed for compression methods that are able to work around this.

For the Burrows-Wheeler Transform, however, the matching process is much simpler, at least in principle, because the encoding is based on sorting every substring of the text into lexical order — we have a sorted list (ideal for binary search) available as a by-product of compression! For example, Figure 1.6 shows some of the sorted strings that are generated during the BWT encoding of Shakespeare's Hamlet. Of course, the full substrings aren't actually generated; they are simply a list of references to positions in the original text. The L column (which shows the BWT output[4]) is really just the character in the original string that comes before the one in the F column. What makes searching in the Burrows-Wheeler Transformed text easy is that using an auxiliary array that is needed for decoding, the rows in the list can be accessed randomly, and characters in each row are easily read off in linear time. Thus, without fully decoding the text we are able to perform a binary search of the original text.

For example, if we were to search for the word "nobler" in the text, we would begin by decoding the middle few characters of the sorted list ("there's a special providence...") and discover that "nobler" is lexically earlier in the file. Carrying on with the binary search brings us to the section in Figure 1.6, and consequently to the line beginning "nobler in the mind to suffer...", which can be decoded for as many characters as are required to show the matched part of the text.

From this point of view, the compressed text is like a wound-up spring, containing lexical energy added by the sorting during encoding, and waiting to be released in a search.

1.7 Organization of this book

Now that we have looked informally at how the BWT can achieve compression, yet still allow efficient searching, in the next chapter we will describe in some detail how the BWT is implemented in practice, including data structures for doing the transformation quickly, and for reversing it efficiently. Chapter 3 will consider what to do with the transformed text, as there are a variety of methods that can be used to code the very repetitive text that is generated.

Chapter 4 looks at suffix trees and suffix arrays, which are important ideas in compression and pattern matching. They pre-date the Burrows-Wheeler

---

[4] The Hamlet text is similar in length to the block size used by BWT coders, so the L column shows the level of repetition typical of the output of a BWT coder.

F	... L
no_sooner_shall_the_mountains	... _
no_spirit_dare_stir_abroad;_T	... _
no_such_stuff_in_my_thoughts.	... _
no_such_thing?_Laer._Know_you	... _
no_tokens._Which_done,_she_to	... _
no_tongue,_Nor_any_unproporti	... _
no_tongue,_will_speak_With_mo	... _
no_tongue:_I_will_requite_you	... _
no_tongues_else_for's_turn._H	... _
no_touch_of_it,_my_lord._Ham.	... _
no_truant._But_what_is_your_a	... _
no_wind_shall_breathe;_But_ev	... _
no_words_of_this;_but_when_th	... _
nobility_of_love_Than_that_wh	... _
noble_Hamlet:_Mine_and_my_fat	... _
noble_and_most_sovereign_reas	... _
noble_dust_of_Alexander_till_	... _
noble_father_in_the_dust:_Tho	... _
noble_father_lost;_A_sister_d	... _
noble_father_slain_Pursu'd_my	... _
noble_father's_person,_I'll_s	... _
noble_heart.--Good_night,_swe	... _
noble_in_reason!_how_infinite	... _
noble_lord?_Hor._What_news,_m	... _
noble_mind_is_here_o'erthrown	... _
noble_mind_Rich_gifts_wax_poo	... _
noble_rite_nor_formal_ostenta	... _
noble_son_is_mad:_Mad_call_I_	... _
noble_substance_often_doubt_T	... _
noble_youth,_The_serpent_that	... _
noble_youth:_mark._Laer._What	... _
nobler_in_the_mind_to_suffer_	... _
noblest_to_the_audience._For_	... _
nocent_love,_And_sets_a_blist	... n
nock_him_about_the_sconce_wit	... k
nocked_about_the_mazard_with_	... k
nocking_each_other;_And_with_	... k
noculate_our_old_stock_but_we	... i
nod,_take_away_her_power;_Bre	... y
nods,_and_gestures_yield_them	... _
noint_my_sword._I_bought_an_u	... a

Fig. 1.6. Another part of the BWT sorted list for Shakespeare's Hamlet; spaces are shown as an underscore

Transform, which is very similar to a suffix array, and it is valuable to study them to help understand the BWT better.

Chapter 5 reviews theoretical results for BWT-based schemes, such as universal compression, optimality issues, and computational complexity. It also covers current challenges in improving the BWT algorithm, with respect to compression performance, theoretical space and time complexity. This chapter also explores the connection between the BWT and other compression algorithms, such as PPM (Prediction by Partial Matching), DMC (Dynamic Markov Compression) and LZ (Ziv-Lempel) coding.

Chapter 6 will discuss other approaches that are very closely related to the BWT. This will include members of the class of compression algorithms that perform compression based on sorted contexts, such as permutation-based coding, block-sorting schemes, and newer approaches such as word-based BWT.

Chapter 7 introduces the problem of pattern matching, and some standard algorithms for searching uncompressed text. We then look at methods that perform searching with the aid of the BWT, including both methods that store indexes as part of the BWT-based compression scheme, and those that perform searching with limited partial decompression of the BWT. These methods exploit the sorted contexts used by BWT and other members of this class of compression algorithm. The remainder of the chapter moves away from exact matching, and presents several algorithms for approximate pattern matching, longest common subsequence and sequence alignment, including algorithms for approximate pattern matching using the BWT. It also briefly considers hardware-based methods for pattern matching.

Chapter 8 explores emerging applications of the BWT, different from text compression and text pattern matching, such as using the BWT for compressed suffix arrays and compressed suffix trees, compressed full-text indexing, image compression, shape analysis, DNA sequence analysis in bioinformatics, and entropy estimation.

We conclude in Chapter 9 with an overview of the BWT with speculation on the short- and long-term direction of research work on BWT.

1.8 Further reading

The "Further reading" section at the end of each chapter will provide key references and tangential information that may be relevant to those wanting to study the topic of the chapter further.

The key reference for this book is Burrows and Wheeler's original 1994 paper titled "A block-sorting lossless data compression algorithm" (Burrows and Wheeler, 1994). Early descriptions of the method were written by Fenwick, initially in three technical reports (Fenwick, 1995b,c, 1996a), and then in a 1996 article in the *Computer Journal* (Fenwick, 1996b). Fenwick's work lead to Julian Seaward's BZIP program, which evolved into BZIP2, a widely used general-purpose implementation based on the BWT. A 1996 article by Mark Nelson in the *Dr Dobb's Journal* (Nelson, 1996) also helped to make the idea public. Soon after that papers about the BWT appeared in the Data Compression Conference (held annually in Snowbird, Utah) and the method became more widely understood. A survey article about the Burrows-Wheeler compression can be found in Fenwick (2003a). A meeting to mark the tenth anniversary of the BWT was held by the DIMACS Center at Rutgers University in August 2004, and a special edition of *Theoretical Computer Science* in November 2007 (volume 387, issue 3) is focused on the BWT. The special edition includes a foreword by Michael Burrows, which gives some interesting background to how the method was developed. It also includes three papers that provide useful overviews and analysis of BWT: Fenwick (2007), Kaplan et al. (2007), and Giancarlo et al. (2007).

The move-to-front (MTF) method used in the original BWT paper is based on work by Bentley et al. (1986) which uses the MTF list for compression, although in this case it was based on coding words rather than characters, and thus the MTF list had to be able to deal with a large vocabulary.

The puzzle at the start of the chapter is an anagram of `data compression`, which can be decoded using the inverse Burrows-Wheeler Transform[5]. It also happens to decode to "don amar to spices". Purists might have preferred us to use the example "The Magic Words are Squeamish Ossifrage" (made famous by the 1977 RSA cipher challenge). Interestingly "Squeamish Ossifrage" has an anagram relevant to data compression: "I squish for a message". However, the BWT of "squeamish ossifrage" is "hreugiassma sfiseoq". The example used from Shakespeare ("To be or not to be...") also has an interesting anagram, discovered by Cory Calhoun: "In one of the Bard's best-thought-of tragedies, our insistent hero, Hamlet, queries on two fronts about how life turns rotten."

Shannon's original 1948 paper that is the basis of much of the work in data compression was published in the *Bell System Technical Journal* (Shannon, 1948), and subsequently in a book by Shannon and Weaver (1949). Other important milestones in data compression prior to the Burrows-Wheeler Transform were Huffman's codes (Huffman, 1952), Ziv and Lempel's methods (Ziv and Lempel, 1977, 1978), arithmetic coding (Pascoe, 1976; Rissanen, 1976; Rissanen and Langdon, 1979), and "Prediction by Partial Matching" (Cleary and Witten, 1984). General texts about data compression include Storer (1988), Bell et al. (1990), Nelson and Gailly (1995), Williams (1991), Witten et al. (1999), Sayood (2000), Moffat and Turpin (2002), Sayood (2003) and Salomon (2004).

---

[5] Actually, the transform gives only the order of the letters; some extra information is needed to establish which letter is the starting point, but it is a puzzle after all!

How the Burrows-Wheeler Transform works

This chapter will look in detail at how the Burrows-Wheeler Transform is implemented in practice. The examples given in Chapter 1 overlooked some important practical details — to transform a text of n characters the encoder was sorting an array of n strings, each n characters long, and the decoder performed n sorts to reverse the transform. This complexity is not necessary for the BWT, and in this chapter we will see how to perform the encoding and decoding in $O(n)$ space, and $O(n \log n)$ time. In fact, using a few tricks, the time can be reduced to $O(n)$.

We will also look at various auxiliary data structures that are used for decoding the Burrows-Wheeler Transform, as some of them, while not essential for decoding, are useful if the transformed text is to be searched. These extra structures can still be constructed in $O(n)$ time so in principle they add little to the decoding cost.

This chapter considers only the transform; in the next chapter we will look at how a compression system can take advantage of the transformed text to reduce its size; we refer to this second phase as the "Local to Global Transform", or LGT.

We will present the Burrows-Wheeler Transform for coding a string T of n characters, $T[1 \ldots n]$, over an alphabet Σ of $|\Sigma|$ characters. Note that there is a summary of all the main notation in Appendix A on page 309.

2.1 The forward Burrows-Wheeler Transform

The forward transform essentially involves sorting all rotations of the input string, which clusters together characters that occur in similar contexts. Figure 2.1a shows the rotations A that would occur if the transform is given T = `mississippi` as the input[1], and Figure 2.1b shows the result of sorting A, which we will refer to as A_s.

---

[1] We will use `mississippi` as a running example in this chapter. This string is often used in the literature as an example because it illustrates the features of

mississippi	imississipp
ississippim	ippimississ
ssissippimi	issippimiss
sissippimis	ississippim
issippimiss	mississippi
ssippimissi	pimississip
sippimissis	ppimississi
ippimississ	sippimissis
ppimississi	sissippimis
pimississip	ssippimissi
imississipp	ssissippimi
(a)	(b)

Fig. 2.1. (a) The array A containing all rotations of the input mississippi; (b) A_s, obtained by sorting A. The last column of A_s (usually referred to as L) is the Burrows-Wheeler Transform of the input

However, rather than use $O(n^2)$ space as suggested by Figure 2.1, we can create an array $R[1 \ldots n]$ of references to the rotated strings in the input text T. Initially $R[i]$ is simply set to i for each i from 1 to n, as shown in Figure 2.2a, to represent the unsorted list. It is then sorted using the substring beginning at $T[R[i]]$ as the comparison key. Figure 2.2b shows the result of sorting; for example, position 11 is the first rotated string in lexical order (imiss...), followed by position 8 (ippim...) and position 5 (issip...); the final reference string is $R = [11, 8, 5, 2, 1, 10, 9, 7, 4, 6, 3]$.

The array R directly indexes the characters in T corresponding to the first column of A_s, referred to as F in the BWT literature. The last column of A_s (referred to as L) is the output of the BWT, and can be read off as $T[R[i] - 1]$, where i ranges from 1 to n (if the index to T is 0 then it refers to $T[n]$). In this case the transformed text is $L = $ pssmipissii. We also need to transmit an index a to indicate to the decoder which position in L corresponds to the last character of the original text (i.e. which row of A_s contains the original string T). In this case the index $a = 5$ is included.

In the above description the transform is completed using just $O(n)$ space (for R). The time taken is $O(n)$ for the creation of the array R, plus the time needed for sorting. Conventionally sorting is regarded as taking $O(n \log n)$ average time if a standard method such as quicksort is used. However, some string sequences can cause near-worst-case behavior in some versions of quicksort, particularly if there is a lot of repetition in the string and the pivot for quicksort is not selected carefully. This corresponds to the traditional $O(n^2)$ worst-case of quicksort where the data is already sorted — if T contains long runs of the same character then the A array will contain long sorted sequences.

---

the BWT well. Note that there is no unique sentinel (end of string) symbol in this example; it is not essential for the BWT, although it can simplify some aspects, particularly when we deal with suffixes later.

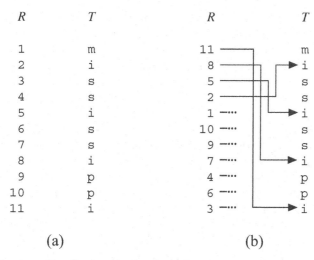

Fig. 2.2. The R array used to sort the sample file `mississippi`

For example, Figure 2.3 shows the A array for the input `aaaaaab`. It is already sorted because of the way the `b` terminates the long sequence of `a` characters. It is possible to avoid this worst case behavior in quicksort with techniques such as the median-of-three partition selection, but the nature of the BWT problem means that even better sorting methods are possible.

Not only can the pre-sorted list cause poor performance in some versions of quicksort, but the long nearly identical prefixes mean that lexical comparisons will require many character comparisons, which means that the constant-time assumption for comparisons is invalid; if all the characters are identical then it could take $O(n)$ time for each of the $O(n^2)$ comparisons, which would be extremely slow, especially considering that for such a case the BWT involves no permutations at all. Long repeated strings can occur in practice in images that contain many pixels of the same color (such as a scan of a black-and-white page with little writing on it) and in genomic data where the alphabet is very small and repeated substrings are common.

aaaaaab
aaaaaba
aaaabaa
aaabaaa
aabaaaa
abaaaaa
baaaaaa

Fig. 2.3. The array A containing all rotations of the input `aaaaaab`

There are several ways to avoid this problem. Burrows and Wheeler observed in their original paper that by having a unique sentinel character, the sorting problem is equivalent to sorting all the suffixes in T, which can be done in linear time and space using a suffix tree. This is discussed in more detail in Chapters 4 and 4, but we should mention that the main drawback of this approach is that although the space requirement is $O(n)$, the constant factor can be significant.

Instead, Burrows and Wheeler proposed a modified version of quicksort that applies a radix sort to the first two characters of each sort key. Each of the two-character buckets now needs to be sorted, but special attention is paid to buckets where the first two characters are the same, since these are likely to indicate long runs of the same character (typically null or space characters), which can take a long time to make a lexical comparison for comparison based sorting, yet are trivial to sort because of how they were generated. Eventually quicksort is only applied to groups of substrings that need sorting within buckets. For example, the strings in Figure 2.3 would be split into three buckets for those beginning with aa, ab and bb respectively. The aa bucket does not automatically have quicksort applied to it because the first two characters are the same, and indeed in this case the bucket happens to already be sorted, and would cause long comparisons between strings because of the long prefixes of runs of the letter a.

Another approach is to eliminate this problem by coding long runs of the same character using a run-length encoding technique, where runs of repeated characters are replaced with a shorter code. This can sometimes even have a positive effect on the amount of compression, although the main purpose is to avoid the poor sorting speed that occurs in the special cases described above by eliminating long runs of the same character. One downside of this is that the original text is no longer available directly in the BWT, which can affect some of the compressed-domain searching methods described later in this book. Also, the run-length encoding will change the context information that the BWT uses, hence the effect on compression is not necessarily positive.

One issue that is inevitable with the BWT is that it requires a large block of memory to store the input string (T) and the index to the strings being sorted (R). If the block is too small the compression will be poor, but if too large, it may use too much memory. Even if the memory is available, there can be issues with caching, and there are performance benefits from keeping blocks within the size of a cache, not just within main memory. The pattern of access to the memory will be random because of the sorting operations that need to be done (the same problem occurs during decoding as well). On modern computers there can be several layers of caching that will be trying to guess the memory access patterns, and these may have complex interactions with the accesses needed for the BWT. This concern needs to be taken into consideration when deciding on the block size; if it fits within the cache (and not just within main memory), it may well be able to operate faster. On the other hand, as parallel machines with on-board memory become more popular the BWT method can potentially be adapted to take advantage of this kind of architecture, and it is even possible that it will have performance benefits in a parallel environment over other popular compression methods. The actual performance in practice will depend on the architecture of the machine, the amount of memory available, and the design of any caches.

Appendix B lists web sites that provide a variety of source code for performing the BWT. Some are suitable for experimenting with the transform and tracing the process, while others are production systems the have optimized the details of coding to perform well in practice.

2.2 The reverse Burrows-Wheeler Transform

The reverse transform — taking a BWT permuted text and reconstructing the original input T — is somewhat more difficult to implement than the forward transform, but it can still be done in $O(n)$ time and space if care is taken. The example given in Figure 1.2 reconstructed the A_s array, but as for encoding, in practice there is no need to store this $O(n^2)$ array. Generally two $O(n)$ index arrays will be needed, plus two $O(|\Sigma|)$ arrays to count the characters in the input. There are several ways that decoding can be done. The original paper by Burrows and Wheeler produces the output in reverse, although it is not difficult to produce the output in the original order. We will show how to generate data structures for both of these cases.

We will use the decoding of the string mississippi as a running example. Figure 2.4 shows the array A_s for this example, with columns F and L labeled. A_s is not stored explicitly in practice, but we shall use it in the meantime to illustrate how decoding can be done. The decoder can determine F simply by sorting L, since it contains exactly the same characters, just in a different order — each column of A_s contains the same set of characters because the rows are all the rotations of the original string. In fact, F need not be stored, as it can be generated implicitly by counting how often each character appears in L.

Looking at A_s helps us to see the information that is needed to perform the decoding. Given just F and L, the key step is determining which character should come after a particular character in F. Consider, for example, the two rows ending with a p (rows 1 and 6). Because of the rotation, the order of these two rows is determined by the characters that come after the respective occurrences of p in T (imi... and pim... respectively). Thus the first occurrence of p in L corresponds to the first occurrence of p in F, and likewise with the second occurrence. This enables us to work through the text backwards: if we have just decoded the second p in L, then it must correspond to the one in row 7 of F. Looking at row 7, the L column tells us that the p was preceded by an i. In turn, because this is the second i in L, it must correspond to the second i in F, which is in row 2. We carry on traversing the L and F arrays in this way until the whole string is decoded — in reverse.

$$F \hspace{12cm} L$$

	F										L
1	i	m	i	s	s	i	s	s	i	p	p
2	i	p	p	i	m	i	s	s	i	s	s
3	i	s	s	i	p	p	i	m	i	s	s
4	i	s	s	i	s	s	i	p	p	i	m
5	m	i	s	s	i	s	s	i	p	p	i
6	p	i	m	i	s	s	i	s	s	i	p
7	p	p	i	m	i	s	s	i	s	s	i
8	s	i	p	p	i	m	i	s	s	i	s
9	s	i	s	s	i	p	p	i	m	i	s
10	s	s	i	p	p	i	m	i	s	s	i
11	s	s	i	s	s	i	p	p	i	m	i

Fig. 2.4. The array A_s for mississipi; F and L are the first and last columns respectively

The correspondence could also have been used to decode the string in its original order. For example, looking at the p in $L[6]$, we can determine that it is followed by $F[6]$, a p. Since this is the first p in F, it corresponds to the first p in L, that is, row 1. That p is followed by an i, and so on. It is marginally simpler to decode the string in reverse order, so usually the BWT literature uses the backwards decoding, although we shall be using both orders in this book.

An easy way to follow the above relationships is to number the appearances of the characters in F and L. Figure 2.5 shows the F and L columns from Figure 2.4, but we have numbered the occurrences of each character in order from first to last using subscripts. This makes the decoded string easy to read off; for example, the fourth row has $L[4] = m_1$, and the corresponding $F[4]$ tells us that it is followed by i_4. Since i_4 is in $L[11]$, we can get the next character from $F[11]$, which is s_4. The entire string is decoded in the order $m_1 i_4 s_4 s_2 i_3 s_3 s_1 i_2 p_2 p_1 i_1$.

In practice the decoder never reconstructs A_s or F in full, but implicitly creates indexes to represent enough of its structure to decode the original string. L is stored explicitly (the decoder just reads the input and stores it in L), but F is stored implicitly to save space and to efficiently provide the kind of information needed during decoding.

Figure 2.6 shows three auxiliary arrays that are useful for decoding. $K[c]$ is simply a count of how many times each character c occurs in F, which is easily determined by counting the characters in L. $M[c]$ locates the first position of character c in the array F, so K and M together effectively store the information in F. $C[i]$ stores the number of times the character $L[i]$ occurs in L earlier than position i; for example, the last character in L is i, and i

F	L
1 i_1	p_1
2 i_2	s_1
3 i_3	s_2
4 i_4	m_1
5 m_1	i_1
6 p_1	p_2
7 p_2	i_2
8 s_1	s_3
9 s_2	s_4
10 s_3	i_3
11 s_4	i_4

Fig. 2.5. Using the character order to perform the reverse transform

occurs 3 times in the earlier part of L. These three arrays make it easy to traverse the input in reverse.

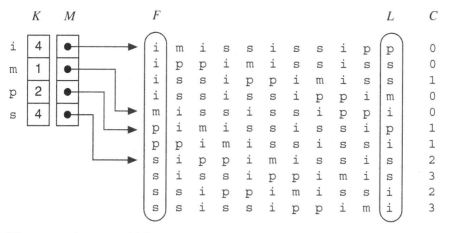

Fig. 2.6. The array (A_s) that is implicitly reconstructed to decode the string pssmipissii

Algorithm 2.1 shows how the input (transformed text L and starting index a) is used to construct these three arrays, which are then used to produce Q, the decoded text. The first step is simply to count the characters into K by going through L (the input), shown in lines 1 to 7 of the algorithm. At the same time, it is convenient to construct C by recording the value of K before each increment. The array M is then constructed in lines 10 to 14 by accumulating the values in C. We now have sufficient structures to decode the text in reverse, which happens in lines 16 to 20.

BWT-DECODE(L, a)
```
 1 for c ← 1 to |Σ| do
 2    K[c] ← 0
 3 end for
 4
 5 for i ← 1 to n do
 6    C[i] ← K[L[i]]
 7    K[L[i]] ← K[L[i]] + 1
 8 end for
 9
10 sum ← 1
11 for c ← 1 to |Σ| do
12    M[c] ← sum
13    sum ← sum + K[c]
14 end for
15
16 i ← a
17 for j ← n downto 1 do
18    Q[j] ← L[i]
19    i ← C[i] + M[L[i]]
20 end for
```

Algorithm 2.1: Reconstruction of the original text

Note that the decoder needs to be given the index a, which is the element in L that corresponds to the end of the text. In our running example a would be 5 — it corresponds to the row in A_s that represents the original string T. $L[5]$ gives us i as the last character of Q. The corresponding value in C is 0, which means that this is the first occurrence of an i in L. Thus it corresponds to the first occurrence of i in F, which is found by adding $C[i]$ to $M[L[i]]$, in line 19 of the algorithm. This proceeds until n characters have been decoded, at which point the whole string is stored in Q.

Reversing the BWT this way requires four arrays (L, K, C and M). K and M contain just $|\Sigma|$ entries (the characters are represented by integers from 1 to $|\Sigma|$) and are likely to be of negligible size; L and C contain n values, and hence use $O(n)$ space. We would normally also have to allow for Q, which uses $O(n)$ space to store the backwards string before it can be stored in the correct order. The time taken is also $O(n) + O(|\Sigma|)$, since the main work is in the two passes through the n input items — once to count them, and once to decode them.

It may be inconvenient that the output is generated backwards, and there are two ways to address this. Below we will look at how to use an extra auxiliary array to do this, but if the goal is simply to decode the input, this is less efficient than using the temporary Q array to store the output. An even simpler approach is to reverse the order of the string at encoding time.

This should not take any extra time, since the whole string must be read into memory anyway — we simply fill the array T in reverse. It may have an impact on compression, depending on the type of data, but for most data there will be no significant impact, and it may even improve compression. The cases where there is an impact tend to be binary files with specific patterns such as leading zeros before numbers. In such cases it is worth being aware of the issue anyway, and the ordering should be chosen to suit the data, since the amount of compression can depend on details such as whether the representation puts the most significant byte of a large number first or last (big- or little-endian). For textual data, reversing the input string means that the system is based around prior contexts of characters, which is how many other compression methods work anyway.

If the transformed text is to be decoded multiple times, it is possible to store one or more auxiliary arrays that enable us to traverse sections of the text at will. This can be useful for pattern matching because it allows segments of the original string to be read off when needed for matching, but still relates the data to the implicit sorted array A_s, which provides access to a sorted list of strings that are useful for searching.

The value $C[i] + M[L[i]]$ is the key to navigating through L to decode the original string, so instead of doing the decoding immediately (which was in lines 16 to 20 of Algorithm 2.1), an array V is created to store the navigation information, shown in Algorithm 2.2. This array can then be used to step backwards through the original characters; the character at $L[i]$ is preceded by the character at $L[V[i]]$. The values of V for our running example are shown in Figure 2.7.

COMPUTE-ARRAY-V(C, M, L) 1 $i \leftarrow a$
2 **for** $j \leftarrow n$ **downto** 1 **do**
3    $V[i] \leftarrow C[i] + M[L[i]]$
4    $i \leftarrow V[i]$
5 **end for**

Algorithm 2.2: Creating the array V to allow for efficient future decoding of the input

It is just as easy to create an auxiliary array that will decode the original text forwards rather than backwards. This array will be called W, and it identifies the position of the character in L that comes *after* the present one, compared with V, which gives the position that comes *before*. As for V, this new array is not essential for decoding, but it can be useful because it preserves access to the sorted structure of L, which can be exploited during pattern matching. Figure 2.7 shows the values of W for the running example.

Algorithm 2.3 shows how the W array can be created. Note that the array M that was created in Algorithm 2.1 is used, and that afterwards its contents

	F										L	V	W
1	i	m	i	s	s	i	s	s	i	p	p	6	5
2	i	p	p	i	m	i	s	s	i	s	s	8	7
3	i	s	s	i	p	p	i	m	i	s	s	9	10
4	i	s	s	i	s	s	i	p	p	i	m	5	11
5	m	i	s	s	i	s	s	i	p	p	i	1	4
6	p	i	m	i	s	s	i	s	s	i	p	7	1
7	p	p	i	m	i	s	s	i	s	s	i	2	6
8	s	i	p	p	i	m	i	s	s	i	s	10	2
9	s	i	s	s	i	p	p	i	m	i	s	11	3
10	s	s	i	p	p	i	m	i	s	s	i	3	8
11	s	s	i	s	s	i	p	p	i	m	i	4	9

Fig. 2.7. The auxiliary arrays V and W which can be used to decode the sample string

are changed so they are no longer valid. Like V, the W array is created in just $O(n)$ time.

COMPUTE-ARRAY-W(M, L)
1 **for** $i \leftarrow 1$ **to** n **do**
2     $W[M[L[i]]] \leftarrow i$
3     $M[L[i]] \leftarrow M[L[i]] + 1$
4 **end for**

Algorithm 2.3: Creating the array W to allow for future decoding of the input

W can then be used to generate the original text in its correct order using the simple sequence shown in Algorithm 2.4.

DECODE-WITH-ARRAY-W(W, L)
1 $i \leftarrow a$
2 **for** $j \leftarrow 1$ **to** n **do**
3     $Q[j] \leftarrow L[i]$
4     $i \leftarrow W[i]$
5 **end for**

Algorithm 2.4: Decoding the original text in its correct order using W

If both forwards and backwards generation of the original text is needed, it is possible to create V and W in one pass as shown in Algorithm 2.5.

V and W are essentially a mapping between F and L in each direction. In some of the pattern matching algorithms in Chapter 7 we will also recreate the array R that was used in the encoder to store the sort order of the substrings, and the reverse mapping of R, called R'. These provide a mapping between F and T; for example, if $R[i]$ is k, then $F[i]$ was the k-th character in T, and $R'[k]$ will be i. All of the arrays for our mississippi example are shown in Figure 2.8, and the algorithm for creating R and R' from W is given in Algorithm 2.6.

i	T	F	L	C	V	W	R'	R
1	m	i	p	0	6	5	5	11
2	i	i	s	0	8	7	4	8
3	s	i	s	1	9	10	11	5
4	s	i	m	0	5	11	9	2
5	i	m	i	0	1	4	3	1
6	s	p	p	1	7	1	10	10
7	s	p	i	1	2	6	8	9
8	i	s	s	2	10	2	2	7
9	p	s	s	3	11	3	7	4
10	p	s	i	2	3	8	6	6
11	i	s	i	3	4	9	1	3

Fig. 2.8. Array values that can be used to do the BWT and searching of the text mississippi

---

COMPUTE-ARRAYS-V-AND-W(M, L)
1 **for** $i \leftarrow 1$ **to** n **do**
2      $V[i] \leftarrow M[L[i]]$
3      $W[M[L[i]]] \leftarrow i$
4      $M[L[i]] \leftarrow M[L[i]] + 1$
5 **end for**

Algorithm 2.5: Creating both the V and W arrays in one pass

2.3 Special cases

In the previous examples the auxiliary arrays traverse each character in L to recreate the original text. There is a special case for the BWT that occurs if the

---

Compute-arrays-R-and-R$'(W)$
1 $i \leftarrow a$
2 **for** $j \leftarrow 1$ **to** n **do**
3      $R'[j] \leftarrow i$
4      $R[i] \leftarrow j$
5      $i \leftarrow W[i]$
6 **end for**

Algorithm 2.6: Construction of R and R' auxiliary arrays in the decoder

input text T is nothing but repetitions of a substring, such as blahblahblah, or even aaaaaaa. If this happens, some of the rotations of the text will be identical, and the reverse transform will end up using only one of the substring occurrences for decoding.

For example, the text cancan results in the decoding arrays shown in Figure 2.9. The arrows show the cycle of three characters that will occur following the V for W links; the other three characters in L are never used. This will still decode correctly; it is just that it is important to decode n times, rather than relying on coming back to the starting point to determine when to stop.

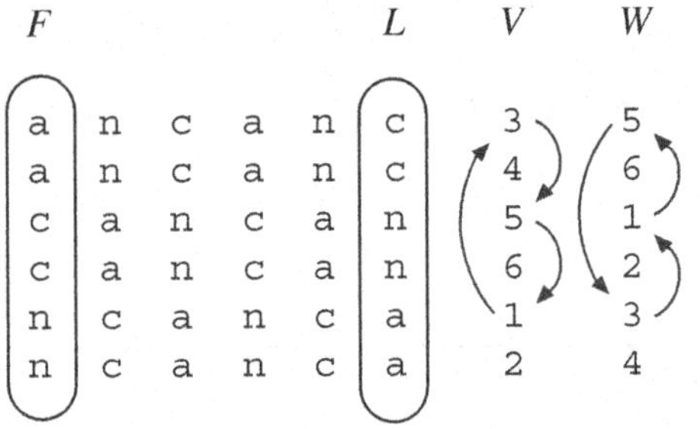

Fig. 2.9. The V and W arrays that are constructed for the string cancan

An even simpler case occurs when the coded text is just one character repeated many times; the decoder will only use the first occurrence of the character for all decoding.

It is worth being aware of this special case because it can also affect pattern matching. Of course, such a case is extremely unlikely to occur in practice. It might happen that a file containing just one repeated value is coded, such as the pixels in a blank image, but even in this case, just one different piece of information in the file, such as the image resolution, will prevent the rotations from being identical. If a particular algorithm is dependent on this not happening, it can be prevented by simply inserting one unique character (such as an end of string sentinel symbol) in T before it is transformed.

2.4 Further reading

The original Burrows and Wheeler paper (Burrows and Wheeler, 1994) remains an excellent explanation of the transform, and includes techniques for implementing the transform efficiently, including using a suffix tree in the forward transform, ways to use quicksort efficiently for the forward transform, and using counting rather than sorting in the reverse transform. Fenwick has published a series of papers which look in detail at implementation of the BWT; four early papers were mentioned in Chapter 1 (Fenwick, 1995b,c, 1996a,b); a summative paper can be found in the November 2007 special issue of *Theoretical Computer Science* about the BWT (Fenwick, 2007), which includes an algorithm for decoding a BWT file in natural order. The proposal for using run-length encoding to avoid the sorting problem in the BWT code was made in (Fenwick, 1996a). Fenwick's report also describes a private communication from Wheeler that gives an effective (if somewhat *ad hoc*) adaptation of quicksort that takes advantage of the particular structures available in the BWT.

The BWT is not the only way to permute texts and still be able to recover them, although other approaches are closely related. A number of such variants are described in Chapter 6.

The names of the arrays used in this chapter, and the rest of the book, differ slightly from some of those used in the BWT literature. This is explained in Appendix A; the main problem is that there is a conflict between the notation used in the pattern matching literature, and that used in the BWT literature. The use of F and L is consistent with Burrows and Wheeler's original paper; however, their T array corresponds to V in this chapter, since we use T for the input text.

3

Coders for the Burrows-Wheeler Transform

Like most transforms, the Burrows-Wheeler Transform does not change the size of the file that has been transformed, but merely rearranges it so that it will be easier to represent it compactly. It then needs to be coded using a second phase which we will refer to as the "Local to Global Transform" (LGT). Figure 3.1 shows a section of the transformed text for Shakespeare's "Hamlet", which reveals the kind of regularities that the BWT exposes. These characters are ones that appear before the context nd; initially the nd is followed by a space, and hence a is very common, but then the character is followed by ndeed, where the i becomes common, and the last few characters precede nder.

Clearly the text in Figure 3.1 contains a lot of patterns, and therefore will be easy to compress. Many sophisticated techniques have been proposed to exploit the regularities of the BWT transformed text, and yet it has emerged that one of the simplest approaches (RLEAC, based on run-length encoding and an order-zero arithmetic coder) gives the best compression and is also very fast compared with more complicated methods. We will begin this section by looking at this simple coder, but later we will also review various other approaches that have been proposed, including Burrows and Wheeler's original "Move to Front" (MTF) list, inversion frequencies, distance coding, frequency counting methods, wavelet trees, and alternative permutations. We will also consider the effect of the block size on compression performance.

3.1 Entropy coding

Before we look in detail at how the structure of a BWT string can be exploited for compression, we will briefly review some fundamentals of how symbols can be converted to bits based on an estimated probability distribution for how likely each symbol is. This process is often referred to as *entropy coding*, because the aim is to represent symbols in as few bits as possible, and the limit of this is dictated by the *entropy*. The BWT-based systems that we will

```
AaaaaaAaaaAaAaAaAeAeiuaaAaoaaiAauaaauiaaaaaieaeeaoeuueauiiiAaaua
aaaaaaaaoaaaaiaaaaaaaaaaaaaaaaaaaaaaaaaaaaaaaaaaaaaAAaAAaAAAAaAaa
AuaeaaaaaaaaaaauaaaaaeaaiaaauueuaeaaaieaaaaaaaaeAAaaaaeaeaaaaaaa
eaaAaaaAaaaaAaaiaaaaaeeiaaaaaaAiaaAaAaiAaAaaaaaaAaaaaaAaaaAAAaAA
aaAAaaaAaaaaoaaaaaAaaAAaAAaaAaaaaaAaaaaaaaaaaaAAaaaaaaAaAaaaaaaa
aaaaaaaaaaaaaaaaiiaAaaAAaaaaeaaaaAaAaaaaaAaaaAAaaaaaaAAAaaaaAaAa
aaaaaaAaaaaaaaaaaaaaaaAaAaauaAAaAaaaAAaAAaaAaaiaaAAAaaaaAAAaaaaa
aaaaaaaaaaaaaaaaaaaaaAAAAAaaAAAauaAauaaaaaaaaaaaAaaaieiiiieeAaaaaa
eeAaiaaoAaAaaaaAAaAoooaiaAaaiAAaaAaAAAAaaaaaaaiiiaeeeaaeAiuiaaaa
aaAaaaaaaaaAAoaaaAAAAaAAAAAAAAaaAiaaaAaaaaAAaaaaAAaaaAaaAaaaoaaAu
aaieaauaeaaAAaaaaaaaaaAaaaaaaaaaaAaaaaaeaaaAaaaaaaAaaauAAaaaaaaa
aAaaAAAAaaAaAaaaaaAAiiiiiiiaieaiaiaaiiAeeaaAaaeaaaaaAaaaaAaoaaiia
aaaaaaaAaaaaaaaAaAaaaaaaAaaaAaaaAaaAiaaaaaAaAoaaaaaaaaaaaaaaoaaaa
AaaaaaaaaAAAaiaaaaaaaAaiaiaAaaAuAaAaaaAaaaaaaaaaaaaaaaaAAaaaaaaAaa
aaaaaAaaaaaaaAaaaAaaAAaaAAaaAAAaAaAaaAaiiiiaaaaauAaaaaaaaaaaaAoae
auaaaaaaaaaaaaieaaaeAAaaAAaAAAaaaaaaAAaAAaAaAAAaaAaaaeaaAAaAaaaAA
aAAAAaeaoaoaaeaaaauaaaaAiAAAuaaaaaaaaaaaaaaaaaauaaaaaeiaAaaAAAaaa
AAAaaaaaaAaaaaAAaAAuaaAAaAaAeAaaaaaAaaaaaAaaaaAAaaAaAAaaaaaaaAAA
aaauuAaAaAAaAAueaaaaaaAaAaaaeAAaAaaaaAaeaaAeeaaaeaaeaauieaaiaeea
aaeeaaaaueiaaeaaaaeeeeeeeeeeeauoueueeeeaeeueuuuaeiiiiiiiIiiIIIiiiI
IiIiiiiiiiiiiIIeieaeoooouuuueaeeoauaeeeaoUUiaeaeoueaoeaeeuauuuu
```

Fig. 3.1. Some of the transformed text generated from Shakespeare's "Hamlet"

be looking at often use entropy coding as their final stage, so it is good to understand the methods that the BWT processing is preparing data for.

In entropy coding, the representation of a symbol is based on some estimated probability of that symbol occurring. The next symbol to be coded will be drawn from a probability distribution that is typically estimated based on previous observations. For example, if the character "e" has occurred in 20 out of the last 100 characters, we might estimate that the probability of the next character being an "e" is 20%.

Shannon (1948) showed that, on average, the optimal representation for a symbol with probability p would use $-\log_2 p$ bits. There are two general approaches to generating the bits given a probability distribution: Huffman coding, and arithmetic coding. Huffman coding can be computed very quickly, but the number of bits used for a particular symbol are whole numbers, and hence won't necessarily be equal to the optimal size of $-\log_2 p$. This is a problem especially when p is close to one; in this case the optimal number of bits approaches zero, but Huffman coding must use at least one bit to represent each symbol. Arithmetic coding overcomes this problem by effectively overlapping the bit representations of successive characters, so one bit in the output might correspond to more than one symbol. Although arithmetic coding is optimal, it is usually an order of magnitude slower than Huffman coding, and hence should be used only in situations where the probability distribution will cause poor behavior in a Huffman coder.

The task of coding using Huffman or arithmetic coding is well understood, and the further reading section at the end of this chapter gives a number of references that explain these techniques in detail. Many BWT-based systems rely on these entropy coders to produce their output. Generally Huffman coding is used if speed is important and the loss of compression is tolerable; otherwise arithmetic coding is used to get the best possible compression. The main property that we need to understand about arithmetic coding is that if it codes a symbol with an estimated probability of p, then the number of bits used will be arbitrarily close to the optimum value of $-\log_2 p$ bits, and thus we can estimate the size of a compressed file without even performing the coding.

Estimating the probability distributions for an entropy coder can be done adaptively or non-adaptively. Non-adaptive systems use the same probability estimates (and therefore the same code) for the entire coding, whereas adaptive systems allow the probability distributions to change from character to character, effectively "learning" during the encoding. Non-adaptive methods would typically scan the entire sequence to be encoded, estimate probabilities, create a code table, and proceed to code the entire sequence using the code table. Adaptive systems don't need to scan the sequence in advance; they generally start with simple assumptions (such as all characters being equally likely), and then change the probabilities as coding proceeds. The decoder is able to adapt in synchronization as long as the adaptation occurs *after* each symbol is encoded, since the symbol can be decoded using the current codes, and the decoder can update the statistics after each character is decoded.

For example, Figure 3.2 shows an adaptive estimation of probabilities for coding the word `mississippi` assuming an alphabet of $|\Sigma| = 4$ characters. The first four columns count how many times each character has been observed so far, although they are initialized to 1 to avoid having zero probabilities. The first row shows that with the initial counts all being equal, the first `m` in the string is given a probability of $\frac{1}{4}$, and is therefore coded in 2 bits, which is what we would expect for an alphabet of four characters if no compression was being attempted. The next line shows the count of `m` incremented, as both the encoder and decoder have observed that one `m` has occurred, and therefore it might be more likely than other characters. Thus the next code, which happens to be for an `i`, gives it a less than even chance of $\frac{1}{5}$ (its count is 1, and the total for all characters is 5). Using Shannon's formula we find that it should be coded in 2.32 bits. The system then "learns" from this, and increases the count of `i` by 1, ready to code the next character. Notice that the second `s` is coded in 1.8 bits, and the fourth one in just 1.32 bits, as the adaptation has given `s` the highest probability.

This example is too short to show the effectiveness of adaptation, but generally after initial poor performance where the probability estimates are very crude, an adaptive system will settle down to represent the statistics of the text it is modeling. The model used in this example is also very simple; it assumes that each character occurs independently of the others. While this is

Character counts				Probability	$-\log_2 p$
i	m	p	s		
1	1	1	1	$p(\texttt{m}) = \frac{1}{4}$	2 bits
1	2	1	1	$p(\texttt{i}) = \frac{1}{5}$	2.32 bits
2	2	1	1	$p(\texttt{s}) = \frac{1}{6}$	2.58 bits
2	2	1	2	$p(\texttt{s}) = \frac{2}{7}$	1.8 bits
2	2	1	3	$p(\texttt{i}) = \frac{2}{8}$	2 bits
3	2	1	3	$p(\texttt{s}) = \frac{3}{9}$	1.58 bits
3	2	1	4	$p(\texttt{s}) = \frac{4}{10}$	1.32 bits
3	2	1	5	$p(\texttt{i}) = \frac{3}{11}$	1.87 bits
4	2	1	5	$p(\texttt{p}) = \frac{1}{12}$	3.58 bits
4	2	2	5	$p(\texttt{p}) = \frac{2}{13}$	2.7 bits
4	2	3	5	$p(\texttt{i}) = \frac{4}{14}$	1.8 bits

Fig. 3.2. Adaptive order zero probability estimation for coding the word `mississippi`

useful (especially for BWT applications), adaptive systems like this generally take account of prior characters when making probability estimates.

In the example some arbitrary choices were made which affect the rate of adaptation. The initial counts need not have been set to 1; a higher value could have been used to make the system take longer to make significant changes in the probabilities, and conversely, instead of incrementing by 1 each time, a higher value could be used to increase the effect of each character arriving. For example, if we were incrementing by 10, then the first m would cause the probability on the next character being an m to be estimated at $\frac{11}{14}$ and the other three characters at $\frac{1}{14}$. This kind of aggressive increment (combined with an aging scheme) is useful for BWT coding because of the strong clustering of similar characters in the input, such as in the example in Figure 3.1.

At the other end of the spectrum from adaptive coding, for the probability distributions that arise in some BWT systems (particularly using MTF) often a simple fixed code can be effective, using the same representations regardless of the statistics. This will inevitably give slightly worse compression performance than if the probability distribution is taken into account, but the gain in speed and simplicity may well justify making the approximation. For example, the codes shown in Table 3.1 can be used to represent values where very small numbers are the most common. For the α code, a value of one is represented using just one bit; a value of two using two bits, and so on. It is sometimes referred to as "unary", because it is based on coding in base 1 (each position is worth 1 times as much as the one to the right). The disadvantage of this code is that larger values will require many bits. Because an event with probability p is ideally represented in $-\log_2 p$ bits, the unary code implies that the probability of a zero is $\frac{1}{2}$, of a one is $\frac{1}{4}$, and so on. The α code strongly favors small values, and is not used so often on its own, although, for example, it is used in BZIP2 to select which Huffman table to use for coding, as there are only six tables to choose from, and 1 and 2 are the most common. A coding that grows in length somewhat slower than this is the γ code, also shown in Table 3.1. The γ code represents a value as its binary number, but because the length of the binary number can vary, a unary code is prefixed to indicate the length of the binary number. Because all of the binary numbers begin with a 1, that bit is omitted. For example, the number 5 has the 3-bit binary representation 101; it is therefore represented as the unary value for 3, followed by the last two digits of its binary representation (01).

value	α	γ	δ
1	1	1	1
2	01	01 0	010 0
3	001	01 1	010 1
4	0001	001 00	011 00
5	00001	001 01	011 01
6	000001	001 10	011 10
7	0000001	001 11	011 11
8	00000001	0001 000	00100 000
9	000000001	0001 001	00100 001

Table 3.1. Two fixed-length codes for the integers

There are many more codes that use this kind of approach; these are often referred to as Elias codes, after the author of a seminal paper on the topic (Elias, 1975). An interesting one is the δ code, which essentially uses a γ code to represent the number of bits in the integer, followed by the binary representation of the integer (again, missing its highest order bit since that will always be a 1). The δ code is a *universal* code, which means that the expected code length is within a constant factor of what would have been assigned by an entropy coder, as long as the ranking of the probabilities is correct.

Codes such as α, γ and δ are fixed, and therefore are completely unresponsive to any probability distribution changes in the input. Their main advantage is that they are very fast, and no code table needs to be stored or transmitted. In contrast, the Huffman and arithmetic entropy coders will use codes that approach optimality for the given probability distribution, although in principle a universal code will also be close to optimal. The further reading section gives references for more information about the implementation and performance of entropy coders and fixed codes, and Section 5.5.2 looks at this kind of code in more detail.

3.2 Run-length and arithmetic coder

One of the simplest ways to code the output of a Burrows-Wheeler Transform is also one of the most effective. In this approach we put the output (such as that shown in Figure 3.1) through a "run-length encoder", which takes advantage of runs of identical characters in a sequence, and then through an arithmetic coder, not unlike the approach shown in Figure 3.2. This method has been labeled RLEAC (Ferragina et al., 2006a).

Traditionally these are combined with other techniques (such as the move-to-front list) that exploit the structure of the transformed text, but a somewhat surprising result is that with properly chosen parameters these two components perform very well on their own. Run-length encoding (RLE) features strongly in much of the BWT research, and can be applied at almost any stage (including before the transform). However, most of the compression is achieved in the arithmetic coding, and there is some evidence that even the run-length encoding isn't necessary if the arithmetic coding is done correctly, although RLE can make implementation simpler and faster.

The run-length encoder simply replaces a run of the same character with a code that specifies what the character is, and how long the run is. For example, in the second line of Figure 3.1 the letter a appears 36 times in a row, which would be replaced with a code; on the other hand, the single occurrences of a letter o are a trivial run of length one, and are not worth replacing. A run-length code generally has three components: a flag to indicate that a run is about to be encoded, the character in the run, and the length of the run. This can be reduced to just two components if it is possible to have a run of length one. In a Burrows-Wheeler transformed file, typically only about 33% of the characters occur in runs of 3 or more, but nevertheless there are some gains to be made as this still represents a significant proportion of the file that occurs in a run.

The key component of the RLEAC backend to a BWT system is the arithmetic coding. This uses a simple adaptive model to count the occurrences of each character in the transformed text, adapting the probability distribution after each character is coded. Adaptive systems are particularly useful when compression must start before the entire input is known, or where only one pass through the input is possible. Because BWT-based systems work with a block of text at a time, adaptive coding is not essential for this purpose. However, another feature of adaptive coding is not just the ability to "learn" new symbols, but to "forget" old ones. Normally this is a side-effect of mechanisms to prevent integer overflow in an arithmetic coder; as symbol frequencies are collected, if the total count of symbols is threatening to cause overflow in the calculations, all individual symbol counts are halved. As well as preventing the overflow, the halving means that subsequent symbol occurrences will have twice the weight of ones prior to the halving. This mechanism can be brought into play more aggressively by incrementing counts by more than one, so that the halving will occur more often, and hence even more weighting is given to recent symbols. A similar effect could be achieved by lowering the threshold for halving, although this means that some accuracy may be lost in rounding during the halving process, since counts are stored as integers. Another possibility is instead of halving the counts, they can be divided by a larger number to "age" them faster.

For example, consider the coding of the characters eeeeaeeueuuuaeiiiiii (taken from the transformed text in Figure 3.1). Figure 3.3 shows them being coded using a very aggressive policy where their counts are incremented by 10, and divided by 3 when the total count exceeds 50 (different figures would be used in practice, and the table shows only four characters, with all "other" characters lumped together in one count, which also is a simplification for the sake of the example). Near the beginning of the sample text the letter e is common. We can see that although at the very start of coding it has an estimated probability of just $\frac{15}{46}$, because its count is incremented by 10 each time it occurs, by the time we get to the fourth e it has a probability of $\frac{28}{39}$, and is coded in just 0.48 bits. Notice also that each time the total count exceeds 50 all the counts are divided by 3, and this means that the relative weight of characters not seen recently is even lower. When dividing by 3 it is important that none of the counts are set to zero, which is why the division is not exact. Toward the end where the character i becomes common, again it only takes a few occurrences (and especially one scaling) before it dominates the probability distribution.

Using an arithmetic coder like this with very rapid adaptation has been found to be very effective for coding the output of the BWT. Ferragina et al. (2006a), for example, suggest incrementing counts by 64, and halving the counts when they get to 16,383. This means that in the steady state counts are being halved every 128 characters (since the total will be ranging from about 8,192 to 16,383) — only the last 128 characters have their full weight, the 128 before them have half the weight, the ones before them only a quarter, and so on.

In principle even the run-length encoding need not be performed separately from the statistical modeling since it simply captures a particularly predictable sequence of characters. However, by using an RLE stage we effectively have two models that are being switched between: the run-length model which places a high probability on the next character being the same as the last character, and the statistical model which places high probability on the next character being the same as some recent characters.

3.3 Move-to-front lists

Traditionally BWT compressors use a "Move to Front" (MTF) list, which essentially ranks characters based on how recently they have occurred. This is done by keeping a list with one entry for each character in the alphabet, and a character is moved to the front of the list each time it is coded, thereby

Character counts						Total Probability	$-\log_2 p$
a	e	i	u	other			
12	15	2	1	16	46	$p(\mathtt{e}) = \frac{15}{46}$	1.62 bits
12	25	2	1	16	56		
4	8	1	1	5	19	$p(\mathtt{e}) = \frac{8}{19}$	1.25 bits
4	18	1	1	5	29	$p(\mathtt{e}) = \frac{18}{29}$	0.69 bits
4	28	1	1	5	39	$p(\mathtt{e}) = \frac{28}{39}$	0.48 bits
4	38	1	1	5	49	$p(\mathtt{a}) = \frac{4}{49}$	3.61 bits
14	38	1	1	5	59		
4	12	1	1	1	19	$p(\mathtt{e}) = \frac{12}{19}$	0.66 bits
4	22	1	1	1	29	$p(\mathtt{e}) = \frac{22}{29}$	0.40 bits
4	32	1	1	1	39	$p(\mathtt{u}) = \frac{1}{39}$	5.29 bits
4	32	1	11	1	49	$p(\mathtt{e}) = \frac{32}{49}$	0.61 bits
4	42	1	11	1	59		
1	14	1	3	1	20	$p(\mathtt{u}) = \frac{3}{20}$	2.74 bits
1	14	1	13	1	30	$p(\mathtt{u}) = \frac{13}{30}$	1.21 bits
1	14	1	23	1	40	$p(\mathtt{u}) = \frac{23}{40}$	0.80 bits
1	14	1	33	1	50	$p(\mathtt{a}) = \frac{1}{50}$	5.64 bits
11	14	1	33	1	60		
3	4	1	11	1	20	$p(\mathtt{e}) = \frac{4}{20}$	2.32 bits
3	14	1	11	1	30	$p(\mathtt{i}) = \frac{1}{30}$	4.91 bits
3	14	11	11	1	40	$p(\mathtt{i}) = \frac{11}{40}$	1.86 bits
3	14	21	11	1	50	$p(\mathtt{i}) = \frac{21}{50}$	1.25 bits
3	14	31	11	1	60		
1	4	10	3	1	19	$p(\mathtt{i}) = \frac{10}{19}$	0.93 bits
1	4	20	3	1	29	$p(\mathtt{i}) = \frac{20}{29}$	0.54 bits
1	4	30	3	1	39	$p(\mathtt{i}) = \frac{30}{39}$	0.38 bits

Fig. 3.3. Aggressive adaptive order zero probability estimation for coding the text
eeeeaeeueuuuaeiiiiii

increasing its rank (and decreasing the corresponding number of bits that will be used to code it next time).

For example, for the Burrows-Wheeler Transform of mississippi, we get the text pssmipissii. The MTF list that is used for coding this is shown in Figure 3.4, assuming only four characters in the alphabet and starting in alphabetical order. The character at the front (left end) of the list is numbered 0, so the first character to be coded (p) has a rank of 2. *After* it has been coded, it is then moved up to rank 0 (the move-to-front step), which in this case happens to be unfortunate because every other character in our small alphabet will be encoded before the next p. Next, the s is coded as rank 3, and then moved up to rank 0. This time it works out well, because the next character is also an s, and is represented by rank 0. The decoder maintains the same list, and after each character is decoded it makes the same updates to the list, so it always has the up-to-date ranking for each character.

MTF list	rank
im(p)s	2
pim(s)	3
(s)pim	0
spi(m)	3
msp(i)	3
ims(p)	3
p(i)ms	1
ipm(s)	3
(s)ipm	0
s(i)pm	1
(i)spm	0

Fig. 3.4. The MTF ranks for the characters in the BWT transformed text $L =$ pssmipissii, assuming that the initial list is imps

In practice the list would typically have 256 entries, one for each possible byte value, and for text such as the example in Figure 3.1 we can see that most of the time we will be dealing with characters with very low ranks, with the occasional high value when a new character is encountered for the first time. Figure 3.3 shows the MTF ranks for a segment of this BWT transformed Hamlet text; for such a text most of the codes are very low values (often 0) because of the clustering of characters. One advantage of the ranks being so low is that linear searches can be sufficient to locate characters in the MTF list if the search starts at rank zero, since most searches will succeed in the first few comparisons.

```
a e e a o e u u e a u i i i A a a u a a a a a a a a a o a a a a i a
2 1 0 1 5 2 4 0 1 3 2 4 0 0 5 3 0 3 1 0 0 0 0 0 0 0 5 1 0 0 0 4 1

a a a a a a a a a a a a a a a a a a a a a a a a a a a a a a a a a
0 0 0 0 0 0 0 0 0 0 0 0 0 0 0 0 0 0 0 0 0 0 0 0 0 0 0 0 0 0 0 0 0

a A A a A A a a A A A A a A a a A u a e a a a a a a a a a a u a a a
0 4 0 1 1 0 1 1 0 0 0 1 1 1 0 1 4 2 5 1 0 0 0 0 0 0 0 0 0 2 1 0 0
```

Fig. 3.5. MTF ranks for a series of characters from Hamlet that occur before the sort key nd

Like the Burrows-Wheeler Transform, the MTF stage is really just another transform, since an input text of n characters will still give us n ranks to encode. However, the ranks are particularly easy to encode because the low numbers are so common. The zero rank is particularly common — typically around half of the ranks are zero — and runs of zeros occur frequently since they correspond to runs of the same character, which is common in a BWT transformed file. For example, in the BWT transformed Hamlet file 76% of the zero ranks occur in runs of three or more, and only 14% occur in isolation. The longest run of 0 ranks is 575 (this occurs because of the character o being common before u). In contrast, the longest run of ranks of 1 is 10, which happens to be caused by alternating "s" and space characters occurring before "how". This is more due to chance than any inherent structure in the text. Because of these kinds of patterns, the MTF ranks are often run-length encoded before any further processing is done.

Eventually (whether or not run-length encoding is used), the ranks are represented using an entropy coder — usually arithmetic coding or Huffman coding. In principle arithmetic coding is best when such high probability symbols need to be represented, but combined with run-length encoding of the output, a Huffman code can be made to work satisfactorily (and in fact this is what is used by BZIP2). Probabilities are estimated using a simple order-0 model; that is, there seems to be little relationship between consecutive MTF ranks apart from the runs of zero ranks. Even a fixed code such as the γ code described in Section 3.1 produces satisfactory results for compressing the output of the MTF, and may be preferred if speed and simplicity are preferred to getting the best possible compression.

The MTF approach is very fast to promote new symbols as they are encountered; in fact, just one occurrence will instantly have a character designated as the most likely to occur next. This is a good assumption much of the time, but the BWT-transformed text will also contain a number of characters that occur in isolation, and promoting these so quickly will result in a higher cost of coding subsequent characters while the one-off character slowly works its way back down the MTF list. A number of variations to MTF have been proposed, such as the "sticky MTF", which checks how often the symbol at the head of the MTF list has been used before demoting it; if it has only been used once then it is moved some distance down the list, whereas if it has occurred twice in succession, it stays at the top of the list and will be demoted slowly in the future.

Recent research has established that the MTF stage may not be needed to compress transformed texts effectively, but instead run-length encoding followed by a fast-adapting entropy coder are sufficient to get excellent compression. This makes sense given the predominance of zero ranks in the MTF output; a zero rank simply means that the previous character has been repeated, and runs of zeros correspond to runs of the repeated character. Hence an appropriately tuned run-length encoder can be expected to pick up this structure.

3.4 Frequency counting methods

Frequency counting methods improve on MTF by basing the ranking of symbols on their frequencies. The simplest approach, to simply give the highest rank to the symbol with the highest frequency, would not be very effective since it would take too long to adapt to favoring symbols that have become popular at the expense of previously popular ones.

The Weighted Frequency Count (WFC) addresses this by defining a function based on symbol frequencies and also the distance to the last occurrence of each symbol within a sliding window, with higher weights being given to more recent occurrences of a symbol. While this approach does give good compression, it is very slow because of the computation involved.

An alternative is the Incremental Frequency Count (IFC) which approximates the WFC by keeping count of character occurrences as they are observed, giving more weight to recent occurrences. This makes computation faster, but at a small cost in compression performance.

3.5 Inversion Frequencies (IF)

The inversion frequencies method is based on the distance between occurrences of symbols in the BWT-transformed text. It relates to an inverted index, which contains a list for each symbol indicating where it occurs in a text.

For example, our sample transformed text `pssmipissii` could be represented by the inverted index shown in Figure 3.6, which gives the number of characters preceding the occurrence of each character named. In the example, "p" occurs after 0 and 5 characters.

```
i: 4, 6, 9, 10
m: 3
p: 0, 5
s: 1, 2, 7, 8
```

Fig. 3.6. Inverted index of the sample transformed text `pssmipissii`

This table can be represented more efficiently by storing the gap since the last occurrence of a character, rather than its absolute position. Furthermore, if the output is being reconstructed by going through the symbols in lexical order, it is only necessary to store the number of intervening symbols that are lexically greater than the current one, as shown in Figure 3.7. From the information in Figure 3.7 the original text is reconstructed by decoding the character i first, then m and so on. The numbers are used to skip only unfilled slots in the decoded text; the last line is not strictly needed, since the character s is simply placed in any unfilled slots.

The inversion frequencies method is comparable in performance to MTF-based methods, performing better on some files and worse on others.

```
i: 4, 1, 2, 0
m: 3
p: 0, 2
s: 0, 0, 0, 0
```

Fig. 3.7. Inversion frequencies representation of the transformed text

3.6 Distance coding

Distance coding has a lot in common with the inversion frequencies method, but is based on encoding the start of each *run* of characters in the transformed text, where a run is a maximal consecutive repetition of the same character, which might be as short as length 1. The end of the run need not be coded, since it will be marked by the start of a run of another character. To seed the decoding, we need to know where the first occurrence of each character is in the text. Subsequent runs are represented as the distance from the previous run of the same character. The distance between two characters is simply the difference between their positions in the array, so two adjacent characters are a distance of 1 apart[1]. A distance of 0 is used to mark the end of the entries for each character.

A simplistic version of distance coding is shown in Figure 3.8, representing the text `pssmipissii`. For example, the first i first occurs at character 5 in the text, and then "runs" of i occur 2 characters later (a single i) and then 3 characters after that (the last two i's in the string). We can detect the end of the first of these "runs" (for example, we know there is a single i because the entry for p shows that there is a p at position 6). The end of each row of distances is marked with a 1.

Character	First occurrence	Distance to next run
i	5	2, 3, 0
m	4	0
p	1	5, 0
s	2	5, 0

Fig. 3.8. Distance coding for the BWT output `pssmipissii`

In addition to this main idea that the ends of runs of a character can be encoded implicitly, there are two other observations that can be used to reduce the amount of information transmitted by this simplified distance coding:

---

[1] A distance of 1 cannot occur in the coding as described so far, since run-lengths are maximal and therefore adjacent runs are not possible, but later we shall see that it is useful.

1. If we know the length of the file to be decoded, the final 0 at the end of each list is sometimes redundant because it will sometimes be the case that there is no more space in the output for any more runs, hence the decoder already knows that there will be no more occurrences of that character.

2. Some of the characters being skipped by the distance code are known to the decoder, and they need not be included in the distance. This enables us to reduce the value representing the distance.

For example, in Figure 3.8 the first occurrence column tells us that the text is of the form ps•mi•••••• (where a dot is an unknown character). The first distance for p is 5 (putting the second p at position 6 in the text), but based on the second rule above we only need to record the distance as 2 (i.e. it is the second *unknown* character). Once that p is decoded we have the text ps•mip•••••, and we know that the only possible character for the first unknown gap is s, yielding pssmip••••• without using any extra information. The distance from i to its next occurrence is 2, but since the p that must be skipped is already known, we can simply record a distance of 1 (the next i is in the next unknown position).

Thus relatively few numbers need be recorded to reconstruct the text, particularly if there are long runs and a limited vocabulary. These numbers are then coded using an entropy coder, yielding good compression results.

3.7 Wavelet trees

Another approach proposed for coding a BWT-transformed text is using *wavelet trees*. Figure 3.9 shows a wavelet tree for our sample transformed text, pssmipissii. The leaves of the tree correspond to the characters that occur in the string to be represented. The root represents the transformed text, and partitions its characters into two groups — those down the left branch and those down the right. This partitioning is represented by the string of bits associated with the node; a 0 means that the corresponding character is in the left branch, and a 1 means that it is in the right branch. The wavelet tree is stored using a binary-heap-like structure; that is, it is a complete tree, with nodes being filled from left to right, top to bottom.

Coding is achieved by applying run-length encoding to the bit patterns for each node; the decoder can reconstruct the original text given those patterns. The run-lengths are coded using the γ code described above in Section 3.1.

Using wavelet trees can be faster than an MTF list, and they have some nice theoretical properties as well as providing a potentially useful structure for searching the text. However, because a simpler coding is used, the compression performance will be slightly less than the best methods, and with MTF, they are likely to be outperformed all round by the simple fast-adapting system described in Section 3.2.

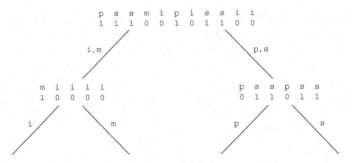

Fig. 3.9. A wavelet tree for the string `pssmipissii`

3.8 Other permutations

The Burrows-Wheeler Transform appears to be the only possible basis of a reversible permutation of the text that can be used for compression; the only other generally reversible transformations are trivial ones that don't usually help with compression performance (such as swapping every second character with its successor). Some variations of the basic BWT are possible. For example, it is possible to limit the size of the substrings being sorted to some constant k characters (typically $k = 2$ to 4). This will inevitably mean that some identical contexts occur, in which case the original order of the substrings is used to resolve the ordering (that is, a stable sort is used). The main advantage of limiting the context size is that it can speed up processing, especially if a very small context is used, since the entire sort can be done using a radix sort. It also avoids the degenerate case where the original text contains many runs of the same character, which can slow down sorting significantly. Contexts of about four characters are enough to capture most of the dependencies in text, and so the loss of compression is very small (typically well under 5% if $k = 4$). A trivial case occurs when $k = 0$, in which case no re-ordering occurs, and the transformed text is the same as the original. Of course, compression performance will be poor in this case. This type of permutation is discussed in more detail in Section 6.1.

A method related to sorting with limited contexts is used in a technique called "Compression boosting", which partitions the BWT transformed text into subsequences of characters that are from related contexts. The value of this can be seen in Figure 3.10, where the sort key initially starts with `tz` and then has a transition to starting with `u_` (a u followed by a space). The `tz` context is primarily preceded by n and i, whereas `u_` is preceded by o. Compression boosting partitions the text so that the bias being used for one context can be dropped when the next one starts, avoiding having to take some time to "learn" that a new set of characters is more likely. An important feature of compression boosting is that it finds the *optimal* partition for a given entropy coder in linear time.

F	L
tz and Guildenstern.] Ros. Wh ...	n
tz and Guildenstern, who go o ...	n
tz: And I beseech you instant ...	n
tz, Courtier. Guildenstern, C ...	n
tz go to't. Ham. Why, man, th ...	n
tz! Good lads, how do ye both ...	n
tz, Guildenstern, and Attenda ...	n
tz, Guildenstern, and others. ...	n
tz, Guildenstern, and some At ...	n
tz, Guildenstern, &c.] Ham. G ...	n
tz.] How now! what hath befal ...	n
tzers? let them guard the doo ...	i
u a daughter? Pol. I have, my ...	o
u a groaning to take off my e ...	o
u a more horrid hent: When he ...	o
u a place. [Danish march. A f ...	o
u a spirit of health or gobli ...	o
u a wholesome answer; my wit' ...	o
u advise me? Laer. I am lost ...	o
u again to bed; Pinch wanton ...	o
u all, If you have hitherto c ...	o
u all without. Danes. No, let ...	o
u alone. Mar. Look with what ...	o
u amble, and you lisp, and ni ...	o

Fig. 3.10. A variation of BWT where the sorting uses only the first two characters to determine sort order

An efficient algorithm for performing the partitioning for compression boosting is available using suffix trees to determine where the partitions should fall. Compression boosting can be applied to various other local-to-global techniques to improve them, but it is still out-performed by a simple arithmetic coder that is set up to adapt quickly because the fast adaptation soon reduces the significance of the change of context.

Variations on the BWT, such as using limited-length sort keys as above, or using English words as the alphabet, are discussed in detail in Chapter 6.

3.9 Block size

Because a BWT-based compression system must have access to a whole text before it can be encoded, a text which is too large to be processed in memory must be broken up into blocks that can be accommodated. These blocks are then compressed independently[2].

So far we have put aside the issue of the size of the blocks to be used. In general, these blocks should be as large as possible to maximize the opportunity to capture patterns in the text, but will be limited by available memory. Typically the amount of memory required is about 5 to 8 times the block size (in bytes), with 1 Mbyte being a reasonable size for blocks (and therefore about 8 Mbyte being used for encoding). An important factor is that the access to memory for BWT is quite random, and implementations should consider how this will interact with caching, since the random access could lead to very slow memory retrieval if the cache cannot store the entire block. Thus the limit in memory size may be more related to cache sizes than the total RAM in a computer.

Burrows and Wheeler's original paper evaluated the effect of block size on compression performance, and found that gains of a few percent were still being made by quadrupling the block size from 16 Mbytes to 64 Mbytes. And of course, gains will be made only if the file being compressed is larger than the block size, and if the material at the start of the file is similar to that much later on.

The BZIP2 program is a general-purpose compression system based on the Burrows-Wheeler Transform. It has a maximum block size of 900 kilobytes, which is larger than many of the files that are likely to be compressed, yet allows the implementation to work with a small footprint in the memory of a standard computer. At this size gains in the order of 1% are made by increasing the block size by about 10%, so larger blocks may well give a little compression gain, but is likely to be at the expense of severe speed deterioration because of cache misses, and may never be noticed since files of that size are more likely to be audio or video rather than text, which are typically compressed with a lossy compression method. Lossless compression would be needed for genomic data, but this kind of file generally does not benefit significantly from larger block sizes.

3.10 Further reading

Entropy coders (especially Huffman and arithmetic coding) are discussed at length in standard texts on lossless compression (see the Further reading section of Chapter 1). They are a particular focus of the book by Moffat and Turpin (2002), and the implementation of arithmetic coding is discussed in Moffat et al. (1995) and Moffat et al. (1998). Some BWT-based systems propose using "range coding", which has similar performance to arithmetic coding, but avoids some potential issues with patents on some versions of

---

[2] This is why BWT-based compression systems are sometimes referred to as "Block-sorting compression".

arithmetic coding; for examples see Foschini et al. (2004) and Ferragina et al. (2006a). Run-length encoding in the context of the BWT is discussed in detail by Deorowicz (2002) and Fenwick (2007).

The classic reference for fixed codes such as the α, γ and δ codes is Elias (1975), which includes universal codes that will be within a constant factor of the entropy even though the probability distribution is not specified. A detailed description of the use of such codes in compression is given in Witten et al. (1999) and Sayood (2003). Fenwick (2002a, 2003c) provides an extensive investigation of the practical use of integer codes with the BWT, and a related code used by Wheeler called the "1/2" code (Fenwick, 1996a, 2007).

The observation that a simple run-length coder with arithmetic coding outperforms many other techniques for compressing a BWT transformed text was made by Ferragina, Giancarlo and Manzini in their 2006 paper (Ferragina et al., 2006a). This paper introduces RLEAC, and compares it empirically with a number of other coders, including "range coding", which is very similar to arithmetic coding. The idea of using a fast adapting arithmetic coder is not a new one; Fenwick (1996a) reported using an arithmetic coder with an increment of 16 and a limit of 8192.

The MTF method was proposed in Burrows and Wheeler's original paper (Burrows and Wheeler, 1994); seminal work on MTF was done by Bentley et al. (1986) and Elias (1987). The proportion of zero ranks after MTF has been applied to a BWT transformed string was reported by Fenwick (1996b) to be about 63%. This paper proposes an approximate entropy coder described as a "unary" model, which takes advantage of the probability distribution of ranks but is simpler and therefore faster than arithmetic or Huffman coding. Balkenhol and Kurtz (2000) explore a number of variations for compressing the transformed text.

Variations on the MTF list which avoid the rapid promotion of one-off symbols were first suggested in Burrows and Wheeler's original paper (Burrows and Wheeler, 1994), but were not evaluated. Subsequently a number of variations have been published, including "Sticky MTF" by Fenwick (2002a, 2003c), Schindler's system (Schindler, 1997a,b), which does not promote a symbol to rank 0 unless it has been seen twice, Balkenhol et al. (1999), where symbols are first promoted to rank 1 before rank 0, and Chapin (2000), which switches between two update algorithms. Wirth (2001) compares the performance of MTF and related approaches on BWT output. Bachrach and El-Yaniv (1997) provide a detailed empirical evaluation of the performance of the MTF and its variations on general text.

The idea of distance coding originated in a posting to the Usenet group comp.compression by Edgar Binder in 2000. It was described and evaluated in Deorowicz (2002), and in Gagie and Manzini (2007). Inversion frequencies (IF) as an alternative to MTF are introduced by Arnavut and Magliveras (1997a) and analyzed by Ferragina et al. (2006b). Improvements for the IF method are noted by Abel (2007b), including changing the order in which characters are stored in the table to achieve slight compression improvements. Coding

BWT-transformed text without ranks is explored by Wirth (2001) and Wirth and Moffat (2001).

The Weighted Frequency Count (WFC) was introduced by Deorowicz (2002) and variations to it are explored by Abel (2007b). A comparison of related methods is given by Abel (2007a). A comparison of move-to-front, distance coding, and inversion frequencies can be found in Gagie and Manzini (2007). The Incremental Frequency Count (IFC) is due to Jürgen Abel (Abel, 2005, 2007a).

"Wavelet trees" are introduced by Grossi et al. (2003) and applied to the BWT in Foschini et al. (2004). Further analysis and application to the BWT is given in Ferragina et al. (2006b).

The observation that limited-length contexts can be used for the BWT sort was published by Schindler (1997a), and is discussed further in Section 6.1. Partitioning the transformed text for "compression boosting" was described in Ferragina and Manzini (2004), Ferragina et al. (2005a), and Ferragina et al. (2006a). Deorowicz describes a system that does not explicitly partition the BWT text according to context, but infers it from the transformed file through a process called "context exhumation" (Deorowicz, 2005). Other work on the Burrows-Wheeler permutation is described by Arnavut (2002) and Crochemore et al. (2005).

A special edition of *Theoretical Computer Science* in November 2007 featured a number of papers about the BWT that are relevant to the material in this chapter.

Suffix trees and suffix arrays

The Burrows-Wheeler Transform has a very close relationship with suffix trees and suffix arrays — the array of indexes to the sorted array of substrings generated during the transform is essentially a suffix array, which in turn is a representation of the information in a suffix tree. As pointed out by Burrows and Wheeler in their original work (Burrows and Wheeler, 1994), the problem of sorting the rotated matrices is the major bottleneck in performing the transformation, and this is essentially an exercise in suffix sorting. This relationship between the BWT and suffix arrays and suffix trees also has important implications in the applications of the BWT, and in its relationship with other compression schemes, such as PPM. Analyzing the performance of the BWT is greatly simplified by an understanding of the construction and complexity of suffix trees and suffix arrays.

In this chapter we study suffix trees and suffix arrays in more detail. While this is motivated by their relationship with the BWT, suffix trees and suffix arrays have become important data structures in their own right, especially for problems in pattern matching, full-text indexing, compression, and other applications.

4.1 Suffix Trees

The suffix tree is a data structure used to represent the set of all suffixes of a string. It has a strong resemblance to the trie data structure (Knuth, 1973; Gonnet et al., 1992). However, unlike the trie, the suffix tree provides a more compact representation of the suffixes. While the size of the trie could be quadratic with respect to the length of the input string, the suffix tree provides a linear space representation of the suffixes.

The suffix tree is efficient in both time and space, and it is used for a variety of applications, such as in pattern matching (Ukkonen, 1993), multiple sequence alignment (Delcher et al., 1999; Kurtz et al., 2004), the identification of repetitions in genome-scale biological sequences (Bieganski et al., 1994;

Volfovsky et al., 2001), and in lossy image compression (Atallah et al., 1999). Apostolico (1985), Giancarlo (1995) and Grossi and Vitter (2005) discussed various applications of the suffix tree. More recently, *Wired* magazine reported the use of the suffix tree data structure in studying an age-old Inca Mystery (Cook, 2007) about the existence of written communication using knots and threads in old Peruvian culture.

Various algorithms have been developed for linear time construction of suffix trees (Weiner, 1973; McCreight, 1976; Ukkonen, 1995). In this section, we will discuss basic algorithms for constructing suffix trees, with an emphasis on newer approaches that lend themselves to direct construction of suffix arrays (without suffix trees). The book by Dan Gusfield (Gusfield, 1997) provides a comprehensive treatment of suffix trees, their construction, and applications.

4.1.1 Basic notations and definitions

We will continue to use $T = T[1\ldots n]$ as our input text. T is a string of length n, over an alphabet Σ. In this book, we assume that for a given string the symbol alphabet is fixed. Thus, we will treat the alphabet size as being constant, unless otherwise stated. Let $T = \alpha\beta\gamma$, for some strings α, β, and γ (α and γ could be empty). The string β is called a *substring* of T, α is called a *prefix* of T, while γ is called a *suffix* of T. The prefix α is called a proper prefix of T if $\alpha \neq T$. Similarly, the suffix γ is called a proper suffix of T if $\gamma \neq T$. We will also use $t_i = T[i]$ to denote the i-th symbol in T — both notations are used interchangeably. We use $T_i = T[i\ldots n] = t_i t_{i+1} \ldots t_n$ to denote the i-th suffix of T. Similarly, we use $T^i = T[1\ldots i] = t_1 t_2 \ldots t_i$ to denote the i-th prefix of T.

For simplicity in constructing suffix trees, we usually ensure that no suffix of the string is a proper prefix of another suffix. This can be done by placing a sentinel symbol at the end of T, such that the sentinel does not appear anywhere else in T. In practice this is often achieved by simply appending a special symbol, say $ to T, such that $ \notin \Sigma$. This constraint implies that each suffix of T will have its own unique leaf node in the suffix tree of T, since any two suffixes of T will eventually follow separate branches in the tree. Unless otherwise stated, we assume that this special symbol has been appended to each string.

Given a string T of length n, its suffix tree $\mathcal{T}_T$ is a rooted tree with n leaves, where the i-th leaf node corresponds to the i-th suffix T_i of T. Except for the root node and the leaf nodes, every node must have at least two descendant child nodes. Each edge in the suffix tree $\mathcal{T}_T$ represents a substring of T, and no two edges out of a node start with the same character. For a given edge, the *edge label* is simply the substring in T corresponding to the edge. We use l_i to denote the i-th leaf node. Then, l_i corresponds to T_i, the i-th suffix of T. Figure 4.1 shows the list of suffixes, the suffix trie, and the suffix tree for an example string $T = \texttt{acracca\$}$.

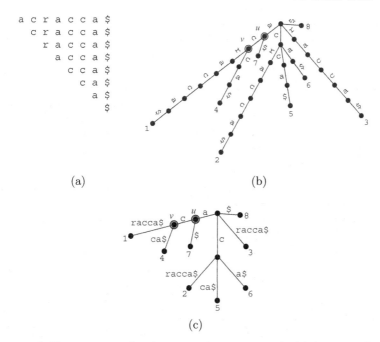

Fig. 4.1. Suffix structures for the string $T = $ acracca$: (a) list of suffixes; (b) suffix trie, and (c) suffix tree. The number at each leaf node corresponds to the starting position of the corresponding suffix in the original string. See the text for explanation of the marked nodes u and v

For edge (u, v) between nodes u and v in $\mathcal{T}_T$, the edge label (denoted $label(u, v)$) is a non-empty substring of T. An edge is called a t-edge if its edge label starts with the symbol t. For a given node u in the suffix tree, its *path label*, $L(u)$ is defined as the label of the path from the root node to u. Since each edge represents a substring in T, $L(u)$ is essentially the string formed by the concatenation of the labels of the edges traversed in going from the root node to the given node, u. The *string depth* of node u, (also called its length) is simply $|L(u)|$, the number of characters in $L(u)$. Using the labels in the suffix tree in Figure 4.1, we will have $L(u) = $ a, $L(v) = $ ac, $label(u, v) = $ c, and the string depth of $v = 2$ (this also applies to the suffix trie). The number at each leaf node corresponds to the starting position of the corresponding suffix in the original string, T.

Properties of a suffix tree

Before discussing the construction of suffix trees, we summarize their basic properties. Given the string $T = T[1 \ldots n]$\$, of length n, but with the end of string symbol appended to give a sequence with a total length $n+1$, the suffix tree of the resulting string T\$ will have the following properties:

1. Exactly $n + 1$ leaf nodes;
2. At most n internal (or branching) nodes (the root node is considered an internal node);
3. Every *distinct* substring of T is encoded exactly once in the suffix tree. Each distinct substring is spelled out exactly once by traveling from the root node to some node u, such that $L(u)$ is the required substring. Note that the node u may be an implicit node (see Section 4.1.3).
4. No two edges out of a given node in the suffix tree start with the same symbol.
5. Every internal node has at least two outgoing edges.

Properties (1), (2), (4), and (5) imply that a suffix tree will have at most $2n + 1$ total nodes, and at most $2n$ edges;

The suffix tree is similar in spirit to the traditional trie data structure (Gonnet et al., 1992). The major difference is the notion of *path-label compression* and *edge-label compression* used in suffix trees. Thus, the suffix tree is generally viewed as a compacted suffix trie, as can be seen in the difference between the two trees in Figure 4.1. Path label compression and edge-label compression are critical for the linear time and linear space complexity of suffix tree construction. The notion of *path-label compression* is related to the requirement that every internal node, except the root node, must have at least two descendants, so we can remove all the internal nodes that have only one descendant in the suffix trie. The characters that make up the labels for the edges linking the removed nodes are concatenated in order, starting from the node nearest to the root. Thus, for the suffix tree, the edge labels can be substrings of the original sequence, rather than single symbols, which will reduce the number of nodes. For *edge-label compression*, rather than writing out the edge label explicitly, we use pointers into the original string to indicate the starting and ending positions of the substring corresponding to an edge label. This requires that the original string T must be available, in order to determine the edge labels explicitly. This reduces the potential $O(n^2)$ space required for suffix trees to $O(n)$, since the maximum number of edges will be $2n$. Figure 4.2 shows the suffix tree representation using edge-label compression for the example string used in Figure 4.1. For example, the edge label c is now replaced with the pair (2,2), while ca$ is replaced with (6,8). Notice that under edge-label compression, the same edge (substring) could be represented with different pairs of pointers, for instance, the edge label c could have been represented with any of the pairs (2,2), (5,5), or (6,6). In practice, the pair representing the first occurrence of the substring in T, or the current occurrence, is generally used.

4.1.2 Construction of a suffix tree

Construction of the suffix tree for a string is not difficult. A simple algorithm that accomplishes this task for any given string is given in Algorithm 4.1. However, building the suffix tree *efficiently* is the key challenge.

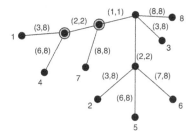

Fig. 4.2. Suffix tree for the string $T = $ acracca$ using edge-label compression

---

SIMPLE-SUFFIX-TREE-ALGORITHM(T)
Create the *root* node, with empty string
for $i \leftarrow 1$ **to** n **do**
    Traverse current tree from the *root*
    Match symbols in the edge label one-by-one with symbols in
        the current suffix, T_i
    if a mismatch occurs **then**
        Split the edge at the position of mismatch to create a new
          node, if need be
        Insert suffix T_i into the suffix tree at the position of mismatch
    end if
end for

Algorithm 4.1: Simple suffix tree construction algorithm

A step-by-step construction of a suffix tree using Algorithm 4.1 is shown in Figure 4.3 for the sample string $T = $ acracca$. First, the root node is created. Then the first suffix $T_1 = T = $ acracca$ is inserted by attaching it to the root node. To insert the next suffix, $T_2 = $ cracca$, the algorithm traverses the edge, matching its edge label symbol-by-symbol. A mismatch occurs at the first position, hence suffix T_2 is attached to the root node. Suffix T_3 is inserted in the same way. To insert suffix $T_4 = $ acca$, we traverse from the root, on the a-edge until the mismatch with the third symbol c. Since the match occurred in the middle of an edge, we split the edge to create a new node at the mismatch position. Then the suffix is inserted by attaching a leaf node to the newly created node. The edge from the node to the leaf is then labeled with the remaining symbols in the suffix being inserted, starting with the mismatched character in the suffix. This process of matching, edge-splitting, and insertion continues until we reach the last suffix (the last symbol) of the string.

The above algorithm, although simple to implement, unfortunately requires construction time that is proportional to the square of n, the length of the string. This $O(n^2)$ complexity may not pose a problem for short sequences

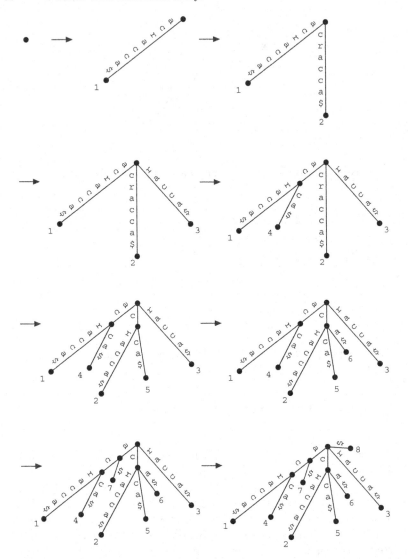

Fig. 4.3. Step-by-step construction of a suffix tree using the simple algorithm

with a few symbols. However, for most practical applications of suffix trees, such as in whole-genome sequence analysis with input strings that could have billions of symbols, more efficient approaches are required.

4.1.3 Ukkonen's suffix tree algorithm

Several methods have been proposed for constructing suffix trees in linear time and linear space. Ukkonen's algorithm (Ukkonen, 1995) is popular mainly because it is easier to understand and implement, and also because of its relatively small memory requirement. Our discussion of Ukkonen's algorithm mainly follows the description in Ukkonen (1995) and Gusfield (1997). Complete details can be found in the book or in the original paper by Ukkonen.

Ukkonen's algorithm is based on an observation on the relationship between the suffixes of substrings from the same string. Given a string $T = t_1 t_2 \ldots t_n$, and the substring $T^i = t_1 t_2 \ldots t_i$ (i.e. the i-th prefix of T), we observe that $T^i = T^{i-1} t_i$. Thus, the suffixes of T^i can be obtained from the suffixes of its longest proper prefix $T^{i-1} = t_1 t_2 \ldots t_{i-1}$ by appending the new symbol t_i at the end of each suffix of T^{i-1}, and by adding the empty suffix. Therefore, the suffix tree of $T = t_1 t_2 \ldots t_n = T^n$ can be constructed using a left to right scan, by first building the suffix tree for T^0, the empty string, expanding this to obtain the suffix tree for T^1, and continuing in this way until we build the suffix tree of $T = T^n$ from that of T^{n-1}. This incremental construction and the left-to-right scanning ability also imply that the method can be used to construct suffix trees online, that is, the algorithm can build the suffix tree piece-by-piece as a new symbol is received, without having the entire input string available at the beginning. To get the algorithm to work in linear time, Ukkonen used various clever ideas based on the properties of suffix trees.

Ukkonen's algorithm starts with an *implicit suffix tree*. Given a string T, and its suffix tree $\mathcal{T}_T$, its implicit suffix tree is obtained from $\mathcal{T}_T$, by removing the special symbol $ from the edge labels, removing each node that has no label, and removing any node that has less than two children. The implicit suffix tree is constructed incrementally as described above. The last implicit suffix tree is then converted to a true suffix tree using a simple linear time traversal of the implicit suffix tree. The implicit suffix tree represents all the suffixes of a string, since each suffix is spelled out by some path from the root, whereby the path can end inside an edge. However, each suffix may not have a unique leaf node in the implicit suffix tree. If the last character in the string is unique (i.e. does not appear anywhere else in the string), then the implicit suffix tree and the true suffix tree will be the same. Figure 4.4 shows the implicit suffix tree for the example string $T = \texttt{acracca}$; notice that nodes 7 and 8 are no longer shown explicitly.

Ukkonen's algorithm also made use of *suffix links*. The notion of suffix links is based on a well-known fact about suffix trees (Weiner, 1973; McCreight, 1976), namely, if there is an internal node u in $\mathcal{T}_T$ such that its path label $L(u) = a\alpha$ for some single character $a \in \Sigma$, and a (possibly empty) string $\alpha \in \Sigma^*$, then there is a node v in $\mathcal{T}_T$ such that $L(v) = \alpha$. A pointer from node u to node v is called a *suffix link*. If α is an empty string, then the pointer goes from u to the root node. In its simplest form, the suffix link from a given leaf node points to the leaf node that corresponds to the longest proper suffix of the suffix represented by the leaf node.

We can now look at Ukkonen's algorithm in more detail. We will give a high level description of the algorithm in terms of its *phases* and the updates in each phase. We then describe the cases involved in performing the suffix updates at each step of the algorithm. Ukkonen's algorithm may be understood by first describing how we can use it to construct a suffix *trie*. We then describe the modifications to the basic algorithm to yield the suffix tree. To explain Ukkonen's algorithm, we use a somewhat longer example string, $T = \mathtt{mississippi\$}$, as this captures all the update cases that will be encountered using the algorithm.

Suffix Trie Construction

Let $\mathcal{J}_T$ denote the suffix trie of the string T. The suffix trie for the string $T = t_1 t_2 \ldots t_n = T^n$ is constructed incrementally, from the suffix trie of its longest proper prefix $T^{n-1} = t_1 t_2 \ldots t_{n-1}$. In turn $\mathcal{J}_T^{n-1}$ is constructed from $\mathcal{J}_T^{n-2}$, and so on. Thus, Ukkonen's algorithm constructs the suffix tree in phases, whereby $\mathcal{J}_T^i$ is constructed in phase i of the algorithm. During phase 1 of the algorithm $\mathcal{J}_T^1$ is constructed from T^0, the empty suffix (empty string). Then $\mathcal{J}_T^2$ is constructed from $\mathcal{J}_T^1$ in phase 2, and so on, until finally, $\mathcal{J}_T^n$, the required suffix trie is constructed from $\mathcal{J}_T^{n-1}$ in phase n. Thus, the major question is how we construct $\mathcal{J}_T^i$, the suffix trie for the prefix $T^i = t_1 t_2 \ldots t_i$ from $\mathcal{J}_T^{i-1}$, the suffix trie of its longest proper prefix.

To construct $\mathcal{J}_T^i$ from $\mathcal{J}_T^{i-1}$, we need to append the next symbol t_i to the end of *each* suffix in $\mathcal{J}_T^{i-1}$, and add the empty suffix. Thus, we visit each suffix of $\mathcal{J}_T^{i-1}$, starting from its longest suffix, walking up to the shortest suffix (which corresponds to the empty string), updating the tree as we walk. Let node u in $\mathcal{J}_T^{i-1}$ be the current node during the walk. How the tree is updated depends on whether or not there is a t_i-edge that starts from node u.

The following update cases can occur:

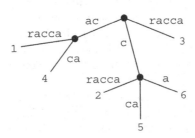

Fig. 4.4. Implicit suffix tree for the string $T = \mathtt{acracca}$

CASE A : Node u does *not* have a path that started with symbol t_i. This could happen in two ways:

1. Node u is a leaf node. Here, we update the tree by appending t_i to $L(u)$, the path label for node u. No new node is created. This can be seen in Figure 4.5 (going from $\mathcal{J}_T^1$ to $\mathcal{J}_T^2$), extending the leaf node with edge label m to mi; or in Figure 4.5 going from $\mathcal{J}_T^8$ to $\mathcal{J}_T^9$, extending the leftmost branch from mississi to mississip.

2. Node u is not a leaf node, but no edge from node u is a t_i-edge. This means that there is at least one edge that continues from node u, but no such edge starts with the symbol t_i. Here, we update the tree by creating a new leaf node starting from u, with edge label t_i. Examples can be seen in Figure 4.5 ($\mathcal{J}_T^1$), creating the leaf node from the root, with edge label m; or in Figure 4.5 ($\mathcal{J}_T^9$), creating the five leaf nodes, each with edge label p, resulting in parent nodes with ≥ 2 outgoing edges.

CASE B : There is a t_i-edge emanating from u. This means that node u is not a leaf node, and the string $L(u)t_i$ has already been added to the suffix trie. Since the end of a suffix need not be explicit in an implicit suffix tree, no update is needed. This can be seen in Figure 4.5 ($\mathcal{J}_T^6$).

The root node, along with the set of nodes with old t_i-edges, the set of nodes with new t_i-edges created from $\mathcal{J}_T^{i-1}$, and the empty string represent $\mathcal{J}_T^i$, the suffix trie of T^i.

Suffix links and boundary paths

Determining which nodes in $\mathcal{J}_T^{i-1}$ should get new t_i edges is performed using suffix links. Given the definition of suffix links, each node in $\mathcal{J}_T^{i-1}$ that represents a suffix of T^{i-1} can be found by traversing a path of suffix links that start from the node with the largest depth (i.e. the node corresponding to the longest suffix $t_1 t_2 \ldots t_{i-1}$), and ends at the shortest suffix (the empty string). This path is called the *boundary path* of the suffix trie $\mathcal{J}_T^{i-1}$. During this traversal, for each node on the boundary path that does not have a t_i-edge, one is created. The new nodes are then connected with new suffix links that form a new path, starting from the suffix $t_1 t_2 \ldots t_{i-1}$. This new path thus corresponds to the boundary path for the new suffix trie, $\mathcal{J}_T^i$.

An important observation is that the traversal of the boundary path of $\mathcal{J}_T^{i-1}$ can be stopped whenever the first node, say u, is found such that node u already has a t_i-edge. This corresponds to CASE B above. We can terminate the traversal at this point because if the string αt_i is a substring of T^{i-1}, for some string α, then each suffix of αt_i (which cannot be longer than $|\alpha t_i|$) must be a substring of T^{i-1}. So, these shorter substrings must have already been added to the suffix trie at some earlier phase. Thus, we can stop the update earlier, whenever CASE B applies. This means that the algorithm creates a new node only when CASE A2 applies.

Figure 4.5 shows the step-by-step construction of the suffix trie for the string $T = \texttt{mississippi}$ using Ukkonen's algorithm. The figure shows all 11 phases of the construction, and the suffix links created at each phase. In some cases, only the suffix links from the current and last phase are included, for ease of presentation. The suffix trie for $T = T^n$ is thus constructed by starting with the empty string, $(\mathcal{J}_T^0 = \epsilon)$. This contains just the root node, and an *auxiliary* node (denoted as $\perp$ in the figures), and the links between them. The auxiliary node makes it possible to avoid an explicit distinction between the root and non-root nodes (i.e. between the empty suffix and non-empty suffixes) in the algorithm. Technically, the auxiliary node is defined as the inverse of any symbol in the alphabet. That is, for all $\sigma \in \Sigma$, $\sigma^{-1}\sigma = \epsilon$, the empty string. Therefore any σ-transition from $\perp$, the auxiliary node should lead to the root node, independent of σ. This is because the root node corresponds to ϵ, the empty suffix.

Figure 4.5 shows the algorithm repeating for each suffix T^i, for $i = 1, 2, \ldots, n$. The algorithm is optimal in the sense that it requires time that is linear with respect to its output size. However, this output size is proportional to the number of substrings in the original string, which could be quadratic with respect to the length of the string. Thus the running time will be in $O(n^2)$.

From suffix trie to suffix tree

The above suffix-trie construction algorithm can be turned into a linear-time algorithm for building suffix trees with some important modifications. The suffix tree of T provides a more compact representation of the suffixes of T by considering only a subset of the nodes in $\mathcal{J}_T$. This subset still includes all the suffixes of T.

Path compression and edge label compression. The first improvement is the use of path compression on the nodes of $\mathcal{J}_T$, which means that only internal nodes with at least two edges are allowed in the tree. The suffix tree $\mathcal{T}_T$ will thus contain only *explicit nodes* in the suffix trie $\mathcal{J}_T$, that is, the set of all branching nodes and all leaf nodes in $\mathcal{J}_T$. By definition, the root node is considered a branching node. The non-explicit nodes (called *implicit nodes*) are not stored in the suffix tree. The use of path compression, however, implies that for suffix tree construction, we may need to split an edge at an implicit node as the algorithm progresses (see below). A second improvement is the use of edge-label compression, whereby each edge label (which is a substring in T) is represented by a pair of pointers, say (p, q), where p and q point respectively to the start and end of the corresponding substring in T. That is, given an edge label, say α, p and q are chosen such that $\alpha = T[p \ldots q] = t_p t_{p+1} \ldots t_q$.

With this indexing, a copy of the original string T is needed as part of the representation of the suffix tree. This means that any substring can be accessed in constant time using its starting and ending pointers. An important advantage here is that we now need only a constant number of symbols (simply

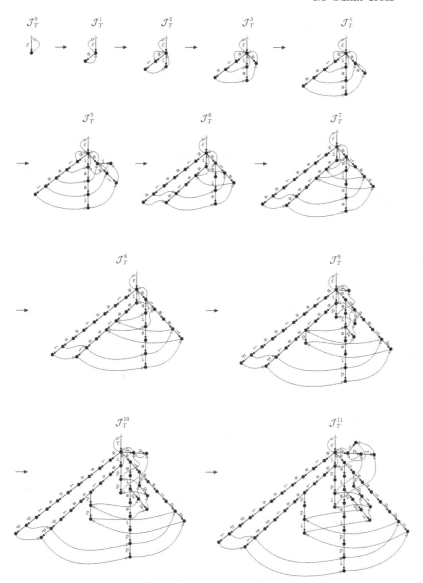

Fig. 4.5. Step-by-step construction of the suffix trie for the sequence $T =$ `mississippi` using Ukkonen's algorithm. The darker (filled) arrows represent transitions from one node to the other; the lighter (open) arrows are suffix links. For clarity, only the last two layers of suffix links are shown in some cases

two pointers) to represent each edge label, rather than requiring memory space that is proportional to the length of the label. Since we have one leaf for each non-empty suffix of T, we can have at most n leaves in the implicit suffix tree. Further, the implicit suffix tree of T can contain no more than $n-1$ branching nodes. The number of edges will be at most $2n - 1$. This means that we can represent $\mathcal{T}_T$ using $O(n)$ space.

The suffix links are now defined only for branching nodes. However, at times imaginary suffix links, called *implicit suffix links*, are used. These links are defined between explicit nodes. This is mandated by the path compression, since some new explicit nodes may need to be created between two implicit nodes.

A leaf node stays a leaf node. Another important observation with the construction algorithm is that, once a leaf node is created and given a label, say l_i, then the node will remain a leaf node with the same label until the end of the algorithm. Thus, the node will never have a descendant node, rather, it can be extended only via character concatenation (update CASE A1 as described previously). As it is sometimes put, 'once a leaf, always a leaf' (Gusfield, 1997). Recall that to extend $\mathcal{J}_T^{i-1}$ to $\mathcal{J}_T^i$, we need to extend the edges to each leaf node by appending the symbol t_i to the edge label. Ordinarily this concatenation will have to be performed for each leaf node at each phase of the algorithm. These extensions can, however, be avoided by a simple modification: whenever a new leaf node is created in phase i, we set its edge label (using the two pointers) to be (i, n), that is, to the substring $t_i, t_{i+1} \ldots t_n$ in T. Therefore explicit updates via character concatenations are no longer required at later phases of the algorithm. When an edge is split, the end point of the leaf node will still be fixed (at n, the end of the string), although the starting position in T may change.

Active point and end point. Ukkonen's algorithm also used the notions of an *active point* and *end point*. During the traversal of the boundary path at the current phase, the first non-leaf node encountered is called the *active point*, while the first node where CASE B applies (i.e. the first node with a t_i transition) is called the *end point*. The active point and end point are key instruments used in achieving the linear time performance of the algorithm. Examples of active and end points are shown in Figure 4.6. We have repeated the suffix trie at some phases in Figure 4.5, but now with the active point and end point clearly marked at each phase. Since we no longer need to perform explicit updates via CASE A1 (from the foregoing discussion), and we had already observed that we can stop traversal of the boundary path whenever CASE B applies (see previous discussion under suffix links and boundary paths), it means that we need to perform updates only on the implicit and explicit nodes on the boundary path between the active point and the end point.

Another important observation here is that the end point in the current phase directly defines the active point in the next phase; the next node on the t_{i-1} edge from the endpoint in $\mathcal{J}_T^{i-1}$ becomes the active point in $\mathcal{J}_T^i$. This

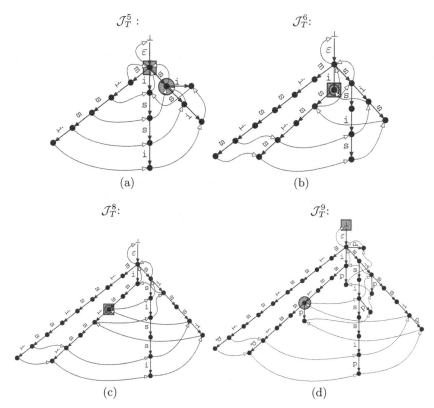

$\mathcal{J}_T^5$: $\mathcal{J}_T^6$:

(a)   (b)

$\mathcal{J}_T^8$: $\mathcal{J}_T^9$:

(c)   (d)

Fig. 4.6. Active points and end points for $\mathcal{J}_T^5$, $\mathcal{J}_T^6$ and $\mathcal{J}_T^8$, and $\mathcal{J}_T^9$ of the sequence $T = $ mississippi. A circle on a node denotes an active point, a box denotes the end point, and a bulls-eye denotes a node that is both an active point and an end point

is very important, as it means that we can avoid a lot of computations that would otherwise be required to update the nodes in the suffix tree. By keeping record of the end point we already know the active point in the next phase. Since updates are performed only between active points and end points, it means that constructing $\mathcal{J}_T^i$ from $\mathcal{J}_T^{i-1}$ requires only one overlapping explicit update (one performed at the end point of $\mathcal{J}_T^{i-1}$, or at the active point of $\mathcal{J}_T^i$). This is shown in Figure 4.6.

Splitting a node. The final issue we need to discuss is how tree updates are performed when the active point is at an implicit node (i.e. between two explicit nodes). Updating the tree in this situation involves three steps: testing the node for possible splitting, splitting the node if necessary, and updating the new explicit node. First, we test to know if the edge needs to be split. If the continuing implicit edge (beyond the active point) is a t_i-edge, we do nothing (since we are working with implicit suffix trees). Otherwise we split the edge at the active point to obtain an explicit node at that point. Then we attach a leaf node to the newly created node. Let edge (u, w) be the edge before splitting, with edge label (p, q). Let v be the newly created explicit node at the active point. Thus, u is the parent node of v, while w is now a child node of v. The label for the upper edge (that is, $label(u, v)$) is given as $(p, |L(v)|) = (p, p + |label(u, v)|)$, while the label for the edge that continues from v (i.e $label(v, w)$) is given as $(|L(v)| + 1, q)$. Then we apply the update cases at this newly created explicit node. This will thus create a new leaf node from the new explicit node (CASE A2). The edge from the newly created explicit node to this leaf node will be a t_i-edge, with edge label $(l_i + |L(v)|, n)$.

Figure 4.7 shows an example of the process for node splitting in Ukkonen's algorithm. The figure shows the suffix tree in phase 5 of the algorithm before node splitting, just after node splitting but before update of the newly created node, and after updating the node. Notice the new suffix link created after node splitting.

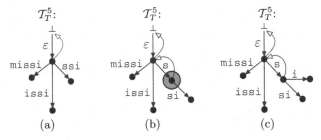

(a)   (b)   (c)

Fig. 4.7. Node splitting during suffix tree construction: (a) tree before node splitting; (b) tree just after node splitting, before node updating; (c) tree after node update. The marked node indicates the node where the splitting occurred

The complete construction phases for building the suffix tree for the running example $T =$ mississippi are shown in Figure 4.8. We have used the substrings as the edge labels for clarity of presentation. In practice, the pair of their starting and ending positions in T will be used.

4.1.4 From implicit suffix tree to true suffix tree

The above algorithm constructs the implicit suffix tree for a given string T. The final step is to convert this implicit suffix tree to a true suffix tree. This can be performed by appending a special end-of-string symbol, $, ($ \notin \Sigma$) to T, and letting the algorithm continue with this new symbol. Alternatively, we can traverse the boundary path from the leaf node of T_T^n up to the root, and make all nodes on the path explicit. Either way, each leaf node in the resulting tree will correspond to one unique suffix in the original string T. The resulting tree is the true suffix tree. The above requires only $O(n)$ time to traverse the

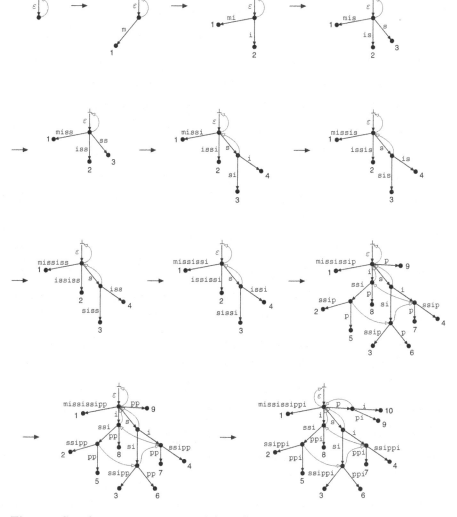

Fig. 4.8. Step-by-step construction of the suffix tree for the string $T =$ `mississippi` using Ukkonen's algorithm

leaf nodes in the tree. Therefore, overall, Ukkonen's algorithm requires $O(n)$ space and time for the construction of the suffix tree for a string of length n.

Figure 4.9 shows the final suffix tree obtained using Ukkonen's algorithm, for $T =$ `mississippi$`. For comparison, we have included the suffix tree with strings for the edge labels, and the final tree with edge-label compression. These can be compared with the suffix trie for the same string shown earlier.

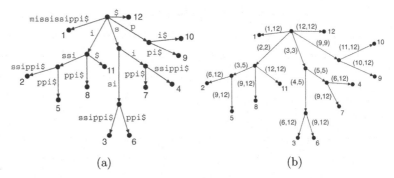

Fig. 4.9. (a) Final suffix tree for the string $T = $ `mississippi` using Ukkonen's algorithm; (b) the same suffix tree represented using edge-label compression

4.1.5 Farach's recursive construction

Farach and colleagues (Farach, 1997; Farach and Muthukrishnan, 1996; Farach-Colton et al., 2000) introduced a fundamentally different method for constructing suffix trees in linear time. Their approach makes use of a recursive decomposition of the original string, whereby the suffix trees of smaller subsets of the suffixes are constructed, and then combined to form the required suffix tree for the original sequence. This new approach has led to some new insights into the properties of suffix trees and their construction. More recently, it has provided a motivation for new methods to construct suffix arrays directly, without first constructing the suffix tree (Kärkkäinen et al., 2006; Kim et al., 2005). This so called *direct suffix sorting* paradigm holds significant promise, especially with respect to efficient computation of the Burrows-Wheeler Transform (both the forward and inverse transformation). We present Farach's suffix tree construction method in detail because of its relationship to some of the direct suffix sorting approaches, and to the BWT.

Basic Algorithm

Farach's algorithm makes use of the relationship between the *longest common prefix* of two strings, and the *lowest common ancestor* of two nodes in a tree. $\text{LCP}(\alpha, \beta)$ denotes the longest common prefix between two strings α and β, and $|\text{LCP}(\alpha, \beta)|$ denotes the length of $\text{LCP}(\alpha, \beta)$. Where the intended meaning is clear from the context, we shall use LCP interchangeably to stand for both the longest common prefix, and its length. $\text{LCA}(u, v)$ denotes the lowest common ancestor of two nodes, u and v, in a tree (that is, $\text{LCA}(u, v)$ is the node furthest from the root that has both u and v as a descendant[1]). An important relationship between the LCP and LCA is the following:

---

[1] The lowest common ancestor is sometimes referred to in the literature as the *least* or *most recent* common ancestor.

$$\text{LCP}(L(u), L(v)) = L(\text{LCA}(v, u)), \text{ for all nodes } u, v \in \mathcal{T}_T.$$

Thus,

$$|\text{LCP}(L(u), L(v))| = |L(\text{LCA}(v, u))|.$$

It has been shown (Harel and Tarjan, 1984; Schieber and Vishkin, 1988; Bender and Farach-Colton, 2000) that after linear-time preprocessing on a tree, the LCA between any two nodes on the tree can be computed in constant time. This means that essentially, after such a linear-time preprocessing, two arbitrary strings can be compared for equality, or to determine if one is a prefix of the other, in constant time.

Let T be the given string. The odd tree of T, denoted $\mathcal{T}_T^o$ is defined as the suffix tree of all suffixes that start at an odd position in T. Similarly, the even tree of T, denoted $\mathcal{T}_T^e$ is defined as the suffix tree of all suffixes that start at an even position in T. Each of $\mathcal{T}_T^o$ and $\mathcal{T}_T^e$ is half the size of $\mathcal{T}_T$, the true suffix tree for T, with each having $n/2$ leaves. Farach's algorithm then proceeds in three steps:

1. Construct $\mathcal{T}_T^o$, the odd tree of T.
2. Using $\mathcal{T}_T^o$, construct $\mathcal{T}_T^e$, the even tree of T.
3. Merge $\mathcal{T}_T^o$ and $\mathcal{T}_T^e$, to form $\mathcal{T}_T$, the final suffix tree for T.

Figure 4.10 shows examples of the odd and even trees, using the example string $T = \text{mississippi}$. We describe each step of the algorithm in more detail below. Farach's algorithm relies heavily on integer sorting to achieve linear time complexity, and assumes an integer alphabet $\Sigma = \{1, 2, 3, \ldots\}$, where $|\Sigma| \leq n$. For a general alphabet, we need to map the symbols in the alphabet to an integer alphabet before applying the algorithm, and after construction we map the integer symbols back to their corresponding symbols in the general alphabet. Since the number of unique symbols in a string cannot be greater than the length of the string, this mapping ensures that the linear time complexity of the algorithm extends to general alphabets.

Constructing $\mathcal{T}_T^o$, the odd tree

Construction of the odd tree is performed in four substeps:

1. **Map pairs of symbols to single characters.** From the original string, $T = t_1 t_2 \ldots t_n$, form $n/2$ pairs of symbols from $t_{2i-1} t_{2i}$, $1 \leq i \leq n/2$ (we can pad the string with an extra '\$' symbol if n is odd). Radix sort the pairs, and remove duplicates, to form a sorted list, SL. This requires only linear time. Then, convert the pairs into their corresponding integers, based on their rank in SL. The result is a string S' of length $n/2$, defined as follows: $S'[i] = \text{rank of } \langle t_{2i-1} t_{2i} \rangle$ in SL. Using the example $T = \text{mississippi\$}$, and assuming the following mapping of the symbols

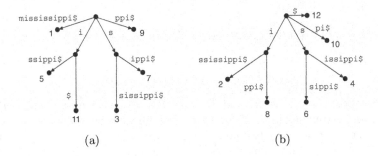

Fig. 4.10. Odd and even trees for the string $T = $ mississippi: (a) odd tree; (b) even tree

to an integer alphabet : $i \to 1, m \to 2, p \to 3, s \to 4$, we get the following result for the mapping: $T = 21441441331\$$; Symbol Pairs = { 21, 44, 14, 41, 33, 1\$ }; $SL = [1\$, 14, 21, 33, 41, 44]$; $S' = 362541\$$;

2. **Recursively construct** $\mathcal{T}_{S'}$, the suffix tree of the mapped sequence, S'. Figure 4.11a shows $\mathcal{T}_{S'}$, the suffix tree for the mapped sequence S'.

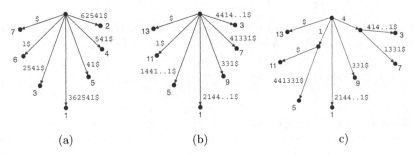

Fig. 4.11. Constructing the odd tree for $T = $ 21441441331\$: (a) suffix tree for the mapped string $S' = $ 362541\$; (b) initial odd tree constructed from (a); (c) final odd tree after adjustments on (b)

3. **Construct** $\mathcal{T}_T^o$ **from** $\mathcal{T}_{S'}$. First, we observe the relationship between T and S'. Each odd suffix in T has a corresponding suffix in S'. In fact, the odd suffix $t_{2i-1}t_{2i}\dots t_n\$$ in T corresponds to the suffix $S'[i]S'[i+1]\dots S'[\frac{n}{2}]\$$ in S'. Thus, the leaf node l_i in $\mathcal{T}_{S'}$ corresponds to the leaf node l_{2i-1} in $\mathcal{T}_T^o$. Any given internal node in $\mathcal{T}_{S'}$ with string depth d becomes an internal node in $\mathcal{T}_T^o$, with depth $2d$. Thus, we can construct $\mathcal{T}_T^o$ from $\mathcal{T}_{S'}$ by replacing the indexes of the leaf nodes and the lengths of the edge labels in $\mathcal{T}_{S'}$ by the corresponding values in $\mathcal{T}_T^o$. However, given that two symbols in T are mapped to one symbol in S', the tree $\mathcal{T}_T^o$

constructed as above may not form a suffix tree, as some nodes may have two edges with edge labels that start with the same symbol (see Figure 4.11b, symbols 1 and 4.) This requires some adjustment to the tree.

4. **Adjust the final suffix tree as needed.** Here, for a given node u, all the edges that start with the same symbol are combined by introducing a new node (say v), between u and the child nodes. The edge (u, v) is then labeled with the symbol shared by the child nodes. If the edge labels for all descendant nodes from u start with the same symbol, the above procedure will imply that node u will have one child node after the adjustment. Thus, node u will be removed from the tree. Of course, this is done while retaining the information in the edge from node u. This adjustment clearly takes linear time with respect to the number of nodes, and the number of edges, each of which is in turn linear with respect to the size of the string, S'.

Figure 4.11 shows $\mathcal{T}_{S'}$, the suffix tree for S', the odd tree constructed from S' (before adjustment), and the final odd tree after adjustment. Let $\varphi(n)$ be the time required to construct the suffix tree for a length-n string, $T = t_1 t_2 \ldots t_n$. Then, the time to construct the odd tree using the above procedure will be given by $\varphi(\frac{n}{2}) + O(n)$.

Constructing $\mathcal{T}_T^e$, the even tree

Constructing the even tree from the odd tree is performed based on the fact that, given an inorder traversal of the leaves of a tree, and the depth of the LCA of adjacent leaves in this ordering, we can re-construct the suffix tree in linear time. Consider the example in Figure 4.9 for $T = \texttt{mississippi}$. Traversing the leaf nodes from left to right in a depth-first manner will produce the following list of leaf nodes: $L_1 = [1, 2, 5, 8, 11, 3, 6, 7, 4, 9, 10, 12]$. Now, the list of LCA depths for the adjacent nodes in L_1 will be: $L_2 = [0, 4, 1, 1, 0, 3, 1, 2, 0, 1, 0]$. With only this information, we can easily re-construct the suffix tree using a simple procedure as shown in Algorithm 4.2.

Figure 4.12 shows the result of the first five steps of the algorithm, using the suffix tree of Figure 4.9. The final result of the algorithm is the suffix tree for the given string. Farach's algorithm constructs the suffix tree such that the resulting leaf nodes are sorted in lexicographic order, based on their corresponding suffixes. That is, the edges emanating from each given node are sorted lexicographically by their edge labels. Notice that the algorithm for constructing the suffix tree using the LCA of adjacent leaf nodes also works for suffix trees with sorted suffixes. Therefore, to construct the even tree from the odd tree, we need to derive the sorted suffixes of the even tree from the odd tree, and also the length of the longest common prefix of adjacent suffixes in this ordering.

Obtaining the sorted even suffixes. The current tree $\mathcal{T}_T^o$ already encodes the odd suffixes in lexicographic order. Thus, a simple inorder traversal

---

SUFFIX-TREE-FROM-LCA-LIST(L_1, L_2)
/* L_1: List of adjacent leaf nodes in a tree: $l_1, l_2, \ldots l_{n+1}$ */
/* L_2: List of depth of LCA of adjacent nodes in the tree */

Create *root* node, with empty string
Set $l_0 \leftarrow root$ node; set $d_0 \leftarrow 0$
for $i \leftarrow 1$ **to** $n + 1$ **do**
    Compute $d_i \leftarrow |\text{LCP}(l_{i-1}, l_i)|$ using L_2
    Starting from the *root*, jump to position d_i along the path $L(l_{i-1})$
    if d_i falls at an edge (i.e. between two nodes) **then**
        Let the edge be (u_{i-1}, v), with edge label (p, q)
        Split the edge (u_{i-1}, v) to create a new node u_i at this position
        Label edge (u_{i-1}, u_i): $label(u_{i-1}, u_i) \leftarrow (p, p + d_i - 1)$
        Label edge (u_i, v): $label(u_i, v) \leftarrow (p + d_i, q)$
    else /*d_i falls at an existing node */
        Call this node u_i
    end if
    Attach a new leaf node l_i at node u_i
    Label edge (u_i, l_i): $label(u_i, l_i) \leftarrow (l_i + d_i, n + 1)$
end for

Algorithm 4.2: Suffix tree from LCA of adjacent nodes

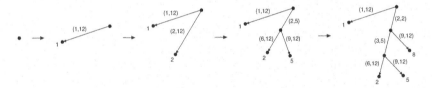

Fig. 4.12. First few steps in constructing the suffix tree from the list of depths for the LCA of adjacent nodes, using $L_1 = [1, 2, 5, 8, 11, 3, 6, 7, 4, 9, 10, 12]$ and $L_2 = [0, 4, 1, 1, 0, 3, 1, 2, 0, 1, 0]$. The final result should correspond to the suffix tree in Figure 4.9b

of the tree will produce a list of the odd suffixes in sorted order. Observe that an even suffix is just one symbol followed by an odd suffix. Thus, to obtain the sorted even suffixes, we form two-element tuples using the pairs $\langle t_{2i}, r_{2i+1} \rangle$, where r_j is the *rank* of suffix T_j in the ordered odd suffixes. The tuples are already sorted by the second element (the odd suffixes). Then, stable-sorting the tuples using radix sort on the first elements will produce the sorted list of even suffixes.

Using the previous example, the ordering of the odd suffixes (the leaves in the odd tree T_T^o) will produce the list: $L_s^o = [13, 11, 5, 1, 9, 7, 3]$. These are then combined with the symbols at the corresponding even positions (left of each odd position) in T to give the tuples: $[\langle 1, 7 \rangle, \langle 4, 3 \rangle, \langle 4, 6 \rangle, \langle 1, 5 \rangle, \langle 3, 2 \rangle, \langle \$, 1 \rangle]$.

Notice that the rank for T_1 (i.e. 4) is not used, since there is no even suffix to the left of position 1 in T. Stable-sorting this list using radix sort with the first element as the key will produce the ordered list: $L_E = [\langle \$, 1 \rangle, \langle 1, 5 \rangle, \langle 1, 7 \rangle, \langle 3, 2 \rangle, \langle 4, 3 \rangle, \langle 4, 6 \rangle]$. We call L_E the sorted even tuples of T. This is the lexicographically ordered list of even suffixes. Using the lists L_E and L_s^o, the corresponding ordered even positions in T can be obtained easily:

$$L_s^e = L_s^o[L_E[i, 2]] - 1, \qquad i = 1, 2, \ldots, \frac{n}{2}.$$

For the running example, the ordered positions will be: $L_s^e = [12, 8, 2, 10, 4, 6]$.

Computing the LCP between the sorted even suffixes. Given the relationship between the LCA and LCP, the LCP between adjacent elements in the sorted even suffixes can be determined based on the LCA between the leaf nodes in the odd tree. After linear time LCA preprocessing (Harel and Tarjan, 1984; Schieber and Vishkin, 1988; Bender and Farach-Colton, 2000) of the odd tree, we can determine the LCP of any two suffixes, represented by two leaves (say, l_{2i}, l_{2j} in T_T^e) using the relation:

$$\text{LCP}(l_{2i}, l_{2j}) = \begin{cases} \text{LCP}(l_{2i+1}, l_{2j+1}) + 1, & : \quad \text{if } t_{2i} = t_{2j} \\ 0 & : \quad \text{otherwise} \end{cases}$$

As described earlier, the value of $\text{LCP}(l_{2i+1}, l_{2j+1})$ can be obtained after linear time preprocessing of the odd tree as follows:

$$\text{LCP}(l_{2i+1}, l_{2j+1}) = \text{LCP}(T_{2i+1}, T_{2j+1}) = L(\text{LCA}(l_{2i+1}, l_{2j+1}))$$

where $L(u)$ is the path label of node u. Thus, given the ordered list of even suffixes and the computed LCP's between adjacent elements in this ordering, the even tree can be easily computed in linear time. The even tree of the running example with $T = \texttt{mississippi}$ is shown in Figure 4.13(b).

Merging the odd and even trees

The final suffix tree T_T is obtained by merging T_T^o and T_T^e , the odd and even tree respectively. This merging process is performed in two steps:

1. **Initial merging.** The first step of the merging process is simple. Farach's merging algorithm uses a *coupled-depth-first* traversal (coupled DFS) of T_T^o and T_T^e. The coupled DFS starts with the root nodes in the two trees. Next, it will take two edges from the respective trees with the same starting symbol, and recursively merge the two subtrees. Repeating this coupled-DFS procedure on each pair of edges with the same starting symbol from the roots of T_T^o and T_T^e produces an initial merged tree. Notice that at any given stage, merging is performed only if both the odd tree and even tree share an edge with the same starting symbol. Otherwise there is nothing to merge.

The only complication in this procedure comes from the fact that we are merging suffix trees (i.e. compacted tries), rather than simple suffix tries. The problem is that even though two edges may start with the same symbol, their edge labels may be different — one edge label could also be a prefix of another. Thus, we may need to stop the merging at the position of first mismatch. To check if the edge labels match symbol-by-symbol would lead to an $O(n^2)$ time for merging. To solve this problem, Farach used a clever approach: at any step during the coupled-DFS merge process, simply merge any two edges that share the same starting symbol. That is, if two edges start with the same symbol, then assume naïvely that the shorter edge is a prefix of the longer edge, break the longer edge, and merge its prefix with the shorter edge. Merging is therefore performed only on equal-length edges. This simple strategy guarantees that we cannot fail to merge any two edges that need to be merged, and requires only linear time to run. However, it could merge more than we need at times. Thus, we have to undo the extraneous merging that may be performed by the algorithm. We call this partial "unmerge" process *merge refinement*.

2. **Merge refinement.** Let $\mathcal{M}_T$ be the resulting merged tree using the simple naïve strategy above. For each node in $\mathcal{M}_T$, we need to determine whether the node requires merge refinement (i.e. merging went too far), and then perform the partial unmerge procedure if needed. First, we pre-process $\mathcal{M}_T$ in linear time, so that LCA queries can be answered in constant time. The path label for each node in $\mathcal{M}_T$ can be determined by using the corresponding node in either T_T^o or T_T^e. Let u be a node in $\mathcal{M}_T$ such that it is the lowest common ancestor of two leaf nodes l_{2i} and l_{2i-1}. Let $L(u)$ be the path label of u in its corresponding node in T_T^o or T_T^e. Let $\hat{L}(u)$ be the current path label of u in $\mathcal{M}_T$. That is, $\hat{L}(u) = \text{LCP}(l_{2i}, l_{2i-1})$, since $u = \text{LCA}(l_{2i}, l_{2i-1})$.

Node u is thus declared as properly merged if $|L(u)| = |\hat{L}(u)|$. Otherwise, $(|L(u)| > |\hat{L}(u)|)$ and merging went too far at the node, and hence we have to perform merge refinement by partially unmerging the merged edges. To do this, we introduce a new node, v in $\mathcal{M}_T$, such that the parent of v is set to the parent of u, and v is the parent of l_{2i} and l_{2i-1}. Node v is sometimes called the *refinement node*. Then, set the path label of node v as $L(v) = \hat{L}(u)$. Unmerge any merged edges between the odd tree and even tree under u. Attach the odd tree and even tree under node u to node v, maintaining the sorted order of the edges from node v. When the unmerge procedure is completed on all nodes that had extraneous merging in $\mathcal{M}_T$, the result will be T_T, the final suffix tree for the input string. The overall unmerging procedure requires linear time processing, which means that Farach's recursive algorithm for suffix tree construction will run in $O(n)$ time.

Figure 4.13c shows the merged tree for the running example, before merge refinement to obtain the final suffix tree in Figure 4.13d. The edges and nodes involved in merge refinement are indicated using an oval. We can notice that the initial merged tree before merge refinement has a structure that is generally similar to the final suffix tree; the difference is only in their edge labels.

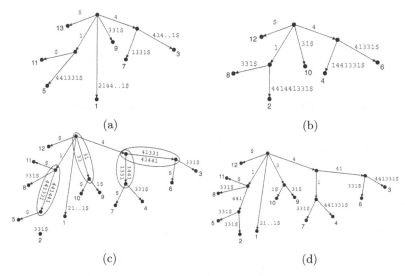

Fig. 4.13. Merging odd and even trees to construct the final suffix tree: (a) the odd tree $\mathcal{T}_T^o$; (b) the even tree $\mathcal{T}_T^e$; (c) the initial merged (overmerged) tree $\mathcal{M}_T$; (d) the final suffix tree $\mathcal{T}_T$ obtained after merge refinement via partial unmerging on $\mathcal{M}_T$. Marked edges with two labels in (c) indicate 'overmerged' edges which require merge refinement. Notice the difference between the LCP of the two labels and the edge length in each case

4.1.6 Generalized suffix trees

For applications involving multiple files, the suffix tree can be constructed for each file independently, and searches or other types of analysis can be performed on each suffix tree. However, for some specific applications, especially for problems such as searching for multiple patterns simultaneously over all the files in a database, a better approach would be to construct a single suffix tree for all the files, and then perform the search on this single tree. Such a single suffix tree constructed for multiple strings is called a *generalized suffix tree* (Gusfield, 1997).

For h multiple strings, $T_1, T_2, \ldots T_h$, building the generalized suffix tree is simple. First, concatenate all the strings into one string: $T = T_1 \$_1 * T_2 \$_2 * \ldots * T_h \$_h$, where the $\$_i$'s are end of string delimiters, and $*$ denotes concatenation. Then, construct the suffix tree of T, the concatenated string. The overall time and space complexity is still linear with respect to $|T|$, the overall length of the concatenated sequence.

4.1.7 Implementation issues

The practical time and space requirements for suffix tree construction, and also the space needed to store the suffix tree after construction, depend on the specific implementation method used. After construction, the required space needed to store the suffix tree will include that for the original text, edge labels, node labels for both branching and leaf nodes, and the space to indicate the parent for each node. During construction (and for some applications), we have to add the space required for the suffix links. In the following discussion, by suffix tree construction, we will assume Ukkonen's algorithm; some methods such as Farach's recursive construction may require more space.

The major consideration is how the outgoing edges from a node in the suffix tree are represented. The three major representations used for outgoing edges are arrays, linked lists, and binary search trees. However, independent of the specific method adopted, we can use a simple analysis to provide an idea of the space requirements of a suffix tree. Assume that a pointer is represented as an integer, and that each integer requires 4 bytes to store. Also, we assume that we are using, say, an ASCII alphabet with 256 symbols; notice that in the worst case we may be looking at an alphabet size as large as n, the size of the sequence, or a system such as Unicode may require two bytes per character, but for the meantime we will assume one byte for each character of the text, which is sufficient to compare memory requirements. Based on the properties of a suffix tree, we can expect to use n bytes for the original text, $2n$ integers for suffix links, $2n$ integers for edge labels, $2n$ integers for node labels (including branching nodes and leaf nodes), and $2n$ integers for indicating node parents. Therefore, we need a total of $8n$ integers plus n bytes, or $33n$ bytes to store the suffix tree with suffix links (for instance during construction), and $25n$ bytes without the suffix links (for instance, for later use, or during search).

Now, consider the effect of the specific representation used for the branching edges at each node. The required cost can be broken down into four components: the cost of storing T, the original sequence ($n/4$ integers); cost of branching nodes, cost of leaf nodes, and cost of edge labels. Let n_d be the number of internal nodes in the suffix tree. The cost of edge labels will be $n + n_d - 1$ integers, independent of the specific node representation. Let c_L, c_P, c_B and c_{SL} be the respective cost (in integers) of representing the node label, parent label, edges at the branching node, and suffix links, at each node. (From the discussion above, $c_L = c_P = c_{SL} = 1$ integer, but we these notations for clarity.) Thus, for all the branching nodes, the space cost will be $n_d(c_L + c_P + c_B + c_{SL})$. For the non-branching (i.e. leaf) nodes, there are no outgoing edges, so the cost will be $n_d(c_L + c_P + c_{SL})$.

With the simple array (also called vector) representation, the first symbols on each branch from a node are represented as an array with $|\Sigma|$ elements.

This gives, $c_{SL} = |\Sigma|$ bytes at each node. Thus, using the array representation at each node, the overall cost of storing the suffix tree will be $(4n + n_d(3 + \frac{1}{4}|\Sigma|) + \frac{n}{4})$ integers. With the linked list representation, the major difference is that the first symbols on each edge at each branching node are now represented using a linked list, rather than an array. The advantage is that we need to provide space for only the symbols that actually appear at the node. Without keeping a record of the count of symbols at each node, we can use the fact that we have a maximum of $2n$ edges in the suffix tree to bound the cost. Thus, we need at most $2n$ pointers (i.e. $2n$ integers) for all the liked lists used for the suffix tree. This can be compared with the $\frac{1}{4}n_d|\Sigma|$ integers required by the vector representation, which can grow as large as $\frac{1}{4}n|\Sigma|$ integers in the worst case. Thus, with the linked-list approach, the total cost for storing the suffix tree will be $(6n + 3n_d + \frac{n}{4})$ integers. Another approach is to use a balanced binary search tree to implement the linked list structure used above. This comes at a slightly reduced performance in search time, but is generally more space efficient than the previous two methods. Use of the binary tree approach makes more sense if the alphabet size is very large.

We can observe the significance of n_d, the number of interior nodes in the tree. Clearly, this number varies with the input string, and could significantly affect the required space. Also, for very large alphabets, the vector representation, in its simplest form as given above, will lead to a huge storage requirement. An improvement could be to use a bit map at each node to indicate which symbols in Σ are the starting symbols for the edge labels for all the edges from the node. This avoids the need to reserve space for the symbols that are not represented at a given node. Results in Manber and Myers (1993) show that the linked-list implementation provided an overall best result with respect to space efficiency. Methods based on hash functions were described by McCreight (1976), while Kurtz (1999) and Andersson and Nilsson (1995) provide more discussions on space-efficient construction and representation of suffix trees.

4.2 Suffix arrays

An important data structure, closely related to the suffix tree, is the *suffix array*. The suffix array simply provides a lexicographically ordered list of all the suffixes of a string. If the element at position i in the suffix array is j, it means that T_j, the suffix starting at position j in T is the i-th smallest suffix of T. This is essentially what the array R is in the Burrows-Wheeler Transform (shown in Figure 2.2b for encoding, and in Figure 2.8 for decoding), except the end of the string is treated slightly differently in each case. Combining the suffix array with the (length of) LCP of adjacent suffixes in this array provides a powerful data structure for pattern matching. With this combination, decisions on the occurrence (or otherwise) of a pattern P of length m in the string T of length n can be made in $O(m + \log n)$ time.

The suffix array can be used in most (though, not all) situations where a suffix tree can be used. However, as was shown in the previous section, given the suffix array and the LCP information, the suffix tree can be constructed in linear time. The major motivation for the use of suffix arrays, rather than suffix trees is their smaller memory footprint. Although the theoretical space complexity is linear for both data structures, typically, the suffix tree requires about three to five times more space than the corresponding suffix array of a string. The construction time for both algorithms is also $O(n)$ on average. For suffix arrays, algorithms that run in $O(n \log n)$ worst case are relatively easy to develop, but $O(n)$ worst case algorithms are much harder to come by. Traditionally, the construction of the suffix arrays have often required more practical running time than suffix trees (see Manber and Myers (1990, 1993) for examples). However, this is now changing, as indicated in the recent survey by Puglisi et al. (2007).

To discuss suffix arrays we will need some more notation. We will continue to use $T = t_1 t_2 \ldots t_n$ to denote the input sequence of length n, with symbol alphabet Σ. For any two strings, say α and β, we use $\alpha \prec \beta$ to indicate that the string α lexicographically precedes the string β. (This includes the case where α and β could be individual symbols, from the same alphabet, i.e. $|\alpha| = |\beta| = 1$.) We use \$ as the end of string symbol, where $\$ \notin \Sigma$ and $\$ < \sigma, \forall \sigma \in \Sigma$. We also use the notion of order-k sorting. We say that a set of strings are order-k sorted if the strings are sorted by their first k symbols. Thus, for any two strings, say α and β, we use the notation $\alpha \prec_k \beta$ to indicate that string α precedes string β in the order-k sorted listing. Further, we use $\mathcal{A}_T$ to denote the suffix array of a string T. Where the string in question is clear from the context, we may drop the T subscript for simplicity.

4.2.1 Traditional string sorting

Sorting a set of strings in a given order is an age-old problem in computer science. A simple approach is to imagine the strings as vectors, with each row corresponding to one of the strings in the set. Then, sorting the strings can be performed by using standard sorting algorithms such as quicksort to sort the vectors. Radix sort can also be easy to apply in this environment, particularly if the alphabet is small, such as in a DNA sequence. Another approach is to sort each column using character-by-character comparisons, starting from the leftmost column. After the k-th iteration, rows that have the same symbol up to the current (i.e. k-th) column are grouped together. At the next iteration, sorting using the next column is then restricted to the rows in the same group (that is, rows that are the same based on order-k sorting). Repeating this process for all the groups of rows with the same symbol at each iteration, and for all the columns, produces a sorted array of the original vector of strings. The column-wise sorts can be performed using a fast character sorting algorithm such as QSORT, an improved quicksort algorithm reported in Bentley and McIlroy (1993). This simple algorithm will lead to an expected time in $O(n \log n)$, with a potential $O(n^2 \log n)$ worst case.

Bentley and Sedgewick (1997) proposed a better approach, based on multi-key quicksort. Using code similar to the QSORT algorithm, they sorted a given set of strings by applying the idea of symbol-by-symbol ternary recursive decomposition on the strings. Basically, given a string α, they group every other string β into three partitions, viz:

$\beta \prec_k \alpha$: strings that are less than α,

$\alpha =_k \beta$: strings that are equal to α, and

$\alpha \prec_k \beta$: strings that are greater than α.

Here ternary partitioning is based on a pivot defined by the first k-symbols in each string. Essentially, k is the number of active dimensions, that is, the number of symbols (starting from the leftmost symbol) that need to be considered for a match. With this partitioning, sorting at any stage involves mainly the strings that remain in the equal partition. Strings in this equal partition can be compared (up to the k-th symbol) without requiring symbol-by-symbol comparisons on the first k symbols. This approach results in a sorting algorithm that runs in $O(n_s \log n_s + kn_s)$ worst case time, where n_s is the number of strings, and k is the required number of active dimensions. When k is small, the time reduces to $O(n_s \log n_s)$. However, for the specific problem of sorting the suffixes of a string, we will have $n_s = n$, and $k = n$, leading to an $O(n^2)$ time for suffix sorting.

In general, the longest common prefix, LCP, (see Section 4.1.5) provides an important mechanism to estimate the level of difficulty in sorting the suffixes of a given string. Define the average LCP, and maximum LCP as follows:

$$meanLCP = \frac{1}{n-1} \sum_{i=1}^{n-1} \text{LCP}(T_{\mathcal{A}[i]}, T_{\mathcal{A}[i+1]}) \tag{4.1}$$

$$maxLCP = \max_{1 \le i < n} \left\{ \text{LCP}(T_{\mathcal{A}[i]}), T_{\mathcal{A}[i+1]}) \right\} \tag{4.2}$$

In Equations 4.1 and 4.2, we have used LCP as the length of the longest common prefix. Usually the average LCP (and also the maximum LCP) between any two adjacent suffixes in the sorted list provides a rough indication of the number of symbol comparisons that will be needed to sort the suffixes. Larger values of these statistics imply more difficulty in performing the suffix sorting. Let $\mu = meanLCP$. For methods that are based on standard string matching using symbol- by-symbol comparisons, the average case complexity will be in $O(\mu n \log n)$. When μ is small, or independent of n, this will result in $O(n \log n)$ time. However, since μ could be in $O(n)$, without careful consideration this could lead to a worst-case complexity of $O(n^2 \log n)$ for such schemes.

4.2.2 Suffix arrays via suffix trees

A theoretically faster approach to construct the suffix array is via the suffix tree. Given the suffix tree, the suffix array can be constructed in linear time by a simple inorder traversal of the suffix tree. For instance, using Farach's recursive construction, all the edges from any given node are implicitly sorted by their edge label. Thus, assuming the edges at each node are sorted from left to right in ascending lexicographic order, a simple depth-first traversal of T_T, the suffix tree of T, will produce the suffix array, $\mathcal{A}_T$, the lexicographically sorted list of all the suffixes in T.

Given the space requirement of suffix trees, there has been interest in direct construction of suffix arrays, without the need to first construct the suffix tree (so called *direct suffix sorting* problem). In the following, we describe some of the proposed methods for direct suffix sorting, starting with the Manber-Myers algorithm (Manber and Myers, 1993).

4.2.3 Manber-Myers suffix sorting algorithm

The problem with using the algorithms that sort a set of strings for the problem of suffix sorting is that they ignore important properties of the suffixes of a string, which are not often shared by a random collection of strings. For instance, suffixes of a string share a lot of common substrings, which can be exploited for more efficient sorting. Moreover, conventional sorting algorithms based on symbol-by-symbol comparisons are often limited to $O(n \log n)$ expected time, with some requiring a quadratic time or more in the worst case[2]. The suffix tree on the other hand, requires much more space than may be needed, and for some applications, avoiding the complications required for efficient suffix tree construction could be advantageous.

Manber and Myers (Manber and Myers, 1990, 1993) were the first to propose an algorithm that directly computes the suffix array for a string, without the need for an initial construction of the suffix tree. Their algorithm performs suffix sorting in phases, using the idea of *successive doubling*, earlier used by Karp et al. (1972) for identification of repeats in a string. Using successive doubling, suffix sorting on a string of length n is performed using a maximum of $\lceil \log n \rceil$ phases. First, the suffixes are placed into buckets according to their first symbols. Essentially, the buckets can be viewed as the first pass on the suffix array $\mathcal{A}_T$, whereby the array is sorted only by the first symbol in each suffix (the $\prec_k$ ordering, with $k = 1$). Thus, consecutive entries in the same bucket will have the same first character.

The above can be accomplished in linear time using a bucket sort. This is phase 0 of the algorithm, and the sorted results correspond to the order-1

---

[2] We note that fast algorithms for suffix arrays can be used to sort a set of strings (in linear time with respect to the total length of the strings), by simply generating the generalized suffix array of the set, and using simple bookkeeping.

sorted suffixes. Then, at each subsequent phase, the buckets are partitioned by sorting according to *double* the number of symbols used in the previous phase. This means that the number of symbols affected in phase i will be 2^i. Therefore, after the i-th phase, ($i = 0, 1, 2, \ldots, \lceil \log n \rceil$), the suffixes will be order-k sorted, where $k = 2^i$. Thus, after the i-th phase in the algorithm, each bucket will hold only suffixes with the same first k symbols, $k = 2^i$. The major challenge is how the elements in each order-k bucket (which are so far sorted according to the $\prec_k$ ordering) can now be sorted to obtain the order-$2k$ buckets (with elements in $\prec_{2k}$ ordering) all in linear time.

The key observation is that, after order-k bucketing, for a given suffix, say T_i, the next k symbols of T_i are just the first k symbols of suffix T_{i+k}. Thus, given two suffixes, say T_i and T_j in the same order-k bucket, (i.e. $T_i =_k T_j$), the relative order of T_{i+k} and T_{j+k} (with respect to the $\prec_k$ ordering) is immediately available. Thus, at phase-$2k$ ($k = 2, 4, 8, \ldots$), in the algorithm (we already have order-1 buckets from the initial bucket sort), we sort the suffixes by starting with the first suffix in the first bucket (which necessarily contains the smallest order-k suffixes). Let this first suffix at $\mathcal{A}_T[1]$ be T_i. Given that T_i starts with the smallest order-k suffix, then, the suffix T_{i-k} must be the first suffix in its order-$2k$ bucket. Therefore, we need to move T_{i-k} to the start of its bucket. Then, take the next suffix according to the $\prec_k$ ordering (i.e. the suffix at $\mathcal{A}_T[2]$, say T_j), and move suffix T_{j-k} to the next available place in its own bucket. The phase continues with this movement of suffixes until all the suffixes in all buckets have been processed. The algorithm will stop when each bucket contains exactly one suffix, which will occur after $\lceil \log_2 n \rceil$ phases at the most. A basic description of Manber and Myers' suffix sorting algorithm is given in Algorithm 4.3.

MANBER-MYERS-SUFFIX-SORTING(T)
/* Returns the suffix array in the array $\mathcal{A}_T$ */
Perform initial bucket sort on T to produce initial sorted array $\mathcal{A}_T$
for $u \leftarrow 0$ **to** $\lceil \log n \rceil$ **do**
    $k \leftarrow 2^u$
    for $v \leftarrow 1$ **to** n **do**
        $i \leftarrow \mathcal{A}_T[v]$
        if $(i - k > 0)$ **or** $(i + k \leq n + 1)$ **then**
            Move suffix T_{i-k} to the next available slot in its bucket (in $\mathcal{A}_T$)
        end if
    end for
end for

Algorithm 4.3: Basic Manber-Myers suffix sorting algorithm

Figure 4.14 shows a run of the algorithm on the example string, $T =$ mississippi\$. For a given suffix T_i, T_i is not moved in its bucket when $i + k > n + 1$, or if $i - k \le 0$. Thus we have:

- In phase $k = 1$, no movement at step $v=6$, since $i - k = 0$.
- In phase $k = 2$, no movement in step 4 ($i - k = 0$), and in step 6 ($i - k < 0$); at step 1, T_{11} was not moved in its current position, since $11 + k > n + 1$, with $k = 2, n = 11$.
- In phase $k = 4$, no movement in steps 4, 6, and 11 ($i - k < 0$), and in step 10 ($i - k = 0$); no more movements within the p-bucket, since for each suffix T_i in this partition, $i + k > n + 1$, with $k = 4, n = 11$.

The final sorted array is given by the values in $\mathcal{A}_T$ at the end of the last phase (the last column in the table): $\mathcal{A}_T = [12, 11, 8, 5, 2, 1, 10, 9, 7, 4, 6, 3]$.

Bucket	Phase $k = 0$ (Bucket Sorting)		Phase $k = 1$			Phase $k = 2$			Phase $k = 4$		
	Suffix	$\mathcal{A}$	Step	Suffix	$\mathcal{A}$	Step	Suffix	$\mathcal{A}$	Step	Suffix	$\mathcal{A}$
\$	\$	12		\$	12		\$	12		\$	12
i	ississippi\$	2	1	i\$	11	◇1	i\$	11	◇	i\$	11
	ississppi\$	5	7	ippi\$	8	8	ippi\$	8	8	ippi\$	8
	ippi\$	8	9	ississippi\$	2	11	ississippi\$	2	9	issippi\$	5
	i\$	11	11	issippi\$	5	12	issippi\$	5	10	ississippi\$	2
m	mississippi\$	1	2	mississippi\$	1	◇4	mississippi\$	1	◇4	mississippi\$	1
p	ppi\$	9	5	pi\$	10	2	pi\$	10	◇	pi\$	10
	pi\$	10	8	ppi\$	9	7	ppi\$	9	◇	ppi\$	9
s	ssissippi\$	3	3	sissippi\$	4	3	sippi\$	7	3	sippi\$	7
	sissippi\$	4	4	sippi\$	7	5	sissippi\$	4	5	sissippi\$	4
	ssippi\$	6	10	ssissippi\$	3	9	ssissippi\$	3	11	ssippi\$	6
	sippi\$	7	12	ssippi\$	6	10	ssippi\$	6	12	ssissippi\$	3

Fig. 4.14. Sample run of Manber-Myers suffix sorting algorithm on the string $T =$ mississippi\$. The final result (the suffix array) is the last column in the figure. The symbol $\diamond i$ indicates that in step i of the current phase, no more comparison is needed. The symbol $\diamond$ (without a number) indicates that the corresponding suffix is now in its final position in the suffix array, and thus requires no more movements

Notice that only pointers to the suffixes need to be moved, there is no need to physically copy the suffixes. Thus, each phase requires $O(n)$ time to complete in the worst case, leading to an overall worst case time of $O(n \log n)$ for the algorithm. On average, however, the algorithm will run in $O(n \log \log n)$ time, since the length of the maximum LCP will be in $O(\log_{|\Sigma|} n)$ on average, for a string with uniformly distributed symbols (Karlin et al., 1983). This can be further reduced to $O(n)$ expected time, using a linear-time mapping of appropriately sized small substrings to integers before sorting begins, for instance, using a hash function (see Section 7.1.4). Further details of these improvements are provided in the original paper (Manber and Myers, 1993).

An improvement and perhaps simplification of the algorithm could be to use radix sort at each phase, rather than the successive doubling and movement of suffixes. That is, after the first phase of bucket sorting, subsequent phases are performed by forming a tuple using the current symbol, and the bucket number of its next symbol in T. Let $\mathcal{A}_T$ be the current suffix array at phase k. This will contain the indexes for the order-k sorted suffixes. As in the original algorithm, $\mathcal{A}_T$ will be progressively sorted as the algorithm progresses. Let $B[i]$ be the bucket number for the i-th suffix in $\mathcal{A}_T$. Suffixes in the same bucket are given the same bucket number. Let $\tilde{\mathcal{A}}_T$ be the inverse of $\mathcal{A}_T$, that is, if $\mathcal{A}_T[i] = j$, then $\tilde{\mathcal{A}}_T[j] = i$. Then, at each phase the tuple is formed as follows: $\langle B[i], B[\tilde{\mathcal{A}}[\mathcal{A}_T[i]+1]]\rangle$. Then we radix-sort the set of tuples in linear time. We continue in this way until each bucket contains exactly one suffix. Overall, the complexity remains the same as in the original algorithm, but using radix sorting will simplify the required movements needed when using successive doubling. On average, this would also require less space in practice, since after the initial bucket sort, radix sorting can be confined to smaller buckets at subsequent phases.

The basic Manber and Myers algorithm has been implemented by McIlroy and McIlroy in the SSORT suffix sorting routine. Larsson and Sadakane (1999, 2007) proposed various improvements to the basic algorithm by combining the successive doubling technique with the ternary-partitioning quicksort proposed by Bentley and Sedgewick (1997).

4.2.4 Linear-time direct suffix sorting

More recently, there has been interest in constructing direct suffix sorting algorithms that do not use the suffix tree data structure, but still run in linear time in the worst case. Example algorithms that achieve this running time complexity can be found in Kärkkäinen et al. (2006), Ko and Aluru (2005) and Kim et al. (2005). Here we describe the KS Algorithm (Kärkkäinen and Sanders, 2003; Kärkkäinen et al., 2006) in more detail, given its simplicity.

The KS suffix sorting algorithm

Kärkkäinen and Sanders (Kärkkäinen et al., 2006) proposed a divide and conquer approach similar to Farach's suffix tree construction method of Section 4.1.5, but for direct construction of suffix arrays. Here, rather than dividing the sequence into two symmetric parts, the sequence was divided into two unequal parts by considering suffixes that begin at positions $((i-1) \bmod 3 \neq 0)$ in the sequence. These suffixes are recursively sorted, and then the remaining suffixes are sorted based on information in the first part which is already sorted. The two sorted lists of suffixes are then combined using a merging step to produce the final suffix array. Thus, a major difference is in the way they divided the sequences into two parts, and in the merging step. Also, the use of a 2/3 recursion (rather than the traditional half recursion) significantly simplified the later merging stage, since a relative order between any conflicting symbols can be found in at most two steps of comparison.

Following Farach's recursive suffix tree construction algorithm (Farach, 1997; Farach and Muthukrishnan, 1996; Farach-Colton et al., 2000) introduced in Section 4.1.5, we describe the basic KS-Algorithm as follows:

1. Classify the suffixes into Type 1 and Type 2 suffixes as follows[3]:
   - T_i is a Type 1 suffix if : $(i - 1) \bmod 3 = 0$
   - T_i is a Type 2 suffix if : $(i - 1) \bmod 3 \neq 0$
2. Sort Type 2 suffixes to form $\mathcal{A}_T^2$.
3. Using $\mathcal{A}_T^2$, construct $\mathcal{A}_T^1$, the sorted order for Type 1 suffixes.
4. Merge $\mathcal{A}_T^2$ and $\mathcal{A}_T^1$ to form $\mathcal{A}_T$, the final suffix array for T.

Sorting Type 2 suffixes. The major problem in the KS Algorithm is the second step – sorting the Type 2 suffixes to form $\mathcal{A}_T^2$. This is performed in a recursive manner. First, the algorithm sorts the Type 2 suffixes based on their first three symbols. For suffix $T_i, (i - 1) \bmod 3 \neq 0$, this will be the trigrams or triplets $[T_i[1], T_i[2], T_i[3]] = T[i \ldots i + 2]$. If all the triplets are unique (and hence have unique ranks in the sorted order), the step is complete. This will mean that the Type 2 suffixes have a maximum LCP of 3. In most general cases, however, the maximum LCP will be more than 3, and hence more computation is required to complete the sorting. To do this, a new string of integers is formed by writing out the triplets from the Type 2 suffixes in their order of occurrence in T, and then replacing each triplet with its rank in the current sorted order. Call this new string S. Notice the similarity between the string S, and the string S' used in Farach's suffix tree construction (see Section 4.1.5). The algorithm is then applied recursively on S to construct its suffix array, $\mathcal{A}_S$. The array $\mathcal{A}_S$ is equivalent to (has a one-to-one mapping with) $\mathcal{A}_T^2$, the required sorted order of the original Type 2 suffixes from T.

Sorting Type 1 suffixes using sorted Type 2 suffixes. After sorting the Type 2 suffixes, $\mathcal{A}_T^1$ the sorted order of the Type 1 suffixes can be deduced from $\mathcal{A}_T^2$ by forming the tuple: $\langle T_i[1], \text{rank of } T_{i+1} \text{ in } \mathcal{A}_T^2 \rangle$ for each $(i - 1) \bmod 3 = 0$. This is equivalent to the pair $\langle T_i[1], \tilde{\mathcal{A}}_S[i + 1] \rangle$, where $\tilde{\mathcal{A}}_S$ is the inverse of $\mathcal{A}_S$. The pairs can then be sorted in linear time, using radix sort to give $\mathcal{A}_T^1$.

Merging sorted Type 1 and Type 2 suffixes. The final step is to merge $\mathcal{A}_T^1$ and $\mathcal{A}_T^2$ to form the required suffix array $\mathcal{A}_T$. The key is that conflicts that can arise during the merging can each be resolved by using $\mathcal{A}_T^2$. To compare a Type 1 suffix T_i with a Type 2 suffix T_j, at the merge stage, we need to consider two cases:

- **1-Compare Case:** If $(j - 1) \bmod 3 = 1$, we compare $\langle T_i[1], \text{rank of } T_{i+1}$ in $\mathcal{A}_T^2 \rangle$, versus $\langle T_j[1], \text{rank of } T_{j+1}$ in $\mathcal{A}_T^2 \rangle$. For this simple case, the relative order of both T_{i+1} and T_{j+1} are available from $\mathcal{A}_T^2$.

---

[3] We use Type 1 and Type 2 for ease of description. These were not necessarily used by the authors in their original work.

- **2-Compare Case:** If $(j-1) \bmod 3 = 2$, we compare $\langle T_i[1], T_i[2], \text{rank of } T_{i+2} \text{ in } \mathcal{A}_T^2 \rangle$, versus $\langle T_j[1], T_j[2], \text{rank of } T_{j+2} \text{ in } \mathcal{A}_T^2 \rangle$. Again, for this more difficult case, the tie is broken using the triplet, since the relative order of both T_{i+2} and T_{j+2} are also available from $\mathcal{A}_T^2$.

Below, we further explain the working of the KS Algorithm using an example. Consider the string $T = \mathtt{mississippi\$}$. First, we group the suffixes into their respective types.

Type 1 suffixes for T: $T_i|(i-1) \bmod 3 = 0$:

$^1\mathtt{mississippi\$}$
$^4\mathtt{sissippi\$}$
$^7\mathtt{sippi\$}$
$^{10}\mathtt{pi\$}$

For Type 1 suffixes, we have used superscripts to indicate their corresponding positions in the parent sequence. Sorting these suffixes will produce $\mathcal{A}_T^1$. Type 2 suffixes use the rule: Type 2 suffixes for T: $T_i|(i-1) \bmod 3 \neq 0$. Table 4.1 shows the Type 2 suffixes, and their sorted order, based on the triplets ($\prec_3$ ordering). Complete sorting of the Type 2 suffixes will produce $\mathcal{A}_T^2$.

Suffix Position	Suffix	Trippes	Sorted Triples	Sorted Positions	Label (Index)
2	ississippi\$	iss	\$\$\$	12	1
3	ssissippi\$	ssi	i\$\$	11	2
5	issippi\$	iss	ipp	8	3
6	ssippi\$	ssi	iss	2	4
8	ippi\$	ipp	iss	5	4
9	ppi\$	ppi	ppi	9	5
11	i\$	i\$\$	ssi	3	6
12	\$	\$\$\$	ssi	6	6

Table 4.1. Type 2 suffixes after the first level of iteration in the KS Algorithm using the example $T = \mathtt{mississippi}$

Since the labels are not unique for all the triplets, we need to construct a new string, and apply the algorithm recursively. The new string will be: $S = 46463521$. We divide S into its Type 1 and Type 2 suffixes. The Type 1 suffixes for S will be the set: { $^1\mathtt{46463521\$}$, $^4\mathtt{63521\$}$, $^7\mathtt{21\$}$ }. Sorting these suffixes will produce the suffix array $\mathcal{A}_S^1$. Table 4.2 shows the Type 2 suffixes for string S, and their sorted order, based on the triplets ($\prec_3$ ordering). A complete sorting of these Type 2 suffixes will produce $\mathcal{A}_S^2$.

From Table 4.2 we have $\mathcal{A}_S^2 = [8, 5, 3, 6, 2]$ and $\tilde{\mathcal{A}}_S^2 = [5, 3, 2, 4, 1]$. We determine the order of the Type 1 suffixes in S by forming the array of tuples: $[\langle 4, 5 \rangle, \langle 6, 2 \rangle, \langle 2, 1 \rangle]$. Sorting these tuples will give $\mathcal{A}_S^1 = [7, 1, 4]$. (In this particular case, the sorted order is available, without forming the tuples.)

The next step is to merge $\mathcal{A}_S^1$ and $\mathcal{A}_S^2$ to form $\mathcal{A}_S = [8, 7, 5, 3, 1, 6, 4, 2]$. These are based on the indexes in the shorter string S. We map these back to their original positions in T to obtain $\mathcal{A}_T^2 = [12, 11, 8, 5, 2, 9, 6, 3]$. Now, we deduce the sorted order for the Type 1 suffixes in T by sorting the tuples: $[\langle m, 5 \rangle, \langle s, 4 \rangle, \langle s, 3 \rangle, \langle p, 2 \rangle]$. The result will be $\mathcal{A}_T^1 = [1, 10, 7, 4]$. Finally, we merge $\mathcal{A}_T^1$ and $\mathcal{A}_T^2$ to form $\mathcal{A}_T$, the required suffix array: $\mathcal{A}_T = [12, 11, 8, 5, 2, 1, 10, 9, 7, 4, 6, 3]$.

Note that the number of Type 1 suffixes is $n/3$, while that of Type 2 suffixes is $2n/3$. This is important, since the recursive call applies only to Type 2 suffixes. Thus, the running time for the algorithm is given by the solution to the recurrence : $\varphi(n) = \varphi(\lceil 2n/3 \rceil) + O(n)$. This gives $\varphi(n) = O(n)$.

The KA algorithm

Ko and Aluru (2005) also used recursive partitioning, but following a fundamentally different approach to construct the suffix array in linear time and space. They use a binary marking strategy whereby each suffix in T is classified as either an S-suffix or an L-suffix, depending on the relative order with its next neighbor. An S-suffix is a suffix that is lexicographically smaller than its right-neighbor in T, while an L-suffix is one that is lexicographically larger than its right-neighbor. That is, T_i is an S-suffix if $T_i \prec T_{i+1}$, otherwise T_i is an L-suffix. This classification is motivated by the observation that an S-suffix is always lexicographically greater than any L-suffix that starts with the same character. The two types of suffixes are then treated differently: the S-suffixes are sorted recursively by performing some special distance computations. The L- suffixes are then sorted using the sorted order of the S-suffixes. The classification scheme is very similar to an approach used earlier by Itoh and Tanaka (1999), (see Section 4.3), but the algorithm in Itoh and Tanaka (1999) runs in $O(n \log n)$ time on average, and $O(n^2 \log n)$ worst case.

Suffix Position	Suffix	Sorted Trippes	Sorted Triples	Sorted Positions	Label (Index)
2	6463521\$	646	1\$\$	8	1
3	463521\$	463	352	5	2
5	3521\$	352	463	3	3
6	521\$	521	521	6	4
8	1\$	1\$\$	646	2	5

Table 4.2. Type 2 suffixes after the second level of recursion in the KS Algorithm using $S = 46463521\$$

4.3 Space issues in suffix trees and suffix arrays

One major motivation for the use of suffix arrays over suffix trees is the small memory footprint of the former. The time and space requirements of the two data structures can be considered from two view points: at the construction stage, and after construction (for storage, or at the time of use, for instance, during search). While the suffix array generally requires a smaller space to store, and less time for searching, traditionally, their construction requires more time than suffix trees (Manber and Myers, 1993). The recent survey in Puglisi et al. (2007), however, shows that some recent suffix sorting algorithms can be faster than suffix arrays, even at construction time. Further, although the suffix array also requires less space than suffix trees during construction, it is still important to consider the actual space needed by a given suffix sorting algorithm. With the increasing input data size for these algorithms (for instance, in genomic applications with potentially billions of symbols in one genome), the space requirement during construction is becoming critical.

There are three major approaches to dealing with the problem of the space required for the construction and use of suffix trees and suffix arrays: (1) space-efficient suffix tree/suffix array construction, (2) compressed suffix trees/suffix arrays, and (3) the construction of suffix trees/suffix arrays in external storage. Below we discuss methods that have been proposed for space-aware suffix sorting. We discuss compressed suffix trees and compressed suffix arrays in Section 8.1, given their very close relationship with BWT-based compressed full-text indexing and other applications discussed in that chapter. The further reading section at the end of this chapter provides some pointers to key references on constructing suffix trees and suffix arrays in secondary storage.

Lightweight suffix array construction

There has been some effort to reduce the actual space requirement in suffix array construction. Algorithms that aim at this reduced space requirement are sometimes called *lightweight* suffix sorting algorithms. More specifically, Manzini and Ferragina (2004) use the term "lightweight" to refer to a suffix sorting algorithm that requires no more than $5n$ bytes plus a small extra space in constructing the suffix array of a string of length n. This is based on the assumption that the alphabet size is no more than 256 characters (which means 1 byte is enough to hold each symbol), and that integers are stored in 4 bytes (32 bits), as is done in most current machine models. Thus, lightweight algorithms require little or no memory beyond those needed to store the text itself (n bytes) and those needed to store the suffix array ($4n$ bytes).

Existing lightweight algorithms can be characterized by the following four steps:

Bucketing. Typically, they start with an initial bucketing to partition the suffixes, usually based on the first one or first two symbols.

Suffix classification. The suffixes are then classified or grouped into different suffix types, often based on their relationship with neighboring suffixes in the string.

Sorting within groups. Based on the suffix group, the lightweight algorithms often use standard string sorting algorithms (such as ternary quicksort (Bentley and McIlroy, 1993), or multikey quicksort (Bentley and Sedgewick, 1997)) to sort suffixes in the same group. Some also use other existing suffix sorting algorithms at this stage, for instance, Seward's COPY algorithm (Seward, 2000) or Larsson and Sadakane's QSUFSORT algorithm (Larsson and Sadakane, 2007).

Derived sorting. Finally, the lightweight algorithms typically exploit the fact that we are sorting suffixes of the same string, by deriving the sorted order of certain buckets or suffixes from previously sorted suffixes.

The difference between the various lightweight suffix sorting algorithms is primarily in the specific approach they used in one or more of the above steps. We describe the popular lightweight algorithms below, with an emphasis on Itoh and Tanaka's TWO-STAGE algorithm, one of the earliest lightweight algorithms.

Itoh-Tanaka Algorithm. Itoh and Tanaka (1999) proposed the TWO-STAGE algorithm for suffix sorting. After initial bucketing based on the first symbol in each suffix, the suffixes in each bucket are then classified into Type A and Type B suffixes as follows:

- T_i is Type A suffix if : $T[i+1] \prec T[i]$
- T_i is Type B suffix if : $T[i] \prec T[i+1]$

The Type B suffixes are then sorted using a standard string sorting algorithm. Specifically, they used a hybrid of sorting algorithms, depending on the size of the group. They proposed simple insertion sort for small buckets, multikey quicksort (Bentley and Sedgewick, 1997) for medium sized buckets, and MSD radix sort (McIlroy et al., 1993) for large groups.

Note that when a Type A and Type B suffix are in the same bucket, the Type A suffix will always precede the Type B suffix. Itoh and Tanaka then used the key observation that, after all Type B suffixes have been correctly sorted, the sorted order of Type A suffixes can be directly derived from the sorted Type B suffixes in one single pass. That is, we simply scan over the suffix array being constructed in ascending order; for a given suffix, say T_i, check if suffix T_{i-1} is Type A; if so, move the suffix T_{i-1} to the first empty position in its bucket. Figure 4.15 shows the result of the Itoh-Tanaka TWO-STAGE algorithm on our sample string, $T = \text{mississippi\$}$.

As can be observed, when the number of Type A suffixes is relatively large compared to the number of Type B suffixes, the algorithm will work faster in practice. To increase the number of Type A suffixes, Itoh and Tanaka suggested the use of buckets based on the first two symbols at the bucketing step (i.e. using $\prec_2$ ordering, rather than $\prec_1$).

Position	1	2	3	4	5	6	7	8	9	10	11	12
Symbol	m	i	s	s	i	s	s	i	p	p	i	$
Type	A	B	B	A	B	B	A	B	B	A	A	−

(a)

Bucket	Position	Suffix	Type	Type B Sorted	Type A (Induced sort)	Merged
$	12	$	−	12		12
i	2	ississippi$	B		11	11
	5	issippi$	B	8		8
	8	ippi$	B	5		5
	11	i$	A	2		2
m	1	mississippi$	A		1	1
p	9	ppi$	B		10	10
	10	pi$	A	9		9
s	3	ssissippi$	B		7	7
	4	ssissippi$	A		4	4
	6	ssippi$	B	6		6
	7	sippi$	A	3		3

(b)

Fig. 4.15. Itoh-Tanaka TWO-STAGE algorithm on the string $T = $ mississippi$: (a) classification of suffixes; (b) sorting process

Two other popular lightweight algorithms are Seward's COPY algorithm (Seward, 2000) and Manzini and Ferragina's DEEP-SHALLOW algorithm (Manzini and Ferragina, 2004). Algorithm COPY performs bucketing on the suffixes based on the first symbols, and for each bucket it further partitions the suffixes into smaller buckets based on their second symbols. It then sorts these smaller partitions using ternary quicksort. When a bucket (say with initial symbol σ) is completely sorted, COPY can deduce the sorted order of all other smaller partitions that have symbol σ as its second symbol directly, by a single pass over the bucket. These are therefore not directly sorted using the string sorting algorithm.

Algorithm DEEP-SHALLOW extends the COPY algorithm in several ways. Rather than use ternary quicksort (Bentley and McIlroy, 1993) for sorting the smaller partitions, they use the multikey quicksort proposed by Bentley and Sedgewick (1997). More importantly, they divide the suffixes within a smaller partition into two parts, based on a threshold on the length of their common prefix. For suffixes with the LCP less than the threshold, they use multikey quicksort as above. For those with LCP beyond the threshold, they abandoned the multikey quicksort, and used a different string sorting algorithm. They call the former approach (for small LCP) *shallow sorting*, and the latter (for smaller partitions with large LCP) *deep sorting*. In Manzini and Ferragina (2004), three algorithms for deep sorting were proposed, one generalizing the idea of direct determination of the sorted order of the smaller partitions based on an already sorted bucket. Recent related work on light-weight suffix sorting has been reported by Maniscalco and Puglisi (2006).

Other algorithms that are closely related to the lightweight algorithms include Larsson and Sadakane's QSUFSORT (Larsson and Sadakane, 1999, 2007), and more recently Schürmann and Stoye's BKPR (bucket-pointer refinement) algorithm (Schürmann and Stoye, 2007). Both algorithms use the successive doubling technique of Manber and Myers as their basic working principle. Both also have a space requirement of $8n$ bytes, with a worst case complexity in $O(n \log n)$ for the former, and $O(n^2)$ for the latter. Schürmann and Stoye focused on strings with variable LCP's as may be needed for applications such as in bioinformatics, using a hybrid of both standard sorting and suffix sorting algorithms.

4.4 Further reading

The suffix tree was originally introduced by Weiner (1973), with space-efficient constructions considered by McCreight (1976). Related data structures such as suffix tries and Patricia trees (Morrison, 1968; Knuth, 1973; Gonnet et al., 1992) have also been studied. Ukkonen (1995) made the suffix tree easier to understand, and showed a simpler method to construct the tree in linear time. Giegerich and Kurtz (1997) showed the close relationship between the seemingly different approaches to suffix tree construction. Farach et al. (Farach, 1997; Farach-Colton et al., 2000) introduced a fundamentally different approach to constructing suffix trees, by simple recursive decomposition. Szpankowski (1993a,b) analyzed suffix trees and the generalized suffix tree. Suffix tree on words are studied in Andersson et al. (1999). Gusfield (1997) provides a detailed study on suffix trees and their various applications. See also Apostolico (1985) for other applications of suffix trees.

The suffix array was introduced by Manber and Myers in the early 1990s (Manber and Myers, 1990, 1993) as a more space efficient alternative to suffix trees. Their algorithm required $O(n \log n)$ time in the worst case, with an average time of $O(n)$. Around the same period, Gonnet et al. (1992) introduced the PAT-array, a very closely-related data structure. Grossi and Vitter (2005) presented various applications of the suffix array data structure. Spurred by the introduction of the BWT in 1994 (Burrows and Wheeler, 1994), which relied heavily on sorting the suffixes of a string, various methods and algorithmic improvements were proposed for the suffix sorting problem (Larsson, 1998; Larsson and Sadakane, 2007; Itoh and Tanaka, 1999; Seward, 2000). While some of the algorithms improved the space needed to construct the suffix array, most of these algorithms still required $O(n \log n)$ time or more in the worst case. It was not until 2003 that algorithms that can construct the suffix array in linear time and linear space in the worst case were introduced (Kärkkäinen and Sanders, 2003; Kärkkäinen et al., 2006; Kärkkäinen, 2007;

Ko and Aluru, 2003, 2005; Kim et al., 2003, 2005; Adjeroh and Nan, 2008). Puglisi et al. (2007) provide a recent survey on suffix arrays. The problem of constructing lightweight suffix sorting algorithms that run in linear time worst case is still open.

Given the problem of space, especially for certain applications that require huge data sizes, more recent efforts have focused mainly on methods to reduce the space requirements for suffix trees and suffix arrays. Space efficient construction of suffix trees were studied in Kurtz (1999) and Andersson and Nilsson (1995). Compressed suffix trees were studied in Munro et al. (2001), Grossi and Vitter (2005), and Kim and Park (2005), while compressed suffix arrays were considered in Grossi and Vitter (2000), Grossi and Vitter (2005), Hon et al. (2003a), and Na (2005). Algorithms that can perform the construction in external storage were proposed in Bieganski et al. (1994), Clark and Munro (1996), Farach-Colton et al. (2000), Hunt et al. (2001), and Cheung et al. (2005) for suffix trees, and in Kärkkäinen et al. (2006) and Crauser and Ferragina (2002) for suffix arrays. Ferragina (2005) looks at the general problem of string searching in external memory. Franceschini and Muthukrishnan (2007) reports on in-place suffix sorting.

5

Analysis of the Burrows-Wheeler Transform

The Burrows-Wheeler Transform performs a permutation of the input string, and thus provides no compression on its own. Rather, the BWT essentially reorganizes the input sequence so that symbols with similar contexts are clustered together in the output stream. In this sense the BWT can be seen as a preprocessing scheme to expose potential redundancies in a given input, and hence enhance later compression, using existing compression algorithms. Thus, the BWT can be viewed as a "compression booster", since it makes it possible for relatively simple compression algorithms to perform better on most input sequences (Ferragina et al., 2005a). Interestingly, some of the better compression methods don't do so well on the BWT output because they are being too "clever" looking for patterns when the patterns are very simple. This ability of the BWT to reorganize (sort) the input sequence based on contexts is central to its relationship with other compression algorithms. It is also the key to its use in various other fields and applications, different from data compression. Not surprisingly, this context sorting stage of the BWT is also the major bottleneck in performing the transformation on a given input sequence.

In this chapter, we analyze the theoretical performance of the Burrows-Wheeler Transform. We consider its performance in terms of its computational complexity (both space and time complexity). We also consider its theoretical performance in data compression, in terms of how close or how fast it could approach the theoretically optimal performance for a given source. We will examine how the theoretical performance of the BWT, be it computational complexity or compression ability, is related to the sorted contexts used by the transform. We will then relate it to other compression methods, especially those based on using contexts, as the BWT approach turns out to effectively be partitioning the input according to contexts in which the characters occur.

Since compression is traditionally the major application of the BWT, it is appropriate to discuss the performance from the viewpoint of the two general stages of BWT-based compression. Thus, our analysis will be based on the general BWT-based compression pipeline introduced in Chapter 3, as shown in Figure 5.1.

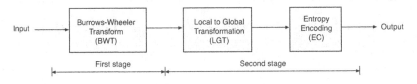

Fig. 5.1. Stages in the BWT compression pipeline

The local to global transform (LGT) converts the local structure induced by the BWT to a global structure that can be exploited by standard entropy encoding algorithms. Let X be some intermediate encoding(s) or transformation(s) on the BWT output. Using the acronyms MTF for move-to-front encoding, RLE for run-length encoding, and EC for order zero entropy coding, we can represent the BWT compression pipeline on an input sequence T as follows: $EC(X(BWT(\text{T})))$. Using specific instantiations of X will generally lead to different compression schemes. Example schemes under this general framework are:

- BWT_{EC}: $\text{EC(BWT}(T))$ (i.e. no MTF, no RLE)
- BWT_{MTF}: $\text{EC(MTF(BWT}(T)))$
- $\text{BWT}_{MTF-RLE}$: $\text{EC(RLE(MTF(BWT}(T))))$
- BWT_{RLE}: $\text{EC(RLE(BWT}(T)))$ (i.e. no MTF)
- BWT_{Z-RLE}: $\text{EC(RLE(Z(BWT}(T))))$
- BWT_{Z}: $\text{EC(Z(BWT}(T)))$)

In the above, Z simply denotes any other local to global structure transformation scheme different from MTF, such as distance coding, or inversion frequencies. We observe that the BWT and EC stages are present in each of the schemes. The variations differ mainly in terms of the further transformations/encodings (such as move-to-front, distance coding and run-length encoding) they apply to the BWT output before final encoding, which uses any order-0 entropy encoder, typically arithmetic coding or Huffman coding. The BWT$_{RLE}$ scheme includes the RLEAC method that was discussed at the beginning of Chapter 3 as one of the best methods overall — the entropy coder in this case is arithmetic coding with the aggressive counting strategy. Some authors have applied the RLE on the input sequence T before passing it to the BWT (Balkenhol and Kurtz, 2000; Fenwick, 1997b). On average, this leads to a reduction in the practical compression time, since the length of the output sequence from the RLE will typically be shorter than the input, and perhaps more importantly, the lack of long runs will reduce the average number of character comparisons required to perform string comparisons. However, the RLE also reorganizes the input string in a way that affects the later stages of the BWT compression. It is not clear whether this initial RLE generally improves or degrades overall compression performance (see Fenwick (1996a,b, 1997b); Deorowicz (2002)). The effect tends to depend more on the specific nature of the input sequence. Furthermore, although the original BWT-based compression introduced by Burrows and Wheeler (1994), which we shall refer to as BWT_0 (corresponding to BWT_{MTF} above), was based on the MTF, there is also the issue of whether the MTF is really necessary in compressing the BWT output close to the source entropy.

5.1 The BWT, suffix trees and suffix arrays

The context clustering stage of the BWT involving sorting the rows of A into the rotation matrix A_s is critical to its performance. This sorting procedure can be performed using suffix trees or suffix arrays, providing an important link between the BWT and these data structures. In fact, an analysis of the BWT can be performed by considering the close relationship between the BWT and suffix trees and suffix arrays because its computational complexity can be traced to the complexity of these important data structures. Similarly, its performance in compression can be analyzed based on its relationship with suffix trees, and the relationship between suffix trees and context trees.

To see the relationship between the BWT and these data structures, consider Figure 5.2, which shows the list of suffixes, the suffix tree, and the BWT sorted rotation matrix for the sample string $T = $ mississippi. In this example a $ symbol is used to denote the end-of-string; it isn't strictly necessary for the BWT, but it does simplify the descriptions by marking the end of each suffix. The L array, the final BWT output, is given in the last column of the table. We have also included the corresponding BWT output symbol (given in brackets) at each leaf node in the suffix tree.

We will assume that the suffix tree of a given input string is available, and that the edges from each node in the tree are sorted in lexicographically increasing order from left to right based on the edge labels, for example using Farach's construction (see Chapter 4). As pointed out in the original work by Burrows and Wheeler (1994), the BWT output can be obtained by a simple traversal of the leaf nodes in the suffix tree from left to right. Let l_i $(1 \leq i \leq n+1)$ be the label of the i-th leaf node in the suffix tree (scanning left to right). Recall that l_i is the starting position of the i-th suffix in the input string T. Thus, at the i-th leaf node, with n as the length of T, we obtain the corresponding BWT output as follows:

$$L[i] = BWT[i] = \begin{cases} T[l_i - 1] & : \quad \text{if } i \neq 1 \\ T[n+1] = \$ & : \quad \text{otherwise} \end{cases}$$

Given that the suffix array records the index of the sorted suffixes of a string, it is easy to see the relationship between the BWT and suffix arrays. If

Suffixes ID	Sorted Suffixes	Suffix Array	Sorted Rotations (A_s matrix)	BWT Output (L)
mississippi\$	1	\$	12	\$mississippi	i
ississippi\$	2	i\$	11	i\$mississipp	p
ssissippi\$	3	ippi\$	8	ippi\$mississ	s
sissippi\$	4	issippi\$	5	issippi\$miss	s
issippi\$	5	ississippi\$	2	ississippi\$m	m
ssippi\$	6	mississippi\$	1	mississippi\$	\$
sippi\$	7	pi\$	10	pi\$mississip	p
ippi\$	8	ppi\$	9	ppi\$mississi	i
ppi\$	9	sippi\$	7	sippi\$missis	s
pi\$	10	sissippi\$	4	sissippi\$mis	s
i\$	11	ssippi\$	6	ssippi\$missi	i
\$	12	ssissippi\$	3	ssissippi\$mi	i

(a)

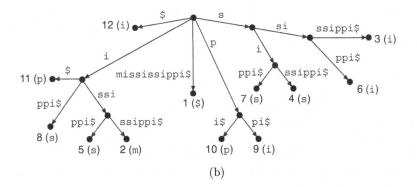

(b)

Fig. 5.2. Relationship between the BWT, suffix trees, and suffix arrays, using the string T = mississippi: (a) the suffixes and the rotation matrix; (b) the suffix tree — the number at each leaf node in the suffix tree corresponds to the suffix ID, which indicates the starting position of the suffix in the original sequence T. The symbol in brackets at each leaf node corresponds to the BWT output symbol for the leaf. The label on each edge corresponds to a substring of T

we ignore the characters after the special symbol \$ in the final results from the BWT rotation and permutation procedures, the sorted suffixes (Figure 5.2a, third column) correspond exactly to the sorted rotated matrix from the BWT (fifth column). Therefore, given A_T, the suffix array of the input string T, the BWT output can be computed as follows:

$$L[i] = \begin{cases} T[A_T[i] - 1] & : \quad \text{if } A_T[i] \neq 1 \\ T[n+1] = \$ & : \quad \text{otherwise} \end{cases}$$

5.2 Computational complexity

To analyze the overall computational complexity of using the BWT, we consider the two major stages in the BWT compression pipeline. The first stage is concerned with the transformation (permutation and sorting) that produces the L array. The second stage concerns the subsequent stage of possibly transforming the local structures in the BWT output into a global structure (for instance, using some recency ranking scheme) and a final entropy encoding using a given variable length code. Thus, stage two corresponds to LGT and EC in the general compression framework. For some applications of the BWT such as in pattern matching, only the first stage is needed, while applications such as biological sequence comparison and phylogeny in bioinformatics may not require the entropy encoding stage. We analyze the computational complexity by considering the two stages in the BWT pipeline.

5.2.1 BWT first stage — the transform

In Chapter 4, we showed that there are algorithms for suffix tree construction that are generally linear in time and space. It is simple to obtain the suffix array from a suffix tree using a simple inorder traversal. However, given the space requirement of suffix trees, various methods have been proposed to perform suffix sorting directly, without the need for initial construction of the suffix tree. Chapter 4 discussed more recent techniques for direct suffix sorting, with worst case time and space complexity in $O(n)$, for a string of length n. Table 5.1 provides a summary of the theoretical time and space complexity of most existing algorithms for suffix sorting. The reported time complexity is with respect to the worst case, while space requirement (in bytes) includes space for both the input string and the suffix array.

Given the relationship between the BWT, suffix arrays, and suffix trees, it is clear that the complexity of the forward Burrows-Wheeler Transform is linear in the length of the input string T, with respect to both time and space. In fact, more recently, Kärkkäinen (Kärkkäinen, 2007) observed that the full suffix array may not even be needed, if one is interested in just the L array, the direct BWT output. This leads to a more memory-efficient algorithm for computing the forward BWT. The resulting algorithm however could not run in linear time.

From Chapter 2, we can observe that given L, the reconstruction of the original sequence T requires the construction of F, the array of first characters, and other count arrays. These can be accomplished in linear time. Hence, the forward BWT and inverse BWT (BWT first stage) can each be performed in linear time and linear space in the worst case.

5.2.2 BWT second stage — coding the transformed text

The second stage of BWT-based compression involves the encoding of the BWT output — the L array and the index value, a. It is easy to see that most

Reference	General methodology	Time complexity	Space needed
Manber and Myers (1993)	successive doubling	$O(n \log n)$	$10n$
Larsson and Sadakane (2007)	successive doubling	$O(n \log n)$	$8n$
Schürmann and Stoye (2005)	bucket pointers	$O(n^2)$	$10n$
Itoh and Tanaka (1999)	binary suffix grouping	$O(n^2 \log n)$	$5n$
Seward (2000)	grouping and copying	$O(n^2 \log n)$	$5n$
Manzini and Ferragina (2004)	deep-shallow sorting	$O(n^2 \log n)$	$5n$
Kärkkäinen and Sanders (2003) and Kärkkäinen et al. (2006)	recursive partitioning	$O(n)$	$12n$
Ko and Aluru (2003, 2005)	recursion with suffix grouping	$O(n)$	$10n$
Suffix tree based methods			
Weiner (1973)	suffix trees	$O(n)$	—
McCreight (1976) and Kurtz and Balkenhol (2000)	suffix trees and hashing	$O(n)$	$28n$
Ukkonen (1995)	suffix trees	$O(n)$	$33n$
Kurtz and Balkenhol (2000)	suffix trees	$O(n)$	$16n$
Farach (1997) and Farach-Colton et al. (2000)	recursive partitioning with odd/even suffix trees	$O(n)$	—

Table 5.1. Worst case time complexity and space complexity for some popular suffix sorting algorithms; the actual space requirement (in bytes) is included where it is known

algorithms at this stage require linear time and linear space (in the worst case) to perform the required encoding. As discussed in Chapter 3, most of the local to global structure transformation (LGT) algorithms (for example recency ranking schemes such as MTF) require only a single pass over the BWT output. For example, consider the i-th step in the MTF algorithm. Let $\sigma = L[i]$, and let the position of σ in the current alphabet list be p_σ. At the i-th step, the MTF algorithm records p_σ on the output stream, and then moves σ to the head of the alphabet list. Thus, the algorithm requires $O(n|\Sigma|)$ time to process all the symbols in the input sequence L. The only additional space required is an $O(|\Sigma|)$ space to maintain the alphabets, where Σ is the symbol alphabet. With a fixed alphabet, the time will be linear with respect to n, the length of the input string. Similarly, the entropy encoding stage can be implemented in linear time and linear space for a given input sequence (see, for instance, Moffat (1990) for arithmetic coding, or Fenwick (2002a) for variable length codes for the integers). The decoding process essentially reverses the encoding steps, and subsequent processing of the output using the inverse LGT. Thus, decoding can equally be performed in $O(n)$ time and space in the worst case.

5.3 BWT context clustering property

An important characteristic of the Burrows-Wheeler Transform is its ability
to find symbols that have similar contexts in the input string and cluster
them together in the output stream. Traditionally, for a given sequence, $T =$
$t_1 t_2 \ldots t_n$, the *context* of symbol t_i is defined by the symbols that immediately
precede t_i in T. This is sometimes called the *preceding context* (or left context),
and is defined by the substring $t_{i-1} t_{i-2} \ldots t_1$. Thus, the context of t_i is defined
by reversing the prefix T^{i-1}. With the BWT, context clustering is performed
based on the *succeeding context* (also called right context, or forward context),
defined by the symbols that immediately succeed t_i in T. Given the cyclic
rotation of the input string by the BWT, the forward context for t_i is therefore
essentially defined by the string $T_{i+1} * T^{i-1}$, where the symbol $*$ denotes
concatenation. When the special end of string terminator $\$$ is used, the forward
context will be determined only by the suffix T_{i+1}.

With the suffix sorting stage of the BWT, suffixes that are similar in the
original sequence will be placed together in the sorted matrix of rotations of
the BWT. From the discussion on the relationship between the BWT and
suffix trees and suffix arrays in Section 5.1, it therefore follows that the BWT
output symbols in the same region of the output array L are likely to have
similar following suffixes, that is, similar forward contexts in the original sequence.

Thus, the output stream can be partitioned into different segments based
on the similarity in the symbol contexts, for instance, based on the LCP between the contexts of nearby symbols in L. Table 5.2 shows the partitioning
that will occur for the example from Figure 5.2 where $T = $ mississippi$\$$
and $L = $ ipsm$\$$pissii, for longest common prefixes greater than 1 and 2. In
the table the output stream L that has been partitioned based on LCP ≥ 1
gives $L_1 = $ [i|pssm|$\$$|pi|ssii]; for LCP ≥ 2, we get the partitioning
$L_2 = $ [i|p|s|sm|$\$$|p|i|ss|ii]. For LCP ≥ 1, we have one of the partitions
being $(L[2], L[3], L[4], L[5])$, which is (p, s, s, m), corresponding to symbols $(T[10], T[7], T[4], T[1])$ each having the same forward context in T, which
is the symbol i in this case, and thus they are in the same partition.

Analysis of the BWT output and the BWT performance in compression
can be performed based on the above context clustering (or partitioning)
property. This can be done by relating the context clustering property of the
BWT with traditional context trees, which are easier to analyze.

5.3.1 Context trees

For a given string T, with symbols taken from the alphabet Σ, the *context tree*
is a rooted tree that records the context of each symbol at any given position
in T. Figure 5.3 shows an example context tree (with compressed paths) for
the string $T = $ mississippi. Each leaf node in the context tree corresponds
to a unique context in T. Contexts are read in reverse from the character of

Position	LCP ≥ 1 Contexts	L	LCP ≥ 2 Contexts	L
1	$	i	$m	i
2	i	p	i$	p
3	i	s	ip	s
4	i	s	is	s
5	i	m	is	m
6	m	$	mi	$
7	p	p	pi	p
8	p	i	pp	i
9	s	s	si	s
10	s	s	si	s
11	s	i	ss	i
12	s	i	ss	i

Table 5.2. Two partitions of the BWT output (the L-array) based on symbol contexts

interest; for example, in Figure 5.3 the context of the 3rd character (s) is mi, so we traverse the tree using this string in reverse (im), which goes down the left-most branches terminated at the leaf labeled with s. Each internal node in an uncompressed context tree has exactly $|\Sigma|$ outgoing edges. Each edge is labeled with a symbol from Σ, and the substring spelled by the path from the root to a given node defines the path label for the node. In the compressed representation, sequences of nodes with only single branches are compressed into a single branch showing the corresponding sequence of characters.

The nodes in a context tree are further decorated with context statistics: for each node, say u, we record the subsequence of symbols that were observed in the context u. These are typically converted to context statistics, which represent the probability distribution of the symbols that were observed following the context u. Thus, at a node, the context statistics describe the distribution of the symbols, given the context represented by the node. Notice that as each leaf node has just one symbol, the count at a leaf node will be just for this symbol, with the counts for the other symbols all zero.

For the example string, Figure 5.3b shows the context tree decorated with context statistics at each node in the tree — the four numbers correspond, respectively, to the number of times each character in $\Sigma = \{$ i, m, p, s $\}$ has been counted. Each node, say u, then corresponds to a subsequence of symbols in T. The root node is taken to have a null context, and corresponds to the entire string. The statistics for the root correspond to the symbol probabilities for the entire sequence. The context statistics of a given node are obtained from the statistics of its descendant nodes, except for the root, which includes the count for the first character in the text, which doesn't occur in any other context.

So far we have considered the unbounded contexts in a given string, which includes all the possible preceding contexts of all lengths to each position in the

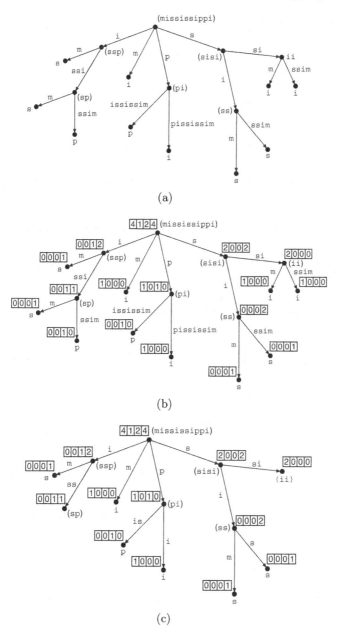

Fig. 5.3. Context tree for the sequence $T =$ mississippi: (a) context tree with path label compression; (b) context tree decorated with context statistics; (c) order-3 context tree. The subsequences at each node in (b) and (c) are the symbols in T that have the path label to the node as their preceding context. The numbers in the boxes at each node are the symbol distribution (as counts) for i, m, p, and s respectively

string. In practice, most context-based systems use *bounded* contexts, that is, they have a maximum number of preceding symbols that can be considered in the context. Thus, an *order-k context* refers to a context of maximum length k, formed using only the first k preceding symbols. Figure 5.3c shows the order-3 context tree for our example. The order-3 context for the first p (position 9) in mississippi will be the three characters preceding it: iss. Thus, the context tree for an order-k context is simply the full context tree truncated to a maximum depth of k. Some of the counts in the original context tree are combined in the order-3 tree.

We can also observe that with the context tree, all the contexts of a given symbol, say t_i in T (independent of the context order or length) will lie along the same path, from the root of the context tree to the leaf node corresponding to t_i. The path itself defines the longest context for t_i so far observed. Any other contexts of t_i can be found as some ancestor of the leaf node. Further, the depth of the lowest common ancestor between any pair of nodes (or equivalently, the lowest common prefix between the contexts) is an indication of the similarity between the contexts.

5.3.2 Estimation using context trees

In data compression, the input string is often considered to be coming from a certain *information source*. The information source is simply a random sequence $\{X_i\}$, where the symbols X_i are taken from a defined alphabet, Σ, with $-\infty \leq i \leq +\infty$.

The information source may be memoryless, that is, each symbol is independent of the previous symbols. It could also have memory, whereby each symbol depends on one or more of the previous symbols. An information source is called *ergodic* if it produces infinitely long sequences of symbols, whereby the statistics of each sequence are generally the same as those from any other sequence generated by the source. Further, an ergodic source is also *stationary*, that is, the distribution of symbols in any sequence generated do not change with time. The parameter θ is used to describe the probability distribution of the symbols in Σ. That is, θ is a $|\Sigma|$-length vector, where the i-th element is the probability that symbol $\sigma_i \in \Sigma$ will be emitted by the source at any given time.

Let $P_a(t_i)$ be the *actual* probability of symbol t_i in the string $T = t_1^n = t_1 t_2 \ldots t_n$ (the subscript a denotes actual probability). For the case of a memoryless source, the probability that the source will generate a particular sequence t_1^n is given by:

$$P_a(t_1^n) = \prod_{i=1}^{n} P_a(t_i)$$

In practice, we may not know θ, the true distribution of the source symbols. This must be estimated at each point as we process the sequence, based on the symbols observed so far. Consider the case of binary symbols. Let x be the number of zeros and y the number of ones so far observed in the string $T^i = t_1^i$. A simple estimate of the probability that the next symbol t_{i+1} will be a one is given by: $P_e(t_{i+1} = 1|t_1^i) = y/(x+y)$. Here, the subscript e denotes estimated probability. The *Krichevsky-Trofimov* (K-T) estimator (Krichevsky and Trofimov, 1981) generally provides a better estimate, as it handles the case when $x = y = 0$. The K-T estimate is defined as follows:

$$P_e(t_{i+1} = 1|t_1^i) = \frac{y + \frac{1}{2}}{x + y + 1}.$$

In general, the K-T estimate for the probability of a string with x zeros and y ones, is calculated iteratively as follows:

$$P_e(0,0) = 1$$
$$P_e(x+1, y) = \frac{x+\frac{1}{2}}{x+y+1}.P(x,y); \quad x, y \geq 0$$
$$P_e(x, y+1) = \frac{y+\frac{1}{2}}{x+y+1}.P(x,y); \quad x, y \geq 0$$

This can be computed using a closed form formula:

$$P_e(x,y) = \frac{(\frac{1}{2}.\frac{3}{2}\cdots\frac{2x-1}{2})(\frac{1}{2}.\frac{3}{2}\cdots\frac{2y-1}{2})}{1.2.3\ldots(x+y)}$$

In most practical situations of interest, however, there is likely to be some dependence between the current symbol and other symbols emitted by the information source — the information source has memory of previous symbols emitted. For such sources with memory, the symbol distribution is not fixed, but could vary from one symbol to the other, depending on the context of the symbol. Thus, the same symbol, say σ observed under two different contexts could potentially have different probabilities (for example, in English, the probability of the character u is quite different if the previous character was a space compared to the previous character having been a q).

The Markov source is a typical example of a source with memory. For an order-k Markov source, the probability of a given symbol depends only on the preceding k symbols, that is, its order-k context. The context tree thus serves as a *model* of the source, and the source is sometimes called a *tree source*. The symbol probability distribution θ is then called the *parameter* of the source. For each node with path label w, the parameter is defined by the probability distribution, $P(.|\hat{w})$, where $\hat{w}$ is the reverse of w. Let c_i denote the path label to the i-th leaf node in the context tree.

For such a source, the actual probability of a particular string $t_1^n \in \Sigma^n$ is given by:

$$P_a(t_1^n) = P_a(t_1 t_2 \ldots t_p) \prod_{i=p+1}^{n} P(t_i|\hat{c}_i) \tag{5.1}$$

where p is the length of the shortest context in the context tree, and c_i is the context of t_i in the string t_1^n, with $c_i = t_{i-|c_i|}^{i-1} = t_{i-|c_i|}t_{i-|c_i|-1}\cdots t_{i-1}$ and $\hat{c}_i = t_{i-1}^{i-|c_i|}$, the reverse of c_i. For order-k Markov sources, $c_i = t_{i-k}^{i-1}$.

For stationary sources, the probability of a symbol depends only on the symbol and its context, and not on the position of the symbol in the text. For such sources, the symbols in t_1^n can be partitioned into different groups based on the similarity of their contexts. Using the context tree, such partitioning is simply performed by considering the leaf nodes that have common ancestors of a given depth. Using this partitioning on the context tree, Equation 5.1 above for the actual probability of the string t_1^n can now be modified as follows:

$$P_a(t_1^n) = P_a(t_1 t_2 \ldots t_p) \prod_{c \in \mathcal{C}} \prod_{t_i \in \mathcal{Q}(c)} P(t_i | \hat{c})$$

where $\mathcal{C}$ is the set of all contexts in the string (essentially, the set of leaf nodes in the context tree), and $\mathcal{Q}(c) = $ set of symbols in t_1^n with the same context, c.

Balkenhol and Kurtz (2000) showed that for a tree source, for each context $c \in \mathcal{C}$, the subsequence of t_1^n formed by the symbols with context c is independent and identically distributed. This is important, as it implies that the subsequence can be encoded based on θ_c, the corresponding symbol distribution under this context, using any locally adaptive encoding scheme, such as arithmetic coding or adaptive Huffman codes.

If we know the model of the tree source, we know at which points to change from one context to the other, thus, we can code the symbols based on their contexts. The model parameter, however, is not always known beforehand. An important issue therefore is how we can estimate the model parameter, θ_c, which defines the probability distribution for the symbols with context c. The K-T estimator described earlier was given just for the case of binary symbols ($|\Sigma| = 2$). Let $T = t_1^n$ be the input string. For general alphabets with $|\Sigma| > 2$, the K-T estimator can be extended to approximate $Pr(T)$ as $Pr(t_1^n)$, the probability of string t_1^n as follows. Let $n_i(\sigma, T)$ be the number of times symbol σ, $\sigma \in \Sigma$ has occurred in the prefix $T^i = t_1^i$, where $n_0(\sigma) \overset{\text{def}}{=} 0$. By definition, the probability of the empty string (the only zero-length string) is taken to be 1. Where it is obvious from the context of discussion, we will drop the T in the notation $n_i(\sigma, T)$.

Then,

$$P_e(t_i | t_1^{i-1}) = \frac{n_{i-1}(t_i) + \frac{1}{2}}{i - 1 + \frac{|\Sigma|}{2}}$$

The required probability $Pr(T) = Pr(t_1^n)$ is then estimated sequentially:

$$P_e(T) = P_e(t_1^n) = \prod_{i=1}^n P_e(t_i | t_1^{i-1}) = \prod_{i=1}^n \frac{n_{i-1}(t_i) + \frac{1}{2}}{i - 1 + \frac{|\Sigma|}{2}} \tag{5.2}$$

This can be written in a closed form formula:

$$P_e(T) = \frac{1}{(n+1)!} \prod_{\substack{i=1 \\ n_n(\sigma_i)>0}}^{|\Sigma|} \frac{1}{2}\frac{3}{2} \cdots \frac{(2n_n(\sigma_i)-1)}{2}$$

For the example with T = mississippi, assuming that $|\Sigma| = 4$, the estimated probability will be:

$$P_e(T) = \left(\frac{\frac{1}{2}}{2}\right)\left(\frac{\frac{1}{2}}{3}\right)\left(\frac{\frac{1}{2}}{4}\right)\left(\frac{\frac{3}{2}}{5}\right)\left(\frac{\frac{3}{2}}{6}\right)\left(\frac{\frac{5}{2}}{7}\right)\left(\frac{\frac{7}{2}}{8}\right)\left(\frac{\frac{5}{2}}{9}\right)\left(\frac{\frac{1}{2}}{10}\right)\left(\frac{\frac{3}{2}}{11}\right)\left(\frac{\frac{7}{2}}{12}\right)$$

$$= 3.3715 \times 10^{-8}.$$

Or, equivalently

$$P_e(T) = P_e([4,1,2,4]) = \frac{\left(\frac{1}{2}\right)^4 \left(\frac{3}{2}\right)^3 \left(\frac{5}{2}\right)^2 \left(\frac{7}{2}\right)^2}{12!}$$

5.3.3 BWT and context trees

There is a striking similarity between the context tree and the suffix tree — in fact, if we ignore the context statistics, the context tree for unbounded contexts as described above is simply the *prefix tree* of T. The prefix tree of a string T is just the suffix tree of $\hat{T}$, the reversed version of T. In the prefix tree, reading the path labels from the leaf to the root gives the corresponding prefix. Figure 5.4b shows the prefix tree for the sequence T = mississippi, that is the suffix tree for the reversed sequence, $\hat{T}$ = ippississim. This can be compared with the context tree of Figure 5.3a. The leaf node with symbol t_i in the context tree corresponds to the leaf node with label $(i-1)$ in the prefix tree.

Thus, by applying the BWT on $\hat{T}$, the reversed version of the input string T, we produce a cluster of contexts. Essentially, this can be viewed as analogous to the context tree of T, based on the relationship between the BWT and suffix trees. The major difference here is that contexts in the context tree formed via the BWT are sorted, which is not necessarily a requirement for ordinary context trees. The BWT also allows us to have contexts of arbitrary order (i.e. unbounded contexts), without needing to keep explicit statistics for each node of the context tree. After applying the BWT, encoding the i-th partition on L requires us to maintain the statistics for only the current context, that is, the i-th context in sorted order.

```
m
mi
mis
miss
missi
missis
mississ
mississi
mississip
mississipp
mississippi
```

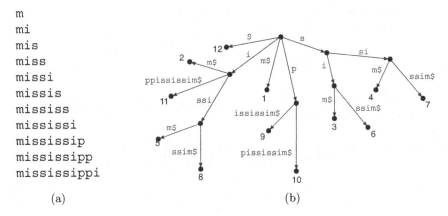

(a)   (b)

Fig. 5.4. The prefix tree: (a) List of prefixes for the string $T = $ mississippi; (b) The corresponding prefix tree — compare with the context tree in Figure 5.3

5.4 Analysis of BWT output

The output of the Burrows-Wheeler Transform can be analyzed both through a theoretical approach (assuming particular kinds of input), and through empirical evaluation. In this section we will review results based on both approaches.

5.4.1 Theoretical distribution of BWT output

A detailed theoretical study of the output distribution of the Burrows-Wheeler Transform (before the application of the local to global structure transformation algorithms) was performed by Visweswariah et al. (2000) and Effros et al. (2002). They showed that, in general, for an input sequence that is independent and identically distributed (i.i.d.), the BWT output is also asymptotically i.i.d. They demonstrated this by showing that the normalized relative entropy (Kullback-Leibler distance) between an i.i.d. distribution and the BWT output distribution tends to zero for an infinitely long input sequence. The i.i.d. nature of the BWT output for i.i.d. input is in line with the results of Balkenhol and Kurtz (2000, 1998), where they argued that the BWT output for a tree source should be i.i.d.

Following a similar line of argument, Visweswariah et al. also showed that for sources with finite-memory, (such as Markov sources), the relative entropy between the BWT output and a source that is piecewise-constant independent and identically distributed (p.i.i.d.) (Merhav, 1993; Willems, 1996) tends to zero in the long run. Thus, the BWT output for a Markov source can be described as a piecewise constant i.i.d. This is a very significant result. Given the sorted nature of the BWT contexts, and the partitioning of the BWT output (the L-array) as induced by these sorted contexts, intuitively, one would expect that the output distribution of the BWT can be modeled by a piecewise constant i.i.d. However, this is the very first theoretical proof of this result. The implication is that, further analysis on the BWT output, for instance, later encoding of the output, can be performed using methods for p.i.i.d. sources.

The results above are without reference to later LGT algorithms. While the MTF and various other LGT algorithms have been proposed, there is not much reported work on a similar theoretical study on the distribution of the BWT output after application of MTF, or other similar transformation, such as interval ranking, inversion frequencies, and so on, although Manzini (2001, 1999) report an initial study on the MTF. Likewise, there is not much reported theoretical study on the nature of the distribution after RLE is applied to the MTF(BWT(T)) results. Clearly, such a theoretical study will be of interest, as it will show clearly the impact the MTF and other LGT algorithms have on the long-term performance of the BWT as a compression booster.

5.4.2 Empirical distribution of BWT output

Motivated by the theoretical study above, it is useful to perform a corresponding empirical study on the nature of the BWT output. To what extent does the output from the BWT come close to the i.i.d. or p.i.i.d. distributions in practice? How does the LGT stage affect the compression performance? Can we do without the LGT stage in its entirety, and code the BWT output directly with an entropy encoding algorithm, perhaps, with appropriate modifications? Various authors have performed an empirical analysis of the BWT output, especially based on the MTF coding (Fenwick, 1996a, 1997b; Deorowicz, 2002).

The last of the questions just posed, about whether we can do without an LGT stage (in particular, dispensing with the MTF transform) has been answered in the positive in recent research, despite the MTF having been strongly associated with the BWT since it was first published. As discussed at the beginning of Chapter 3, it is possible to have the entropy coder itself model the recency effect simply by having it use an adaptive counting system where the probability of a character is estimated from its count, but the count is heavily weighted toward recent occurrences of that character. For example, Ferragina et al. (2006a) describe their FAST adaptation system where the count of a symbol is incremented by 256 each time it is encoded, and all symbol counts are halved if the total count reaches 65,536. This means that after the first 256 symbols have been coded, each 128 symbols will have double the weight of the previous 128 symbols, and so on. They use a run-length encoder on the output of the BWT, which will pick up immediate repetitions of characters, but apart from this simple pre-processing, the BWT output is only processed by the arithmetic coder, which means that processing time is very good. Looking at the output sample in Figure 3.1 on page 34, we can see that the window of 128 symbols (runs) corresponds to just a few lines of text, so a small set of symbols will very quickly dominate the statistics. Changes in the input (such as the large number of "i" characters in the last line of the figure) will also be acquired very quickly. Ferragina et al. (2006a) reported that the FAST adaptation system performed better than the equivalent MTF-based system; for example, using RLE(BWT(T)) with the FAST adaptation compressed a large collection of files to an average of 1.126 bits per character, whereas the equivalent MTF system compressed them to 1.158 bits per character. Fenwick (1996a) also reported good results using an arithmetic coder with an increment of 16 and a limit of 8192.

We are interested in the empirical behavior of the BWT output not just for compression performance, but for other applications that take advantage of the structure that it finds in its input. In the remainder of this section we report experimental results that help us to understand the nature of the BWT, and how it behaves on data that might be encountered in practice. We do this using five files with different content characteristics. Some details of the files are described in Table 5.3. The first three files are from the Canterbury corpus (http://corpus.canterbury.ac.nz, "large" collection), while "lena" is a widely-used test image for image processing, and "random16" is a random sequence over an alphabet of 16 symbols, which should be compressed to 4 bits per byte.

File name	Size (bytes)	Description
bible	4,047,392	King James Bible (English text).
E.coli	4,638,690	Complete genome of the *Escherichia coli* bacterium, stored with 1 symbol per byte. This file is known for its low level of redundancy.
world192	2,473,400	The CIA world fact book (English text).
random16	10,000,000	A sequence of random 4-bit numbers generated using the uniform distribution.
lena	262,322	Test image from the USC collection, 512×512 pixels, 8 bit gray scale. Raw gray scale values, not pixel differences or prediction errors.

Table 5.3. Files used for empirical analysis of BWT output

First we look at the statistics and nature of the direct output from the BWT (the L array), the output when L is passed through MTF:

$$L_{MTF} = \text{MTF}(\text{BWT}(T)),$$

and the result when L_{MTF} is passed through RLE:

$$L_{RLE} = \text{RLE}(\text{MTF}(\text{BWT}(T))).$$

For each representation of the original sequence we consider the direct probabilities (bigrams, trigrams, and so on), the order-k entropy, the Zipf's law fit, and the effect of each stage on compression, via context-based entropy estimation. We also considered what happens when the four sequences T, L, L_{MTF}, and L_{RLE} are passed through some other popular compression schemes. In a sense, this last experiment provides a simple method to check the compression boosting performance of the BWT.

We begin by looking at bigrams (pairs of characters) in the transformed files, as these reflect higher-order dependencies. Figure 5.5 shows the bigram frequencies for each file, using the four representations indicated above, and Figure 5.6 shows an enlargement of the detail of these graphs. In this and other figures from experiments discussed in this section, we use *txt* to denote T, the original sequence; *bwt* for L, the direct BWT output; *mtf* for L_{MTF}, the MTF results, and *rle* for L_{RLE}, the resulting sequence after applying the RLE on the MTF output. Figure 5.5 shows that for the textual files, the original sequence tended to have fewer bigrams than the other representations. For the genome sequence, the MTF output and the original sequence seemed to have a higher occurrence of repeated bigrams. The L_{RLE} sequence had more than 16 distinct bigrams, which is because new symbols are included as part of the encoding process for RLE. For the image file, the MTF and the RLE seem to be necessary to achieve higher proportions of repeated bigrams, yet the actual percentages are quite low. For the random sequence, L_{RLE} produced much higher occurrences of repeated bigrams, although we can also observe the piecewise linear nature of the probability in this case. Overall, the BWT-based sequences L, L_{MTF}, and L_{RLE} tended to produce a higher probability of bigrams for the first few most frequent bigrams, although in some cases, T, the original sequence had a comparable number.

Similar trends can be observed for other q-grams, with $q > 2$. We have shown the results for bigrams ($q = 2$) only, since any repetition for q-grams with higher values of q will always include the bigrams by necessity; the results on q-gram probabilities provide an indication on the compressibility of the sequences. Each q-gram will provide an indication of the nature of the q-order entropy. Rather than focusing on the q-grams, we will consider how the BWT stages affect the higher order entropy of the original sequence. Figure 5.7 shows the order k entropy for the representations for small values of k. For text data, the best results (lower values) were produced using L and L_{MTF}. For the genome sequence, all the representations produced similar results, except the RLE output, L_{RLE}. For the image sequence, the lowest entropies were produced using either the direct BWT output or the original pixel sequence; the BWT isn't well suited to compressing raw photographic images because very few patterns are repeated *exactly* in such files. As with the genome sequence, all four representations produced similar higher-order entropies on the random sequence, with L_{RLE} producing a slightly lower value at $k = 2$ and 3. Apart from the random sequence, the L_{RLE} sequence almost always resulted in the highest entropy. However, in practice the best BWT coders do not simply use the entropy (which is based on the relative frequencies of the symbols), but they use the adaptive system described at the start of this

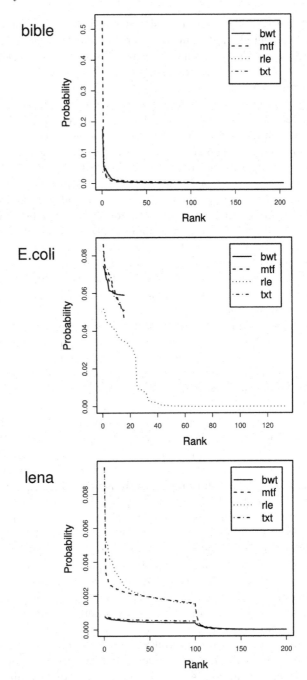

Fig. 5.5. Bigram frequencies for different BWT-based representations of the original sequence (continued on next page)

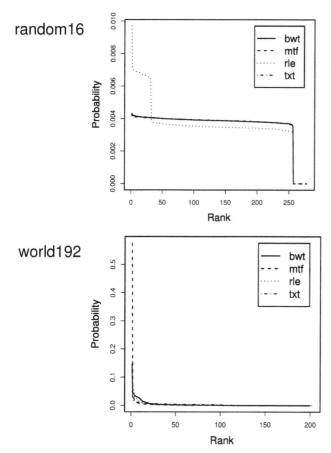

random16

world192

Fig. 5.5 continued: Bigram frequencies for different BWT-based representations of the original sequence

section. This has the important property of halving counts frequently, so that recent symbols will have more weight than older ones. If this is done aggressively enough then it achieves a recency effect, similar to the MTF system, and thus gives comparable compression.

Another way to consider the BWT output is by looking at how different words or substrings are distributed within each representation. One way to do this would be to consider the distribution of the frequency counts for the substrings, which gives an indication of the level of repetition of these substrings in a given sequence. Zipf's law (Zipf, 1949) provides a way of viewing such frequencies for the ensemble of words or substrings in the sequence (rather than for an individual word). Essentially, the law states that given a set of words from a natural language, ranked by their probability of occurrence, the probability of any word is inversely proportional to its rank. That is, the word

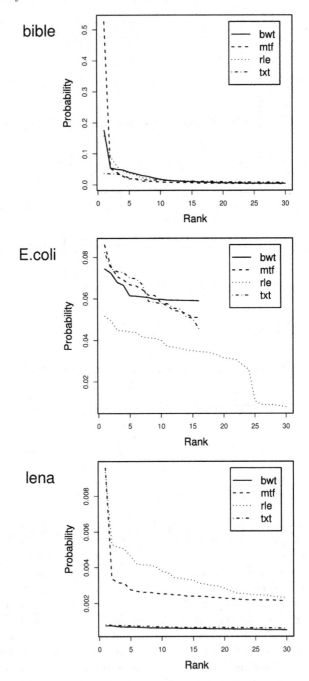

Fig. 5.6. Expanded view of bigram frequencies in Figure 5.5 (continued on next page)

random16

world192

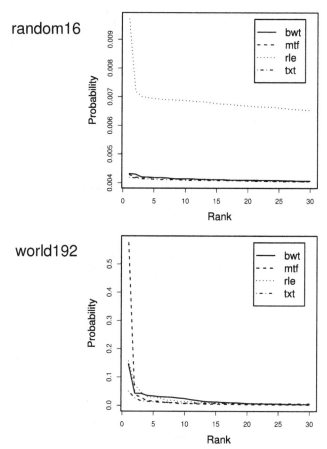

Fig. 5.6 continued: Expanded view of bigram frequencies in Figure 5.5

with the highest probability will occur about twice as frequently as the second most probable word, which in turn will occur twice as frequently as the third most probable word. More specifically, if n is the number of words or phrases, k is their rank order, and s is an exponent parameter used to characterize the distribution, the generalized Zipf's law predicts that the probability of the word with rank order k will be given by $p_{k,s,n} = \frac{1/k^s}{\sum_{i=1}^{n} 1/i^s}$. The classic Zipf's law is a special case with $s = 1$. Different data sets could follow Zipf's law, but with different exponents. Thus, although originally motivated by observations on words in a natural language, Zipf's law provides another way to study the structure of a given data ensemble, be it natural language texts, biological sequences, or general sequences.

Figure 5.8 shows the Zipf's law fit for each representation, with an expanded view of the graphs shown in Figure 5.9 — Zipf's law is characterized by straight lines on a log-log graph. The figures indicate that for text se-

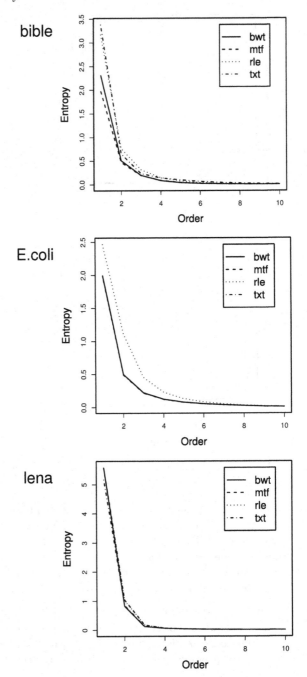

Fig. 5.7. Order-k entropy for T, L, L_{MTF}, and L_{RLE} (continued on next page)

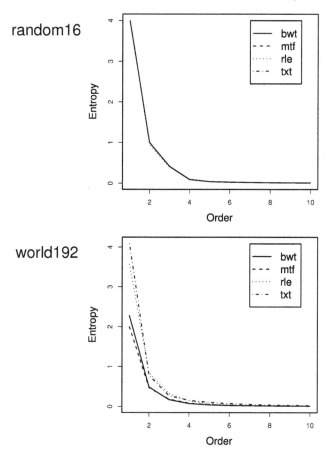

Fig. 5.7 continued: Order-k entropy for T, L, L_{MTF}, and L_{RLE}

quences, the frequency versus rank order plots follow Zipf's law for all the representations, perhaps with different exponents. For the genome sequence, again L_{RLE} was distinct from the rest, which seemed to have a similar behavior. The results for L_{MTF} and L_{RLE} were quite similar on the image data, while L and T were closer to each other. Again, all the representations had similar characteristics on the random sequence, except for L_{RLE}. Generally, the plots for this sequence were unusual compared with those from other types of data, with a seemingly piecewise-linear characteristics.

Figure 5.10 shows the estimated entropy using order-k contexts for each of the representations. Here, entropy estimation is performed using k-order contexts as defined by the BWT. To do this, symbols in the L array that have the same order k following context (that is, the same order-k common prefix starting in their corresponding rows in the A array) are grouped together, and their statistics used to compute the entropy for that region in L. We apply the

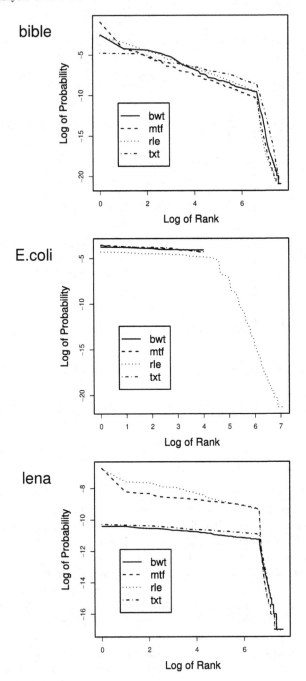

Fig. 5.8. Zipf's law fit for T, L, L_{MTF}, and L_{RLE} based on order-k sorted contexts (continued on next page)

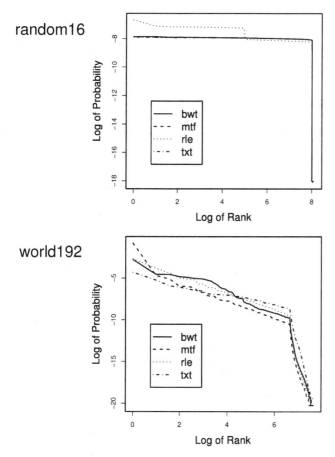

Fig. 5.8 continued: Zipf's law fit for T, L, L_{MTF}, and L_{RLE} based on order-k sorted contexts

same method to L_{MTF} (and L_{RLE}). This means that rather than passing one long sequence to the MTF or RLE, we pass chunks of adjacent symbols from L (or L_{MTF}). The estimated entropy using this scheme can be compared with the entropy results shown earlier (Figure 5.7), and the practical compression results shown in Table 5.4. The estimated entropy doesn't include the space for storing the statistics, so this level of compression is not possible in practice.

Table 5.4 shows the results obtained when the four representations of the sequence (T, L, L_{MTF} and L_{RLE}) are each passed to different compression schemes, namely simple arithmetic coding, GZIP and PPMC. The first row (T) in each table corresponds to not using the BWT. All other results are with inputs as the output at some given stage in the BWT compression pipeline. In almost all cases, the BWT-based representations led to improved compression, even when used on other compression schemes. In general, L_{RLE} did not do

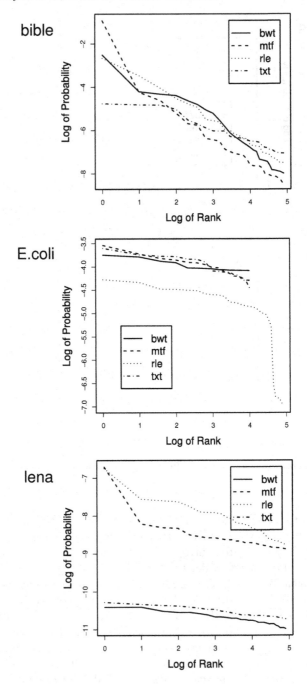

Fig. 5.9. Zipf's law fit — expanded view of Figure 5.8 (continued on next page)

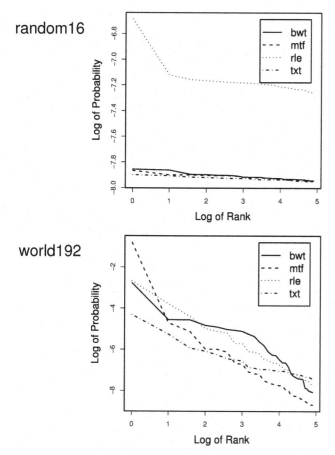

Fig. 5.9 continued: Zipf's law fit — expanded view of Figure 5.8

well on the random sequence, although it produced the best overall result across different compression schemes. In particular, L_{RLE} with PPMC resulted in some compression on the genomic sequence, and significant compression of the text sequences.

Table 5.5 shows the corresponding results when the order-1 context partitions on these representations are used. These results can be compared with those in Table 5.4, which did not use context partitions. Context partitions are formed based on the L array, as described above for context-based entropy estimation. Thus, this does not apply to the original sequence T, so there are no results for *txt*. We can notice the general improvement of compression performance, especially for the text sequences, and the DNA sequence.

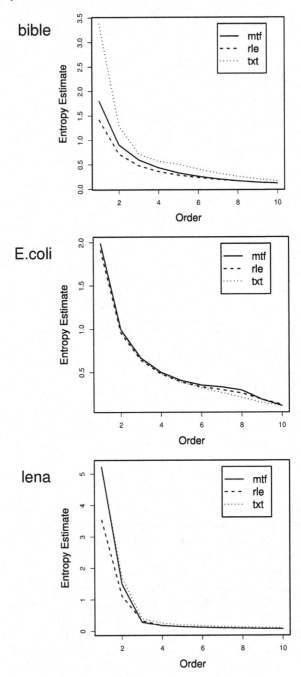

Fig. 5.10. Estimated entropy for L, L_{MTF}, and L_{RLE} based on order-k sorted contexts (continued on next page)

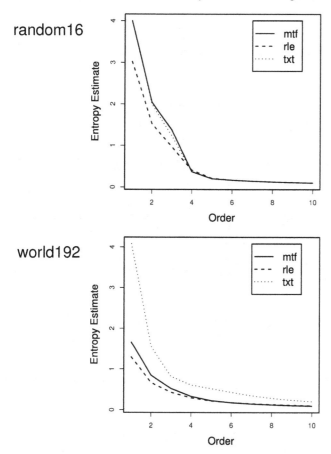

Fig. 5.10 continued: Estimated entropy for L, L_{MTF}, and L_{RLE} based on order-k sorted contexts

5.5 Analysis of BWT compression performance

The Burrows-Wheeler Transform performs a permutation of the input sequence, and thus provides a one-to-one mapping between the input symbols and the output symbols. Since symbol permutations do not change the order-zero entropy, in principle, the BWT cannot change the minimal code lengths that can be used to describe the source, at least for an order-zero model where context and locality are ignored. However, the BWT makes it easier to approach the limits of achievable compression performance. In this section we describe some methods for analyzing the theoretical performance of compression schemes that are based on the BWT. The description in this section borrows a lot of terminology and notation from information theory, and we start by defining some of these. Details and proofs of the relations can be

arith	bible	E.coli	lena	random16	world192
txt	0.5440	0.2537	0.9293	0.5041	0.6248
bwt	0.4888	0.2518	0.7669	0.5041	0.5558
mtf	0.2652	0.2530	0.7112	0.5041	0.2729
rle	0.2511	0.3558	0.7246	0.5286	0.2549

(a)

GZIP	bible	E.coli	lena	random16	world192
txt	0.2907	0.2801	0.8940	0.5708	0.2893
bwt	0.2959	0.2848	0.7639	0.5705	0.3025
mtf	0.2889	0.2849	0.7426	0.5706	0.2940
rle	0.2841	0.3220	0.7577	0.5852	0.2866

(b)

PPMC	bible	E.coli	lena	random16	world192
txt	0.2948	0.2502	0.8493	0.6313	0.3141
bwt	0.2981	0.2499	0.8511	0.6316	0.3266
mtf	0.2681	0.2518	0.8558	0.6276	0.2828
rle	0.2172	0.2445	0.7943	0.6312	0.2205

(c)

Table 5.4. Using BWT-based representations of a sequence $(T, L, L_{MTF}$, and $L_{RLE})$ as the input to different compression algorithms: (a) arithmetic coding; (b) GZIP; (c) PPMC

found in any standard text on information theory, such as Cover and Thomas (2006).

5.5.1 Definitions and notation

In this section we will take some liberties with the notation, and use $T = t_1^n = t^n$. The three will be used interchangeably, depending on ease of presentation in the context of the discussion. Let Y be a discrete random variable with values taken from an alphabet $\Sigma = \{\sigma_1, \sigma_2, \ldots, \sigma_{|\Sigma|}\}$. Let $p(\sigma) = Pr\{Y = \sigma\}$, $(\sigma \in \Sigma)$ be the probability mass function. The *entropy* of the random variable Y, denoted $H(Y)$, is a measure of the amount of uncertainty in the random variable, or equivalently, the minimum number of bits we need to describe the random variable, on average. The entropy is defined as[1]:

$$H(Y) = \sum_{i=1}^{|\Sigma|} p(\sigma_i) \log \frac{1}{p(\sigma_i)}$$

The entropy depends only on the probability of symbols in Σ, and not on their actual values. The n-th order entropy, denoted $H(Y^n)$, indicates the

---

[1] In this book, all logarithms are to base 2, unless otherwise indicated.

arith	bible	E.coli	lena	random16	world192
bwt	0.3587	0.2480	0.7251	0.5088	0.4497
mtf	0.2264	0.2523	0.7731	0.5094	0.2276
rle	0.2162	0.2775	0.7882	0.5338	0.1965

(a)

GZIP	bible	E.coli	lena	random16	world192
bwt	0.2438	0.2923	0.7421	0.5827	0.2233
mtf	0.2493	0.2924	0.7898	0.5834	0.2291
rle	0.2459	0.3143	0.8074	0.5995	0.2221

(b)

PPMC	bible	E.coli	lena	random16	world192
bwt	0.2440	0.2474	0.8169	0.6529	0.2334
mtf	0.2480	0.2495	0.8707	0.6536	0.2499
rle	0.2381	0.2571	0.8847	0.6621	0.2305

(c)

Table 5.5. Using order-1 context partitions of the BWT-based representations $(L, L_{MTF},$ and $L_{RLE})$ as the input to different compression algorithms: (a) arithmetic coding; (b) GZIP ; (c) PPMC. Order-1 contexts are determined based on the L array, as was done for context-based entropy estimation

uncertainty in the outcome of a sequence of n experiments with Y. The n-th order entropy is given as :

$$H(Y^n) = \sum_{y^n \in \Sigma^n} p(y^n) \log \frac{1}{p(y^n)}$$

where $y^n = (y_1, y_2, \ldots, y_n) \in \Sigma^n$ is an n-length sequence.

For stationary ergodic sources we can define the *entropy rate*, given as follows:

$$H(\Sigma) = \lim_{n \to \infty} \frac{1}{n} H(Y^n).$$

In practice, the true probability distribution of the source symbols may not always be known with complete accuracy. Thus, the probabilities may have to be approximated based on previous observations on the symbols from the source. For a given input sequence, the probabilities can be estimated using the frequency of occurrence of each symbol, computed based on symbols observed so far in the sequence. Thus, sometimes, we make use of the *empirical entropy* of the source, rather than the true entropy, which may not be known.

Recall that $n_j(\sigma)$ is the number of times symbol σ has been observed just after we consider the j-th symbol in the sequence. Suppose we have n observations of the random variable Y, recorded as the n-sequence $y^n = (y_1, y_2, \ldots, y_n)$. Then, the empirical entropy is given by:

$$\tilde{H}(Y) = \sum_{i=1}^{|\Sigma|} \frac{n_n(\sigma_i)}{n} \log \frac{n}{n_n(\sigma_i)} \tag{5.3}$$

Suppose we have chosen a source coding strategy for Y, say code C, such that symbol $\sigma \in \Sigma$ is coded with a codeword with length $\ell(\sigma)$. Then the expected code length for the random variable Y using this coding strategy will be $\ell(C) = \sum_{i=1}^{|\Sigma|} p(\sigma)\ell(\sigma)$. Similarly, we can define the code length when the coding strategy is used on a sequence of n symbols from Y. Let $\ell_n(y^n) = \ell(y_1, y_2, \ldots, y_n)$ be the code length for the codeword assigned to the n-sequence y^n. Then, the expected code length for an n-sequence will be:

$$\ell_n(C) = \sum_{y^n \in \Sigma^n} p(y^n)\ell_n(y^n).$$

Thus, the per-symbol code length will be:

$$\ell_n = \frac{\ell_n(y^n)}{n} = \frac{1}{n} \sum_{y^n \in \Sigma^n} p(y^n)\ell_n(y^n).$$

For an optimal coding strategy, the average code length per symbol ℓ_n will be bounded as follows:

$$H(Y) \leq \ell_n \leq H(Y) + \frac{1}{n}$$

Thus, by using increasingly long sequences (large values of n), we can get the average code length per symbol to approach the entropy of the source as close as we wish. For a stationary stochastic process, $\lim_{n \to \infty} \ell_n = H(\Sigma)$, the entropy rate of the process.

The *coding redundancy* is a measure of the performance of a coding strategy. It indicates to what extent the average code length per symbol achieved by the coding strategy differs from that of the optimal code. Various expressions are used for coding redundancy. In this section we use the simple form: $\rho_n = \ell_n - H(Y)$, or $\rho_n = \ell_n - H(\Sigma)$, for stationary stochastic sources. The rate at which ρ_n, the coding redundancy, converges to zero is an important theoretical performance measure for a lossless source coding strategy.

The divergence between two distributions is measured by the relative entropy between them. The relative entropy (also called the *Kullback-Leibler distance*) between two distributions $p(y)$ and $q(y)$ is defined as follows:

$$D(p(y)\|q(y)) = \sum_{y \in \Sigma} p(y) \log \frac{p(y)}{q(y)}$$

The KL-distance is not symmetric. A symmetric distance can be obtained by using the average:

$$D(p,q) = (D(p\|q) + D(q\|p))/2$$

Given a source with a known symbol probability distribution, say $p(y)$, arithmetic coding or Huffman coding are two simple methods that can be used to encode a given sequence from the source to a size close to the entropy. If however, we assume an incorrect distribution, for instance, $q(y)$, then, coding with Huffman coding or arithmetic coding will result in an additional code length of $D(p(y)\|q(y))$ per symbol. This sensitivity to the accuracy of the distribution motivated the need for source coding methods that can still code the source close to the entropy without necessarily knowing the true symbol distribution. A coding strategy that achieves an average code length $\ell_n = \lambda H(Y) + \gamma$, where λ and γ are constants, without prior knowledge of the symbol probabilities, is called a *universal code*. Typical examples of such universal codes are the Elias γ- and δ-codes (Elias, 1975). Values for the Elias γ code for sample inputs are given in Table 3.1. Lengths for Elias codes for different input values are given in Section 5.5.2 (Table 5.6). A comparison of integer codes can be found in the paper by Fenwick (2002b).

Some of the results in this section will make use of Jensen's inequality (Cover and Thomas, 2006), an important inequality in information theory. Let x be a random variable, and let f be a concave function. The inequality states that

$$\sum_{i=1}^{h} p_i f(x_i) \leq f\left(\sum_{i=1}^{h} p_i x_i\right),$$

where the p_i's are positive weights, such that $\sum_{i=1}^{h} p_i = 1$. Figure 5.11 illustrates Jensen's inequality for $h = 2$ and $p_1 = p_2 = \frac{1}{2}$ — the average of the function values is less than the function of the average values.

5.5.2 Performance using recency ranking

As can be seen in the basic BWT compression pipeline (see Figure 5.1), the transformation of local structure to global structure is an important stage in most BWT-based coding schemes. This can be traced back to the original paper by Burrows and Wheeler (1994), where they suggested the use of MTF for post-processing on the BWT output before final encoding. Most practical BWT-based compression schemes have thus followed this paradigm, so not surprisingly, this basic EC(MTF(BWT(T))) approach has also received the most attention in terms of theoretical analysis of BWT compression performance (Arimura and Yamamoto, 1998; Effros et al., 2002; Balkenhol and Kurtz, 2000; Manzini, 2001). Thus, we start our analysis of BWT performance in compression by considering this basic compression scheme, with special emphasis on symbol ranking schemes, such as the MTF (also called recency ranking) (Bentley et al., 1986; Elias, 1987). Our discussion below follows the approach used by Arimura and Yamamoto (1998) and Effros et al. (2002).

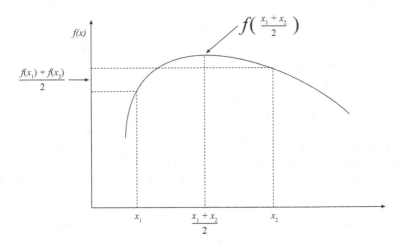

Fig. 5.11. Illustration of Jensen's inequality

With the MTF, the symbols in the BWT output (the L-array) are coded as integers, such that the i-th symbol in L is coded based on the last time it was observed. Specifically, at step i, the MTF transmits the number of *distinct* symbols observed since the last occurrence of symbol $L[i]$, and then moves the symbol to the front of its list. We can analyze the BWT performance using recency ranking by considering three major components:

1. Choice of the universal code for the integers to be used;
2. Performance of the chosen universal integer code with recency ranking on general sequences; and
3. Performance of the scheme on BWT output sequences, considering the nature of such sequences.

Choice of universal codes

To code the results generated by the MTF, we need a specific prefix-free code for the integers. Here we will use the Elias γ-code and δ-code (Elias, 1975), which we will denote as c_1 and c_2, respectively[2]. Let $f_1(x)$ and $f_2(x)$ be the corresponding code length functions that give the number of bits required to represent the integer x using codes c_1 and c_2 respectively. The γ-code (c_1) describes a positive integer x using $f_1(x)$ number of bits, using a two part code, where

$$f_1(x) = 1 + 2\lfloor \log x \rfloor$$

The first part is a prefix with $\lfloor \log x \rfloor$ zeros. The second part is the binary representation of x, which requires $1 + \lfloor \log x \rfloor$ bits. Concatenating the second

---

[2] These have been introduced already and are shown in Table 3.1 on page 37.

part to the first gives the C_1 code for x. The δ-code (C_2) is obtained by re-using the C_1 code as follows. Replace the $\lfloor \log x \rfloor$ zeros followed by a 1 using the C_1 encoding of $(1 + \lfloor \log x \rfloor)$. The result will be a code that uses $f_2(x)$ bits to represent the integer x, where

$$f_2(x) = 1 + \lfloor \log x \rfloor + 2\lfloor \log(1 + \log x) \rfloor$$

We can apply the method again to define the C_3 code, a slightly improved representation with code length function:

$$f_3(x) = 1 + \lfloor \log x \rfloor + \lfloor \log(1 + \log x) \rfloor + 2\lfloor \log(1 + \log(1 + \log x)) \rfloor$$

This process can be applied again and again to get a family of codes with successively improved representation of the integer. Each member of the family of C_i codes, $i = 1, 2, \ldots$ is a prefix code. However, as can be observed from the code length functions, for most practical purposes, the improvement may not be very significant, except for very large integers. Table 5.6 shows example code lengths using the C_i-family of codes for some sample input values.

x	$\log_2(x)$	$f_1(x)$	$f_2(x)$	$f_3(x)$	$G_1(x)$	$G_2(x)$	$G_3(x)$
1	0	1	1	1	1.0000	1.0000	1.0000
2	1	3	4	5	3.0000	4.0000	5.0000
10	4	7	8	8	7.6439	8.5453	9.7090
100	7	13	11	11	14.2877	13.5125	14.5304
256	8	17	15	16	17.0000	15.3399	16.2900
1000	10	19	16	17	20.9316	17.8757	18.7315
10000	14	27	20	21	27.5754	21.9611	22.6725
100000	17	33	25	25	34.2193	25.8862	26.4705
1000000	20	39	28	28	40.8631	29.7068	30.1785
10^9	30	59	38	38	60.7947	40.7962	40.9923
10^{15}	50	99	60	59	100.6578	62.1641	61.9708
10^{20}	67	133	79	77	133.8771	79.5896	79.1597
10^{25}	84	167	96	94	167.0964	96.8345	96.2137
10^{30}	100	199	112	110	200.3157	113.9645	113.1833
10^{50}	167	333	181	180	333.1928	181.8655	180.6164

Table 5.6. Code lengths and their bounds for the C_i-family of codes

Performance of integer codes with MTF

The performance of MTF using the family of C_i codes was analyzed in Bentley et al. (1986), while Elias (1987) performed a similar analysis for both recency ranking (MTF) and interval codes. Let $u^n \in \Sigma^n$ be a sequence of length n, with symbols from the alphabet Σ. Let $\ell_n(u^n)$ be the total length (in bits) of the sequence u^n after it is encoded with MTF and a chosen integer code.

They showed that using the C_i family of codes with code length function $f_i(x)$ bits, then $\ell_n(u^n)$ is bounded by:

$$\ell_n(u^n) \le nG_i(H(u^n)) \text{ bits,}$$

where $G_i(x)$ is related to $f_i(x)$, with $f_i(x) \le G_i(\log(x))$. For example,

$$G_1(x) = 1 + 2x;$$
$$G_2(x) = 1 + x + 2\log(1+x),$$
$$G_3(x) = 1 + x + \log(1+x) + 2\log(1+\log(1+x)).$$

Thus, with the C_2 code for instance, we have

$$\ell_n(u^n) \le n\left(H(u^n) + 1 + 2\log(1 + H(u^n))\right).$$

Performance on BWT output

Given the foregoing, we can now analyze the effect of MTF when presented with the output stream from the BWT (the input string is assumed to be reversed before applying the BWT). The major issues here are the partitioned nature of the BWT output, and the need to send the row index a for the BWT. With $|C|$ context partitions, the subsequences of the L-array that are in the same partition can each be coded using the MTF independently. Suppose we use C_2 as the integer code, and let S_i denote the subsequence in the i-th partition. Then, coding the BWT output using this strategy will result in an overall code length (in bits) for the input sequence $T = t^n$ bounded by:

$$\ell_n(t^n) \le \sum_{i=1}^{|C|} |S_i| \left[H(S_i) + 1 + 2\log(1 + H(S_i))\right] + (\log(n+1) + 1)$$

The last component is needed to code a, the row index of the original string in the sorted BWT rotation matrix. Expanding and dividing through by n, we get

$$\ell_n = \frac{\ell_n(t^n)}{n} \le \sum_{i=1}^{|C|} \frac{|S_i|}{n} H(S_i) + \sum_{i=1}^{|C|} \frac{|S_i|}{n} + 2\sum_{i=1}^{|C|} \frac{|S_i|}{n} \log(1 + H(S_i)) + \frac{\log(n+1)}{n} + \frac{1}{n}$$

Since the log is a concave function, we can use Jensen's inequality (Cover and Thomas, 2006) to pull the log function outside the summation to obtain:

$$\sum_{i=1}^{|C|} \frac{|S_i|}{n} \log(1 + H(S_i)) \le \log\left(\sum_{i=1}^{|C|} \frac{|S_i|}{n}(1 + H(S_i))\right) = \log(1 + H(t^n))$$

Thus the bound on per-symbol code length can be simplified to:

$$\ell_n \leq H(t^n) + 1 + 2\log(1 + H(t^n)) + \frac{\log(n+1) + 1}{n}$$

Or,

$$\ell_n = H(T) + 2\log(1 + H(T)) + 1 + O\left(\frac{\log n}{n}\right)$$

With the $2\log(1 + H(T))$ term in the result, the above bound may not attain the entropy, even for very long sequences. While we can reduce this term by using, say, C_i codes with higher values of i, the $O(\log(1 + H(T))$ term will still persist. To get the average code length to approach the entropy of the source, we can apply the BWT on k-extensions of the source (Cover and Thomas, 2006). That is, symbols in the original sequence are now grouped into $\frac{n}{k}$ blocks of size k each, such that a symbol block in T now maps to one symbol in the extended sequence. For an original sequence Y with symbols in Σ, and its k-th extension, Y^k, with symbols in Σ^k, the following relation holds:

$$H(Y^k) = H_k(Y) = kH(Y).$$

Applying this to the BWT code above, the average code length for each k-length block will be:

$$\ell_n^k(T) = \ell_n^k(t^n) \leq H_k(t^n) + 1 + 2\log(1 + H_k(t^n)) + \frac{\log(n/k + 1) + 1}{n/k}.$$

Thus, the average code length for the original symbols in T using this k-extension will be:

$$\ell_n = \frac{\ell_n(t^n)}{n} = \frac{\ell_n^k(t^n)}{k} \leq H(t^n) + \frac{1}{k} + \frac{2}{k}\log(1 + kH(t^n)) + \frac{\log(n/k + 1) + 1}{n/k}\frac{1}{k}.$$

Taking the limits as $k \to \infty$ gives the final result:

$$\ell_n \leq H(t^n) + \epsilon + O\left(\frac{\log(n/k + 1) + 1}{n}\right) = H(T) + \epsilon + O\left(\frac{\log(n/k + 1) + 1}{n}\right).$$

where ϵ is a small constant. Observe that $k \leq n$.

Analysis of BWT-based coding using the extended alphabet Σ^k with blocks of k symbols was originally performed in Arimura and Yamamoto (1998), and studied in detail by Effros et al. (2002). Effros et al. also discussed various options for the choice of k the extension parameter, and their implications in the redundancy of the BWT-code. They observed that for a string $T = t^n$, the BWT output obtained when T is treated as a sequence of symbols from Σ is very closely related to the BWT output that will result if we consider T as a sequence of n/k symbols from the extended alphabet Σ^k. In particular, for each row in the BWT sorted rotation matrix A_s using Σ^k, there is a corresponding row in the A_s matrix using Σ. Further, the ordering of the rows is also the same in the two matrices. Thus, the BWT output for T using extended symbols in Σ^k can be obtained from the BWT of T using the original symbols in Σ. This relationship is demonstrated in Figure 5.12. This has an important implication in implementing the approach using extended sources, since we can now use the transformation on the extended source, while maintaining the same general time and space complexity as with the original sequence. In practice though, alphabet extension can create a problem for using entropy coding (such as Huffman coding or arithmetic coding) after MTF, since the coding tables could become quite large. BWT-based compression by alphabet extension which is usually used to obtain theoretical bounds on compression performance is somewhat similar in concept to the more practical technique of word-based BWT (see Chapter 6).

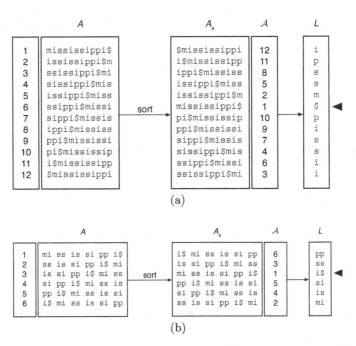

(a)

(b)

Fig. 5.12. Using the BWT on extended alphabets, using the example $T =$ mississippi: (a) original BWT matrix of sorted rotations; (b) BWT matrix of sorted rotations for extended alphabet, Σ^2. The BWT on the extended alphabet Σ^2 (b) can be obtained from the BWT output on the original alphabet Σ by removing the even rows in (a). The arrowhead indicates the row that corresponds to the original sequence T

The analysis above closely follows the performance analysis of MTF and recency ranking given in Bentley et al. (1986) and Elias (1987). In fact, Bentley et al. (1986) showed that the MTF algorithm can achieve universal coding performance via alphabet extension. Thus, the MTF does not necessarily need the BWT to achieve universal coding performance. Yet, while it may be difficult to exactly quantify the impact of the BWT on MTF, especially given the sorting performed by the BWT, it is, however, clear that the BWT can help the MTF converge faster to the source entropy, especially for smaller sequences. This is supported by the fact that for most practical input sequences, applying the MTF to the L-array (the BWT output) leads to a smaller integer output, on average, when compared to using the MTF directly on the original sequence T.

The above results have been obtained based on a reversed version of the original sequence. Although reversing the string before applying the BWT made the analysis somewhat easier, time reversal is not a necessary condition to achieve the coding performance results reported. This is supported by the fact that the entropy of a source is not affected by time reversal (Cover and Thomas, 2006):

$$H(Y) = \lim_{n \to \infty} \frac{1}{n} H(Y_1 Y_2 \ldots Y_n) = \lim_{n \to \infty} \frac{1}{n} H(Y_n Y_{n-1} \ldots Y_1). \tag{5.4}$$

Fenwick (2002a) studied the performance of BWT using integer codes, rather than entropy encoding. He showed that integer codes can produce competitive practical compression results, comparable with results obtained with entropy codes. In his earlier work on a detailed analysis of the empirical performance of BWT, Fenwick (1996b, 1997b) showed that there is no significant performance difference whether the BWT is applied directly, or on a reversed sequence. This is to be expected given the relationship in Equation 5.4.

5.5.3 Performance without LGT

An interesting debate has been whether the MTF or other variants of the local to global transformation (LGT) are really necessary for BWT-based compression (Wirth and Moffat, 2001; Effros et al., 2002; Giancarlo and Sciortino, 2003; Ferragina et al., 2005a). In particular, for some applications, such as in lossless image compression, the use of the MTF on BWT output does not seem to provide much improvement in compression, when compared with direct coding of the BWT output using arithmetic codes (Arnavut and Magliveras, 1997a; Arnavut, 2002). Given the observed partitioning of the BWT output based on sorted contexts, it becomes possible to analyze the performance of the BWT in compression by coding directly on the L-array, without the need for local to global structure transformation algorithms, such as MTF. If we know the boundary for each partition of the BWT output, it becomes possible to code the partitions independently, for instance, by using possibly different universal codes for the subsequences contained in different partitions.

For the unbounded contexts, each context partition could contain just one symbol. Thus, for this approach to work, we need to choose contexts with a specific order. For a given context order, say k, the encoder can determine all the order-k forward contexts that appeared in the original data sequence, by an iterative use of the L-array, and F-array, using a process similar to the BWT decoding procedure. Thus, we can determine the number of times each context occurred (i.e. the size of the context). Given the sorted nature of the contexts, this essentially gives the boundary (or transition) points between adjacent contexts or partitions in the L-array, the BWT output. We can then encode the BWT output by explicitly encoding the boundary points (or analogously, the length of each partition), and then encoding the subsequence in each partition independently, using any universal encoder, such as arithmetic coding. The parameters of each partition still need to be estimated, which can be done using the Krichevsky-Trofimov (K-T) estimator as described previously.

Let B_i be the lower boundary point for the i-th context (i.e. the i-th partition). Let S_i be the subsequence in the i-th partition of the L-array. That is, the symbols in S_i all have the same k-order forward context in T. We can analyze the performance of the above coding strategy by considering the three major components:

1. The cost of encoding a, the row index of the original string in the sorted rotation matrix of the BWT;
2. The cost of describing $B_i, i = 1, 2, \ldots, |\mathcal{C}|$, the boundary points, or alternatively the size of each context partition; and
3. The cost of encoding $S_i, i = 1, 2, \ldots, |\mathcal{C}|$, the subsequence in each context partition.

The BWT index a can be encoded using no more than $\lfloor \log n \rfloor + 1$ bits. Rather than coding the boundary points (B_i's) directly, it may be more efficient to code the length of the context partitions — that is, the difference between adjacent boundary points. Thus, for the i-th partition, we code its size using $B_i - B_{i-1}$, where $B_0 = 0$ by definition. Using the example in Table 5.2 (page 98), with $k = 1$, we have 5 partitions, with boundary points given by: $B = [1, 5, 6, 8, 12]$, and partition sizes given by: $B_i - B_{i-1} = [1, 4, 1, 2, 4]$, with $i = 1, 2, 3, 4, 5$. Similarly, with $k = 2$, we will have 9 partitions, with sizes defined similarly. We observe that, given the nature of the BWT output, the context in the first partition always starts with \$, the special end of string symbol. Its size must always be 1, since the symbol appears only once in the input string to the BWT. Thus, we do not really need to send boundary information about this context. Similarly, we do not need to send the last boundary point, since it must always be $n + 1$. Thus, the size of the last partition can be computed, if we already know the size of all the other partitions, since the sum of all the partition lengths must be $n + 1$. Therefore, we need to encode only $|\mathcal{C}| - 2$ integers representing the size of the partitions, $i = 2, 3, \ldots, |\mathcal{C}| - 1$. Thus, the total cost of explicitly coding the partition sizes will be:

$$\sum_{i=2}^{|\mathcal{C}|-1} (\lfloor \log(B_i - B_{i-1}) \rfloor + 1) \leq (|\mathcal{C}| - 2)(1 + \log n) \tag{5.5}$$

To code the symbols in the L-array, we can consider each S_i, $i = 1, 2, \ldots, |\mathcal{C}|$, the subsequence for the i-th partition individually, using arithmetic coding, with the K-T estimator for the symbol probabilities.

Let $H_{\hat{\theta}}(t^n)$ be the first order entropy of the sequence $t^n \in \Sigma^n$, with the empirical distribution given by $\hat{\theta}$. Krichevsky and Trofimov (1981) showed that using the K-T estimator as given in Equation 5.2 to determine $P_e(T) = P_e(t^n)$, the estimated probability of the sequence $T = t^n$, the resulting description length will be bounded by:

$$nH_{\hat{\theta}}(t^n) + \frac{|\Sigma| - 1}{2} \log n - d \leq \log \frac{1}{P_e(t^n)} \leq nH_{\hat{\theta}}(t^n) + \frac{|\Sigma| - 1}{2} \log n + d \tag{5.6}$$

where d is a small constant.

Thus, if we code each S_i independently, using the K-T estimate to determine the probability distribution for the symbols in each partition, we obtain an overall coding length for describing the original sequence $T = t^n$ after the BWT transformation on $\hat{T}$, the reverse of T. Using Equation 5.5 and the inequality on the right-hand side of Equation 5.6 above, we can bound the overall coding length as follows:

$$\ell_n(t^n) \leq (1 + \log n) + (|\mathcal{C}| - 2)(1 + \log n) + \sum_{i=1}^{|\mathcal{C}|} \left(|S_i| H_{\hat{\theta}}(S_i) + \frac{|\Sigma| - 1}{2} \log |S_i| + d_i \right)$$

$$\leq (|\mathcal{C}| - 1)(1 + \log n) + \sum_{i=1}^{|\mathcal{C}|} |S_i| H_{\hat{\theta}}(S_i) + \frac{|\mathcal{C}|(|\Sigma| - 1)}{2} \log |n| + d$$

Dividing through by n, and after a little manipulation we obtain the bound on the average code length per symbol:

$$\ell_n = \frac{\ell_n(T)}{n} = \frac{\ell_n(t^n)}{n} \leq \frac{1}{n} \sum_{i=1}^{|\mathcal{C}|} |S_i| H_{\hat{\theta}}(S_i) + \frac{|\mathcal{C}|(|\Sigma| + 1)}{2} \frac{\log n}{n} + \frac{d}{n}$$

$$\leq H_{\hat{\theta}}(T) + \frac{|\mathcal{C}|(|\Sigma| + 1)}{2} \frac{\log n}{n} + O\left(\frac{1}{n}\right).$$

The first component is simply the empirical entropy of the input string, while the last two components represent the extra cost incurred in using this coding strategy. Thus, the redundancy in using this coding strategy on the BWT output is simply:

$$\rho_n(\theta, T) = \frac{|\mathcal{C}|(|\Sigma| + 1)}{2} \frac{\log n}{n} + O\left(\frac{1}{n}\right)$$

In terms of the dominant components, the above result is very close to the optimal rate of convergence for finite memory sources as described by Rissanen (1986). The difference is only by a constant factor of $\frac{|\Sigma|+1}{|\Sigma|-1}$. The largest difference will be for the case of binary strings when $|\Sigma| = 2$. For larger alphabets, the difference becomes insignificant. The above results show that the BWT output can in fact be coded for optimal compression performance (for finite memory sources), without the need for MTF or other local to global structure transformation algorithms. Here, universality was obtained without the need for alphabet extension, as was required for coding with MTF (see the previous subsection). More importantly, for applications like image compression where the alphabet size could be relatively large, for example 256 for gray scale images, or 511 for their pixel differences, one should expect a relatively better performance from the BWT. Interestingly, MTF-based approaches typically do not perform well on images.

5.5.4 Performance using piecewise constant parameters

Given the p.i.i.d. nature of the BWT output as described earlier, it is no surprise that methods used for efficient coding of sources with piecewise and identically distributed distributions can be adapted for equally efficient coding of the BWT output. Thus, Effros et al. (2002) studied the performance of BWT-based coding when the BWT output is coded using published methods for coding p.i.i.d. sources (Shamir and Merhav, 1999; Willems, 1996). They showed that, for finite memory sources with unknown state space and unknown memory constraint (i.e. essentially, unknown $|\mathcal{C}|$, the number of contexts, and unknown k, the context order), using p.i.i.d. parameters, the coding length of the BWT-output can be bounded, depending on the specific p.i.i.d. coding algorithm. In particular, they showed that, when using Willems' algorithm (Willems, 1996), which runs in $O(n^3)$ time, the following bound can be obtained:

$$\ell_n = \frac{\ell_n(T)}{n} \leq H_{\hat{\theta}}(T) + \frac{|\mathcal{C}|(|\Sigma| + 1)}{2} \frac{\log n}{n} + O\left(\frac{1}{n}\right).$$

They also showed that, using Shamir and Merhav's algorithm (Shamir and Merhav, 1999) that runs in $O(n^2)$ time, the bound will be:

$$\ell_n = \frac{\ell_n(T)}{n} \leq H_{\hat{\theta}}(T) + \frac{|\mathcal{C}|(|\Sigma| + 1)}{2} \frac{\log n}{n} + O\left(\frac{\log \log n}{n}\right).$$

As before, the coding redundancy in each case is given by the last two terms in the right hand side of the inequality. Thus, while the p.i.i.d. approaches can provide universal coding performance, in general, they are no better than coding directly, using an explicit description of the boundary points and the subsequences within each partition. Further, the time complexity for the p.i.i.d. approaches is generally worse than the linear time complexity required by the method that uses explicit boundary point description. However, the p.i.i.d.-based methods could be seen as more general, since they assume no knowledge of the memory constraint (the context order), or the specific contexts.

5.5.5 Performance on general sources via empirical entropy

Some of the analysis results above are valid only for finite memory sources, such as Markov sources. In practice, some parameters of such sources, such as the true number of states, (that is, the number of contexts) may not be easily available. Further, some practical data may be difficult to model using such finite state sources. Also, the analysis so far has ignored run-length encoding on the MTF output, an important component of some of the best performing BWT-based practical compression schemes. Manzini (1999, 2001) took a fundamentally different approach to the analysis of BWT performance, addressing the problems listed by analyzing the performance of BWT without any assumptions on the probability distribution of the symbols. Rather, he used the empirical entropy as defined previously, and in a modified form that is more realistic for BWT coding.

Starting with the empirical entropy defined in Equation 5.3, Manzini defined a modified zero-order empirical entropy:

$$H_0^*(T) = \begin{cases} 0 & : \text{ if } |T| = 0, \\ \frac{1 + \lfloor \log |T| \rfloor}{|T|} & : \text{ if } |T| \neq 0 \text{ and } H_0(T) = 0, \\ H_0(T) & : \text{ otherwise} \end{cases} \tag{5.7}$$

where $H_0(T)$ is the zeroth-order empirical entropy of T using Equation 5.3.

Clearly, $H_0(Y) \leq H_0^*(Y)$. The motivation for this modification is the observation that the empirical entropy as defined in Equation 5.3 could underestimate the length required to represent certain inputs, such as the string $T = a^n$, with n repetitions of the same symbol. Here, $H_0(T) = 0$, while $H_0^*(T) = \frac{(1 + \lfloor \log n \rfloor)}{n}$. Thus, the modified empirical entropy ensures that the entropy should contain enough information to recover the length of the input sequence.

Using $H_0(T)$, Manzini defined an analogous quantity for $H_k^*(T)$, the k-th order modified entropy of T, as the minimum length per symbol that can be achieved by using, for each symbol in T, a codeword that is based on a context order of at most k (see Manzini (2001)). This is quite different from the traditional definition that codes the sequence in blocks of fixed size k.

Manzini's analysis also made use of results on the performance of arithmetic coding (Howard and Vitter, 1993), where it was shown that the code length per symbol obtained using arithmetic coding on a sequence $Y = y^n = (y_1, y_2, \ldots, y_n)$ can be bounded by:

$$\frac{\ell_n(Y)}{n} \leq H_0(Y) + \mu_1 + \frac{\mu_2}{n}$$

where μ_1 and μ_1 are constants, with $\mu_1 \approx \frac{1}{100}$. This result is different from (but similar to) the usual bound on arithmetic coding performance using $\frac{\ell_n(Y)}{n} \leq H(Y) + 2$ bits.

Based on the above, the general approach is then similar to the approach described earlier that uses the partitioned nature of the BWT output. First, Manzini performed a detailed theoretical study on the nature of the MTF output. Let $T = t_1 t_2 \ldots t_n$ be a given string, with $t_i \in \Sigma = \{\sigma_1, \sigma_2, \ldots, \sigma_{|\Sigma|}\}$. Let $\bar{T} = MTF(T)$, and let $T = S_i S_2 \ldots S_u$ be some partition of T, where each S_i is a subsequence of T. Notice that $|\bar{T}| = |T| = n$, and that $\sum_{i=1}^{u} |S_i| H_0(S_i) \leq n H_0(s)$. He showed that the entropy of the MTF output can be bounded as follows, using the *empirical* entropy:

$$n H_0(\bar{T}) \leq 8 \left(\sum_{i=1}^{u} |S_i| H_0(S_i) \right) + \frac{2}{25} n + u(9 + 2|\Sigma| \log |\Sigma|)$$

Based on this result, Manzini showed that for any context length, $k \geq 0$, the performance of $\mathrm{BWT_0}$, (the BWT-based compression scheme originally proposed by Burrows and Wheeler) which uses the $\mathrm{EC(MTF(BWT}(T)))$ model (where EC is an order-0 arithmetic coder) can be bounded as follows:

$$\ell_n(t^n) = \ell_n(\bar{L}) \leq 8n H_k(t^n) + \left(\mu_1 + \frac{2}{25} \right) n + |\Sigma|^k (9 + 2|\Sigma| \log |\Sigma|) + \mu_2 \quad (5.8)$$

where $\bar{L} = \mathrm{MTF}(L)$.

In practice, the bound can be improved slightly by observing that, rather than all the $|\Sigma|^k$ possible subsequences, we may need to consider only the order-k subsequences that actually appear in T. Although the constants in the bound are admittedly high for most practical purposes, it still provides another proof that the BWT can, at least in theory, provide competitive results over very long sequences.

So far the analysis has used the empirical entropy, but a problem with this approach is that the definition of empirical entropy implies that certain strings can be "coded for free", which may not be true in practice. Manzini used the modified empirical entropy (Equation 5.7) to alleviate this problem.

For BWT-based compression using the model $\mathrm{EC(RLE(MTF(BWT}(T)))))$, Manzini used the modified empirical entropy to show that

$$\ell_n(t^n) = \ell_n(RLE(\bar{L})) \leq (5 + \varepsilon) n H_k^*(t^n) + g_k \quad (5.9)$$

where g_k is a constant.

The result was based on the use of c_2 codes for the run-lengths, after MTF. Essentially, the use of RLE has improved the bound in Equation 5.8 by eliminating the constant overhead per symbol, and by reducing the multiplicative constant on the entropy.

The Manzini bounds in Equation 5.8 and 5.9 have been improved by more recent work (Giancarlo and Sciortino, 2003; Ferragina et al., 2005a; Kaplan et al., 2006, 2007). For instance, in Giancarlo and Sciortino (2003), using a different partitioning technique, the multiplicative constant was reduced from $(5 + \varepsilon)$ to $\frac{5}{2}$, while in Kaplan et al. (2006, 2007), the factor was reduced further to 1.7286. In theory, as with the previous analysis on MTF output (see Section 5.5.2), the bounds could possibly be further improved with the extra overheads made as small as we wish, by applying the analysis using alphabet extensions on the original sequence.

5.6 Relationship with other compression schemes

Although the encoding and LGT stages of the BWT-compression pipeline are generally sequential, the overall BWT-based compression is still non-sequential because the BWT requires access to the complete string during its computation. This is one core difference between the BWT and most other compression algorithms, especially those discussed in this section, which are generally sequential, with coding statistics being updated adaptively as more and more of the input string is observed[3]. We start our discussion of the relationship between BWT and other compression schemes by considering the class of context-based compression schemes.

5.6.1 Context-based schemes

Most compression methods predict the probability of the next symbol based on an observation of the previous symbols. An order-k finite-context compression scheme is one that performs symbol predictions based on the preceding k symbols observed in the input stream. Among compression schemes that are members of this class are the PPM-family, the Associative Coder of Buyanovsky (ACB), context-tree weighting (CTW) method, and Dynamic Markov Coding (DMC). The LZ family of compression methods have also been shown to relate to context prediction (Langdon Jr., 1983; Bell, 1987; Bell et al., 1990; Bell and Witten, 1994; Yokoo, 1997), and variations have been explored that incorporate explicit contexts (Hoang et al., 1995, 1999).

Not surprisingly, given the sorted contexts used by the BWT, we can expect a strong relationship with this class of compression algorithms. In this subsection, we explore the link between the BWT and some members of the class of finite-context compression schemes.

---

[3] See Chapter 6 on sequential variants of the BWT.

PPM — Prediction by Partial Matching

For lossless compression, the PPM family of compression algorithms (Cleary and Witten, 1984; Bell et al., 1990; Moffat, 1990) is known to be among the best in terms of data compaction ability, and are rivaled only by BWT-based methods, which appeared nearly a decade after PPM was developed. The PPM compression scheme uses a symbol-wise model that adaptively generates the statistics of the input text sequence as the sequence is being compressed. Given a current symbol t_i, and its k-th order context c_i, with $c_i = t_{i-k}t_{i-k+1}\cdots t_{i-1}$, a key problem in symbol-wise compression schemes is to generate a prediction of t_i based on its context c_i. These predictions are used to compute the conditional probability $P(t_i|c_i)$ for each input symbol, which is then used by an entropy encoder — typically an arithmetic coder, which will code a probability p in close to $-\log_2 p$ bits.

Rather than using a single fixed-order context to generate the required prediction, the PPM scheme uses a set of finite order contexts that can range over different values of k (this is the "partial matching" referred to in the name). By using an "escape" mechanism, it carefully switches from the highest order context to lower order contexts, depending on the input data. Coding a single character is done by sending a series of messages to the decoder to inform it which size context is being "escaped" to, before coding the character in that context. This mechanism is equivalent to a blend of the different contexts, although implementations generally code a symbol in just one context, augmenting the alphabet with an "escape" symbol ⟨esc⟩, which is used to tell the decoder to change to the next smaller context. Initially the context size k is set to the maximum order context (typically about 3 to 5 characters). At the i-th coding step, PPM tries to use its maximum order context to predict the next symbol, t_i. If the symbol has appeared previously in this k-order context, the symbol is coded with an estimated probability $P(t_i|t_{i-k}t_{i-k+1}\cdots t_{i-1})$. If the symbol has never appeared in this context, an escape symbol is sent, and the context order is reduced to $k-1$. The process is repeated with this reduced-order context. If the model reaches the lowest-order context, the symbol is encoded based on a fixed pre-determined probability distribution. By convention, the lowest order context is denoted with $k = -1$, with symbol probabilities typically defined by the uniform distribution, $p(\sigma) = \frac{1}{|\Sigma|}$ for all $\sigma \in \Sigma$.

For example, suppose PPM is coding the sequence $T = \mathtt{mississippi}$, and it is up to the first $\mathtt{p}$, which has a 5th order context of $\mathtt{sissi}$. The sequence of decisions made to code the $\mathtt{p}$ is shown in Table 5.7. With $k = 5$, the context $\mathtt{sissi}$ has not occurred before, so both the encoder and decoder know to switch down to $k = 4$ without an information being sent. $\mathtt{issi}$ has occurred once, where it was followed by $\mathtt{s}$. If we use a simple scheme that allocates a count of 1 to ⟨esc⟩, then we have $p(\mathtt{s}) = \frac{1}{2}$ and $p(\langle\mathrm{esc}\rangle) = \frac{1}{2}$. We take the latter because we want to code a $\mathtt{p}$, not an $\mathtt{s}$. (If the next character had been an s, it would have been coded at this point with a probability of $\frac{1}{2}$, which requires

1 bit.) The $\langle\mathrm{esc}\rangle$ means that both encoder and decoder switch to $k = 3$, ssi. This has occurred once before, but it only predicts an s which would have already been coded, so $p(\langle\mathrm{esc}\rangle) = 1$ (the s is excluded), and we shift to $k = 2$, si. This also generates $p(\langle\mathrm{esc}\rangle) = 1$, shifting to $k = 1$, which is the context of i. This has occurred twice, but in both cases predicts s which has already been coded, so again, we escape to $k = 0$. Note that these escapes will add 0 bits to the output, since their probability is 1. In the zero order context we have 3 occurrences of i, 1 occurrence of m and 4 of s. s is excluded since it would have already been coded, giving $p(\mathrm{i}) = \frac{3}{5}, p(\mathrm{m}) = \frac{1}{5}$ and $p(\langle\mathrm{esc}\rangle) = \frac{1}{5}$. If the next symbol was i or s, it would be coded at this point, but since it is p, we escape to $k = -1$, where all symbols are equally likely. At this point we code the p with $p(\mathrm{p}) = \frac{1}{|\Sigma|}$ (note that in this context exclusions are not applied even though the other characters would never be coded here; although it would be beneficial for this small example, in practice it is not worth the effort).

context	σ	count	prob	next context
sissi →				→ issi
→	issi → s	1	$\frac{1}{2}$	
	→ $\langle\mathrm{esc}\rangle$	1	$\frac{1}{2}$	→ ssi
→	ssi → s	×	×	
	→ $\langle\mathrm{esc}\rangle$	1	1	→ si
→	si → s	×	×	
	→ $\langle\mathrm{esc}\rangle$	1	1	→ i
→	i → s	×	×	
	→ $\langle\mathrm{esc}\rangle$	1	1	→ ε
→	ε → i	3	$\frac{3}{5}$	
	→ m	1	$\frac{1}{5}$	
	→ s	×	×	
	→ $\langle\mathrm{esc}\rangle$	1	$\frac{1}{5}$	→ (−1)
→	(−1) → i	1	×	
	→ m	1	×	
	→ p	1	$\frac{1}{4}$	
	→ s	1	×	

Table 5.7. PPM procedure for coding the first p in $T = $ mississippi, with the context reducing through $k = 5, 4, 3, 2, 1, 0, -1$. At the lowest context order ($k = -1$), the symbol is coded based on the uniform distribution ($p = \frac{1}{|\Sigma|}$). Exclusions are indicated by a cross

Different variants of the PPM model exist, such as PPMA, PPMB, PPMC, PPMD, and PPM* (Cleary and Witten, 1984; Bell et al., 1990; Moffat, 1990; Cleary and Teahan, 1997; Witten et al., 1999). The models differ mainly in the way the escape probability is determined, which is a manifestation of the *zero-frequency problem* — estimating the probability of an event for which there are no samples on which to base the estimate (Witten and Bell, 1991).

Table 5.7 uses the simple idea of assigning a count of 1 to the escape symbol (sometimes referred to as PPMA), but a better way that works well is based on the number of distinct symbols seen so far — effectively it is estimating the probability of a novel symbol occurring based on how often novel symbols have occurred in the past; the more novel symbols we have seen, the more likely it is that the next symbol is novel, and vice versa. One could argue the opposite of course; if many novel symbols have occurred, perhaps it is less likely that a new one will occur in the future. However, this approach works well in practice, and is supported by statistically sound approaches to estimating novel events (Witten and Bell, 1991). This is the idea behind the PPMC model (Moffat, 1990), where escape probabilities are assigned as $P(esc|c) = \frac{v}{v+x}$, where v is the number of distinct symbols so far observed in the context c, and x represents the total number of symbols observed in the context c. Under the PPMC model, symbol t_i with z counts in context c will be assigned the probability $P(t_i|c) = \frac{z}{v+x}$. The probability is further modified by the exclusion mechanism mentioned in the example; there is no point allocating probabilities to symbols that will not be coded in the current context, as this will always make compression worse, although keeping track of excluded characters can slow the system down. Another variation is "update exclusions", which updates the count of a character only in the context in which it would be coded; this speeds up compression, and can have a positive effect on the amount of compression obtained too (Bell et al., 1990; Moffat, 1990; Cleary and Teahan, 1997).

In principle the performance of PPM should always improve with a higher maximum context order. However, empirical results show that while the performance improves as we increase the maximum from 0, the best results are achieved with a maximum of about 5 or 6, beyond which the compression performance starts to degrade slowly. The main reason is that although longer contexts can provide more reliable predictions, they often lead to more escape symbols, since we are less likely to be able to find samples for longer contexts. Fenwick (2007) reports that if PPM uses high-order contexts, as much as 95% of the output is accounted for by the cost of identifying the context; very few bits are needed to identify the character once the decoder knows the context that it occurs in.

The PPM* algorithm (Cleary and Teahan, 1997) addresses this problem by removing the need to specify the maximum context order beforehand. This allows the algorithm to automatically adapt to contexts of arbitrary order, essentially giving the PPM algorithm the ability to use contexts of unlimited order (that is, unbounded contexts). The key idea used in PPM* to support unbounded contexts is the concept of "deterministic contexts". A context is said to be deterministic when it gives a unique prediction. Thus, a deterministic context will have only one following symbol. The deterministic contexts are then exploited using the following strategy: at a given step, first, check if there are already some deterministic contexts in the current context list; if so, choose the shortest deterministic context; if no deterministic context is found, then choose the longest context in the list. Then, apply the PPM algorithm starting from the chosen context. The result is that the PPM* approach generally leads to a significant reduction in the number of novel characters observed, and hence, the number of escape symbols, leading to an overall improved compression.

Of course, maintaining unbounded contexts for PPM* requires the ability to access every possible context already observed, all the way back to the first symbol. A simple approach would require an $O(n^2)$ time and space. To solve the associated computational problem with maintaining unbounded contexts, PPM* uses a context trie, which is very similar to the context tree. The key idea is that whenever a unique context is observed, a leaf node in the context trie is allowed to point back into the original string. Extending a context thus requires only that the pointer be moved forward by one position. Figure 5.13 shows the PPM* context trie for the example sequence mississippi. Non-unique contexts observed so far in the string extend downwards until they become unique. At this point, a pointer is inserted to point to the start of the context in the input string.

Some variants of the PPM have also been implemented using compacted suffix tries and suffix pointers (Bunton, 1997; Cleary and Teahan, 1997). Figure 5.14 shows the suffix tree representation of the PPM context tree of Figure 5.13. The PPM context tree can be compared with the standard context tree of the same sequence, discussed earlier (see Section 5.3).

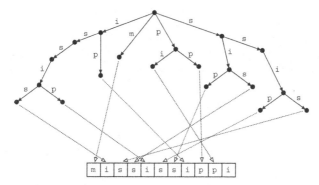

Fig. 5.13. PPM* context trie for the string mississippi; the edge labels start from the root until the context is unique, at which point the leaf node is made to point to the starting position of the context in the original string

Relationship between PPM and BWT

When one considers a version of PPM implemented with suffix tries or suffix trees (and context tries), and the context-tree view of the BWT explored earlier in this chapter, the similarity between the two compression methods

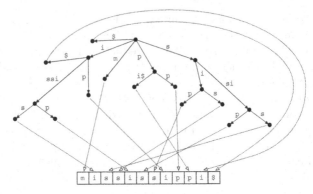

Fig. 5.14. Suffix tree representation of the PPM context shown in Figure 5.13. Only the edge labels that lead to unique contexts are used. The suffix links are not shown

start to emerge. The connection between the PPM family and the BWT was initially observed by Cleary et al. (1995); Cleary and Teahan (1997), and later studied by Larsson (1998). Effros (2000) further studied the relationship between the PPM and BWT, with the objective of improving the computational efficiency of PPM (using ideas from BWT), while maintaining its superior compression performance.

To see the relationship, consider Figure 5.15, which shows the BWT transformation matrices for $T = $ mississippi\$, as used earlier. In addition, we have added the matrix A_{ss}. A_{ss} is obtained from A_s, the original BWT sorted rotation matrix, but each row contains only just enough symbols to make the context represented by the row to be unique. Thus, the unique contexts in A_{ss} form a one-to-one mapping with the leaves of the PPM context tries (see Figures 5.13 and 5.14). The BWT output (the L-array) is also shown. It can be observed that, for any given row, the element in L is simply the symbol that immediately precedes the corresponding unique context in the same row using A_{ss} (the PPM context). This corresponds to the forward context used by the BWT. Essentially, this means that both the BWT and the PPM use the same contexts, up to the length of the deterministic context used by the PPM. Thus, while the BWT sorts its contexts, and exploits the unbounded contexts after observing the complete input string, PPM* adaptively predicts the next symbol, based on an unbounded context, as determined by its shortest deterministic context.

Context Tree Weighting

The context tree was introduced earlier in Section 5.3. It was assumed that the tree (the model of the source) is known, and the problem was to estimate the parameter, θ, the symbol distribution. In general, neither the model nor the parameter will be known at the time of compression, and thus will need to be estimated by the compression algorithm. The context tree weighting

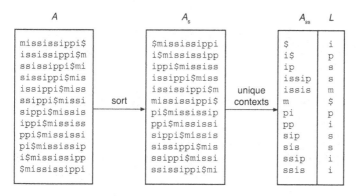

Fig. 5.15. Relationship between PPM and BWT; the unique unbounded contexts of the PPM correspond one-to-one with the unbounded contexts of the BWT

algorithm (CTW) provides a method to estimate both the model and the model parameter (Willems et al., 1995).

First, the context tree is constructed based on the part of the input sequence observed so far. For an order-k model, the context tree is truncated at a maximum depth of k. At the heart of the CTW algorithm is the computation of weighted probabilities for each node in the context tree. Recall that at each node, say u, in the context tree, we have a record of the number of occurrences of each symbol in the subsequence associated with u. Rather than using $P_e(u)$ (Equation 5.2) to compute the estimated probabilities directly, for each node u in the context tree, the CTW method computes a weighted probability, denoted P_w^u. This is the probability that is then used to encode the subsequence associated with node u. Let $S(u)$ be the subsequence.

For simplicity in notation, we let $n_u(\sigma) = n_{|S(u)|}(\sigma, S(u))$. Then, we can write $P_e(u) = P_e([n_u(\sigma_1), n_u(\sigma_2), \ldots, n_u(\sigma_{|\Sigma|})])$. The CTW algorithm starts at the leaf nodes; these will be at depth k for an order-k model. Consider the leaf node u. At this node, we have available the counts

$$[n_u(\sigma_1), n_u(\sigma_2), \ldots, n_u(\sigma_{|\Sigma|})].$$

Since we do not have much more information beyond the counts, the best we can do is to assume that the subsequence associated with each leaf is memoryless. Therefore, the weighted probability for this node is best determined using the K-T estimator. Thus, we should have:

$$P_w^u = P_e(u) = P_e\left([n_u(\sigma_1), n_u(\sigma_2), \ldots, n_u(\sigma_{|\Sigma|})]\right) : \text{ if } \mathrm{depth}(u) = k$$

This computation is performed for each leaf node, and the resulting probabilities are then used to recursively compute the weighted probabilities for the internal nodes. Now consider the internal node u. Let $u_1, u_2, \ldots u_{|\Sigma|}$ be its children. We already know the weighted probabilities for the child nodes. The subsequence associated with u could be memoryless, and hence the K-T estimate, $P_e(u)$, will be a good estimate. If the subsequence is not memoryless, the CTW algorithm then uses the product $\prod_{i=1}^{i=|\Sigma|} P_w^{u_i}$ as the best estimate for the probability. Since we are not sure of which of the two cases holds, the CTW algorithm chooses the simple average of the two. Thus, we have:

$$P_w^u = \frac{P_e\left([n_u(\sigma_1), n_u(\sigma_2), \ldots, n_u(\sigma_{|\Sigma|})]\right) + \prod_{i=1}^{i=|\Sigma|} P_w^{u_i}}{2} : \text{ if depth}(u) < k.$$

where u_i is the child node on the σ_i-edge starting from node u. Figure 5.16 shows the weighted context tree for the order-3 context tree of Figure 5.3. For the sequence $T = \text{mississipi}$, we have $P_e(T) = P_e([4, 1, 2, 4]) = 3.3715 \times 10^{-8}$, and $P_w^T = 1.3008 \times 10^{-6}$.

The next question is how we update the tree when the next symbol is observed. Interestingly, the CTW algorithm has a simple way to do this, and hence can compute the weighted probability of the new sequence incrementally based on the current weighted probabilities. Let the encoded sequence be $T = t_1 t_2 \ldots t_{i-1}$ and the new symbol be $t_i = \sigma$. Thus we need to update the context tree of T to derive the tree for $T * \sigma$. Let U be the set of nodes on the path in the context tree (starting from the root) defined by symbols preceding the next symbol, $t_i = \sigma$. The update is performed as follows:

For each node $u \in U$,

1. Increment $n_u(\sigma)$;
2. Update $P_e([n_u(\sigma_1), n_u(\sigma_2), \ldots, n_u(\sigma_{|\Sigma|})])$;
3. Update P_w^u.

Figure 5.16b shows the updated tree, for the tree in Figure 5.16a when the new symbol is $\sigma = \text{s}$. The path that contains the nodes in U has been highlighted. It is easy to see that, for each update, a maximum of k nodes will need to be visited. Thus, the context tree weighting algorithm requires time and space that is linear, for a fixed context order k.

Traditionally, text compression with the CTW is usually performed by applying the CTW independently on each bit plane for the symbols involved. For instance, 7 binary planes are used for the ASCII symbols (assuming 7-bit ASCII symbols); that is, the text is sliced into 7 strings, each consisting of the bits from each position of a byte. Thus, seven context trees will be needed, and the results can be combined for the final compressed data. The use of binary CTW may be attributed to the fact that any symbol alphabet can be converted to an equivalent binary alphabet. Moreover, the original CTW paper (Willems et al., 1995), and most of its extensions (Willems et al., 1996; Willems, 1998) have been based on the binary alphabet. However, with the formulation above which is based on the general K-T estimator for fixed alphabets of arbitrary size, it becomes possible to apply the CTW algorithm to compress sequences from a general alphabet.

In terms of theoretical performance, it was shown in Willems et al. (1996) that the CTW algorithm can achieve Rissanen's theoretical bound for finite

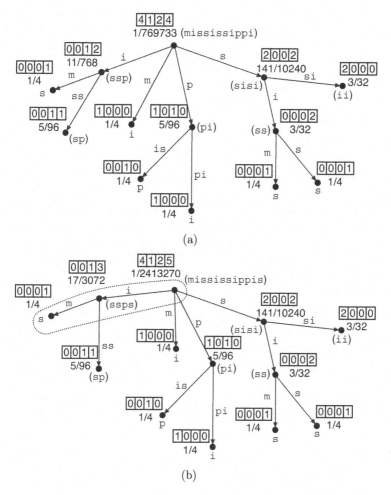

Fig. 5.16. Context tree weighting method: (a) Weighted context tree for the context tree of Figure 5.3 using $T = \mathtt{mississippi}$; (b) updated context tree when the next symbol is **s**. In (b), the path that contains nodes that require updating have been highlighted. Fractions at each node correspond to the weighted probability at the node

memory sources. The CTW also provides very good compression performance in practice. Results on practical compression experiments using the CTW method have been reported for general text (Tjalkens et al., 1997; Volf, 1997), genomic sequences (Chen et al., 2002), and map images (Kopylov and Fränti, 2005).

Section 5.3 showed the close relationship between the BWT and context trees. This implies that the BWT and the CTW methods are equally closely related. Again, the major difference is the fact the BWT sorts its contexts, while the CTW does not require that the contexts be sorted. Further, while the BWT makes use of unbounded contexts, data compression with the CTW requires that the context order be stipulated beforehand, and should remain fixed during the compression. Thus the context order has to be transmitted to the decoder. The results of Section 5.5 show that BWT (using context partitions without LGT, or with p.i.i.d. parameters) can achieve the same theoretical compression performance bounds as the CTW method.

Ziv-Lempel (LZ) coding

The family of Ziv-Lempel codes (abbreviated as LZ due to some historical confusion) are widely used in data compression, most notably in the ZIP and GZIP utilities, and in the GIF and PNG image compression formats. LZ coding is based on replacing strings in a text with references to where the string has occurred earlier in the text. This means that they are adaptive; even if the text is about an unusual topic, once a relevant phrase or component of a word has been introduced then it can be used for future reference. The LZ family of methods can generally be divided into two groups: the "LZ77" group, which allow pointers to reference substrings at any position in the recent text, and the "LZ78" group[4], which parse the text into substrings that are numbered and can be referenced simply with the number, as the length is determined when the phrase is parsed. The LZ77 group tend to be slow for encoding and fast for decoding, while the LZ78 tend to be moderately fast for both encoding and decoding. Over the years the LZ77 based methods, in combination with Huffman coding, have emerged as giving the best compression performance.

The LZ77 group have pointers with two components; the first identifies which previous substring is being referenced, and the other gives the length of the match that should be copied. For example, the word mississippi could be coded as miss(3,4)ppi, where the pointer (3,4) means to count back 3 characters (to the first i in the text), and then copy 4 consecutive characters (issi). This particular example uses a recursive pointer; the decoder must begin copying the 4 characters before the 4th one is known, but it will be available by the time it is needed. Recursive pointers are particularly good for simulating run-length encoding; for example, a(1,19) represents the letter a repeated 20 times. LZ77 methods usually put a limit on how far back the pointer can reach; this limits the search that must be made to find a match, and it also allows the pointer component to be a fixed size. It also means that adaptation focuses on recent history so that if the text gradually changes (is not stationary) then older text will be lost from this "window" of available characters.

The LZ78 group generally parse the input using a trie structure. For example, the LZW method (based on LZ78) starts with a trie that contains

---

[4] LZ77 and LZ78 are named for the years in which they were first published; they are sometimes referred to as LZ1 and LZ2 respectively (Ziv and Lempel, 1977, 1978).

all symbols in the alphabet, and then grows branches of the trie as the text is encoded. The initial LZW trie for the alphabet {i,m,p,s} is shown in Figure 5.17a. Nodes in the trie contain the code that will be used to encode a string represented by a path from the root to that node, so initially we just have the codes from 0 to 3 for the four characters respectively. If we are compressing the input mississippi, the first m will be coded as a 1, and then we extend this branch of the trie by one character using the next input character (i), giving us node 4 which can be seen in Figure 5.17b. The second i has not been coded yet, and it in turn is coded as 0. The 0 node is then extended using the third character, s. This continues, giving the coded form as shown in Figure 5.17c. Of course, the example is too short to show any good compression, but notice that the trie is building up a collection of useful phrases that can be used to represent substrings of the text with just one number. The trie itself is a good structure for finding the longest match for substrings in the text, since one just follows the path from the root until a leaf is reached. At this point we have the phrase number for coding, and it is also the place where the tree is extended by one character. There is a minor problem if a leaf node is used for encoding as soon as it is generated, as the decoder does not have the next character available. However, it turns out that in this situation the first and last character of the phrase will be the same, so the unknown character can be obtained from the first character of the phrase that was just used.

Even at a simplistic level both LZ77 and LZ78 have strong commonalities with the Burrows-Wheeler Transform. The LZ77 method searches for the longest match for the upcoming characters, and the pointer back to a previous occurrence of that phrase is effectively linking together maximally matching phrases that would have been brought together in the Burrows-Wheeler Transform. LZ78 based methods use the trie structure shown in Figure 5.17b, which is an abbreviated suffix tree being used to find longest matches, and the branches from any node share the common context represented by the path to that node.

Yokoo (1997) presents an approach to compression that bridges the gap between BWT-based methods and Ziv-Lempel methods; it is based on the binary search tree used for LZ77 style coding in Bell (1986) which was used to find the longest match in the previous text for LZ coding. Yokoo uses a variant of the binary search tree, which groups similar contexts together in lexical order (an inorder traversal of the tree gives the prefixes of the text in lexical order). These prefixes are searched to make predictions about what the next character can be (which is similar to PPM), but the idea is extended if the characters beyond the first one being predicted are also strongly predicted to occur next, in which case more than one character is encoded at that step. The group of characters coded in one step require a reference to where they have occurred before, and hence we end up with a kind of LZ coding, but with a context to predict which sequence of characters is likely to occur next. Yokoo's approach is described in more detail in Section 6.4.

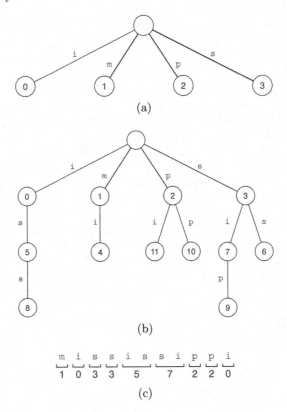

(a)

(b)

(c)

Fig. 5.17. Coding `mississippi` using LZW: (a) the initial trie; (b) after coding the text; (c) how the text is coded

This is not the only way the LZ coding has been related to finite context predictions. Langdon Jr. (1983) showed a model based on the trie of an LZ78 compressor which assigned probability distributions to individual input symbols in a way that the number of bits coded was identical to what it would have been for the LZ78 coding. This established that LZ78 coding is equivalent to a predictive model; the weakness of the model that was revealed is that it doesn't use a maximal context for prediction, but instead starts with a zero-order prediction for one character, then first-order *for the next character*, and so on until no prediction can be made. At this point it resets to the zero-order context for prediction and restarts. This contrasts with PPM (and BWT), which use the longest possible context for predictions. The idea of finding an equivalent predictive model was extended to the LZ77 family by Bell (1987).

Dynamic Markov Compression (DMC)

The Dynamic Markov Compression (DMC) method (Cormack and Horspool, 1987) is a relatively simple method to implement, yet gives compression comparable to the PPM- and BWT-based methods. Its main disadvantage is that it is relatively slow because it codes only one input bit at each step, when most methods code a byte at a time. It is based on a Finite State Machine which models the text as a Markov model, with each state storing a probability distribution to code the next character, and a transition to the next state to be used depending on which character is encoded. DMC is most easily implemented using a binary alphabet, and files with larger alphabets are simply read one bit at a time.

Figure 5.18 shows a small model generated as part of DMC. For example, state 1 has a transition to state 2 on a 0, and its count is 25. A 1 from the same state has a count of 10, and so for this state we can estimate $p(0) = 25/35$ and $p(1) = 10/35$. After a transition is followed, its count is incremented for future probability estimates. A key idea in DMC is that new states are added to the model by a process called "cloning"; a heuristic is used to determine if a state and a transition into it are heavily used, in which case a copy of the state is made so that more detail can be stored in that part of the model. As cloning continues, the size of the model can grow very large (typically the number of states is comparable to the number of characters in the input).

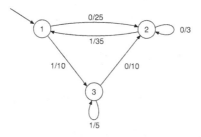

Fig. 5.18. A small DMC model

Although in general the state that a finite state machine is in depends on the whole input string prior to the current character, in practice the cloning heuristic proposed for DMC ensures that only a finite number of previous bits from the input string need to be known to determine the state of the system, and hence which probability distribution will be used (Bell and Moffat, 1989). For example, in Figure 5.18, if the previous character(s) are 01 then we will always end up in state 1, and conversely, if we are in state 1 then the string must have ended with the characters 01.

This result means that the DMC model is effectively implementing a finite context model (based on a finite number of previous bits), and the coding of a symbol depends entirely on a finite prior context. Thus it is closely related to the BWT, where the context is used to partition characters into different areas of the transformed string, and their coding depends on what other characters have been seen in a similar context.

5.6.2 Symbol ranking schemes

The general family of symbol-ranking text compression algorithms provide another way to consider the relationship between the BWT and other popular compression algorithms. In his original work on entropy of the English language, Shannon (1951) performed experiments to predict the information content of an English text by using humans (who are well experienced with English) to guess the next symbol. Shannon's idea was to use human subjects to predict the contents of a passage (character by character), and from that estimate the best possible compression that might be obtained if a computer was able to predict English text as competently as a human. There are two versions of the experiment.

1. **Type-1**: In the first version, the subject is asked to guess the next character in the text. The subject is then informed whether the guess is correct, or if not, the correct answer is revealed to the subject.
2. **Type-2** In a second version, the subject is asked to continue guessing until the correct answer is obtained.

Thus, the human subjects make use of knowledge of the preceding symbols (that is, the context) to predict the next symbol. This is essentially an unbounded context, the performance of which is, perhaps, only limited by a person's memory capacity, patience and experience.

Table 5.8 shows the results of this experiment as reported by Shannon (1951) for the Type-2 experiment. Notice the significant skew in the distribution of the number of guesses, which implies a potential for significant compression — the table shows that, on average, 79% of the symbols are predicted correctly at the first guess. By considering the sequence of successful and unsuccessful guesses, Shannon was able to estimate the entropy of English text. His estimate of 0.6 to 1.3 bits per symbol for English is still a challenge for most practical compression algorithms.

Number of guesses (or symbol ranking)	1	2	3	4	5	> 5
Probability (%)	79	8	3	2	2	5

Table 5.8. Shannon's results for the probability of correct guesses for English text

Fenwick (1997a,b, 1998, 2003b) was the first to make the connection between some of the popular compression algorithms and Shannon's original experiment, leading to a family of "symbol ranking" text compression algorithms. Members of this class include most of the high-performing text compression algorithms available today, such as the BWT, ACB, LZP, the MTF, and Elias' recency and interval ranking schemes. In general, symbol-ranking compression algorithms work in two steps.

1. **Ranking Phase:** This is the symbol ranking step, where the ranked list of symbols is generated. For each context, we maintain a list of symbols ranked in order of their probability of appearing in the given context. Any input symbol is then placed into its correct rank in the sorted list. It is this rank that is then transmitted as the code for the symbol. An identical list is maintained at the decoder, and can be used to recover the correct symbol based on the transmitted rank.

2. **Coding Phase:** This phase performs the final encoding of the sequence of ranks produced by the ranking phase. In general, the recorded sequence of ranks often have a highly skewed distribution, which can be exploited by entropy coding algorithms, such as arithmetic coding or Huffman codes. The sequence of ranks can also be coded with simple integer codes, such as the Elias γ-codes or δ-codes.

With respect to the BWT, symbol ranking comes into play at two stages. The context sorting stage groups symbols with similar contexts together in one partition of the BWT output. Thus, adjacent contexts in a partition should have sequences with similar ranks. In the second stage, BWT-based methods often use a move-to-front (MTF) list to maintain one single ranked list (with the same size as the alphabet), transmitting the rank of the current output symbol in the list, before the symbol is moved to the front of the list. The MTF list changes to adapt to changing symbols observed in the L array, the BWT output. Given the similarity of nearby contexts in the BWT output, the nearby symbols in the BWT output are expected to be similar. Thus, changes in the MTF list will mainly be gradual.

Methods that belong to this class of symbol ranking compression algorithms can also be seen as preprocessors, whereby the output of the preprocessor can be sent to another compression algorithm for final compression. Some recent work has viewed the BWT as a "compression booster" (Ferragina et al., 2005a), whereby the output of the BWT can be passed on to a potentially low-performing basic compression algorithm for improved performance of the basic algorithm, for instance, without the MTF.

5.7 Further reading

The computational complexity of the BWT is typically analyzed by considering the complexity of suffix tree or suffix array construction algorithms. (Kurtz and Balkenhol, 2000) described improved suffix-tree based algorithms for computing the BWT. Kärkkäinen (Kärkkäinen, 2007) also provided a new scheme that is specifically tuned for computing the BWT, without computing the complete suffix array. Szpankowski (1993a) analyzed the height of suffix trees for data compression. Suffix trees were surveyed in Giegerich and Kurtz (1997), while more recent surveys on suffix arrays appear in Puglisi et al. (2005, 2007). Chapter 4 on suffix trees and suffix arrays provides more details on suffix sorting and suffix trees.

The only major work on the output distribution of the BWT was performed by Visweswariah et al. (2000) and Effros et al. (2002). Yokoo (1997) was among the first to provide some theoretical analysis of block-sorting text compression. Other earlier work on theoretical analysis of the performance of the BWT in universal source coding was performed by Arimura and Yamamoto (1998), Sadakane (1998), Balkenhol and Kurtz (1998, 2000), Effros (1999) and Effros et al. (2002). Manzini (1999, 2001) took a comparatively different approach, using the notion of empirical entropy (Bentley et al., 1986) and its modifications to obtain bounds on the compression ratio of BWT-based compression schemes. More recent work in this area has followed Manzini's approach (see Giancarlo and Sciortino (2003); Ferragina et al. (2005a); Kaplan et al. (2006)). Fenwick (1998) studied the empirical performance of BWT compression using universal codes for the integers, after the MTF, rather than the more traditional approach of using entropy coding. Kaplan and Verbin (2007) is a another recent paper analyzing BWT-based compression systems.

The PPM method was presented by Cleary and Witten (1984), with further descriptions and development provided by Bell et al. (1990) and Moffat (1990). The LZ compression methods originally appeared in Ziv and Lempel (1977) and Ziv and Lempel (1978). The LZW method is by Welch (1984). The DMC method appeared in Cormack and Horspool (1987). More information about these methods can be found in Witten et al. (1999), and in other general compression books listed in the "Further reading" section at the end of Chapter 1.

The relationship between the BWT (and sorted-context based methods in general) and other well-known compression schemes, such as the LZ family was initially pointed out by Yokoo (1997). Larsson (1998), Cleary and Teahan (1997), and Effros (1999, 2000) studied the close relationship between the BWT and PPM-family, especially the PPM* algorithm with unbounded contexts. Fenwick (2007) presents a more recent work on the relationship between BWT and PPM. Larsson (1998) also studied the close relationship between the BWT and context trees, although without relating it to the CTW (contexttree weighting) approach. He described heuristics for generating pruned context trees needed for compression, based on the expected compression gain in including a given node in the PPM context tree. Context-tree weighting is described in detail in the classic paper by Willems et al. (1995). The K-T estimator was originally proposed by Krichevsky and Trofimov (1981) for binary sources.

The discussion on BWT and symbol ranking compression schemes is mainly due to Fenwick (1998). There is related information about compression methods that are similar to the BWT in Chapter 6. The experiments on estimating the entropy of English by human guesses were performed by Shannon (1951). The entropy of English was further studied by Cover and King (Cover and King, 1978) using a gambling estimate.

6

Variants of the Burrows-Wheeler Transform

With the huge excitement that was generated by the publication of the original paper on the Burrows-Wheeler Transform in 1994, followed by a more detailed empirical study by Fenwick between 1995 and 1996 (Fenwick, 1995b,c, 1996a,b), it did not take long before researchers started considering different variations, extensions and generalizations of the transform. There were many questions to ask; for instance, given the sorted BWT rotation matrix, is the array of last characters (the last column L of the matrix A_s) selected by the BWT as its output the only possible choice? And if other choices are possible, might they give better compression? The first column (F) would be an attractive choice if it were possible to recover the original text from this column, since it can be represented very efficiently. It would seem that there is insufficient information to recover the text T from F, and we know how to recover it from L, but what of the columns between them?

Another debate was about the transformation itself. Do we need a complete sorting of all the cyclic rotations of the original text, or can we make do with a limited-length key comparison — for instance, sorting based on the k-length prefix of each row, for an arbitrary k? Can we recover the original text without error from such limited-order sorting? Given that sorting is the major bottleneck in BWT-based analysis, if this simplified sort were possible it could have a significant advantage with respect to computational complexity; but what will be the impact on compression? Other questions included whether the BWT can be applied to a word-based alphabet, especially given that the original paper that proposed the MTF algorithm for compression (Bentley et al., 1986) used word-based alphabets.

In this chapter we address the above issues and more by considering various published extensions and generalizations of the BWT. Where possible, we include empirical performance of the BWT variant or generalization.

6.1 The sort transform

One generalization of the BWT is found by considering the number of characters used to compare lines in the array A. With the BWT, the position of a given symbol in the output list is determined by its unbounded context. That is, sorting a row in A uses as many symbols as are needed to compare it with another row, so the character in the L column (BWT output) has its position based on an unbounded number of following characters, which we regard as its context. One question is whether one can recover the original string from an L-array formed using only a limited-length context, rather than unbounded contexts. The question was settled in the affirmative by Michael Schindler (Schindler, 1997a,b, 2001), who showed that for a given k, a transformation similar to the BWT can be performed using only order-k contexts. He demonstrated that with only small values of k, for instance $k \leq 16$, the compression loss when compared with using the full unbounded contexts (i.e. with $k = n$) can be minimal. Schindler's algorithm, called the *Sort Transform*, can be viewed as a generalization of the BWT with parameter k, where the original BWT corresponds to the case of $k = n$. In fact, with a k value greater than the maximum LCP between any two suffixes in the original string, the output of the sort transform will be identical to that of the BWT. The sort transform algorithm is implemented in the compression program SZIP.

6.1.1 Forward sort transform

We will use the symbols L_k and V_k to denote the corresponding BWT arrays L and V respectively when using the sort transform with order-k contexts. Similarly, we use a_k to denote the corresponding starting index using the order-k sort transform, and A_k to denote the sorted matrix or rotated substrings (at $k = n$, we have $L_k = L, a_k = a, V_k = V$, and $A_k = A_s$). The forward sort transform is simple. For a text T with $|T| = n$, and the parameter k for the size of the sort context, the steps are similar to the forward BWT described in Chapter 2:

1. Perform cyclic rotations of the input string T to form the rotation matrix A;
2. Sort the rows in A based only on the first k symbols in each row; if there are ties, use the position in T of the starting symbol in each row involved in the tie as the tie breaker. Call the resulting order-k sorted rotation matrix A_k.
3. Record the pair (L_k, a_k) as the output of the sort transform, where L_k is the last column of A_k, and a_k is the row index of the original string T in A_k.

Figure 6.1 shows a run of the sort transform on a sample string $T = $ banana for different values of k. In general, whenever k is greater than the maximum LCP between any adjacent rows in the BWT sorted rotation matrix, then the results from the k-order sort transform become identical to those of the BWT. This can be observed at $k = 4$ in the example ($maxLCP$, the maximum LCP is 3).

With the limited-context sorting there are likely to be duplicate sort keys — for example, with $k = 1$ there can only be $|\Sigma|$ different keys. Schindler (1997b) suggested that the sort order for duplicate keys should follow the reverse order of the substrings in T; that is, the index to the substring in T is used as the tie-breaker for key comparisons. However, with appropriate modifications to the transformation arrays, this is not a necessary condition for the algorithm to work.

One major attraction of sorting with limited-order contexts is computational efficiency. With small values of k it is easy to use a simple radix sort to provide a fast transformation, leading to $O(kn)$ time in the worst case. When k approaches n, this defaults to quadratic time with respect to the length of the input string. In practice though, only small values of k are required, and hence the algorithm is fast. Further, for random text where the $maxLCP$ is expected to be small compared with the length of the text, the algorithm can be expected to provide superior speed performance.

6.1.2 Inverse sort transform

The major problem is how to recover the original T, given only L_k and a_k. As with the original BWT, it is quite remarkable that, indeed, there is an algorithm to perform this recovery. However, unlike the BWT, which has a relatively simple inverse transformation, computing the inverse of the Schindler's sorting transform is quite involved, and can be more time consuming than the forward transform (Schindler, 1997a,b). Although Schindler showed empirical results of his algorithm, his descriptions are not sufficient to clearly understand how the inverse transformation is performed.

Inverting the sort transform generally requires two stages:

- **Sorting stage:** From L_k generate all the order-k contexts, and sort these contexts lexicographically. When there is a tie, use the position of the symbols to break the tie as was done during the forward transform.
- **Retrieval stage:** Using the sorted order-k contexts, generate new transformation vectors. Using these vectors, sequentially retrieve the symbols in T.

The sorting stage can be performed in a manner very similar to the BWT inversion procedure shown in Figure 1.2 (page 4). Starting with the L_k-array, we can reconstruct the initial order-k sorted rotation matrix. From L_k, the last column of the matrix, construct F by simply sorting L_k. Construct the order-2 contexts by concatenating $L_k[i]$ to $F[i]$ for each i, $1 \leq i \leq n$. Sort the resulting bigrams to obtain the order-2 sorted contexts. Repeat this concatenation and sort process to obtain the order-3, order-4, ..., order-k sorted contexts. Figure

```
banana
ananab
nanaba
anaban
nabana
abanan
```
(a)

Position	A_1	V_1	Index	C_1	M_1
2	ananab	4	1	3	4
4	anaban	5	2		5
6	abanan	6	3		5
1	banana	1	4	1	1
3	nanaba	2	5	2	1
5	nabana	3	6		1

(b)

Position	A_2	V_2	Index	C_2	M_2
6	abanan	5	1	1	5
2	ananab	4	2	2	4
4	anaban	6	3		5
1	banana	1	4	1	1
3	nanaba	2	5	2	2
5	nabana	3	6		2

(c)

Position	A_3	V_3	Index	C_3	M_3
6	abanan	5	1	1	5
2	ananab	4	2	2	4
4	anaban	6	3		6
1	banana	1	4	1	1
5	nabana	2	5	1	2
3	nanaba	3	6	1	2

(d)

Position	A_4	V_4	Index	C_4	M_4
6	abanan	5	1	1	5
4	anaban	6	2	1	6
2	ananab	4	3	1	4
1	banana	1	4	1	1
5	nabana	2	5	1	2
3	nanaba	3	6	1	3

(e)

Fig. 6.1. Example of Schindler's sort transform, for four values of k: (a) the unsorted rotation matrix A; Sorted rotation matrix for (b) $k = 1$; (c) $k = 2$; (d) $k = 3$; (e) $k = 4$. For this particular example, we have $a_k = 4$ for each value of k. The transform vectors required for the inverse sort transform are also included. Position indicates original row indexes before sorting. See the text for definitions of C_k and M_k

6.2 shows how the sorting stage is performed during the inversion process, using the example in Figure 6.1.

Step: 1	2	3	4	5	6
L_3	sort	concatenate $L_3 * F$	sort	concatenate	sort
n	a...n	na	ab...n	nab	aba...n
b	a...b	ba	an...b	ban	ana...b
n	a...n	na	an...n	nan	ana...n
a	b...a	ab	ba...a	aba	ban...a
a	n...a	an	na...a	ana	nab...a
a	n...a	an	na...a	ana	nan...a

Fig. 6.2. Sorting stage in performing the inverse sort transform; this is based on the example in Figure 6.1, for $k = 3$

The retrieval stage is the major challenge. Schindler (1997a,b) gave a high-level description of the above inversion procedure. In his patent on the sort transform (Schindler, 2001), he described the possibility of using various data structures, such as hash tables and tries to implement the inversion procedure. More recently, Chan and Nong (2005) and Nong and Zhang (2006, 2007a) provided a more detailed study of the Schindler's sorting transform, especially its inversion. They showed that given the output of the sort transform, the original inverse BWT algorithm can be modified to compute the inverse of the sort transform.

To understand the inverse transformation we need to consider the properties of the arrays and the sorted rotation matrix involved in limited-order sorting. The properties generally follow those of the original BWT, with some important differences in certain cases. Recall that V_k maps the symbols in L_k to F, such that $L_k[i] = F[V_k[i]]$. The first observation is that, similar to the original BWT L and F arrays, when the same symbol, say σ, occurs in two positions in L_k, their relative order in L_k is maintained in F, the array of first characters. That is, if the same symbol appeared in $L_k[i]$ and $L_k[j]$, and $i < j$, then, their respective positions in F as defined by the mapping vector V_k must be such that $V_k[i] < V_k[j]$.

As with the original BWT matrices, we can also notice that, for a given position $i, i = 1, 2, \ldots, n$, $A_k[V_k[i], 1] = L_k[i]$. Thus we should have, for $j = 2, 3, \ldots, n$, $A_k[V_k[j], 1 \ldots k] = L_k[j] * A_k[V_k[j], 1 \ldots k - 1]$. Chan and Nong (2005) proved an important theorem about limited-order sorting. Consider two positions i, j ($1 < i < j$) in L_k with $L_k[i] = L_k[j] = \sigma$. They showed that, if rows $V_k[i]$ and $V_k[j]$ have the same first k symbols, that is, $\text{LCP}(A_k[V_k[i], 1 \ldots n], A_k[V_k[j], 1 \ldots n]) \geq k$ (or equivalently, $A_k[V_k[i], 1 \ldots n] =_k A_k[V_k[j], 1 \ldots n]$), then, for any position, say r, $i < r < j$, if $L_k[r] = L_k[i] = \sigma$, the corresponding row in A_k, starting at $V_k[r]$ must have the same first k symbols as the row starting at $V_k[i]$. This means that the rows $V_k[i] \ldots V_k[r] \ldots V_k[j]$ in A_k must all have the same k-order context, and hence must belong to the same group or contiguous region in F. This relationship is the key to correct inversion of the sort transform, given only the pair (L_k, a_k). Furthermore, when the sentinel symbol $ is appended to the end of the string T before the transform, it is easy to see that the matrix A_{n-1} will be identical to $A_n = A_s$, the original BWT sorted rotation matrix.

The retrieval stage is then performed using a modified BWT inversion procedure. Following the methods proposed in Chan and Nong (2005) and Nong and Zhang (2006, 2007a), we can modify the BWT inversion algorithms of Section 2.2 to realize the inversion procedure for limited-order sort transform.

To invert the original BWT we used two primary arrays. One was the array C, such that $C[i]$ is the number of instances of symbol $L[i]$ in $L[1 \ldots i-1]$. The second array M contained the cumulative count of each symbol in L. Essentially M recorded the starting position in F of *each distinct symbol* in the alphabet. To use the same general approach for the limited order contexts used in the sorting transform, we must modify the above arrays, to reflect the fact that the sorting now uses only the order-k contexts along with position sorts, and not the unbounded contexts used by the BWT.

Consider each distinct order-k context as forming a partition of the matrix A_k, or equivalently of F, the array of first characters. Let C_k be a count array, such that, $C_k[i]$ gives the size of the i-th *distinct* order-k context partition in A_k. Thus, all positions in F that share the same order-k context in A_k will have one $C_k[i]$ value. Therefore, $C_k[i]$ is defined only for rows in F (and hence A_k) that represent the starting position of a new order-k context. Thus, in Figure 6.1 the C_k entries mark the start of each partition, with just 3 partitions for $k = 1$, and every row being a partition for $k = 4$. M_k is another array with the cumulative count of contexts in each context partition. More specifically, $M_k[i]$ is the cumulative number of order-k contexts in the context partition to which symbol $L[i]$ belongs; that is, the order-k context partition containing row $V_k[i]$ in A_k (or equivalently, row $V_k[i]$ in F). Thus, M_k is also defined with respect to order-k context partitions. All rows in A_k that belong to the same context partition share the same values for C_k and M_k, respectively. Both C_k and M_k are easy to compute — after generating the order-k sorted context, both vectors can be computed in $O(n)$ time. Figure 6.1 shows values for C_k and M_k for a sample run. Notice how the elements in the vector C_k progressively tend to unity as k approaches the value of $(1 + maxLCP)$. Similarly, the vector M_k becomes identical to V_k, which in turn will be equal to V, the original BWT vector, whenever k is greater than the $maxLCP$.

Using the new vectors, the retrieval stage needed to recover the symbols in T when inverting the sort transform can be performed by modifying the retrieval segment of the BWT reconstruction procedure (lines 16 to 20 in Algorithm 2.1 on page 26). This modification is shown in Algorithm 6.1.

The following is a run of the above algorithm for the retrieval stage of the sort transform inversion procedure, after the initial sorting stage. We continue

---

INVERSE-SORT-TRANSFORM(L_k, a_k, C_k, M_k)
16 $j \leftarrow a_k$
17 **for** $i \leftarrow n$ **down to** 1 **do**
18     $T[i] \leftarrow L_k[j]$
19     $j \leftarrow M_k[j] + (C_k[M_k[j]] - 1)$
20     $C_k[M_k[j]] \leftarrow (C_k[M_k[j]] - 1)$
21 **end for**

Algorithm 6.1: Inverse sort transform after initial sorting

with the example used earlier in Figure 6.1, and consider the case with $k = 2$, and $a_k = 4$.

$j = a_2 = 4;$
$i = 6 : T[6] = L_2[4] = \mathsf{a}; j = M_2[4] + C_2[M_2[4]] - 1 = 1 + 1 - 1 = 1; C_2[1] = 1 - 1 = 0;$
$i = 5 : T[5] = L_2[1] = \mathsf{n}; j = M_2[1] + C_2[M_2[1]] - 1 = 5 + 2 - 1 = 6; C_2[5] = 2 - 1 = 1;$
$i = 4 : T[4] = L_2[6] = \mathsf{a}; j = M_2[6] + C_2[M_2[6]] - 1 = 2 + 2 - 1 = 3; C_2[2] = 2 - 1 = 1;$
$i = 3 : T[3] = L_2[3] = \mathsf{n}; j = M_2[3] + C_2[M_2[3]] - 1 = 5 + 1 - 1 = 5; C_2[5] = 1 - 1 = 0;$
$i = 2 : T[2] = L_2[5] = \mathsf{a}; j = M_2[5] + C_2[M_2[5]] - 1 = 2 + 1 - 1 = 2; C_2[2] = 1 - 1 = 0;$
$i = 1 : T[1] = L_2[2] = \mathsf{b}; j = M_2[2] + C_2[M_2[2]] - 1 = 4 + 1 - 1 = 4; C_2[4] = 1 - 1 = 0;$

We can see that at the last step, the value of the index variable j becomes $j = a_2 = 4$, the original starting value, indicating a complete cycle for the retrieval stage.

With the above approach, the sorting stage can be performed in $O(kn)$ time, which could be quadratic as k tends to n. The retrieval stage can be performed in $O(n)$. Given the discussion on suffix sorting in Chapter 4, it may be possible to perform the sorting stage in $O(n)$ time, leading to an overall linear time algorithm for both the forward sort transform, and the inverse sort transform.

6.1.3 Performance of the sort transform

Figure 6.3 compares the performance of Schindler's sort transform with the original BWT method. The figure shows results for different input sequences for different values of k, up to $k = 100$. The files used are described in detail in Section 5.4.2, on page 106, and were chosen because of the variety of the nature of their contents. To clearly show the effect of a limited-order transform on the compression performance these tests use the same second stage algorithms (simply MTF followed by run-length encoding and the arithmetic coding) for both BWT ($k = n$) and Schindler's sort transform ($k < n$). As can be seen from the figure, the compression performance becomes almost indistinguishable from that of the original BWT from around order $k = 8$.

Figures 6.4 and 6.5 show the performance of the sort transform with respect to compression and decompression time[1]. The graphs show an essentially

---

[1] The times are for a 2.4GHz dual-core processor.

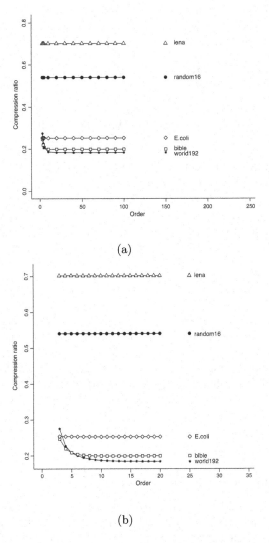

(a)

(b)

Fig. 6.3. (a) Compression performance of Schindler's sort transform for different values of k; (b) an expanded view of the graph. Results using the original BWT are indicated at order $k = 150$ in (a) and at $k = 25$ in (b). The compression ratio is given as (compressed size) / (original size)

linear relationship between the compression or decompression time and the sorting order, k. In general, the compression time for the original BWT corresponds to around the time needed between order $k = 10$ and order $k = 17$ with the sort transform. However, for decompression, the original BWT was always a lot faster than the sort transform, even for very small k values. This

is borne out by the relative performance of the implementations of SZIP and
BZIP, which use Schindler's method and the original BWT method respectively; SZIP is a little faster for compression but does not reduce the file size
as much, whereas BZIP is faster for decompression.

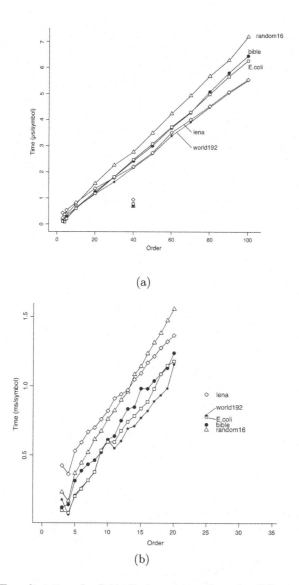

(a)

(b)

Fig. 6.4. (a) Encoding time for Schindler's sort transform for different values of k;
(b) detailed view for smaller values of k. The original BWT results are shown at
$k = 40$ and $k = 25$ respectively

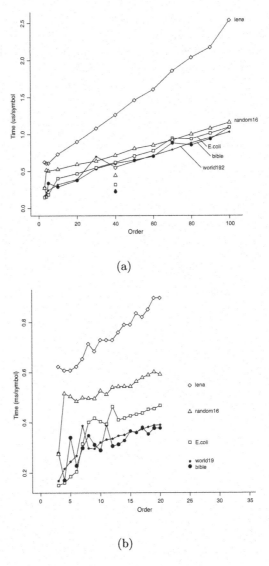

(a)

(b)

Fig. 6.5. (a) Decompression time for Schindler's sort transform for different values of k; (b) detailed view for smaller values of k. The original BWT results are shown at $k = 40$ and $k = 25$ respectively

The results highlight differences depending on the nature of the files being compressed. The textual files give good compression, and benefit the most from higher values of k. The "E.coli" file compressed to just over 25% of its original size, which is what would be expected since there are only 4 symbols in its alphabet — beyond the two bits per symbol the BWT and related systems find few patterns in such files without being adapted for genomic data. The "lena" file was difficult to compress because the compression is lossless, and such images really require a lossy method, or at least one that does not rely on patterns being repeated exactly (no spatial error prediction stage was used for the results reported here). The compression and decompression speeds for this file are quite variable, largely because it is a small file and compression time is influenced more by overheads than the main processing time. The "random16" file was compressed close to a half of its size, as should be expected, and this was achieved even with very small values of k. Because the characters are random, contexts would have been evenly distributed with small LCPs, and this is reflected in it being the fastest file to encode and decode.

6.2 Lexical permutation sorting

Another possible generalization of the BWT can be found by considering the choice of the specific column to select after the BWT sorting stage. Traditionally the BWT selects L, the last column of the sorted rotation matrix A_s, as its output, accompanied by the index of the original string in the matrix. Compression is then performed by further post-processing of the selected column, for instance, using the MTF algorithm and entropy coding. There is therefore the question of whether we can choose any other column of A_s and still recover the original sequence without error. This was exactly the problem studied by Arnavut and Magliveras in the late nineties in lexical permutation sorting (Arnavut and Magliveras, 1997a,b; Arnavut and Arnavut, 2004). They showed that, indeed, for a certain class of strings, it is possible to choose some other columns, and still recover the data. For general strings, which can be considered as multiset permutations, this can also be done, but with some added overhead. Before we get into details of their lexical permutation sorting algorithm (LPSA), we introduce some further notation.

Given n distinct objects, a *permutation* of the objects is simply a linear arrangement of the objects. Thus, for a collection of n distinct objects, we have $n!$ possible permutations of the collection. A permutation can also be considered as a re-labeling of the objects in the collection, i.e. a one-to-one and onto mapping of the n objects. Let χ be a set of objects. Then a permutation π of χ is a bijection from χ onto χ, $\pi : \chi \to \chi$. Suppose $\chi = \{a, b, c, d, e, f\}$. An example permutation π is denoted as follows:

$$\pi = \begin{pmatrix} a & b & c & d & e & f \\ d & f & b & c & a & e \end{pmatrix}$$

This corresponds to the mapping, $a \to d, b \to f, c \to b, d \to c, e \to a, f \to e$, or equivalently $\pi(a) = d, \pi(b) = d$, etc. The permutation is not affected if we swap the columns, or more generally, if we change the order of the columns. Thus, the permutation above could be written as :

$$\pi = \begin{pmatrix} a & d & c & b & e & f \\ d & c & b & f & a & e \end{pmatrix}$$

However, if we impose a fixed order on the elements in χ, we can denote the permutation by simply writing out only the second row. For instance, if we choose $[a, b, c, d, e, f]$, the lexical ordering of the elements of χ, then the permutation above will be $\pi = (d\ f\ b\ c\ a\ e)$. The result is sometimes called the Cartesian form of the permutation. A permutation can sometimes be decomposed into a product of disjoint cycles. For example, the permutation $\pi = (a\ e\ d\ f\ b\ c)$ can be depicted using the equivalent notation: $\pi = (a)(b\ e)(c\ d\ f)$.

To every permutation π, there is a corresponding *inverse*, denoted π^{-1}. Every permutation has a unique inverse. For the example above, we have

$$\pi = \begin{pmatrix} a & b & c & d & e & f \\ d & f & b & c & a & e \end{pmatrix} \text{ and } \pi^{-1} = \begin{pmatrix} d & f & b & c & a & e \\ a & b & c & d & e & f \end{pmatrix} = \begin{pmatrix} a & b & c & d & e & f \\ e & c & d & a & f & b \end{pmatrix}$$

In Cartesian form, we have $\pi^{-1} = (e\ c\ d\ a\ f\ b)$. This inverse permutation can be used to undo the effect of the permutation. The *identity* permutation is obtained by multiplying a permutation with its inverse, that is, the product $\pi^{-1}\pi$. This notation applies the inverse permutation *after* applying the original permutation. In general, the order of the permutations is important in computing the product of two permutations. For two permutations π_1 and π_2, we use the notation $\pi_3 = \pi_1\pi_2$ to represent $\pi_3(i) = \pi_1(\pi_2(i))$. Notice that for the identity permutation, $\pi\pi^{-1} = \pi^{-1}\pi$.

6.2.1 Sorting permutations

Consider what happens when we apply the BWT on a permutation. For instance, suppose we are given the permutation $T = (d\ f\ b\ c\ a\ e)$, with $n = 6$. We obtain the BWT rotation matrix A, and its sorted form A_s as follows:

$$A = \begin{bmatrix} d\ f\ b\ c\ a\ e \\ f\ b\ c\ a\ e\ d \\ b\ c\ a\ e\ d\ f \\ c\ a\ e\ d\ f\ b \\ a\ e\ d\ f\ b\ c \\ e\ d\ f\ b\ c\ a \end{bmatrix}, \quad A_s = \begin{bmatrix} a\ e\ d\ f\ b\ c \\ b\ c\ a\ e\ d\ f \\ c\ a\ e\ d\ f\ b \\ d\ f\ b\ c\ a\ e \\ e\ d\ f\ b\ c\ a \\ f\ b\ c\ a\ e\ d \end{bmatrix}.$$

Each column in A (also A_s) is a permutation of the original sequence, and so is each row. Since the symbols in a permutation are unique, to sort A, we need to consider only the first symbol in each row. The original permutation T occurs at row 4 in A_s (i.e. $a=4$). Let C_i be the i-th column in the sorted rotation matrix A_s. That is, $C_1 = F$ and $C_n = C_6 = L$. Observe that if we view the columns as permutations, $C_1 = F$ is the identity permutation. Further, $C_2 = (e\ c\ a\ f\ d\ b)$ (the second column) and $C_n = (c\ f\ b\ e\ a\ d)$ (the last column) are inverses ($C_2 C_n = C_1 = F$). That is, $\forall i, j$, if $C_2[i] = j$, then $L[j] = i$. Also notice that $C_{2+1} = C_3$ and $C_{n-1} = C_5$ are inverses.

With the BWT, we would choose the pair $(L, a) = (C_n, a)$ as the BWT output. Given the above relationship between L and C_2 however, it means that we can as well choose (C_2, a) as the BWT output, and still be able to recover the original string. In fact, there is a simple procedure to perform this recovery, given in Algorithm 6.2.

INVERSE-BWT-FROM-SECOND-COLUMN(C_2, a)
  $T[1] \leftarrow C_2[a]$
  for $i \leftarrow 2$ **to** n **do**
    $T[i] \leftarrow C_2[T[i-1]]$
  end for

Algorithm 6.2: Inverse BWT from second column

Now consider the general case. T is the given permutation, with $n = |T|$. A is the BWT rotation matrix, and A_s is its sorted form. The permutation π_i denotes the i-th column of A. That is,

$$A = [\pi_1, \pi_2, \ldots \pi_i, \pi_{i+1}, \ldots, \pi_n].$$

We can observe that A is symmetric, and hence $\pi_1 = T$, the original input permutation. Also, to sort A, all that is required is to rearrange the rows such that the first column after the rearrangement is the identity permutation. Based on these observations, Arnavut and Magliveras (1997a,b) proved an important lemma about sorting a matrix of cyclic permutations, such as A. They showed that the columns in A_s, the sorted rotation matrix, can be described using a simple form: $C_i = \pi_1^{-1} \pi_i$. That is, $C_i[k] = \pi_i(\pi_1^{-1}[k])$. Hence, the sorted matrix will be:

$$A_s = [\pi_1^{-1}\pi_1, \pi_1^{-1}\pi_2, \ldots, \pi_1^{-1}\pi_i \quad \pi_1^{-1}\pi_{i+1}, \ldots, \pi_1^{-1}\pi_n].$$

For the previous example, we have $T = \pi_1 = (d\ f\ b\ c\ a\ e)$ and $\pi_1^{-1} = (e\ c\ d\ a\ f\ b)$. We can then compute any of the columns, for instance, $C_3 = \pi_1^{-1}\pi_3 = (e\ c\ d\ a\ f\ b)(b\ c\ a\ e\ d\ f) = (d\ a\ e\ b\ f\ c)$. From the above, we can see that with $C_n = L = \pi_1^{-1}\pi_n$, and its inverse, $C_n^{-1} = \pi_n^{-1}\pi_1$, we should have $T[i+1] = C_n^{-1}[T[i]]$.

Let the permutation $\theta = C_2$. Any column of A_s can be derived as some power of θ. For example, $C_3 = \theta^2$. More specifically, $C_k = \theta^{k-1}$. Thus, the columns of A_s form a cyclic group of order n. More generally, let $\mathcal{G}$ be the set of columns of A_s that are generators of the cyclic group $\langle \theta \rangle$. Then, both $\theta = C_2$ and its inverse $\theta^{-1} = L = C_n$ can be completely specified as an integer power of any column, $C_k \in \mathcal{G}$. Further, since any column can be specified as an integer power of θ, it follows that any column of A_s can be specified as an integer power of any column in $\mathcal{G}$.

The number of such generators for a cyclic group is given by *Euler's phi function*:

$$\phi(n) = n \prod_{p|n} \left(1 - \frac{1}{p}\right),$$

where p runs over all primes that divide n (n inclusive, if n is prime). Thus, whenever n is prime, we have $\phi(n) = n - 1$, otherwise, $\phi(n) < n - 1$.

Since the C_i's, the columns of A_s, form a group, each column must be an inverse of some column in A_s. We can observe the following relationship about the sorted permuted matrix, A_s: The columns C_i and $C_{n-(i-2)}$ are inverses, where $2 \le i \le (\frac{n+2}{2})$ when n is even, and where $2 \le i \le (\frac{n+1}{2})$ when n is odd. Thus, when n is even, we must have $C_k = C_k^{-1}$, where $k = \frac{n+2}{2}$. That is, ignoring C_1, the middle column in A_s will be the inverse of itself.

Consider the example permutation $\pi = (3\ 1\ 5\ 4\ 2)$. Applying the BWT to this permutation will produce the A and A_s matrices as follows:

$$A = \begin{bmatrix} 3\ 1\ 5\ 4\ 2 \\ 1\ 5\ 4\ 2\ 3 \\ 5\ 4\ 2\ 3\ 1 \\ 4\ 2\ 3\ 1\ 5 \\ 2\ 3\ 1\ 5\ 4 \end{bmatrix}, \quad A_s = \begin{bmatrix} 1\ 5\ 4\ 2\ 3 \\ 2\ 3\ 1\ 5\ 4 \\ 3\ 1\ 5\ 4\ 2 \\ 4\ 2\ 3\ 1\ 5 \\ 5\ 4\ 2\ 3\ 1 \end{bmatrix}.$$

Table 6.1 shows the permutations generated when we choose δ as each column in A_s, $\delta = C_i, i = 2, 3, \ldots 5$ and the corresponding results for δ^q, where $q = 1, 2, \ldots, 5$. Thus, we have 4 generators ($\phi(5) = 4$), and in every single case in the table, we can observe that each column of A_s is generated by some power of δ. This can be compared with the previous example with $T = (d\ f\ b\ c\ a\ e)$, where $n = 6$, and hence we again have 4 generators. In that case, C_4 is not a generator as it is the inverse of itself.

$\delta = C_2$					$\delta = C_3$					$\delta = C_4$					$\delta = C_5$				
δ	δ^2	δ^3	δ^4	δ^5	δ	δ^2	δ^3	δ^4	δ^5	δ	δ^2	δ^3	δ^4	δ^5	δ	δ^2	δ^3	δ^4	δ^5
5	4	2	3	1	4	3	5	2	1	2	5	3	4	1	3	2	4	5	1
3	1	5	4	2	1	4	3	5	2	5	3	4	1	2	4	5	1	3	2
1	5	4	2	3	5	2	1	4	3	4	1	2	5	3	2	4	5	1	3
2	3	1	5	4	3	5	2	1	4	1	2	5	3	4	5	1	3	2	4
4	2	3	1	5	2	1	4	3	5	3	4	1	2	5	1	3	2	4	5
↑	↑	↑	↑	↑	↑	↑	↑	↑	↑	↑	↑	↑	↑	↑	↑	↑	↑	↑	↑
2	3	4	5	1	3	5	2	4	1	4	2	5	3	1	5	4	3	2	1

Table 6.1. Generating columns in the BWT, starting from different columns (different generators) in the sorted rotation matrix; the up arrows indicate the corresponding columns in A_s generated at the indicated power of δ

For cases with $\delta \neq C_2$, we can find some q, such that $\delta^q = \theta = C_2$. In fact, given n, the chosen column C_i (i.e. $\delta = C_i$), and the power p, we can determine the value of k, the column index of the permutation that will be generated, such that $C_k = \delta^q$. The above results imply that, for the special case where the input string T represents a permutation of distinct characters, we can choose any column of A_s, the BWT sorted rotation matrix, as the BWT output, and still recover the data without error. This approach implies the possibility of selecting a column that could lead to more compression than the L array (last column) which is always chosen by the BWT.

6.2.2 Lexical permutation sorting algorithm

To apply the idea of permutation sorting for the more general case of text strings, we consider *multiset* permutations. A multiset is similar to a set, however, elements in a multiset can be repeated, which corresponds to the more normal situation of having strings over an alphabet where symbols from the alphabet can be used more than once in a string. A multiset permutation is an ordered arrangement of the elements in a multiset. For example, if $\chi = \{a, a, a, b, b, c\}$ is a multiset then $\pi = (a\ b\ b\ a\ c\ a)$ is a permutation of χ. Let $T = t_1 t_2 \ldots, t_n$ be a given text string, with symbols from an alphabet Σ. Then, we can consider T as a multiset permutation: $T = (t_1, t_2, \ldots, t_n)$. Suppose we apply cyclic rotations on the string T. Let $T^{(i)}(1 \leq i \leq n)$ denote the result obtained after left-cyclic shifts on T by $(i-1)$ positions. The *lexical index permutation* for T, denoted λ_T, is defined by the permutation $\lambda_T = \rho^{-1}$, where $\rho^{-1}(j) = i$ iff $T^{(i)}$ is, lexically, the j-th string among $\{T^{(h)}\}_{h=1}^{h=n}$, the n strings formed from the cyclic rotations of T.

Using the example multiset permutation above as T, that is, $T = (a\ b\ b\ a\ c\ a)$, we have $\rho^{-1} = \lambda_T = (2\ 5\ 4\ 3\ 6\ 1) = (1\ 2\ 5\ 6)(3\ 4)$, and $\rho = \lambda_Y^{-1} = (6\ 1\ 4\ 3\ 2\ 5) = (1\ 6\ 5\ 2)(3\ 4)$. Thus, the lexical index permutation of the string T is a sorting permutation, and essentially corresponds to the lexicographic sorting of the resulting strings from the left-cyclic rotations of T. We can thus observe the relationship with the BWT: λ_T^{-1}, the inverse of the lexical index permutation, basically maps T to F, the array of first characters.

Hence by considering strings as multisets, we can cater for the more general case of text strings where symbols in the alphabet can be repeated. The input T, and the BWT output L, each represents a different multiset permutation of the input. Arnavut and Magliveras (1997a,b) extended the idea of permutation sorting to multisets. They showed that if the symbols in T are taken from an integer alphabet, and $F = (1\ 2\ \ldots n)$ is the identity permutation after sorting T lexicographically, then $A_s[i, j] = F[A_s[i, j]]$.

For text strings, which are generally multisets rather than ordinary sets, Arnavut and Magliveras (1997a,b) proposed the *lexical permutation sorting algorithm* (LPSA). The LPSA works as follows: first transmit the F array (the sorted symbols in T), for instance, by simply sending the count of each symbol. Then, transmit λ_T, the lexical index permutation of T. Observe that for most practical cases, this will generally lead to worse compression performance than the BWT. The problem of applying LPSA to multisets is that, in general, the BWT (or the LPSA) on multisets is not always *surjective* over Σ^*. That is, they may be one-to-one but not onto, and hence, no longer bijective. Therefore, it is possible to have a multiset from the same symbol alphabet such that no input string can be mapped to it using any multiset permutation, so given only the multiset permutation of the input string, it may not always be possible to reconstruct the original string.

6.3 The extended BWT

Another way to generalize the Burrows-Wheeler Transform is to consider the ordering required at the sorting stage. This addresses the question of whether the BWT output is more useful given a specified sort-order for the symbols in the alphabet other than that imposed by the particular alphabet representation used, such as ASCII. Obviously, the lexicographic ordering used in the original BWT (and the LPSA) is just one example of a possible ordering of the alphabet. In an attempt to address this issue, Mantaci et al. (2005, 2007) proposed an extension of the BWT that uses an ordering different from the lexicographic ordering. The new ordering allows the BWT to be extended to handle a multiset of strings (rather than just a single string which is a multiset of symbols).

The extended BWT also has the nice property that it is surjective: that is, for any string in Σ^*, there will always be some input multiset of strings that will map to it via the extended BWT.

6.3.1 Sort order between strings

Before describing the new sort order between strings and the extended BWT, we introduce some more definitions. Given the symbol alphabet Σ, two strings $S_1, S_2 \in \Sigma^*$ are called *conjugate* if $S_1 = uv$ and $S_2 = vu$, for some strings $u, v \in \Sigma^*$. Notice that two conjugate strings will be cyclic rotations of each other. The string u is said to be *primitive* if $u = v^k$ iff $u = v$ and $k = 1$. For any given string u, there is a unique primitive string s, and an exponent k, such that $u = s^k$. For the string $u = s^k$, we use the notations: $s = \texttt{root}(u)$ and $k = \texttt{exp}(u)$. The string $u^\omega = uuuu\ldots$ is used to denote a string formed by infinitely iterating u. Clearly, two strings u^ω and v^ω are equal iff $\texttt{root}(u) = \texttt{root}(v)$. That is, u and v are powers of the same primitive string.

In Chapter 4, we introduced the $\prec$ relation as corresponding to the lexicographic ordering. That is, for $u = u_1 u_2 \ldots$, and $v = v_1 v_2 \ldots$, we have $u \prec v$ iff there exists some index j, such that $u_i = v_i, \forall i = 1, 2, \ldots, j$, and $u_{j+1} < v_{j+1}$.

Using the above notations, Mantaci et al. introduced the following relation between strings $u, v \in \Sigma^*$:

$$u \preceq_\omega v \iff \begin{cases} \mathtt{exp}(u) \le \mathtt{exp}(v) & \text{if } \mathtt{root}(u) = \mathtt{root}(v) \\ u^\omega \prec v^\omega & \text{otherwise} \end{cases}$$

We can observe that the relation $u \preceq_\omega v$ enforces a total order between u and v. Clearly, $u \preceq_\omega v$ is different from the lexicographic ordering $u \prec v$ in general. For instance, with $u = \mathtt{ab}$ and $v = \mathtt{aba}$, we have $u \prec v$, but $v \preceq_\omega u$. The periodicity lemma (Smyth, 2003) shows that, in practice, when $\mathbf{u} \neq \mathbf{v}$, we can decide if $u \preceq_\omega v$ by considering only the $\mathtt{pref}_k(u)$ and $\mathtt{pref}_k(v)$, the respective k-length prefix of u^ω and v^ω, where $k = |u| + |v| - \gcd(|u|, |v|)$. That is,

$$u \preceq_\omega v \iff \mathtt{pref}_k(u) \prec \mathtt{pref}_k(v)$$

Or equivalently, using the notation of Section 4.2:

$$u \preceq_\omega v \iff u^\omega \prec_k v^\omega$$

Using the previous example $u = \mathtt{ab}$ and $v = \mathtt{aba}$, we have $k = 2 + 3 - \gcd(2,3) = 4$. Thus, we can differentiate between $u^\omega = \mathtt{abababab}\ldots$ and $v^\omega = \mathtt{abaabaaba}\ldots$ by considering only their first 4 symbols. Thus we have $v \preceq_\omega u$ in this case.

6.3.2 Performing the extended BWT

Based on the above order relation, Mantaci et al. (2005, 2007) proposed an extension of the BWT to a multiset of primitive strings. When it is required, each string can be made primitive by simply appending an end of string symbol. Let $T = \{S_1, S_2, \ldots S_s\}$ be a multiset of s primitive strings. The extended transformation is performed on T using the following steps:

1. Compute the conjugates of each element of T. Form an array of conjugates A, whereby each element in A corresponds to exactly one of the conjugates computed. Notice that here the rows do not necessarily have the same number of columns. We can pad the rows so that they all have the same number of columns, without affecting the results.
2. Sort A, the array of conjugates according to the new order relation. Let $A_s = w_1, w_2, \ldots, w_m$ be the list of conjugates in sorted order. That is, for $1 \le i < j \le m$, $w_i \preceq_\omega w_j$.
3. Let $a = \{a_1, a_2, \ldots, a_s\}$ be the set of indexes representing the respective positions in A_s of the original strings in T. That is, a_i is the position of S_i in A_s.
4. Let L be the array of last characters of the elements in A_s. That is, for $1 \le i \le m$, $L[i] = w_i[|w_i|]$, the last symbol in the string w_i. Similarly, we define F, such that $F[i] = w_i[1]$, the first symbol in string w_i.
5. The output of the extended transformation is the pair (L, a).

To make the similarity with computing the BWT clearer, we have deliberately modified the description given by Mantaci et al. by using notation and terminology similar to the usual Burrows-Wheeler Transform. The BWT is a special case of the extended transformation, where $s = 1$; that is, when we have only one single string in T. Table 6.2 shows the results of applying the extended BWT to an example multiset of strings: $T = \{S_1, S_2, S_3, S_4\} = \{\mathtt{ab}, \mathtt{aba}, \mathtt{cbac}, \mathtt{bac}\}$. We have included the F and L arrays, the permutation π that maps F to L, and its inverse. From the table, the results of the extended BWT will be:

$(L, a) = (\mathtt{babbbaaccaca}, \{3, 2, 11, 8\})$.

Conjugates, A	Index A_s		F	L	π	π^{-1}
ab	1	aab	a	b	2	6
ba	2	aba	a	a	6	1
aba	3	ab	a	b	7	7
baa	4	acb	a	b	10	8
aab	5	accb	a	b	12	9
cbac	6	baa	b	a	1	2
bacc	7	ba	b	a	3	3
accb	8	bac	b	c	4	10
ccba	9	bacc	b	c	5	11
bac	10	cba	c	a	8	4
acb	11	cbac	c	c	9	12
cba	12	ccba	c	a	11	5

Table 6.2. Example transformation using the extended BWT on a sample multiset of strings, $T = \{\mathtt{ab}, \mathtt{aba}, \mathtt{cbac}, \mathtt{bac}\}$

For comparison, Table 6.3 shows the corresponding results using the original BWT on the same multiset of strings (assuming the individual strings are concatenated, i.e. $T = S_1 * S_2 * S_3 * S_4 = \mathtt{ababacbacbac}$). Comparing Tables 6.2 and 6.3 we can see that the extended BWT will require less time and space to perform the required sorting, since each conjugate will be shorter than any given concatenated rotated sequence.

6.3.3 Inverting the transform

The extended BWT is reversible; as with the forward transformation, the inversion procedure closely follows that of the original BWT. Let $n = |T| = |L|$ be the total number of symbols in the multiset T. Two key observations used in inverting the BWT can be used in performing the required inversion (with slight modifications):

- For each $i, 1 \leq i \leq n$, if $i \notin a$, then $F[i]$ succeeds $L[i]$ in one of the strings in T.

A	Index A_s		F	L	π	$\pi^{-1} = V$
ababacbacbac	1	ababacbacbac	a	c	6	10
babacbacbaca	2	abacbacbacab	a	b	9	6
abacbacbacab	3	acababacbacb	a	b	10	7
bacbacbacaba	4	acbacababacb	a	b	11	8
acbacbacabab	5	acbacbacabab	a	b	12	9
cbacbacababa	6	babacbacbaca	b	a	2	1
bacbacababac	7	bacababacbac	b	c	3	11
acbacababacb	8	bacbacababac	b	c	4	12
cbacababacba	9	bacbacbacaba	b	a	5	2
bacababacbac	10	cababacbacba	c	a	1	3
acababacbacb	11	cbacababacba	c	a	7	4
cababacbacba	12	cbacbacababa	c	a	8	5

Table 6.3. Using the original BWT on the sample multiset of strings, $T =$ {ab, aba, cbac, bac} used in Table 6.2, assuming the strings are concatenated to one string: $T =$ ababacbacbac

- The order of appearance of a particular symbol from the alphabet is the same in both F and L. That is, the j-th instance of symbol σ in L corresponds to the j-th instance of σ in F.

The following steps can be used to perform the reverse transformation:

1. Sort the elements in L, the output of the transform, to obtain F, the array of first characters.
2. Define a permutation π on $\{1, 2, \ldots, n\}$ that maps F to L, computed as follows: $\pi(i) = j$ if $F[i]$ and $L[j]$ refer to the same symbol in T. Thus, π^{-1} is analogous to the BWT transformation vector V that maps L to F.
3. Decompose the permutation π into disjoint cycles: $\pi = \pi_1 \pi_2 \ldots \pi_k$. Each cycle π_i corresponds to a conjugacy class of a component string in the multiset T. Since the strings in T are primitive, then for each $i, 1 \leq i \leq k$, there exists a unique index that is moved by π_i. Each index in a, the set of starting indexes, appears in one and only one disjoint cycle.
4. Let a_i be an index such that $a_i \in a$ and $a_i \in \pi_i$. Then, for each $i, 1 \leq i \leq s$, S_i, the i-th string in T is reconstructed as follows:

$$S_i = F[a_i] * F[\pi(a_i)] * F[\pi^2(a_i)] * \ldots * F[\pi^{l_i}(a_i)]$$

where $l_i = |\pi_i|$, the length of the disjoint cycle π_i.

Continuing with the previous example, we have $F =$ aaaaabbbbccc and $L =$ babbbaaccaca, giving the following mapping:

$$\pi = \begin{pmatrix} 1\ 2\ 3\ 4\ 5\ 6\ 7\ 8\ 9\ 10\ 11\ 12 \\ 2\ 6\ 7\ 10\ 12\ 1\ 3\ 4\ 5\ 8\ 9\ 11 \end{pmatrix}$$

with

$$\pi^{-1} = \begin{pmatrix} 1\ 2\ 3\ 4\ 5\ 6\ 7\ 8\ 9\ 10\ 11\ 12 \\ 6\ 1\ 7\ 8\ 9\ 2\ 3\ 10\ 11\ 4\ 12\ 5 \end{pmatrix}$$

These can be decomposed into their respective disjoint cycles:

$$\pi = (1\ 2\ 6)(3\ 7)(4\ 10\ 8)(5\ 12\ 11\ 9)$$

$$\pi^{-1} = (1\ 6\ 2)(3\ 7)(4\ 8\ 10)(5\ 9\ 11\ 12).$$

Based on the permutations, we can recover the original strings as follows:

$$
\begin{aligned}
a_1 &= 3; S_1 = F[3] * F[7] = && \text{ab} \\
a_2 &= 2; S_2 = F[2] * F[6] * F[1] = && \text{aba} \\
a_3 &= 11; S_3 = F[11] * F[12] * F[5] * F[9] = && \text{cbac} \\
a_4 &= 8; S_4 = F[8] * F[4] * F[10] = && \text{bac}
\end{aligned}
$$

Alternatively, we could use $\rho = \pi^{-1}$, and then reconstruct the strings using L:

$$S_i = L[\rho^{l_i}(a_i)] * L[\rho^{l_i - 1}(a_i)] * \ldots * L[\rho^2(a_i)] * L[\rho(a_i)]L[a_i]$$

where $l_i = |\rho_i|$, the length of the cycle ρ_i. Thus, just as with the original BWT, we can use L and π^{-1} to reconstruct the original strings, starting with the last symbol, and ending at the first.

Mantaci et al. showed that, for any given string $S \in \Sigma^*$, there must exist some multiset of primitive strings, T, and a set of indexes a, such that applying the extended BWT on T will produce the result (S, a). That is, any given string has some input multiset of strings that maps to it via the extended BWT. Thus the extended BWT is one-to-one and onto, and hence bijective. For example, the string $S = $ bccaaab has no corresponding string T that maps to it via the BWT. However, with the extended BWT, we can see that $T = \{$ab, abcac$\}$ maps to S. This important distinction from the original BWT provides a link with a known theorem in string combinatorics, due to Gessel and Reutenauer (1993): given a symbol alphabet Σ, there exists a bijection between Σ^* and the family of multisets of conjugacy classes of primitive strings in Σ^*.

In practical experiments, Mantaci et al. showed that when the multiset of strings corresponds to the blocks used in BWT-based block-sorting, the extended BWT performed better than the usual block-sorting using the same size of blocks. When the block size is set to be the same as the size of the original sequence, both the BWT and extended BWT produced the same result. There is a potentially simpler approach to compressing a multiset of strings, though. One can simply concatenate them, and then use the BWT to compress the concatenated sequence. The length of each component string can then be transmitted to the decoder to determine the beginning and end of each component. The major advantage of the extended BWT appears to be in its use of a smaller memory footprint, and potentially faster sorting stage on average, since the complete BWT rotation matrices will not be needed. However, in the worst case, the complexity will still be quadratic with respect to the total number of symbols in the multiset of strings.

6.4 Sort-based context similarity measurement

The sorting stage of the BWT orders the cyclic rotations such that symbols with a similar forward context are brought closer in the BWT output. This essentially provides a form of context sorting for the input symbols, and is a fundamental step in the Burrows-Wheeler Transform. One major criticism of the BWT is its *offline* nature, requiring all the data to be available before the transformation can be performed. In an independent, but very closely related work, Yokoo (1996, 1997) proposed a sort-based context similarity measurement suitable for use in data compression. The method is adaptive and *online*, and performs the required context sorting as each symbol is observed. Given its use of context sorting as a primary mechanism in the compression process, this method is sometimes viewed as an online variant of the Burrows-Wheeler Transform. In this section we will have a closer look at Yokoo's original method, its later improvements, and their relationship with the BWT.

6.4.1 Context similarity measurement and ranking

The similarity of two contexts is measured simply by the longest common suffix between the contexts. If we consider the contexts in reversed order, this similarity measurement becomes the same as the LCP between the reversed contexts. Just as we defined order-k contexts, we can equally define the context similarity measure based on the lexicographic order of the first k symbols, where the symbols are read in reverse order.

Yokoo (1996, 1997) described a method to use the context similarity measurement in lossless compression. The idea is very closely related to symbol-wise ranking methods, whereby for each context the encoder maintains a list of candidate symbols, with each symbol assigned some rank, based mainly on the likelihood of the symbol being observed in the given context. Using the above similarity measure, and given previously observed contexts, we can sort the contexts in reverse-lexicographic order.[2] Using this ordering, a rank can be assigned to the symbol following each given context. Based on these ranks, we can encode each incoming symbol once it is observed (i.e. one symbol at a time, without the need to observe all the symbols as in BWT). When the next symbol is observed, its corresponding rank is written to the output stream for subsequent entropy encoding. For a novel symbol which has not yet been observed in the existing contexts, the rank is assigned $(1 + x)$, where x is the

---

[2] Recall that our definition of contexts in Chapter 5 already embodies prefix reversal.

number of distinct symbols so far observed. This rank and the raw symbol are then written to the output stream.

Figure 6.6 shows an example using the sequence mississippi. The figure shows the list of contexts (the prefixes) and the sorted contexts in reverse-lexicographic order. The similarity measurement (and hence, the ranking) in the table is based on similarity with respect to the current context, which corresponds to the entire string (read in reverse order). In this particular case the first three contexts each have the length of 1 as the longest common suffix with mississippi, hence their similarity measurement is 1. After the LCP criteria on the reversed prefixes, we use the simple alphabetical listing to break possible ties, and hence define a total order on the contexts. The final ranks for each symbol are given in the rightmost column in Figure 6.6b.

Context	Symbol
ϵ	m
m	i
mi	s
mis	s
miss	i
missi	s
missis	s
mississ	i
mississi	p
mississip	p
mississipp	i
mississippi	σ

(a)

Similarity	Context	Symbol	Rank
	mississippi	σ	
1	mi	s	1
	missi	s	
	mississi	p	2
0	ϵ	m	3
	m	i	4
	mississip	p	
	mississipp	i	
	mis	s	
	missis	s	
	miss	i	
	mississ	i	

(b)

Fig. 6.6. Context similarity and ranking using an example string $T =$ mississippi: (a) context list; (b) sorted contexts with similarity value and rank

Consider what happens when we observe the new symbol σ. To encode σ, we check the ranks. If σ is one of the four symbols so far observed (that is, $\sigma \in \{m,i,p,s\}$), the corresponding rank is transmitted. For example, if $\sigma = m$, the number 3 is transmitted. However, if $\sigma \notin \{m,i,p,s\}$ (for example $\sigma = e$), then the symbol is novel, so the *virtual rank* (5 in this case) is transmitted, followed by the raw novel symbol e. Figure 6.7 shows how the similarity measurement and the ranks change after observing two instances of the next symbol, one for when the next symbol has previously been observed, and the other for when the next symbol is novel. Notice that after observing a novel symbol, the context sorting is not affected by the current context, but rather depends on the lexicographic order of the symbols.

6.4.2 The prefix list data structure

In the original implementation of the sort-based context similarity method (Yokoo, 1997), the context-symbol pairs were maintained in reverse lexicographic order using a binary search tree. This required the use of doubly-linked lists to connect the nodes in the tree, which made it easier to compute the ranks. The idea was motivated by the method initially proposed in Bell (1986) for implementing LZ-based compression, by storing strings in lexical order. However, the complexity of the scheme was still relatively high, requiring time in $O(k^2 \log |\Sigma|)$ for inserting a context-symbol pair in the tree, for an order-k context similarity, assuming a balanced tree. Thus, the method could be implemented only for limited-order contexts (for example, with k limited to 8).

In a later work, Yokoo (1999) proposed the *prefix list* as a data structure to maintain all prefixes of a given string in reverse-lexicographically sorted order. Let T^i and T^j be two adjacent suffixes in the prefix list. T_j is called an *immediate predecessor* of T^i if T^j immediately follows T^i in the prefix list. Conversely, T^j is called an *immediate successor* of T^i.

The prefix list is a doubly-linked list, whereby each node in the list contains an integer index and three pointers, *succ, pred,* and *next*. Every prefix in the string is represented by one node in the prefix list. If a node, say P, contains the i-th prefix, $T^i = T[1 \ldots i]$, then the integer index $P.index$ will be the position index i. The pointers $P.succ$ and $P.pred$ respectively point to the immediate successor and immediate predecessor nodes in the list. The pointer $P.next$ points to the next prefix in the original string, starting from the current prefix. That is, at the node for T^i, $P.next$ will point to the node for prefix T^{i+1}. For the original string $T = T^n$, the pointer $P.next$ is NULL. The list head, the empty string T^0, is denoted by a special symbol H. The end of the list (list tail) is indicated by another special symbol E.

Table 6.4 shows the list of prefixes for $T = \mathtt{mississippi}$, sorted in reverse lexicographic order. Observe the difference from the result in Figure 6.6, where the prefixes were arranged with respect to their similarity to the current context. Figure 6.8a shows a representation of the notation described above for

Similarity	Context	Symbol	Rank
	mississippis	σ	
2	mis	s	1
	missis	s	
1	miss	i	2
	mississ	i	
0	ϵ	m	3
	mi	s	
	mississippi	s	
	missi	s	
	mississi	p	4
	m	i	
	mississip	p	
	mississipp	i	

(a)

Similarity	Context	Symbol	Rank
	mississippie	σ	
0	ϵ	m	1
	mi	s	2
	mississippi	e	3
	missi	s	
	mississi	p	4
	m	i	5
	mississip	p	
	mississipp	i	
	mis	s	
	missis	s	
	miss	i	
	mississ	i	

(b)

Fig. 6.7. Context similarity and ranking for example string $T =$ mississippi, for two cases of the next symbol: (a) next symbol $\sigma =$ s has been observed previously; (b) next symbol $\sigma =$ e is novel, and has not been observed so far in the string

the prefix list, while Figure 6.8b shows an example prefix list for the sequence $T =$ mississippi. The prefix list can be constructed incrementally as we observe the symbols in T. Suppose we have inserted $T^0, T^1, \ldots, T^i$, the prefixes at the initial segment of the input string (T^0 is the empty prefix). If the incoming symbol t_{i+1} is lexicographically smaller than all symbols seen so far, then the prefix T^{i+1} should be inserted just to the right of the list head, H. Conversely, if t_{i+1} is lexicographically greater than all symbols seen so far, then T^{i+1} should be inserted just to the left of the list tail E. Otherwise, if the symbol t_{i+1} does not occur in the prefix $T[1 \ldots i]$, then we must have some unique position in the prefix tree corresponding to some node Q, such that:

$$T[Q.index] \prec t_{i+1} \prec T[Q.succ.index].$$

Thus, the new node for T^{i+1} should be inserted between the nodes pointed to by Q and $Q.succ$.

Sort ID	Sorted prefixes	Original position	Following symbol
0	ϵ	0	m
1	mi	2	s
2	mississippi	11	$\sigma =?$
3	missi	5	s
4	mississi	8	p
5	m	1	i
6	mississip	9	p
7	mississipp	10	i
8	mis	3	s
9	missis	6	s
10	miss	4	i
11	mississ	7	i

Table 6.4. Sorted prefixes for the string $T =$ mississippi

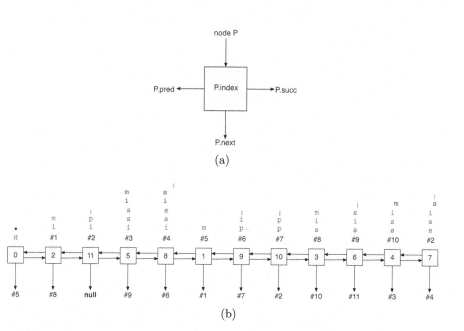

Fig. 6.8. The prefix list data structure: (a) basic structure of a node in the prefix list; (b) prefix list for the sample string $T =$ mississippi

The case where t_{i+1} has already appeared in $T[1 \ldots i]$ involves more work, since the inequalities above may turn into equalities. However, notice that since the list is already in sorted order, we need to compare only the incoming symbol t_{i+1} with the last symbol of the existing prefixes. In this case, the immediate successor or predecessor of T^{i+1} has the same last symbol as T^{i+1}, namely t_{i+1}. Let T^{j+1} be the immediate predecessor of T^{i+1}. If T^{j+1} has the same last symbol as T^{i+1}, (that is $t_{j+1} = t_{i+1}, 0 \le j < i$), then $T^j = T[1 \ldots j]$ must precede $T^i = T[1 \ldots i]$ in the prefix list. Thus, in moving from the current node towards H, the head of the list, the node representing T^j should be the first node with the same following symbol t_{j+1} as t_{i+1}. This can be tested by following the *next* pointer. Similarly, let T^{j+1} be the immediate successor of T^{i+1}. If the last symbol t_{j+1} of T^{j+1} is the same as t_{i+1} (the last symbol of T^{i+1}), then in moving from the current node toward the list tail E, the node representing T^j should be the first node such that $t_{j+1} = t_{i+1}$. Therefore, starting from the node for the current prefix T^i, we need to search forward and backward, looking for the node T^j, while comparing the last symbols t_{j+1} with the incoming t_{i+1}. Once we find the node representing T^j we can follow the *next* pointer to reach the node to get T^{j+1}. Then, the new node (for T^{i+1}) should be inserted adjacent to the node representing T^{j+1}.

Using the prefix list, it is simple to compute the symbol ranks required in compression with context-based similarity measurement. On average, the prefix list can be constructed in linear time for Markov sequences (Yokoo, 1999), however, the worst case complexity for general sequences could be quadratic in the length of the string.

6.4.3 Relationship with the Burrows-Wheeler Transform

The first connection between the BWT and the sort-based context similarity approach is clearly the fact that both methods use sorted contexts. Earlier, it was noted that after a novel symbol is observed, the context sorting result no longer depends on the current context, but rather on the lexicographic order of the symbols. This provides a simple link with the BWT: if we append the special end of sequence symbol $ to the string being compressed, the list of symbols obtained after context similarity sorting corresponds exactly to the BWT output (L-array) when the input is the reversed string. The use of ranks as a primary step in Yokoo's approach also connects the method with the second stage of the BWT, where the BWT output is passed though the LGT (local to global transformation) stage to produce ranks, which are subsequently coded using entropy coding, or some integer codes.

A more direct relationship with the BWT can be established using the prefix list data structure. Using the previous notation for the prefix tree, the BWT can be realized using the procedure shown in Algorithm 6.3. Consider the example with $T = \texttt{mississippi\$}$. The corresponding reversed string will be $\hat{T} = \texttt{reverse}(T) = \texttt{\$ippississim}$. Applying the BWT on this reversed string will produce the sorted suffixes and the final BWT output array shown in Table 6.5.

COMPUTE-BWT-FROM-PREFIX-LIST(T, H, E)
  $P \leftarrow H$
  $i \leftarrow 1$
  while $P \neq E$ **do**
    if $P.next = $ NULL, **then**
      $L[i] \leftarrow \$$
    else
      $L[i] = T[P.next.index]$
    end if
    $P \leftarrow P.succ$
    $i \leftarrow i + 1$
  end while

Algorithm 6.3: Algorithm to compute the BWT from a prefix list

Sort ID	Sorted suffixes	Original position	BWT output, L
0	$\$\ldots$	0	m
1	im$\ldots$	10	s
2	ip$\ldots$	1	$\$$
3	issim$\ldots$	7	s
4	issis$\ldots$	4	p
5	m$\$\ldots$	11	i
6	pi$\ldots$	3	p
7	pp$\ldots$	2	i
8	sim$\ldots$	9	s
9	sis$\ldots$	6	s
10	ssim$\ldots$	8	i
11	ssis$\ldots$	5	i

Table 6.5. BWT sorted rotation matrix and L-array for $\hat{T}$ = reverse(mississippi$) = $ippississim

Using the above algorithm on the example in Figure 6.8, we obtain the following first few results:

$L[1] = T[\#5.index] = T[1] = $ m;
$L[2] = T[\#8.index] = T[3] = $ s;
$L[3] = \$$, since $T[\#1.succ.next] = $ NULL;
$L[4] = T[\#9.index] = T[6] = $ s; etc.

Thus, the final result will be $L = \texttt{ms\$spipissii}$, which is exactly the BWT output when the input string is $\texttt{reverse}(T) = \texttt{\$ippississim}$.

Yokoo (1997, 1999) also described the strong relationship between the sort-based similarity method and LZ-family of compression algorithms. This could be seen as another indirect link between the BWT and the LZ-family. Also, the phrase sorting and ranking steps of the ACB compression scheme (a variant of the LZ-family) makes the ACB compression scheme (Salomon, 2004) another closely related method to the BWT.

6.4.4 Performance of the prefix list

The compression performance on the Calgary corpus[3] as reported in Yokoo (1997) using the Method C encoding scheme is shown in Table 6.6. The other methods given for comparison are BZIP and SZIP (two of the best implementations of BWT-based compression), GZIP (the widely used LZ-based gzip utility with default settings), and "PPMC" (one of the better implementations of PPM). The parameters indicated in the table for each method are the default values which give good speed and compression performance for each method.

The results for Yokoo's prefix list method are worse than standard BWT results (BZIP and SZIP), but for the natural language text files it is generally better than GZIP. Given the online nature of the context-based sort similarity measurement approach, the compression performance is reasonable. The results could be further improved by passing the ranks to an MTF algorithm, or some other LGT schemes.

In terms of encoding time, Yokoo (1997) reports that compression using only order-k context sorting (with $k = 8$) was about 20 times slower than GZIP. Using the prefix data structure, the time required was reduced ten-fold (Yokoo, 1999).

6.5 Word-based compression

So far we have described the BWT with an input string that is considered to be made up of tokens, where the tokens are simply individual characters or symbols, typically from a small alphabet. Like most other data compression schemes, the BWT can also be applied when the tokens are a sequence of symbols (for example, words in a language), rather than the individual characters. With word-based approaches we have the immediate problem of very large alphabets, and hence efficiency considerations in terms of both space

---

[3] The corpus and evaluations on a number of compression methods are available from http://corpus.canterbury.ac.nz/. Note that Yokoo (1997) did not report results for two of the files in the corpus, and hence Table 6.6 shows only 12 of the 14 files in the corpus.

Method:	BZIP	GZIP	PPMC	SZIP	YOKOO	YOKOO
Parameter:	-6	-d	-896		C_8	C_∞
bib	1.95	2.52	2.12	1.98	2.53	2.40
book1	2.49	3.26	2.52	2.36	2.83	2.78
book2	2.06	2.71	2.28	2.03	2.53	2.44
news	2.51	3.07	2.77	2.50	3.00	2.87
paper1	2.46	2.79	2.48	2.50	2.84	2.76
paper2	2.42	2.90	2.46	2.44	2.81	2.75
progc	2.50	2.68	2.49	2.52	2.89	2.81
progl	1.72	1.82	1.87	1.75	2.30	2.12
progp	1.71	1.82	1.82	1.82	2.34	2.13
Average (text files)	2.20	2.62	2.31	2.21	2.67	2.56
geo	4.48	5.35	5.01	4.29	6.18	6.07
obj1	3.87	3.84	3.68	3.78	4.88	4.74
obj2	2.46	2.65	2.59	2.48	3.17	2.96
Average (all files)	2.55	2.95	2.67	2.54	3.19	3.07

Table 6.6. Comparative compression performance using sort-based context similarity measurement

and time become important. Word-based compression using the BWT can be viewed as another variation of the general theme of Burrows and Wheeler, and has been studied in detail in Isal and Moffat (2001a,b) and Isal et al. (2002). We begin this section by first reviewing the general concept of word-based compression, and then we explain how word-based BWT fits into the general framework.

6.5.1 General word-based compression

The first problem in word-based compression schemes is how to define what is a *word* and what is not. This is required when parsing the input, before applying the particular compression scheme. For text strings, such as English text, we can use natural words in the language, and hence use natural delimiters such as the space character to indicate the end of a word. However, this overlooks other special symbols and punctuation marks. A simple approach to the problem is to simply divide up the input into bigrams, trigrams, or general q-grams, where $q = 2, 3, \ldots$, and then assume that each q-gram is a word. Using $q = 1$ corresponds to the usual case of treating each character or symbol as the elementary token. Of course, the q-gram approach may not be able to exploit the structure and dependencies between words in the sequence, for instance if the input sequence is from an English text. Another way to handle the problem is to use two dictionaries, one for alphanumeric words, and a second dictionary for non-alphanumeric symbols, such as punctuation and the space character. With this scheme, for any given input, the parsed sequence will thus contain a strict alternation of words from the two dictionaries. A third approach is to use one dictionary and a pre-specified delimiter, and thus consider any combination of symbols between two consecutive instances of the delimiter to be a word. This results in an immediate saving, as the delimiter need not be transmitted to the decoder, since the decoder already knows the delimiter, and hence can re-construct the sequence. When the delimiter is the *space* character, this corresponds to the *spaceless word model* proposed in de Moura et al. (2000). For non-text data such as images, or genomic sequences, it is not so clear how the sequence should be split into words. For images for instance, one can consider the most frequently used symbols as the delimiter. Thus, if the sequence to be compressed represents prediction errors for an image, the symbol "0" represents a good choice.

As an example, suppose we are given the following input text (which uses "_" as the space symbol):

$$\texttt{this\_one,\_this\_one,\_is\_the\_one}$$

The alternating dictionary approach will produce the following (using "|" to separate entries):

Word list: `this|one|this|one|is|the|one`
Non-word list: `_|,_|_|,_|_|_|`

The *q*-gram approach (using 2-grams) will produce the parsing:

`th|is|_o|ne|,_|th|is|_o|ne|,_|is|_t|he|_o|ne`

The spaceless word model will give :

`this|one,|this|one,|is|the|one|`

After initial parsing into words, the next issue is how to represent the dictionary and the parsed sequence. One method is to use a two-pass approach using an *explicit dictionary*. Here, unique items in the lists are given integer numbers, and these numbers are then used to replace the items in the list. The resulting list of integers is then coded using an entropy encoder, and transmitted to the decoder. For the decoder to be able to recover the transmitted data, the list of unique items (the dictionary) must also be transmitted to the decoder. For the alternating dictionary approach, for instance, we must transmit two dictionaries, and two coded integer lists. For the example we would need to transmit the word list : {`this|one|is|the`} with the corresponding numbers $\{1, 2, 3, 4\}$, and the parsed word list: $\langle 1, 2, 1, 2, 3, 4, 2 \rangle$. Similarly, for the non-word list, the dictionary will be: {`_|,_`}, with corresponding numbers $\{1, 2\}$, and the parsed non-word list: $\langle 1, 2, 1, 2, 1, 1 \rangle$.

Although using explicit dictionaries is simple to understand and implement, the two pass requirement may make it less attractive for some applications. More importantly, the overhead of the dictionary may have a significant impact on the achievable compression, especially for short sequences, where most of the words will occur only a few times. With an *implicit dictionary*, the dictionary is constructed adaptively as the text is being parsed and then embedded into the parsed sequence without the need for explicit transmission of the dictionary. In this case the first occurrence of each word (sequence of two or more symbols) will be coded using a sequence of its constituent symbols in order. Subsequent occurrences are then coded as an integer number. For an original symbol alphabet $\Sigma = \{\sigma_1, \sigma_2, \ldots, \sigma_{|\Sigma|}\}$, the dictionary entries are numbered starting from $|\Sigma| + 1$, so that all the alphabet symbols are available regardless of what else is in the dictionary. For English text and assuming an alphabet of 8-bit symbols (numbered 0 to 255), the dictionary elements will be given integer numbers starting from 256.

Using the above scheme on the running example,

"this_one,_this_one,_is_the_one"

the three parsing strategies described above will produce the following results:

The alternating dictionary approach will produce the following, where words are spelled out the first time they occur, and a space is used to mark the end of a new word:

Word list: t|h|i|s|_|o|n|e|_|256|257|i|s|_|t|h|e|_|257
Non-word list: _|_,|255|256|255|255|

Using 2-grams we get the following (where 256 is allocated to the first pair, th, 257 to the second pair, is, and so on):

t|h|i|s|_|o|n|e|,|_|256|257|258|259|260|257|_|t|h|e|258|259

The spaceless word model produces the following (where a new word is delimited by a space, so 256 is allocated to this, 257 to one, 258 to is and so on):

t|h|i|s|_|o|n|e|,|_|256|257|i|s|_|t|h|e|_|257|

6.5.2 Word-based Burrows-Wheeler Transform

After the parsing stage, the resulting parsed sequence(s) can be used as an input to any standard compression scheme, such as the LZ or PPM families. For BWT-based compression schemes, after the parsing stage the resulting sequence(s) of integer codes could be passed directly to the BWT compression pipeline. This means that, in principle, for word-based BWT, all that is needed is a kind of preprocessing scheme on the input, and then the BWT is applied on the resulting sequence(s). This view is depicted in Figure 6.9, where we have inserted a parsing stage between the input and the BWT first stage. Given that the MTF algorithm (Bentley et al., 1986) was originally described using words as the basic token, in principle, the MTF can equally be used with little modification for the word-based BWT.

Practical implementation, however, could become an issue. Given the significantly expanded alphabet size in word-based schemes, the standard BWT

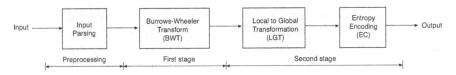

Fig. 6.9. The BWT pipeline, modified for word-based BWT

procedure may become difficult to use. For instance, the large alphabet may become a major problem for the sorting stage, as most algorithms assume that the alphabet is small compared to the input size. This may no longer hold for word-based schemes, and could result in more complications in both space and time requirements. In particular, methods based on suffix trees as the basic mechanism for sorting the suffixes must find mechanisms to combat the potential space problem. Similar problems can also arise for the MTF implementation, which again assumes that the alphabet is small, and this can be implemented using simple arrays.

Isal and Moffat performed detailed studies on word-based BWT, and proposed various mechanisms for its implementation, especially for the BWT-second stage. They proposed a variant of the MTF that uses a forest of search trees, specifically, multiple splay search trees (which was also suggested in the original paper on MTF (Bentley et al., 1986)). Each tree in the forest contains information about a range of current MTF rank values, such that the first tree contains records about the most recently accessed items, the second tree contains records about the second most recently accessed items, and so on. The ordering of items within a given tree depends on both the integer value that is being represented, and also on the standard MTF list. The challenge is how items are moved from one tree to the other, and how the exact rank of each item is computed. Details on various methods for moving items between the trees, and for getting (moving) items to (off) the head of the list are discussed in Isal et al. (2002). Isal et al. also considered improvements on the entropy coding stage when large alphabets are involved, as is the case in word-based BWT. In particular, they proposed modifications of arithmetic coding to provide methods for coding with large alphabets, which can be used for word-based compression schemes.

An approach related to word-based BWT is the word-based FM index (WFM) (Ferragina, 2007), which is a combination of the BWT-based FM index (see Chapters 7 and 8), and a byte-aligned Huffman coding (Navarro et al., 2000; de Moura et al., 2000). One major advantage here is that since queries are usually word-oriented, using a word-based FM index avoids the need for later post-processing. Furthermore, only a few (3 or 4) random accesses are required, independent of the query word, since the maximum codeword length is typically small.

6.6 Further reading

The Burrows-Wheeler Transform has generated a lot of interest since its initial publication in 1994, perhaps based on its simplicity, and the existence of efficient algorithms for its computation. There have been several variations on the original theme by Burrows and Wheeler. Early attempts at generalizing the BWT were made by Arnavut and Magliveras (Arnavut and Magliveras, 1997a; Arnavut, 2002) on the choice of the particular column to use after the sorting, and by Schindler (1997a,b) on the order of the contexts required for the sorting stage. The work by Schindler has been discussed in detail by Chan and Nong (2005) and Nong and Zhang (2007b). An approach similar to the permutation-based approach adopted by Arnavut and Magliveras (1997a,b) was followed in more recent work by Mantaci et al. (2005, 2007), where they extended the BWT to a multiset of strings. Their approach resulted in a transformation of multistrings that is bijective, unlike the original BWT. There is a growing body of work in this direction, and the extended BWT provides a strong link between the BWT and other known theorems and structures in string combinatorics, such as the relationship between the BWT and Sturmian strings (Mantaci et al., 2003), and the connection between the BWT and combinatorics of multiset permutations (Gessel and Reutenauer, 1993; Crochemore et al., 2005). Multiset permutations are discussed in Knuth (1973). The idea of changing the sort ordering has been used in constructing suffix arrays that sort using ordering relations different from the lexicographic order (Franek and Smyth, 2006). This provides another avenue to investigate the performance of BWT in compression and other applications, with alternative sort orderings.

Yokoo's context-based similarity measurement (Yokoo, 1997) was another early work that is very closely related to the block-sorting nature of the BWT. The prefix list data structure was proposed in Yokoo (1999), as an efficient data structure for implementing the context-based similarity measurement approach. Yokoo reported that using the prefix list resulted in a ten-fold improvement in the efficiency of sort-based context-based sort similarity measurement. The ACB (Associative Coder of Buyonoski) is described in Salomon (2004) and Fenwick (2003b). The sorting stages used by the ACB make it a very close cousin of the BWT.

Moffat and his group (Isal and Moffat, 2001a,b; Isal et al., 2002) proposed the word-based BWT, as a way to use the BWT on natural text. In Wirth (2001) and Wirth and Moffat (2001) they also studied segmentation methods for coding the BWT output, without the need for MTF. The word-based approach can be viewed as a preprocessing scheme on the input string before the application of the BWT. Abel and Teahan (2005) present a detailed study on various preprocessing schemes that can be applied before actual compression, including results on BWT performance after preprocessing. Grabowski (1999) also described initial ideas on preprocessing, by converting capital letters to small letters, and adding a flag, as a way to improve BWT compression.

Kruse and Mukherjee (1998, 1999) studied the use of the STAR family of transformation schemes as an initial preprocessing stage for general compression algorithms, including the BWT. Related work reported in Awan et al. (2001), Awan and Mukherjee (2001), Sun et al. (2003a,b) and Mukherjee and Awan (2003) describes a "Length Index Preserving Transform" (LIPT), which uses a static English dictionary to boost compression.

Another recent variation of the Burrows-Wheeler Transform is the XBW (XBW transform) of Ferragina et al. (2005b, 2006c). While the BWT works on strings, the XBW applies to labeled trees, after appropriate linearization. Using path-label sorting and grouping, the XBW transforms a labeled tree into two components; the first captures the structural properties of the tree, and the second captures the tree labels. After path linearization, the XBW basically sorts the nodes in the tree based on their node labels. From one view point, the XBW provides a compressed representation of the suffix tree, and provides facilities for supporting different types of navigational, visualization, and subpath queries on the tree.

7

Exact and approximate pattern matching

A fundamental operation with strings is determining whether a *pattern* of characters or symbols occurs as a *substring* in a larger string called the *text*, or as an approximate *subsequence* in the text. This problem has been investigated since the early 1960s, not only for its theoretical importance in computer science but because it has many applications in information processing and biological sciences. In computer science, string pattern matching algorithms are used in database search and retrieval, text processing and editing, lexical analysis of computer programs, data compression, cryptography and other applications. In recent years, string matching algorithms have been used as powerful tools in the study of genomics and proteomics, in finding genes and regulatory motifs, and in comparative genomics, gene expression analysis and molecular evolutionary theory.

As noted in Chapter 1, pattern matching and data compression are intimately related, and at the same time they can work against each other. The process of compression removes redundancies in a text by replacing data with smaller and irregular bit patterns, which unfortunately also destroys the natural structure of the text and makes it harder to search for patterns and retrieve information.

A simple solution is a *decompress-then-search* approach that involves restoring the original data before a search is performed with a pattern matching algorithm. The decompression process, however, can be time consuming, and is likely to be doing work to decompress material that won't be of interest in the pattern matching. A better solution would allow a direct search of the compressed data with minimal or no decompression. Searching without any decompression is called *fully-compressed pattern matching*, or sometimes just *compressed pattern matching*. This process involves compressing the pattern and matching it to the compressed text representation. Of course, for many compression methods this is not possible, particularly with compression algorithms that use different representations for a substring depending on its context. This is the case with adaptive compression algorithms, and also occurs with some coders, including arithmetic coders, where there is no unique representation for a particular character. An alternative technique is *compressed-domain pattern matching*, which performs partial decompression of the text to remove some of the obstacles that the compression has introduced, while still providing the advantages of avoiding complete decompression.

Another approach is to construct a secondary index data structure to accelerate searching, which would seem to increase the space used, although it is possible to take advantage of the relationship between the index and the text to improve both compression and searching. This approach is commonly used for full-text retrieval (FTR) applications such as search engines. Normally an FTR system will identify *terms* in the text that can be indexed (typically English words). However, in this book we are focusing on pattern-matching, in which *any* substring of the text might be matched; traditionally this involves processing the entire text looking for the pattern, but it is also possible to construct various kinds of index to support the pattern matching, particularly if multiple patterns are to be located, in which case the effort used in building the index can be amortized over the multiple searches. Adapting the Burrows-Wheeler Transform for this sort of application is particularly attractive because the compression process automatically provides a sorted index of the text, and thus we have a nice compromise between avoiding doing extra work to create an index, yet we can benefit from such information being available.

In this chapter we will begin in Section 7.1 by looking at classic exact pattern matching algorithms for uncompressed text, as some of the compressed-domain methods build on these. The section also looks at algorithms for pattern matching with "don't-care" characters, which allow for uncertainty in the search. We then discuss the compressed domain pattern matching problem in Section 7.2, with the main emphasis on the use of the Burrows-Wheeler Transform to aid compressed-domain pattern search. We will then move on to approximate pattern matching algorithms (Section 7.4), including "k-mismatch algorithms" which allow a fixed number of characters to be different between a pattern and the text it matches. Some uncompressed-domain approximate matching methods are introduced, and then implementations of BWT domain approximate pattern matching are described. It is also possible to design hardware algorithms to accelerate pattern matching, and these will be discussed briefly in Section 7.5.

7.1 Exact pattern matching algorithms

The problem of searching a text for occurrences of a given pattern is well understood, and this section reviews the most commonly used methods.

First we will define some terms and notation that will be used in the descriptions. We will represent the pattern being searched for as an array or string $P[1 \ldots m]$, containing m characters over an alphabet Σ, where $\Sigma =$

$\{\sigma_1, \sigma_2, \ldots \sigma_{|\Sigma|}\}$, with $|\Sigma|$ representing the size of the alphabet. We will refer to the input text as an array $T[1 \ldots n]$ of n characters over the same alphabet, $(m, n \geq 1$ and $n \geq m)$. The *pattern matching* problem is to determine whether pattern P occurs as a substring in text T. If P occurs in T then we also want to determine the position(s) in T of the occurrence(s) of P.

There are several ways to tackle this problem. In the well-known Knuth-Morris-Pratt (KMP) (Knuth et al., 1977) and Boyer-Moore (BM) (Boyer and Moore, 1977) algorithms, the pattern is pre-processed off-line to identify useful structures in the pattern, and the text is used as an *input string* to the algorithm. Another approach is to pre-process the text into a data structure which expedites the search of pattern(s) in the text. Suffix trees (Section 4.1), suffix arrays (Section 4.2), and the Burrows-Wheeler Transform are typical examples of this approach. A third approach is to transform both the text and the pattern into numeric or binary strings, and the computation is performed in this transformed domain. The Karp-Rabin algorithm (Karp and Rabin, 1987) is the most well-known method that uses the numeric transformation via a hash function, and Baeza-Yates and Gonnet (1992) have developed methods that use bitwise operations on binary strings. A few other relevant methods will be mentioned, although this section is not exhaustive as this topic is not the main focus. The descriptions of the algorithms are based on Gusfield (1997) where a comprehensive discussion of other algorithms can be found.

In the analysis of these algorithms we will use the standard random access machine (RAM) as our model of computation, and quantify the performance of the algorithms in terms of the asymptotic time and storage complexity by using the standard "Big-O" notation. We will also occasionally constrain our complexity measures by imposing additional properties such as whether the algorithm can operate *on-line* (in a single pass of the text) or in *real time* (each character in the text T can be processed only once, and the processing time must be bounded by a constant). The complexity is also sometimes parameterized by the alphabet size.

7.1.1 Brute force matching

The most obvious approach for pattern matching is to compare the given pattern characters $P[1 \ldots m]$ with the first m characters of the text $T[1 \ldots m]$ stored in a buffer, and compare the corresponding pairs of characters. If all character pairs match, the algorithm reports that P has been found in T, and notes the text position where the first pair of characters matched. Whether or not a match is found, the pattern characters are then compared with the characters starting at the next position in T (i.e. $T[2 \ldots m+1])$ to see if every pair matches. This process is iterated $n - m + 1$ times, and then terminates. Pseudo-code for this method is given in Algorithm 7.1.

This algorithm takes $O(nm)$ time. An example of the worst case is when $T = \mathsf{a}^{n-1}\mathsf{b}$, and $P = \mathsf{a}^{m-1}\mathsf{b}$. For the first $n - m$ attempts the character comparison fails at the last (m-th) character position of the pattern after $m-1$

BRUTE-FORCE-PATTERN-MATCHING(P, T)
  $i \leftarrow 1$ /* pointer to a character in pattern P */
  $j \leftarrow 1$ /* pointer to a character in text T */
  while $(i \leq m$ **and** $j \leq n)$ **do**
    if $P[i] = T[j]$ **then**
      $i \leftarrow i + 1$
      $j \leftarrow j + 1$
    else
      $j \leftarrow j - i + 2$
      $i \leftarrow 1$
    end if
    if $i > m$ **then** report P found in T, beginning at position $j - m$
  end while

Algorithm 7.1: Brute force pattern matching algorithm

successful matches. The last iteration leads to a successful match which needs an additional m comparisons, giving a total of $(n - m)m + m = nm - m^2 + m$ character comparison operations. The algorithm needs $O(m)$ storage to hold the pattern and m text characters buffered from the input. For random text, the time required by the brute force algorithm is in $O(n)$. Thus, for such text, and in most practical situations, the brute force algorithm generally performs as well as the theoretically optimum algorithm of Knuth-Morris-Pratt (described next), because pattern matches will usually fail early in the character-by-character comparison process.

7.1.2 The Knuth-Morris-Pratt Algorithm

The worst case inefficiency of the brute force algorithm arises because it does not use the information that it has already encountered during the partial match between the pattern and the text. When a mismatch occurs at the j-th input character of the text, the text pointer does not necessarily have to be reset back to $j - i + 2$ because the algorithm already "knows" the previous $i - 1$ characters of the pattern P. More precisely, if we imagine placing the pattern under the text and sliding it right during the matching process, the brute force method blindly slides the pattern by just one character right whenever a mismatch occurs, but it may be possible to slide it further than that — for example, if the pattern abc has just mismatched with the text abd... we know that none of the first three starting positions will be a match because of the nature of the two strings. What is the maximum amount of right shift that can be made without missing the occurrence of the pattern in the text? If this can be answered, we can use the general approach in Algorithm 7.2 to find the first occurrence of the pattern.

To determine the appropriate amount of right shift, we need to define the concept of a *border*. A border of a pattern $P[1 \ldots i]$ is any prefix of $P[1 \ldots i]$

GENERAL-PATTERN-MATCHING($pattern, text$)
  align the pattern at left of text
  while (all pattern characters have not been compared with text characters
      and text is not exhausted) **do**
    while (a pattern character mismatches with the current text character)
    do
      right shift pattern **appropriately**
      resume matching operation with the text
    end while
    if pattern is exhausted **then** report pattern found
    else report not found
    end if
  end while

Algorithm 7.2: A general pattern matching algorithm

that is equal to a proper suffix of $P[1 \ldots i]$. The longest border for $P[1 \ldots i]$ will be denoted as b_i with a length l_i. The sequence of l_i's for $i = 1$ to n is called the *border array*. If we add the constraint that $P[i+1] \neq P[l_i+1]$, then the border will be denoted as B_i and its length will be denoted as L_i (Figure 7.1a). As an example, if $P = $ xxxccaexxxcaxd, then the single character x is a border for position $i = 10$, the longest border for $i = 10$ is $b_{10} = $ xxx with $l_{10} = 3$, and $B_{10} = $ xx with $L_{10} = 2$. Suppose for a given alignment of the pattern with the text, the first mismatch between the text and the pattern occurs at the k-th character in the input text, $T[k] = $ z, and the $(i + 1)$-th character of the pattern $P[i + 1] = $ y as shown in Figure 7.1b.

This means that the first L_i characters of the pattern P match the same number of characters preceding $T[k] = $ z. This is significant because, unlike the brute force method, we can right-slide the pattern by $i - L_i$ places so that the next comparison operation will be between the characters $P[L_i + 1] = $ x and $T[k] = $ z. Note that the amount of this shift depends only on the pattern P, and is independent of the text T. We can pre-compute and store in an array the values of L_i for each value of i ($1 \leq i \leq m$) for a given pattern P. We formally define the *failure function* for $1 \leq i \leq m + 1$ as $F[i] = L_{i-1} + 1$, and define $L_0 = 0$. Thus, if a mismatch occurs in position $i + 1 > 1$ of P with $T[k]$, the pattern is right shifted so that the next comparison takes place between position $T[k]$ and the character in position $L_i + 1 = F[i + 1]$. This can be done by setting a pointer p to $F[i + 1]$ in the pattern. There are two special cases: if a mismatch occurs at position $i = 1$, set $F[1] = 1$; and if the entire pattern matches and we are interested in continuing the search process to find all matches in the text, we right shift the text by $(m - L_m)$. This is done by setting $F[m + 1] = L_m + 1$. A formal proof of the fact that no actual occurrence of a pattern in the text will be missed by such a right shift is omitted here. The computation of the failure function F takes $O(m)$ time (this is explained below). The KMP algorithm is given in Algorithm 7.3.

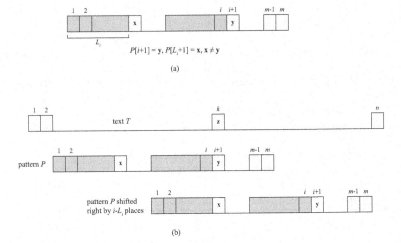

Fig. 7.1. Knuth-Morris-Pratt Algorithm: (a) definition of border B_i with length L_i; (b) Knuth-Morris-Pratt shift

The critical lemma that allows $O(m)$ computation time to pre-process the pattern to determine the failure function is the following.

Lemma 1 *For any i, $l_{i+1} \leq l_i + 1$. The equality holds if and only if $P[l_i + 1] = P[i + 1]$.*

The following is an intuitive explanation of the lemma. It is obvious that if $P[l_i + 1] = P[i + 1] = x$, then x contributes to incrementing l_i by 1, that is, if the border is l_i at position i we will be able to find a longer border at position $i + 1$ (see Figure 7.1b). Now, assume $P[i + 1] = y$ and $x \neq y$. If y does not appear to the left of x between locations 1 through l_i, then obviously $l_{i+1} = 0$. If y appears to the left of x, possibly more than once, then l_{i+1} will have a non-zero value. The problem essentially has now been reduced to finding a border on an instance of the original problem on a smaller string $P[1 \ldots l_i]$. This process can be recursed until either a valid prefix b_{i+1} is found or the beginning of the pattern is reached. In this case, if $P[1] = y$ then $b_{i+1} = y$ and $l_{i+1} = 1$. Otherwise, $l_{i+1} = 0$, as noted earlier.

To illustrate this idea, as an example we will use a Fibonacci string, which is defined as: $F_0 = b$, $F_1 = a$ and for $q > 2$, $F_q = F_{q-1} * F_{q-2}$, where $*$ denotes the concatenation operation. This gives F_6 as **abaababaabaab**. Suppose, by using some algorithm, we have obtained the value of the border for $i = 11$ as $b_{11} = abaaba$ with $l_{11} = 6$. We now want to obtain l_{12} and b_{12}. First, we try to extend the border by one character by checking whether $P[l_{11} + 1] = P[i + 1]$ which is not true for our example because $P[l_{11} + 1] = b$ and $P[i + 1] = a$. Let's assign a variable $v = l_{11}$. If $P[v + 1] = P[i + 1]$ were true, we could have immediately set $l_{12} = l_{11} + 1$ and proceeded to compute l_{13}. But, since

---

KMP-STRING-MATCHING (P, T)
pre-process pattern P to compute the failure functions:
  $F[j] = L_{j-1} + 1$ for $1 \leq j \leq m + 1$
$p \leftarrow 1$ /* a pointer into the pattern P */
$k \leftarrow 1$ /* a pointer into the text T */
/* The pattern is aligned at the left of the text */
while $(k + (m - p) \leq n)$ **do** /* T matches P so far */
  while $(P[p] = T[k]$ **and** $p \leq m)$ **do** /* match continues */
    $k \leftarrow k + 1$
    $p \leftarrow p + 1$
  end while
  if $p = m + 1$ **then**
    report pattern P occurs at position $k - m$ in the text T
  end if
  if $p = 1$ **then**
    /* a special case when mismatch occurs at position 1 of P */
    $k \leftarrow k + 1$
  end if
  $p \leftarrow F[p]$
end while

Algorithm 7.3: KMP pattern matching algorithm

$P[v+1] \neq P[i+1]$, we repeat the procedure with respect to the smaller string by "bouncing" back to location 6 where the prefix b_{11} ends. Now we have $l_6 = 3$ and $b_6 =$ aba. Actually, l_6 is already available since, as we will see soon, the computation of borders proceeds from left to right in the main algorithm. We can now extend $v = l_6$, because $P[v+1] = P[4] =$ a and $P[i+1] = P[12] =$ a. Thus, $l_{12} = 4$.

This discussion leads to an $O(m)$ algorithm to find all the b_i's and l_i's as shown in Algorithm 7.4. For positions 1 to 13 for the string abaababaabaab the algorithm will give the border length values (0,0,1,1,2,3,2,3,4,5,6,4,2), respectively.

The **for** loop is executed $m - 1$ times. The variable v is assigned a new value $m - 1$ times each time this loop is executed, where its value either increases by one or remains unchanged. The variable v is also assigned new values in the **while** loop a variable number of times corresponding to the number of times a pointer "bounces" back, each time working with a reduced length prefix whose minimum value is 0. Thus the total reduction of the value of v is also bounded by $m - 1$, which is the maximum number of times its value is assigned in the **while** loop. This yields a total complexity of $O(m)$ for Algorithm 7.4.

The constrained values of the borders B_i and their lengths L_i can be computed similarly, as shown in Algorithm 7.5. The algorithm assumes that the unconstrained values of border lengths computed by Algorithm 7.4 are avail-

---

COMPUTE-FAILURE-FUNCTION (P, T)
$l_1 \leftarrow 0$
for $i \leftarrow 1$ to $m - 1$ **do**
   x $\leftarrow P[i + 1]$
   $v \leftarrow l_i$
   while $(P[v + 1] \neq$ x and $v \neq 0)$ **do**
      $v \leftarrow l_v$
   end while
   if $P[v + 1] =$ x **then**
      $l_{i+1} \leftarrow v + 1$
   else
      $l_{i+1} \leftarrow 0$
   end if
end for

Algorithm 7.4: Computing the KMP failure function for pattern P

able to this algorithm. The proof of correctness and the complexity analysis are left as exercises. Note that the KMP algorithm, Algorithm 7.3 that we presented earlier, uses these constrained values.

COMPUTE-CONSTRAINED-FAILURE-FUNCTION (P)
$L_1 \leftarrow 0$
for $i = 2$ to m **do**
   $v \leftarrow l_i$
   if $P[v + 1] \neq P[i + 1]$ **then**
      $L_i \leftarrow v$
   else
      $L_i \leftarrow L_v$
   end if
end for

Algorithm 7.5: Computing the KMP *constrained* failure function for pattern P

In the KMP algorithm, when there is a mismatch between a pattern and a text character, the pattern is shifted right as specified by the failure function. But, failures may repeat and in the worst case this may happen $|\Sigma|$ times. Thus, in the worst case the KMP algorithm has complexity $(O(m|\Sigma| + n)$. If we assume that $|\Sigma|$ is constant the complexity is $O(m+n)$. But, the possibility of multiple comparisons makes the algorithm non-real time. To be real time, the time between two successive comparisons with text characters cannot exceed a prescribed constant amount of work and once a text character has been examined, it cannot be seen again. This can be achieved by modifying the definition of B_i to a specific character x in the alphabet in Figure 7.1, and denoting it by $B_{i,\mathbf{x}}$ and its corresponding length by $L_{i,\mathbf{x}}$. Algorithm 7.3 remains essentially unchanged except that in the case of a mismatch, it is shifted right by an amount $i - L_{i,\mathbf{x}}$.

7.1.3 The Boyer-Moore algorithm

The Boyer-Moore algorithm is currently considered to be one of the most efficient pattern matching algorithms for searching an ordinary text and has become the practical exact pattern matching algorithm of choice. Using shift heuristics, it is able to avoid making comparisons with some parts of the text and can therefore produce a sub-linear performance of $O(\frac{n}{m})$ in the best case, although on average it requires $O(m + n)$ comparisons and in the worst case deteriorates to $O(mn)$ time complexity. The algorithm, however, requires access to the text in a particular order and is not suitable for on-line or real time applications. Although it is not strictly on-line or real time, in practice it needs a buffer of only $O(m)$ characters, so in practice it can be adapted to work through a text in a single sequential pass.

The algorithm scans the characters right to left starting with the right-most character of the pattern P, but the pattern is shifted left to right as in the KMP algorithm. When a mismatch is found, the maximum of two pre-computed shifts obtained by two rules, called the *good-suffix rule* and *bad-character rule*, are used to determine how far to shift the pattern before beginning the next set of comparisons. This shifts the pattern along the text from left to right, without missing possible matches, until the required patterns have been located or the end of the text is reached.

The *good-suffix rule* is used when a suffix s of P has already been matched to a substring of the text T, but the next comparison results in a mismatch between the text character z and the pattern character x (see Figure 7.2). The set of diagrams shown in Figure 7.2 illustrates the ideas. There are several cases to be considered.

The first case is when there is a rightmost copy of s, denoted s', which is not a suffix of P, and the character to the left of this copy, y, is not equal to the character x. In this case we shift the pattern right until s' aligns with s of T. We continue the matching operation from the rightmost character of P and proceed left one character at a time if characters match. Note the strings s and s' could partially overlap each other as shown in Figure 7.2b.

The second case is when the copy s' satisfying the above conditions does not exist. In this case we shift the left end of P past the left end of s in T by the least amount so that a proper prefix of the shifted pattern matches a suffix t of s in T (see Figure 7.3).

If neither of the above two cases apply, we shift the entire pattern P right m places.

Now consider the case when the pattern matches entirely and we are interested in finding all occurrences of the pattern. In this case, we right shift the

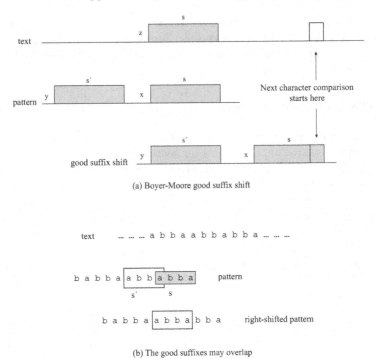

(a) Boyer-Moore good suffix shift

text   … … … a b b a a b b a b b a … … …

b a b b a a b b a b b a   pattern
        s′   s

b a b b a a b b a b b a   right-shifted pattern

(b) The good suffixes may overlap

Fig. 7.2. The Boyer-Moore shift rules

pattern by the least amount such that a proper prefix of the pattern matches a suffix of matched portion s in the text T. If no such suffix exists, then we shift the entire pattern to the right of the mismatched character.

The *bad character* heuristic is illustrated in Figure 7.4. If the first mismatch occurs as $(P[i] = \mathbf{b}) \neq (T[j] = \mathbf{a})$, then we shift pattern P so that the closest $\mathbf{a}$ to the left of position i in P is aligned with position j in the text. If no such $\mathbf{a}$ appears in the pattern, then we shift the pattern to the right of the mismatched character (see the examples in Figure 7.4). A formal description of the algorithm in the context of compressed-domain pattern matching is given in Algorithm 7.7 with only one change: in line 6 for the *while* statement the condition should be replaced with $(i > 0$ and $P[i] = T[k])$.

A table of shift distances for the good-suffix rule can be computed before searching begins in $O(m)$ amortized time, and requires $O(m)$ space. A table for the bad-character rule can be calculated before searching begins in $O(m+|\Sigma|)$ time and requires $O(m + |\Sigma|)$ space. The original Boyer-Moore algorithm required an overall time of $O(mn)$, but this has since been improved to $O(m + n)$ by various authors. The good suffix heuristic is essential for the linear time worst case performance. The book by Smyth (2003) provides a detailed treatment and analysis of different variants of the BM algorithm.

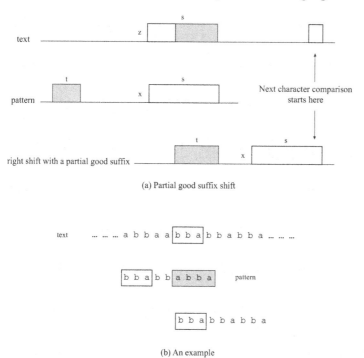

(a) Partial good suffix shift

(b) An example

Fig. 7.3. Partial Good Suffix rule: (a) Partial Good Suffix shift; (b) an example

7.1.4 The Karp-Rabin algorithm

The Karp-Rabin algorithm (Karp and Rabin, 1987) converts the successive m-character substrings of the text into a sequence of $n - m + 1$ numbers, called *fingerprints*, with the help of a *hash* function h that interprets the substring as an integer in a $|\Sigma|$-radix number system, where the alphabet of the characters is assumed to be $\Sigma = \{0, 1, \ldots, |\Sigma - 1|\}$. Thus, for binary strings with $\Sigma = \{0, 1\}$, the integer associated with the m-length binary string $s = s_1 s_2 \ldots s_m$ is $h(s) = \sum_{i=1}^{m} 2^{m-i} s_i$. Similarly, an integer associated with a m-length substring in the text T starting at location r, denoted as $t_r = T[r \ldots r + m - 1]$, is given by:

$$h(t_r) = \sum_{i=1}^{m} 2^{m-i} T[r + i - 1].$$

Thus, if we take s to be the pattern P, and $h(s) \neq h(t_r)$, then we can immediately conclude that the pattern (P) cannot possibly match the m-character segment of text at location r. One of the problems with this approach is that the integers generated by the simple hash function h can be extremely large in any practical situation for a reasonably-sized alphabet and pattern

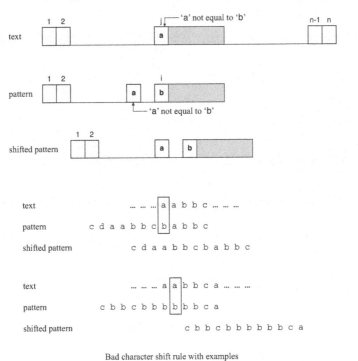

Bad character shift rule with examples

Fig. 7.4. Boyer-Moore Bad Character rule

length, and the representations of these large numbers may violate the random access computation model. Karp and Rabin tackled both of these problems by using a *fingerprint* $h_p(x)$, rather than $h(x)$. The fingerprint $h_p(x)$ is defined as $h_p(x) = h(x) \bmod p$, where p is a suitably chosen prime number and $x = x_1 x_2 \ldots x_m$ is a string of m integers in the range 0 to $|\Sigma| - 1$.

There are two tricks to implementing this efficiently. First, we can take advantage of the associative property of the modulo operation and compute the fingerprint using Horner's rule for a binary string x:

$$h_p(x) = (x_m + 2(x_{m-1} + 2(x_{m-2} + \ldots + 2(x_2 + 2(x_1) \bmod p) \bmod p) \ldots$$
$$\bmod p) \bmod p) \bmod p$$

For an alphabet of size $|\Sigma|$, the multiplicative factor 2 should be replaced by $|\Sigma|$. This approach means that no number at any intermediate stage of computation will exceed $|\Sigma| p$. The expression takes $O(m)$ multiplication and addition operations. A second optimization can be done when we first compute $h_p(t_1)$ by taking $O(m)$ time, which will then enable us to obtain $h_p(t_2), h_p(t_3), \ldots h_p(t_{n-m-1})$ in a constant amount of time each. The idea of this optimization can be explained by a simple example using a binary string. We take an example text $T = \cdots 111011 \cdots$, a sample pattern length

$m = 5$, with $t_{r-1} = 11101$ corresponding to the start of the substring of T, and therefore $t_r = 11011$. Thus, $h(t_{r-1}) = 2^4 + 2^3 + 2^2 + 0.2^1 + 2^0 = 29$ and $h(t_r) = 2^4 + 2^3 + 0.2^2 + 2^1 + 2^0 = 27$. If we take $h(t_{r-1})$, multiply it by 2 (adds a zero on the right-hand side), subtract 1.2^5 (remove the first bit) and add 1.2^0 (add the last bit), we get $h(t_r) = 29.2-32+1=27$. In general, for a binary text string we can write

$$h(t_r) = 2h(t_{r-1}) - 2^m t_{r-1}[1] + T[r + m - 1]$$

Now we can apply the mod operation to obtain the final recurrence relation

$$h_p(t_r) = [(2h(t_{r-1}) \bmod p) - (2^m \bmod p)t_{r-1}[1]) + T[r + m - 1]] \bmod p$$

However, if $h(s) = h(t_r)$ under modulo p, we cannot guarantee that the pattern occurs unless we compare the pattern with t_r character by character. If such comparison gives a mismatch, it is said to be a *false match*. Choosing a prime number p so that it is not too large, yet gives a low probability of false match, is a challenging one. Karp and Rabin proposed a randomized procedure using a number theoretic approach to establish that a random prime can be chosen which is less than mn^2 and which yields a very low probability of false match. For example, the probability is less than 0.001 for a 32-bit fingerprint. In the worst case, the Karp-Rabin algorithm takes $O(mn)$ time, and in the average case it takes $O(m + n)$.

7.1.5 The shift-and method

The basic operations in the Knuth-Morris-Pratt and the Boyer-Moore methods are comparisons of characters. Baeza-Yates and Gonnet (1992) published an exact pattern matching algorithm that is based on *bitwise* operations. The method is very efficient for small patterns, although it has $O(mn)$ time complexity in the worst case.

We define a binary matrix M with m rows and n columns such that $M[i, j] = 1$ if and only if the prefix of the pattern $P[1 \ldots i]$ equals the suffix $T[j - i + 1 \ldots j]$ in the text at the j-th position. For a text $T = $ xabxabaaca and a pattern $P = $ abaac, the matrix M is shown in Figure 7.5.

Note that if there is a diagonal of 1's starting from row 1 and ending in row m, it means the pattern has occurred in the text. The algorithm can be defined formally after we define two binary column vectors. The first is *Pos*, which stores a bit vector for each character in the alphabet. $Pos[x]$ is an m-bit vector whose i-th position is set to one if the character x occurs in the i-th position of the pattern P, $1 \leq i \leq m$. The second column vector is *Bitshift*$[j - 1]$, and is the $(j - 1)$-th column of M shifted downward by 1 bit with an appended one as the first bit and the overflowed last bit discarded. Column 1 is initialized to all zeros if $P[1] \neq T[1]$; otherwise its row 1 entry is one and rest are zero bits. To compute M, the j-th column is obtained from the $(j - 1)$-th column by bitwise logical AND operation of $Pos[T[j]]$

```
      x a b x a b a a c a
a 0 1 0 0 1 0 1 1 0 1
b 0 0 1 0 0 1 0 0 0 0
a 0 0 0 0 0 0 1 0 0 0
a 0 0 0 0 0 0 0 1 0 0
c 0 0 0 0 0 0 0 0 1 0
```

Fig. 7.5. Matrix M for the shift-and method on text $T = $ xabxabaaca and a pattern $P = $ abaac

with $Bitshift[j - 1]$. The operation is repeated n times until the last column is obtained. If at any time during construction of M, the bit in the last m-th row becomes one, it implies the pattern must have occurred in the text. The worst case computation time is $O(mn)$, although only a linear amount of storage is needed since we need keep only the previous column and the current column at any time during the execution. One big advantage of the software implementation is that if m is small and fits into a computer word (32 to 128 bits which fits most practical situations for pattern lengths), the bitwise logical AND operation can be performed very quickly, yielding a very fast algorithm.

A hardware implementation of this idea is described at the end of this chapter, in Section 7.5.1.

7.1.6 Multiple pattern matching

A generalization of the pattern matching problem is to search for *sets* of patterns. Given a set of patterns $P = [P_1, P_2, \ldots, P_k]$ and an input text string T of length n, we need to determine whether some pattern P_i occurred as a substring in T. We will assume that the total length of the patterns is m, and the text is longer than the shortest pattern in the set P. We also assume that the patterns in the set are distinct. A straightforward approach to this problem is to apply either the KMP or Boyer-Moore algorithm for each pattern in the set over the text T. This will take $O(m + kn)$ time in total.

Aho and Corasick (1975) solved the multiple pattern matching problem using only $O(n+m)$ time. If the number of patterns k is large, this is a significant improvement. The idea of their algorithm is to generalize the KMP approach using a finite state machine. A similar approach was originally developed by Knuth following a theorem by Cook (1972) which proved the existence of a linear pattern matching algorithm from language theoretic considerations. The state transition rules of this automaton were realized by the KMP shifts that we discussed earlier. Aho and Corasick adopted a similar approach but we will present a better known formulation using a *digital trie* or *digital search tree*, and a variation of a trie known as a *keyword tree*. The term *keyword* sim-

ply refers to a pattern being searched for, and so in the following the terms
pattern and *keyword* are used interchangeably.

The *digital trie* is a data structure developed by Knuth in 1973, and is
very useful for pattern matching. An example of a kind of trie that is being used as a keyword tree is shown in Figure 7.6a containing the keywords
{abca, aca, acabb, bcb, bcc}. The branch factor of the tree can be up to the
size of the alphabet ($|\Sigma|$), with each branch corresponding to the next charac-
ter in a substring. In the case of a keyword tree, the substrings represented in
the tree are the set of patterns that are to be matched (in other applications
a digital trie stores substrings of the text rather than the patterns). A subset
of nodes in the tree represents a given set of keywords over the finite alphabet
Σ. The concatenation of characters from the root to the nodes spell out the
keywords. Each edge is labeled by a character, and sibling edges must have
distinct characters.

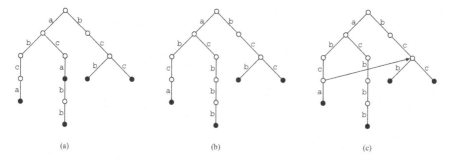

(a)   (b)   (c)

Fig. 7.6. (a) Keyword tree for {abca, aca, acabb, bcb, bcc}; (b) digital search tree
(trie) for the patterns {abca, acbbb, bcb, bcc}; (c) one of the failure links; solid nodes
correspond to the keywords

In Figure 7.6a the keywords are marked by solid nodes. Every node v
in the tree represents a string of characters from Σ corresponding to the
concatenation of characters on the path from the root to v, and this string
will be denoted as $path(v)$. The root represents the null string ϵ. Note that the
keyword aca is a proper prefix of the keyword acabb. If no pattern is allowed to
be the prefix of another, then each terminal node represents a pattern, and the
tree is called a *digital search tree*, although the terms *keyword tree* and *digital
search tree* are sometimes used interchangeably. An example of a digital search
tree is shown in Figure 7.6b for the pattern set {abca, acbbb, bcb, bcc}. The
construction of the tree takes $O(m)$ time. This is easy to see: the tree for P_1
is simply a path with edges labeled by the characters of P_1. Suppose we have
the tree of the first i patterns in the tree. To add the pattern P_{i+1}, just trace
the path using the letters in P_{i+1} as far as possible. At some point a distinct
sibling edge has to be added, which will lead to a sub-path terminating in a
terminal node representing the pattern. Thus the work involved is bounded

by the length of the pattern P_{i+1}. Adding all the pattern lengths gives us m characters, so the total construction time is $O(m)$.

A *brute force method* to search a text for any of the patterns in the set is to start at each position in the text and trace a unique path from the root, matching text characters with the characters labeling the edges in the path until a failure occurs or a node representing a pattern is reached. For a keyword tree, a node representing a pattern may be reached more than once if some patterns in P are prefixes of other patterns in P. For example, as a special case, all the patterns occur in just one path in the keyword tree if the patterns P consists of all the prefixes of a given string. In general, to find all patterns for a given position in the text the tree traversal time is bounded by the length of the longest pattern which could be $O(m)$. Since there are n positions in the text, the brute force algorithm thus takes $O(nm)$ time in the worst case. The Aho-Corasick algorithm generalizes the KMP algorithm for a keyword tree and reduces this time to $O(n + m + \eta_{occ})$, where η_{occ} is the number of occurrences of the patterns in P in T.

To motivate the idea, we will use the example text abcbcaabcc and try to find the patterns in the digital search tree of Figure 7.6b. After matching the first three characters abc of $P_1 = $ abca, the search fails so the process needs to be started from the root beginning with the second character of the text, b. We cannot make a KMP-like shift since no suffix of abc is a proper prefix of abc. However, the third pattern in the set, bcb, has a prefix bc which matches with the suffix bc of abc. So, the "border" of the KMP algorithm is now located in a different pattern, bcb, and therefore rather than starting the search process at the root node, it should skip the first two edges labeled by bc and proceed to find the pattern bcb after just one more character comparison operation. This can be achieved by storing a *failure link*, as shown in Figure 7.6c (note that not all the failure links are shown).

More formally, for the node v, define $lp(v)$ to be the length of the longest proper suffix of $path(v)$ that is a prefix pr_i of some pattern P_i in P. The unique node in the tree that has a path label pr_i will be denoted as $link(v)$. The ordered pair $(v, link(v))$ will be called a *failure link*. If $lp(v) = 0$, then $link(v)$ will be the root node; in this case it need not be stored, as nodes that do not have an explicit failure link will have an implicit failure link to the root node. Now, suppose we are tracing a text T on the digital tree to find patterns and come to node v after matching with the character $T[c-1]$ of text, and there is a mismatch with character $T[c]$, where c points to a position in the text. Then, by the definition of the failure link $(v, link(v))$, it is guaranteed that the characters $T[c - lp(v) \ldots c - 1]$ will match the characters of $path(link(v))$. We can then proceed to compare the character $T[c]$ with the next character after $path(link(v))$. This is a generalization of the notion of shifting the pattern in KMP algorithm as discussed earlier in the chapter.

Before we give the final algorithm, we need to resolve the situation where one pattern is a substring of another pattern in P. For example, consider $P = (\text{abacc}, \text{ba})$ and $T = \text{abacd}$. The tree for P will have two separate paths leading to two terminal nodes. After traversing the path abac, it will fail and start from the root and then encounter the character d of text; it will fail again and never find the pattern ba even though it is present in the text. This happened because the pattern ba is embedded in abac but is not a suffix of abac. This can be taken care of easily by noting that if there is a failure link or a directed path of failure links from *any* node v in the tree to a terminal node corresponding to pattern P_i, then whenever the node v is reached during the tree traversal, one can conclude that the pattern P_i has occurred in the text ending at the current text position (c) when v was reached. Thus we can modify our algorithm by stating that if a node v is reached at $T[c]$, and if v is either a terminal node, a link or a directed path of links from v that leads to a terminal node, then a pattern must have occurred in the text ending in position c. We can now state the Aho-Corasick algorithm as shown in Algorithm 7.6.

MULTIPLE-PATTERN-MATCHING $(T, KeywordTree)$
   $c = 1$ /* a pointer into the text */
   $v = root$ /* search begins at root node */
   repeat
      while (v is root node **and** $T[c]$ does not match with
           any character labeling outgoing edges (v, v') from v) **do**
         $c \leftarrow c + 1$
      end while
   until character of outgoing edge $(v, v') = T[c]$ **or** $c > n$
   if $c > n$ **then** report *no pattern found* and **quit**
   repeat
      while ($T[c]$ matches the character labeling
           outgoing edges (v, v') from v) **do**
         if v' corresponds to a pattern P_i or there is a directed path of
            failure links from v' to a node associated with a pattern P_i **then**
           report P_i occurs in T ending at position $c - 1$
         end if
         $v \leftarrow v'$
         $c \leftarrow c + 1$
      end while
      $v \leftarrow link(v)$
   until $c > n$

Algorithm 7.6: Aho-Corasick multiple pattern matching algorithm

Several improvements of the KMP, Boyer-Moore and Aho-Corasick algorithms have been reported in the literature; see the further reading section for more information.

7.1.7 Pattern matching with don't-care characters

A fixed length *don't-care* or *wild-card* character, which we will refer to as the $FLDC$ character ϕ, is a symbol that does not belong to Σ but matches with every character in Σ including ϕ itself. However, the "match" relation is no longer *transitive*. For example, ab matches with aϕ which matches with ac, but b $\neq$ c. This creates problems if one attempts to apply the KMP or Boyer-Moore shifts for pattern matching. For example, if P = babϕab and T = babcbaab, using the KMP algorithm when the pattern is aligned with the beginning of the text, ϕ matches with c. The KMP algorithm will now right shift the pattern by two places and the pattern is found because after the shift, ϕ matches with a. This is a *false match* because a $\neq$ c, and we have mistakenly assumed transitivity.

Another variation of the pattern matching problem is when the pattern has a *variable length don't-care* or VLDC character, denoted as θ, which matches with any string of characters of arbitrary length. For example, the pattern a θ b matches with any string that starts with a and ends with b. Another variation is to use both *fixed length* and *variable length* don't-care characters together, for example, aθb$\phi\phi$c. Normally it is assumed that θ has at least one character but patterns described by regular expressions can handle the case when null strings have to be embedded.

If the pattern has a bounded constant number k of don't-care characters, then there are $O(n + m)$ algorithms to find the pattern in the text. The basic idea of one approach is to define an integer array C of length $|T|$ which is initialized to all zeros. From a single pattern P with don't-care characters we construct an ordered sequence of substrings $M = [P_1, P_2, \ldots, P_s]$ in P that do not contain any wild-card characters. These can be obtained in $O(m)$ time by scanning the pattern P left to right and noting down the pairs of transitions in order from a don't-care character to a character in Σ immediately followed by a transition from a character from Σ to a don't care character with some special attention to the beginning and end of P. The maximum value of s is k. Also note some patterns may be repeated in M. Let l_i be the starting location of P_i in P. Using the Aho-Corasick algorithm, we now find, for each P_i, all starting positions of P_i in T. Suppose a starting location of P_i is found in T at position w. Then, add 1 to $C[w - l_i + 1]$. The incremented value of C in this location acts as a witness that P_i occurred at a distance l_i from this location in C. If this happens to cell $C[w - l_i + 1]$ for all patterns P_i in M, then the count of $C[w - l_i + 1]$ will be exactly s and the pattern P has occurred in T at position $T[w - l_i + 1]$. The time to find patterns of P in T is $O(n + m + s)$ for one occurrence of P in T. The quantity s depends on the number k of FLDC characters in relation to m, the total length of the pattern P. Assuming k to be a constant, we can also assume s to be bounded by a constant. Thus, the complexity is $O(n + m)$. Since each cell of C can have a maximum value of s, if P appears in each location in T, incrementing all the cells in C will involve $O(sn)$ amount of work, giving a total complexity of

$O(sn + m)$. Since s is assumed to be a constant, the worst case complexity is $O(n + m)$.

If the number of don't-care characters in the pattern is not a constant, we can use a method proposed by Pinter (1985) as follows: let $d_{i,j} = p_i - p_j$ denote the distance between the pattern P_i and P_j, where p_i and p_j denote the positions of P_i and P_j, respectively, in P. Using the Aho-Corasick algorithm, obtain the lists $L_1, L_2, \ldots L_s$ corresponding to patterns $P_1, P_2, \ldots, P_s$ where the list L_i contains the positions of occurrences of P_i in the text T. Then, the *intersection* of the two lists L_i and L_{i+1} is obtained by keeping only those positions in L_i that are at a distance $d_{i,i+1}$ to the left of the positions in list L_{i+1}. This intersection list is denoted $L_{i,i+1}$. A set of intersection lists $L_{1,2}, L_{3,4}, \ldots, L_{s-1,s}$ is then obtained. Without loss of generality, assume that s is an even number. The computation is now done hierarchically upwards by computing lists $L_{i,i+1.i+2,i+3}$ by *intersecting* two lists $L_{i,i+1}$ and $L_{i+2,i+3}$ by retaining the positions in list $L_{i,i+1}$ that are at a distance $d_{i,i+1} + d_{i+2,i+3}$ to the left of positions in $L_{i+2,i+3}$. This process is continued until the list $L = L_{1,2,\ldots,s-1,s}$ is obtained. If L is a non-empty list then the pattern P occurs in T and the entries in L give the beginning positions where P occurs in T. The proof of correctness of this algorithm is left to the reader as an exercise. The time complexity of the algorithm is $O(m^{1.5} + n\sqrt{m})$.

If both the pattern and the text contain don't-care characters, the problem can be reduced to multiplying an m-bit number by an n-bit number (Fischer and Paterson, 1974). If the time for this multiplication is $t(m, n)$, it can be shown that the complexity of pattern matching with don't-cares is given by $O(t(n, m) \log m \log |\Sigma|)$. Using the Schönhage-Strassen integer multiplication algorithm, (Strassen, 1969; Schönhage and Strassen, 1971) the time becomes $O(n \log^2 m \log \log m \log |\Sigma|)$. This is a theoretical result and the algorithm has not been implemented in practice.

We will conclude this section with a previously unpublished method for matching with don't-care characters. Consider first the case when the pattern has both the fixed length don't-care character ϕ as well as the variable length don't-care character θ, the text has no don't-cares, and the size of n is small enough that computation using position index numbers in the text can be performed in a RAM model of computation. As before, we first extract the ordered sequence of substrings $M = [P_1, P_2, \ldots, P_s]$ in P that do not contain any wild-card characters in $O(m)$ time. For each pattern P_i, we determine the *ranges*, that is, the beginning position $tail_i$ and the end position $head_i$ of all P_i in T. We create a sorted tail array $TL_i = [tail_i]$ and a sorted head array $HL_i = [head_i]$ for each P_i. For example, let the pattern be $P = \text{ab}\theta\text{bc}\theta\text{ca}\phi\phi\text{aa}$. Without loss of generality, assume that the first and the last characters of P are from Σ. Let $T = \text{ababbcaabcabbccaabaab}$. The component patterns are $P_1 = \text{ab}$, $P_2 = \text{bc}$, $P_3 = \text{ca}$ and $P_4 = \text{aa}$. The sorted tail and head arrays are shown in Table 7.1. During the execution of the Aho-Corasick algorithm, these sorted lists can be derived as auxiliary outputs without going through separate sorting algorithms to sort these arrays, and thus it takes only $O(m)$ time to compute them.

Pattern	TL_1	HL_1
ab	[1,3,8,11,17,20]	[2,4,9,12,18,21]
bc	[5,9,13]	[6,10,14]
ca	[6,10,15]	[7,11,16]
aa	[7,16,19]	[8,17,20]

Table 7.1. The head and tail arrays for $P = \mathsf{ab}\theta\mathsf{bc}\theta\mathsf{ca}\phi\phi\mathsf{aa}$

We now draw a *range order graph* using the following procedure (an example is shown in Figure 7.7). For each component P_i, we create a row of vertices in order from left to right, where a vertex v corresponds to the range $TL_i[r] - HL_i[r]$. The range vertices for patterns P_i and P_{i+1} are placed in consecutive rows. The vertices in the second to last row are connected by a *thin* directed edge from the r-th range to the $(r+1)$-th range. The first vertex in any row does not have any incoming edge, and neither do any of the edges in the first row. A vertex in row j ($1 \le j \le (s-1)$) is connected by a *thick* directed edge to the left-most node in row $j+1$ if the head value of the vertex is less than or equal to the tail value of the vertex in row $j+1$ *and* there is a variable length don't-care character between pattern P_j and P_{j+1} in P. On the other hand, if there are δ don't-care characters ϕ between pattern P_j and P_{j+1} in P, then the vertex in row j is connected to a vertex in row $(j+1)$ if and only if the tail value in the $(j+1)$-th row is exactly equal to the head value of the vertex in row j plus $\delta + 1$. Such a j-th row is designated in the graph by writing "$+\delta$" beside the row (shown beside row 3 in Figure 7.7).

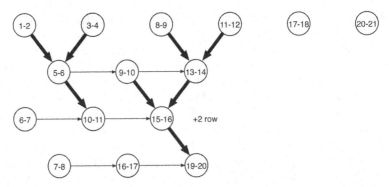

Fig. 7.7. The range order graph for $P = \mathsf{ab}\theta\mathsf{bc}\theta\mathsf{ca}\phi\phi\mathsf{aa}$ and $T = \mathsf{ababbcaabcabbccaabaab}$. Each row corresponds to some pattern P_i in P. Each node corresponds a pairs of (tail – head) for some pattern in P

It is easy to prove that if one can find a path in this graph which originates in the first row and terminates in a node in the last row, then the pattern P occurs in T. The thick edges encountered in the path correspond to the matches with the P_i substrings. The rows (linked by thin lines) indicate the following property: if an edge from row j terminates in a left-most vertex in row $j+1$, then there are also thick edges from this vertex to all the vertices to the right of this left-most vertex connected by thin edges. One can now verify that for our running example there are 8 occurrences of P in the text T by following all possible paths from the top to bottom row. One of them is (1-2,9-10,15-16,19-20) which corresponds to P_1=ab, θ=abbcaa, P_2=bc, θ=abbc, P_3=ca followed by $\phi\phi$ = ab and aa at positions 19-20.

The time complexity of the construction of the range graph is $O(n \log n)$. This is because there can be at most n range values and the left most thick edges can be found by doing an $O(\log n)$ search on the sorted tail array, which can also have $O(n)$ values. The graph also requires $O(n)$ storage since each vertex can have a maximum of one outgoing thick edge and one outgoing thin edge. Searching for a thick edge from row j to row $j + 1$ begins at the left most vertex with an incoming thick edge, and proceeds by tracing the path on thin edges until a node is found that has an outgoing thick edge. Thus this step takes $O(m)$ time. So, to find just one occurrence of P in T, the algorithm takes $O(m + n \log n)$ time, which is $O(n \log n)$ if n is large compared to m (this is the case in most practical situations). If there are η_{occ} occurrences of P in T, the algorithm requires $O(n \log n + m\eta_{occ})$ time. The algorithm can also handle $FLDC$ characters in the text but in the worst case the number of occurrences of component patterns might become $O(n^2)$ which will cause the range graph to have $O(n^2)$ size.

References for other approaches for pattern matching with don't-care characters are given in the "Further reading" section of this chapter.

7.2 Pattern matching using the Burrows-Wheeler Transform

Pattern matching in the compressed domain can have the advantage of avoiding having to fully decompress a file before it is searched, and potentially it can be faster because there is less data to search. Many methods for compressed-domain pattern matching have been proposed for a variety of compression methods, but are generally based on transforming the pattern into the compressed domain and performing a linear search on the compressed file. In contrast, compressed-domain pattern matching using the Burrows-Wheeler Transform has the potential to accommodate a *binary* search, because the compressed domain under the BWT provides a representation of the substrings of the text in sorted order. This represents a significant potential performance improvement, since it could potentially support searching in logarithmic time rather than linear time. Of course, in practice it isn't quite that simple!

When discussing pattern matching in the compressed-domain, particularly with Burrows-Wheeler Transform algorithms, we classify the algorithms as either *index-based* or *non-index based*. An algorithm is index-based if it precomputes and stores information beyond the compressed representation of the text, before search time, for the purpose of facilitating later search on the text. In this chapter we will discuss both non-index based algorithms (such as one based on binary search of the transformed file), and index-based algorithms (such as the *FM-index* algorithm). There are many approaches to searching Burrows-Wheeler transformed files; in addition to binary search, it is possible to do pattern matches based on "*q*-grams" (substrings of length q, typically just a few characters long) which also make *approximate* matching possible; and the Boyer-Moore algorithm can be adapted for compressed-domain BWT matching.

In this section we first look at exact matching algorithms for BWT compressed files, and evaluations of their performance; we then move to approximate matching in the BWT domain, which is considerably harder to evaluate because of the many possibilities for what we mean by "approximate" matches. This book focuses on BWT-based compression methods. References are provided in the further reading section at the end of this chapter for pattern matching based on other compression methods. Full-text indexing based on the BWT is described in Chapter 8.

The formal definitions of the Burrows-Wheeler Transform, the inverse transform and their associated arrays have been described in Chapter 2. A summary of the arrays is given in Appendix A on page 309. Many of these arrays are used for compressed-domain pattern matching. The ones that are used the most are L, which is the transformed text (last column of the sorted array A_s which contains the n rotated substrings from the text T); F, which is the first column of A_s and is simply the characters of the text sorted into lexical order; R, an index showing the permutation caused by sorting the texts i.e. it is a mapping from the rows of A to those of A_s; and V and W, which are used to navigate through the transformed text to produce the original text both backwards and forwards (respectively).

The search algorithms described in this section (excluding the FM-index), will work with any post-transform compression scheme suitable for BWT because they work on the BWT transformed text, L. This means we must reverse the compression (typically a combination of move-to-front coding, run-length encoding, and/or order-0 arithmetic/Huffman coding) to retrieve the permuted string L before searching can begin. The evaluations reported in this chapter will use BSMP, the BWT-based compression technique reported in Bell et al. (2002) when we compare the different approaches. BSMP is a fairly traditional approach to encoding Burrows-Wheeler Transform files, involving three stages. The first stage passes the BWT output through a move-to-front (MTF) coder (Bentley et al., 1986) to take advantage of the clustering of characters. The resulting output is then given to a run-length coder to remove long sequences of zeros, and finally an order-0 arithmetic coder compresses the run lengths.

The compression for the FM-index method described later is provided by a move-to-front coder, followed by a multiple table Huffman coder (Wheeler, 1997). Although this results in a lower compression ratio than BSMP, it is faster and allows random access into the compressed file, which permits searching without reversing the compression of the entire file. As well as the compressed text, auxiliary indexing information is also stored to improve search performance at a small cost to the size of the resulting file.

7.2.1 Boyer-Moore pattern matching using the BWT

To be used in the compressed-domain, the Boyer-Moore algorithm must be able to access the text in the correct order. For BWT-based compression, this is achieved by decoding parts of the text, as needed, through the F array and R' arrays as shown in Algorithm 7.7. In this algorithm, the variable k represents the position in the original text (from 1 to n), and is incremented using the Boyer-Moore rules. The text T isn't available of course, but because $T[k] = F[R'[k]]$, each value is easily obtained by making two index lookups instead of one.

Compared with decompress-and-search, this approach is generally a little faster because the array T does not need to be generated, and the extra auxiliary information needed can be generated faster than the time it would have taken to create T. However, two array references are needed to access each character for comparison, and if several patterns are to be matched, it will probably be more efficient to decode T than to work in the compressed domain.

7.2.2 BWT-based exact pattern matching with binary search

The output of the Burrows-Wheeler Transform is remarkable in that it provides access to a list of all suffixes of the text in sorted order. This makes it possible to use a binary search on the list that operates in $O(m \log n)$ time.

For example, Figure 7.8 shows the sorted list of suffixes for the text mississippi. This is basically the same as the sorted matrix A_s (shown in Figure 2.1b), but strings are not wrapped around to the start of the text. If a search pattern appears in the text, it will be located at the beginning of one or more of these lines. Additionally, because the list is sorted, all occurrences of a search pattern will be located next to each other; for instance, si appears at the start of lines 8 and 9. In principle, A_s is represented using the array R, but this would require access to T to match the characters. Below we shall see how intermediate arrays from the BWT decoding can be used to access the rows of A_s.

COMPRESSED-DOMAIN-BOYER-MOORE-SEARCH(P, F, R')
1   COMPUTE-GOOD-SUFFIX(P)
2   COMPUTE-BAD-CHARACTER(P)
3   $k \leftarrow 1$
4   **while** $(k \leq n - m + 1)$ **do**
5       $i \leftarrow m$
6   **while** $(i > 0$ **and** $P[i] = F[R'[k + i - 1]])$ **do**
7           $i \leftarrow i - 1$
8   **end while**
9   **if** $i = 0$ **then**
10   Report a match beginning at position $k - 1$
11          $k \leftarrow k +$ <*shift proposed by the good-suffix rule*>
12   **else**
13          $s_G \leftarrow$ <*shift proposed by the good-suffix rule*>
14          $s_B \leftarrow$ <*shift proposed by the extended bad-character rule*>
15          $k \leftarrow k + \text{MAX}(s_G, s_B)$
16   **end if**
17 **end while**

Algorithm 7.7: Boyer-Moore search using the Burrows-Wheeler Transform

```
1   i
2   ippi
3   issippi
4   ississippi
5   mississippi
6   pi
7   ppi
8   sippi
9   sissippi
10  ssippi
11  ssissippi
```

Fig. 7.8. Sorted substrings for the text mississippi

In practice, this structure is accessed through the M array, which stores the starting locations of each group of characters in F, and thus provides a "virtual index" to the first character of each row in the sorted substring list. The remaining characters in a row are decoded as needed using the W transform array (see Appendix A for its definition; Figure 7.9 shows the BWT arrays for this example, including W — it is the same as Figure 2.8, repeated here for ease of reference). A row from A_s needs to be decoded only if it is needed to perform a string comparison as part of the binary search (that is, a maximum of $\log n$ rows need to be decoded), and even then only enough is decoded to make the comparison decision. This comparison is shown in Algorithm 7.8, where i is the number of the row in A_s being compared to the pattern, P. If t is a string representing that row, the return value of the function is 0 if P is a prefix of t, negative if $P < t$ and positive if $P > t$.

i	T	F	L	C	V	W	R'	R
1	m	i	p	0	6	5	5	11
2	i	i	s	0	8	7	4	8
3	s	i	s	1	9	10	11	5
4	s	i	m	0	5	11	9	2
5	i	m	i	0	1	4	3	1
6	s	p	p	1	7	1	10	10
7	s	p	i	1	2	6	8	9
8	i	s	s	2	10	2	2	7
9	p	s	s	3	11	3	7	4
10	p	s	i	2	3	8	6	6
11	i	s	i	3	4	9	1	3

Fig. 7.9. Array values that can be used to do the BWT and searching of the text `mississippi`

BINARY-SEARCH-STRCMP(P, W, L, i)
1 $m \leftarrow$ LENGTH(P)
2 $j \leftarrow 1$
3 $i \leftarrow W[i]$
4 **while** $(m > 0$ **and** $L[i] = P[j])$ **do**
5     $i \leftarrow W[i]$
6     $m \leftarrow m - 1$
7     $j \leftarrow j + 1$
8 **end while**
9 **if** $m = 0$ **then**
10   **return** 0
11 **else**
12   **return** $P[j] - L[i]$
13 **end if**

Algorithm 7.8: String comparison function for binary search of BWT-transformed text; pattern P is being matched against the characters starting at position i in L (i.e. row i of A_s)

For example, if row $i = 9$ of A_s is being compared with the pattern $P =$ `sip`, the comparison algorithm uses W to change i from 9 to 3 to identify the first character of row 9, which is at $L[3]$. This character is `s`, which matches $P[1]$, and so i is changed to 10, and $L[10]$ is `i`, which matches $P[2]$. Finally, i is changed to 8, and $L[8]$ is `s`, which is greater than the character `p` at $P[3]$.

A negative value is returned, indicating that sip comes before row 9 if it is in A_s.

The use of the M array to index the substrings allows an improvement on the $O(m \log n)$ performance of binary search by narrowing the initial range of the search. If c is the first character of the pattern[1], the initial lower and upper bounds for a binary search are given by $M[c]$ and $M[c+1] - 1$. For instance, in the example in Figure 7.8, if the search pattern begins with the letter s, M tells us that it can occur only between lines 8 and 11. This range contains $\frac{n}{|\Sigma|}$ rows on average and therefore reduces the search time to $O(m \log \frac{n}{|\Sigma|})$ in the average case.

Binary search on a BWT-compressed file is illustrated in Algorithm 7.9 (Bell et al., 2002). It operates by performing a standard binary search on the range $M[c] \ldots M[c+1] - 1$, which results in a match with one occurrence of the pattern if any exists. It is also necessary, however, to locate other occurrences. This could be done by a simple linear search backward through the sorted substrings until the first mismatch is found, as well as forward to find the first mismatch in that direction (thus, identifying the first and last occurrence of the pattern). If there are η_{occ} occurrences of the pattern in the text, this would take $O(\eta_{occ})$ time, however, and would be rather time consuming if there are many occurrences. Instead, it is more efficient to apply two further binary searches. The first search locates the first substring that has P as a prefix and operates on the range $M[c] \ldots p-1$, where p is the location of the initial match. Like a standard binary search, each step compares the midpoint of the range to the pattern, however, if the comparison function returns a negative value or zero, it continues searching the range $low \ldots mid$; otherwise, it searches the range $mid + 1 \ldots high$. The second search locates the last occurrence of P and is performed in the range $p + 1 \ldots M[c+1] - 1$, but this time choosing the range $low \ldots mid - 1$ for a negative comparison result and $mid \ldots high$ for a positive or zero result. A further improvement can be made by basing the ranges for the two subsequent searches on mismatches of the initial search. The first of the two extra searches operates in the range $q \ldots p - 1$ where q is the largest known mismatched row in the range $M[c] \ldots p - 1$, that is, the last low value of the range. A similar range can be identified for the second search.

Finally, after all occurrences have been found in the sorted matrix, the corresponding matches in the text must be located. This is achieved using the R array. If the pattern matches lines $i \ldots j$ of the sorted matrix A_s, then the indexes for the matches in the text are identified by $R[i \ldots j]$, because R maps from F (the first characters of A_s) to T.

The version of the BWT-based binary search presented here uses W and L to compare the sorted strings of A_s, but the comparison could alternatively have been based on R' and F, since R' is the sorted array, and $F[R'[i]]$ gives

---

[1] We will assume that the alphabet can easily be mapped to integers, as is the case with codes such as ASCII.

BINARY-SEARCH(P, W, L, R)

```
 1  c ← P[1]
 2  P′ ← P[2...m]
 3  low ← M[c]
 4  high ← M[c + 1] − 1
 5
 6  while (low < high) do
 7      mid ← (low + high)/2
 8      cmp ← BINARY-SEARCH-STRCMP(P′, W, L, W[mid])
 9      switch cmp
10        case = 0 : break
11        case > 0 : low ← mid + 1
12        case < 0 : high ← mid
13      end switch
14  end while
15
16  if cmp = 0 then
17      h ← mid − 1
18      while (low < h) do
19          m ← (low + h)/2
20          if BINARY-SEARCH-STRCMP(P′, W, L, W[m]) > 0 then
21              low ← m + 1
22          else
23              h ← m
24          end if
25      end while
26      if BINARY-SEARCH-STRCMP(P′, W, L, W[low]) ≠ 0 then
27          low ← mid  /* No matches in low...mid − 1 */
28      end if
29
30      l ← mid + 1
31      while l < high do
32          m ← (l + high + 1)/2  /* Round up */
33          if BINARY-SEARCH-STRCMP(P′, W, L, W[m]) ≥ 0 then
34              l ← m
35          else
36              high ← m − 1
37          end if
38      end while
39      if BINARY-SEARCH-STRCMP(P′, W, L, W[high]) ≠ 0 then
40          high ← mid  /* No matches in mid + 1...high */
41      end if
42      return R[low...high]
43  else
44      return NULL  /* No matches found */
45  end if
```

Algorithm 7.9: BWT-based binary search algorithm

$T[i]$. This different formulation is used for inexact matching using q-grams, and it is closely related to pattern matching with suffix arrays (see Section 7.2.3), which also use the R array in place of W to determine the position for a comparison.

7.2.3 BWT-based exact pattern matching with suffix arrays

Suffix arrays (described in Section 4.2) are a useful tool for pattern matching, and the Burrows-Wheeler Transform naturally provides a suffix array because of the sorting that occurs during encoding. A suffix array is an index to all suffixes of a text sorted in the lexicographical order of the suffixes, and therefore allows patterns to be located in the text through a binary search of the index. This array is very similar to the sorted context structure used by binary search. However, the suffix array approach discussed in this section is really an *indexed-decompress-then-search* approach because it fully decodes the original text, T. The cost of constructing the index is trivial because it is just the R array (defined in Section 2.1), which can be produced as a by-product of decoding. The R array corresponds directly to a suffix tree; the suffix $T[R[i]\ldots]$ is the i'th entry in the suffix array.

Unlike the BWT-based binary search approach, the suffix array needs more work to set up searching, since it decodes the entire text T. However, it will be faster to perform matches, because the characters in T are accessed directly, whereas the binary search had to go through the W array for every character access.

Algorithm 2.6 shows how to construct R. Although this is shown as a separate operation from the decoding, it is possible to combine the two operations to reduce the number of passes through the text and avoid having to generate the W array. This is shown in Algorithm 7.10, which replaces the last loop in Algorithm 2.1.

SUFFIX-ARRAY-FROM-L-ARRAY (C, M, L)

```
16  i ← a
17  for j ← n downto 1 do
18      R[i] ← j + 1
19      if R[i] = n + 1 then
20          R[i] ← 1
21      end if
22      Q[j] ← L[i]
23      i ← C[i] + M[L[i]]
24  end for
```

Algorithm 7.10: Suffix array construction as the text is decoded (replaces lines 16 onwards from Algorithm 2.1)

Pattern matching with this structure can be performed in a manner similar to that of the BWT binary search approach. In fact, the steps described in Algorithm 7.9 can be reused, the only alterations being to the calls to BINARY-SEARCH-STRCMP. These calls are replaced with:

$$\text{SUFFIX-ARRAY-STRCMP}(P', T, R[x])$$

where x is the line in the suffix array to be compared with P'. This string comparison function for suffix arrays is much simpler than that of binary search because the text has already been decoded and is referenced directly — hence only the single array T is used for comparison, whereas binary search used the array L to get the text characters, and W to navigate around L. The suffix array comparison differs from an ordinary string comparison that might be found in a standard programming language library only in that it also reports that a match exists if the first string (the pattern) is a prefix of the second — they are not required to have the same length.

The suffix array approach (and indeed, the binary search method) can be adapted to be case insensitive. The general idea is quite simple: the comparison method is changed to ignore case when comparing two characters. However, this can't be done at just decode time; the encoder must also use the case-insensitive comparison, since the R array is based on the sort order of the encoding, and therefore both encoding and pattern matching must use the same rules for comparison so that they have the same lexical ordering for strings.

7.2.4 Pattern matching using the FM-index

The *FM-index* approach to compressed-domain pattern matching uses a combination of the Burrows-Wheeler Transform compression algorithm and a suffix array data structure to obtain a *compressed* suffix array (Ferragina and Manzini, 2000, 2001b, 2005). It is called FM-index because it is a **F**ull-text index that occupies a "**m**inute" amount of space[2]. The authors refer to it as an "Opportunistic Data Structure" because it reduces the storage requirements of the text without lowering the query performance. Indexing is added to the compressed BWT file to allow random access into the compressed data without the need to decompress completely at query time. This is an attractive property, since it avoids the pre-processing needed by the methods described earlier to obtain the BWT arrays.

The FM-index is a forerunner of what has become a relatively large family of compressed full-text indexes based on the BWT. A broad survey that covers related methods has been published by Navarro and Mäkinen (2007), and the "pizzachili" website (see Appendix B) is an ongoing source for evaluating related research. Chapter 8 has a section on compressed suffix trees and compressed suffix arrays.

---

[2] Coincidentally, "FM" also matches the initials of its authors, Ferragina and Manzini.

Searching using FM-index

Searching with the FM-index is performed through two key functions: COUNT and LOCATE. COUNT determines how many matches there are for the pattern in the text, and LOCATE identifies where they can be decoded from. Both use the OCC function, which for $\text{OCC}(c, k)$ returns the number of occurrences of the character c in $L[1 \ldots k]$. In principle this can be done directly using the C array generated during BWT decoding, but because FM-index avoids decompression, this information must instead be stored with the compressed file, and therefore it needs to be represented as efficiently as possible. We shall see in the section below on compression and auxiliary information that it is possible to store this auxiliary information compactly with the compressed file, and still retrieve it in $O(1)$ time.

The OCC function is an important feature of the FM-index because it allows random entries of the V array[3] to be calculated as needed (see Appendix A for a definition of V, and Figure 7.9 for its values for our running example). Thus, unlike the other algorithms in this section, the transform arrays need not be constructed in their entirety before searching begins; only the M array is required[4]. Access to M is described in the section below on compression and auxiliary information; it has just one entry for each character in the alphabet, so is very small. When required, an entry in V is calculated as

$$V[i] \leftarrow M[c] + \text{OCC}(c, i) - 1, \text{ where } c = L[i].$$

This is equivalent to line 19 of Algorithm 2.1.

The function COUNT identifies the starting position sp and ending position ep of the pattern in the rows of the sorted matrix. For example, if we are searching for occurrences of ssi in the text $T = \text{mississippi}$ then the relevant matches are at the start of rows in the range from 10 to 11 in the suffix array, as shown in Figure 7.10, so the COUNT function will return $sp = 10$ and $ep = 11$. The number of times the pattern appears in the text is $ep - sp + 1$.

The COUNT function can be implemented in $O(m)$ time as illustrated in Algorithm 7.11. Matching is performed from right to left along the pattern, taking advantage of the grouping of all occurrences of a character in F. There are m phases, whereby, at the i-th phase, sp points to the first row of the suffix matrix that has $P[i \ldots m]$ as a prefix and ep points to the last row that has $P[i \ldots m]$ as a prefix. Thus, after the m phases, the first and last occurrences of the pattern are referenced. For example, when searching for the phrase ssi in the text mississippi (Figure 7.10), in the first phase the range (sp to ep)

---

[3] Papers about the FM-index method refer to V as LF, since it maps the L array to the F array.

[4] Instead of M, papers about FM-index use an array called C, for which $C[i] = M[i] - 1$. For consistency with other algorithms in this book, we use M, and have changed the FM-index algorithms accordingly.

1 i
2 ippi
3 issippi
4 ississippi
5 mississippi
6 pi
7 ppi
8 sippi
9 sissippi
→ 10 ssippi
→ 11 ssissippi

Fig. 7.10. Looking for matches for ssi in the text mississippi using the FM-index method

is 1 to 4 (rows starting with i), in the second phase it is 8 to 9 (rows starting with si), and the third time it is 10 to 11 (rows starting with ssi).

COUNT(P, M)
1 $i \leftarrow m$
2 $c \leftarrow P[m]$
3 $sp \leftarrow M[c]$
4 $ep \leftarrow M[c + 1] - 1$
5 **while** ($sp \leq ep$ **and** $i \geq 2$) **do**
6      $c \leftarrow P[i - 1]$
7      $sp \leftarrow M[c]+ \text{OCC}(c, sp - 1)$
8      $ep \leftarrow M[c]+ \text{OCC}(c, ep) - 1$
9      $i \leftarrow i - 1$
10 **end while**
11 **if** $ep < sp$ **then**
12   **return** $ep - sp + 1$
13 **else**
14   **return** 0
15 **end if**

Algorithm 7.11: Counting pattern occurrences with FM-index

For some applications it may be sufficient just to count the number of occurrences of the pattern, but generally we will want to read the text surrounding the pattern. This is done by the LOCATE function, which takes the index of a row in the sorted matrix A_s and returns the starting position of the corresponding substring in the text. Thus, an iteration over the range $sp \ldots ep$ identified by COUNT, calling LOCATE for each position, will result in a list of all occurrences of the pattern in the text. Normally we could just use the array R to locate the position, but because the text is still compressed at this point and R would be too large to store, the LOCATE function is used. Instead of storing all of R, only a small number of selected values are stored, and the positions that they correspond to are "marked". The technique for determining which rows are marked and how they are represented is discussed in the section below on compression and auxiliary information, but the main point is that the LOCATE function simply works backwards through the text until it finds a "marked" position i' for which $pos(i')$ is available, and from that $pos(i)$ can be determined.

The method for locating the position $pos(i)$ using the auxiliary information is shown in Algorithm 7.12. The location of row i is denoted by $pos(i)$, and if it is a marked row, the value is available directly. If i is not marked then, M and OCC are used to locate the previous character, $T[pos(i) - 1]$, in the text (each loop in the algorithm is just calculating the entry $V[i']$ on the fly). For example, for Figure 7.10, if we wish to locate where the first match for ssi occurs in the text, we will call LOCATE(10) since it appears in line 10 of A_s. If row 10 is not "marked", then the iteration will change i' to 3, because $L[3]$ is the character in T that comes before $L[10]$. If row 3 isn't marked then it will continue back with i' going through 9, then 11, 4, and so on. Note that this is equivalent to setting $i' \leftarrow V[i']$, but does not need the V array to be stored explicitly. This is repeated v times until a marked row, i_v, is found. The marked row is therefore v characters earlier in the text than the one we wanted to locate, so at this point we can return $pos(i) = pos(i_v) + v$. Using this algorithm, $pos(i)$ has calculated $R[i]$ based on a small subset of the R array which was stored as "marked" nodes.

LOCATE(i)
1 $i' \leftarrow i$
2 $v \leftarrow 0$
3 **while** (*row i' is not marked*) **do**
4     $c \leftarrow L[i']$
5     $m \leftarrow Occ(c, i')$
6     $i' \leftarrow M[c] + m - 1$
7     $v \leftarrow v + 1$
8 **end while**
9 **return** $pos(i') + v$

Algorithm 7.12: Locating the position of a match in the original text for FM-index

In many respects, the search algorithm of the FM-index is very similar to that of the BWT binary search, but where binary search first locates one instance of the pattern in the sorted matrix and then uses another two binary searches to locate the first and last instances, the FM-index uses an incremental approach, identifying the first and last occurrences of the suffixes of the pattern, increasing the size of the suffix until the locations have been found for the entire pattern. Lines 8 and 9 of Algorithm 7.11 effectively perform mappings using the V array rather than W, which was used by the BWT binary search. This is because V corresponds to processing the text in reverse. Also, binary search is able to report the location in the text of a match with one array lookup to the R auxiliary array, instead of the more complex operations employed by the LOCATE function, which effectively reconstructs parts of R as needed. The price paid by binary search is that it must decompress before pattern matching can begin.

Compression and auxiliary information

The compression process used by the FM-index method is different from the other algorithms in this section because it needs to allow random access into the compressed file. Additional indexing information is also stored with the compressed file so that the search algorithm may perform the OCC function efficiently and report the location of matches. The file structure is designed so that the extra information takes up little space.

To compress the text, the Burrows-Wheeler Transform permuted text, L, is created and partitioned into segments of size ℓ_{sb} which are referred to as *superbuckets*, with each superbucket being partitioned into smaller segments of size ℓ_b which are referred to as *buckets*. The buckets are then compressed individually using multiple-table Huffman coding (Wheeler, 1997).

Random access is available to the start of a superbucket, and in turn to one of the buckets within it. Thus if the buckets are too large then the access time will be slow because of having to decode irrelevant material to get to the desired location; however if they are too small then compression performance will be poor because coding is done independently in each bucket. Ferragina and Manzini performed extensive experiments with the FM-index and found that 16 kilobyte superbuckets and 1 kilobyte buckets provide a good compromise between compression and search performance in general; these are the values used for the evaluation of this method.

For each superbucket, a header is created that stores a table of the number of occurrences of all characters in the previous superbuckets. That is, the header for superbucket S_i contains the number of occurrences for each character $c \in \Sigma$ in $S_1 \ldots S_{i-1}$. Each bucket has a similar header, but contains character counts for the buckets from the beginning of its superbucket. Thus, OCC(c, k) can be calculated in $O(1)$ time by decompressing the bucket containing $L[k]$ and counting the occurrences in that bucket up to $L[k]$, then adding the values stored for c in the corresponding superbucket and bucket headers. To increase search performance, a *bucket directory* has also been proposed. This directory records the starting positions in the compressed file of each bucket, so that any bucket may be located with a single directory lookup.

This auxiliary information can also be compressed because, as described in Section 7.2, the L array often has clusterings of characters, which means that the range of characters in each superbucket will usually be small. A bitmap is stored to identify which subset of characters appears in each superbucket. Thus, a header needs to contain only counts for characters that are recorded in the corresponding superbucket's bitmap. Furthermore, variable integer coding may be used to reduce the space required for the entries that are stored.

One further structure that must be considered contains the information about the marked rows that identify the location in the text of some of the rows in the sorted matrix. Empirical results have shown that marking 2% of the rows provides a suitable compromise between storage requirements and search speed when using a superbucket size of 16 kilobytes and a bucket size of 1 kilobyte (Ferragina and Manzini, 2001b). A number of marking schemes have been proposed to determine which of the rows should be marked. One possibility marks rows at evenly spaced intervals, where the interval is determined by the percentage of rows that are marked. However, an alternative scheme was favored (which is also used in the discussion of performance later in this chapter) to make the search algorithm simpler even though it performs poorly in some circumstances. It takes advantage of the fact that each character in the alphabet appears roughly evenly spaced throughout an ordinary English text. The character c that appears in the text with the frequency closest to 2% is selected, and any row ending with c is marked by storing its corresponding location using $\log n$ bits. This simplifies the searching because, if i is a marked row, $pos(i)$ is stored in entry $\text{OCC}(c, i)$ of the marked rows, whereas the former strategy requires extra information to be calculated or stored to relate a marked row to the position where its value is stored. The latter strategy, however, relies heavily on the structure of the text and performance deteriorates significantly if characters are not evenly spaced.

Finally, we note that the search algorithm also requires access to the M array. This is not defined in the original FM-index papers, although it contains only $|\Sigma|$ entries and so will have an insignificant effect on the size of the compressed file. In principle it could be constructed with a single pass over the auxiliary information before searching begins, but this is unlikely to be justified given that it is such a small array.

7.2.5 Algorithm improvements with overwritten arrays

This section describes a way to improve some of the pattern matching algorithms, both in memory requirements and search time, by introducing *overwritten* arrays.

Overwritten arrays are a simple modification to the BWT-based suffix arrays and binary search algorithms that re-use the space allocated to one of the temporary BWT arrays rather than allocate more memory for a new array. They are able to reduce search time, and for suffix arrays, reduce memory usage.

Algorithm 7.10 showed the method for constructing the R array construction as the text is being decoded. During one iteration of the **for** loop, the

i-th element of C is read and a value is stored in the i-th element of R. The suffix array method does not require the C array after R has been constructed, so it is possible to write the entry for $R[i]$ into $C[i]$ at the end of each loop, avoiding the need to allocate a separate area of memory for a second array. Furthermore, if the computer is using a cache then this approach can reduce the number of cache misses during the creation of R, which means that the modification increases the speed as well.

Binary search uses Algorithm 2.6 (page 30) to create R (note that line 3 can be omitted because R' is not needed). The array W will be needed afterward as part of the searching process, so we cannot overwrite it. However, it turns out that because of caching, it can be more efficient to create W, then copy its values to another array and overwrite that copy with R. This is because the loop in Algorithm 2.6 is now only reading and writing sequentially from one array, providing excellent locality of reference. This provides a faster search performance, but unlike the suffix array method, does not reduce memory usage.

7.3 Performance of BWT-based exact pattern matching

In this section we will compare the different approaches for using BWT-coded files for pattern matching. Results for a decompress-then-search approach (using the standard Boyer-Moore algorithm described in Section 7.1.3) have also been included to provide a reference point. Boyer-Moore was selected as the reference because it is currently considered to be one of the most efficient pattern matching algorithms for searching an ordinary text file. For more extensive and updated comparisons the reader is referred to the sites mentioned in Appendix B, particularly the "pizzachili" site.

The implementations reported here employ the improvements introduced in Section 7.2.5, since these make a worthwhile improvement to both the speed and memory performance. Unless stated otherwise, the tests were performed on "bible.txt", a 4 Mbyte English text file from the Canterbury corpus[5]. The nature of the BWT output for this file was studied in Section 5.4. For most experiments, patterns were selected randomly from the set of words that appear in the text being searched. Of course, some selected words will appear as substrings of other words, and so the substrings will also be located by the search algorithms. For the experiment on pattern length (Section 7.3.2), the search patterns were not restricted to English words; they could be any string that appeared in the text that had the required length. Because different selections of search patterns will take different amounts of time, error bars are shown in graphs that report the speed of each method. These are based on 50 repetitions of each search, and the error bars show the confidence intervals one standard deviation above and below the mean. Unless otherwise stated,

---

[5] http://corpus.canterbury.ac.nz

the reported times include the time for full or partial decompression (that is, construction of the auxiliary arrays) as is required, as well as the time for searching. Section 7.3.3 investigates the time required to construct the auxiliary arrays, without searching.

7.3.1 Compression performance

The compression performance of BWT-based systems for pattern matching is reported in this chapter using files from the Canterbury corpus. A brief description of the files is given in Table 7.2. Some of the files (such as the large "E.coli" file, which uses only the four characters a, c, g and t) are not conventional text, and provide a good test of the systems for more unusual kinds of inputs.

Table 7.3 compares the compression ratio of the pattern-matching based methods with BZIP2. BZIP2, a production-quality compression program that uses the Burrows-Wheeler Transform, and represents the state-of-the-art in terms of a practical system that has been developed with both speed and compression in mind. The BSMP method is the compression approach used to evaluate the binary search and suffix array pattern matching algorithms in this chapter; in principle the methods from BZIP2 could have been used to get better performance, but we are mainly concerned with relative performance, and the simpler BSMP suffices for this. The table also gives the compression performance of the FM-index method (abbreviated as FM-i), which must store auxiliary information with the compressed text.

File name	Size (bytes)	Description
alice29.txt	152,089	English text ("Alice in Wonderland")
asyoulik.txt	125,179	Shakespeare ("As you like it")
bible.txt	4,047,392	King James Bible
cp.html	24,603	HTML source
E.coli	4,638,690	Complete genome of the E. Coli bacterium
fields.c	11,150	C source code
grammar.lsp	3,721	LISP source code
lcet10.txt	426,754	Technical writing
plrabn12.txt	481,861	Poetry
world192.txt	2,473,400	The CIA world fact book
xargs.1	4,227	GNU manual page

Table 7.2. The files in the Canterbury corpus

In most cases, BZIP2 provides the best compression, closely followed by BSMP. The exception is "E.coli" where BSMP is marginally better. This file contains genetic data, which has little structure that the Burrows-Wheeler Transform can exploit, and thus is only compressible due to the ability to store the characters in two bits (because the alphabet has a size of four)

File	Size	Compression Ratio BZIP2	BSMP	FM-i
alice29.txt	152,089	2.27	2.56	3.52
asyoulik.txt	125,179	2.53	2.85	3.79
bible.txt	4,047,392	1.67	1.79	2.58
cp.html	24,603	2.48	2.72	4.26
E.coli	4,638,690	2.16	2.12	2.69
fields.c	11,150	2.18	2.43	3.88
grammar.lsp	3,721	2.76	2.92	4.65
lcet10.txt	426,754	2.02	2.30	3.30
plrabn12.txt	481,861	2.42	2.74	3.57
world192.txt	2,473,400	1.58	1.60	2.66
xargs.1	4,227	3.33	3.54	5.24
mean		2.31	2.51	3.65

Table 7.3. Compression achieved by algorithms based on the Burrows-Wheeler Transform. Size is in bytes and compression ratio is in bits per character

instead of the eight bits used in the uncompressed file. In this situation, the technique used by BSMP of compressing the entire file in one block has a lower overhead than that of BZIP2, which segments the file into 900 kilobyte blocks and compresses each block independently of the others.

In all cases, the FM-index produces the largest files. Their size, on average, is more than one bit per character larger, which is due to the additional indexing information that is stored (see Section 7.2.4). This compares favorably, however, to full-text retrieval systems such as MG (Witten et al., 1999), which is an offline system for compressing and indexing text. MG uses an inverted file for indexing, which, for "bible.txt", occupies 14.4% of the space of the original file. In contrast, the index structure of the FM-index occupies less than 10%. The FM-index also saves a small amount of space by compressing the text using a BWT-based method, as opposed to the word-based Huffman coder used by MG. Overall, the FM-index uses 0.68 bits per character less than MG when the auxiliary files of MG are ignored, and 1.56 less, when they are included.

Table 7.4 shows the time taken by the three compression approaches to compress and decompress the files in the large collection of the Canterbury corpus[6]. The large collection was used because some of the running times on smaller files are too short to make significant comparisons. Note that the speed of BSMP is poor simply because the implementation has not been tuned carefully. In particular, it treats the file as a single block, and most of the encoding time is spent sorting the block, which can be several megabytes for the test files. In contrast, BZIP2 limits blocks to 900 kilobytes. The BSMP

---

[6] The times reported in this section are based on experiments run on a 1.4GHz AMD Athlon with 512 Mbytes of memory, running Red Hat Linux 7.2. The CPU had a 64 kilobyte first level cache and a 256 kilobyte second level cache.

File	Size	Compression Time BZIP2 BSMP	FM-i	Decompression Time BZIP2 BSMP	FM-i
bible.txt	4,047,392	3.29 48.62	6.98	0.98 4.05	1.68
E.coli	4,638,690	4.01 64.45	6.96	1.39 5.53	2.17
world192.txt	2,473,400	2.06 33.14	4.24	0.66 2.39	0.95

Table 7.4. Speed of the compression and decompression algorithms; size is in bytes and times are in seconds

method could easily be improved by using smaller blocks, and a better sorting algorithm.

In all cases, BZIP2 has the best compression time. The FM-index was slightly slower, partly because it is not as highly optimized as BZIP2, but also because of the additional time required to create the necessary indexing information.

The decompression time is the more important measurement, because all of the search methods require at least partial decompression for searching. When decompressing, the performance of BSMP was comparatively closer to that of the FM-index, with most of the difference caused by the slower nature of an arithmetic coder (used by BSMP) over a Huffman coder (used by the FM-index). Again, the highly tuned BZIP2 significantly outperforms the other two approaches.

7.3.2 Search performance

Search performance is often reported in terms of the number of comparisons required for a search, although in practice other metrics may be more meaningful. As shown in Section 7.2, the index-based algorithms that use binary search (binary search and suffix arrays), require $O(m \log \frac{n}{|\Sigma|})$ comparisons. The remaining two index-based algorithms evaluated here — BWT-BM and the decompress-then-search approach (both based on Boyer-Moore) — use $O(m+n)$ comparisons on average. These analyses consider only the searching process, however, and ignore the requirements of some algorithms to create indexes or decompress the text before searching begins. A better measure of search time would be $O(n + sm \log \frac{n}{|\Sigma|})$ and $O(n + s(m + n))$, respectively, where s is the number of searches performed, and the additional $O(n)$ term covers the decompression and indexing steps, which operate in linear time.

Although the FM-index method also uses a binary search, comparisons are made in a linear fashion during both the OCC function and the LOCATE function. In OCC, a bucket is decompressed and the occurrences of a particular character in the required portion of the bucket are counted. Each step of the LOCATE function involves determining whether the given row is marked. For the marking scheme described in Section 7.2.4 (Compression and auxiliary information), this involves a comparison of the last character in the row with the character used for marking. Thus, FM-index requires only $O(m)$ time and in $O(\frac{n}{\log n} \log \log n)$ bits of extra space to count the number of occurrences of a single pattern in the text. If the pattern occurs η_{occ} times, FM-index will require $O(m + \eta_{occ} \log^2 n)$ time, using space bounded by $5H_k(T) + O(\frac{\log \log n}{\log m})$ bits to locate all the η_{occ} occurrences, where $H_k(T)$ is the k-th order entropy.

Figure 7.11 shows the mean number of comparisons, plotted against pattern length, to search for all words in "bible.txt" — that is, the text sequence was the contents of "bible.txt", and each distinct word in "bible.txt" was used as a pattern.

The binary search and suffix array methods based on BWT work particularly well, which is not surprising given the logarithmic effort required — the text had about 4 million characters, which implies only about 22 substring comparisons, and each string comparison involves just a few characters. In contrast, the FM-index method requires a lot of comparisons to locate a word because it must search linearly back through the text to find a marked entry.

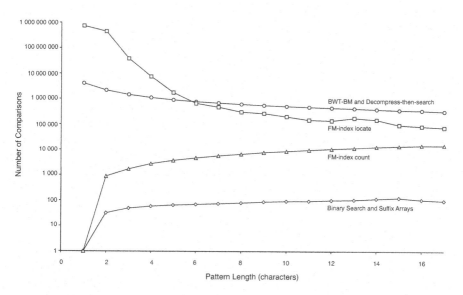

Fig. 7.11. Mean number of comparisons by pattern length for "bible.txt"

Interestingly, for patterns of length one, no comparisons are required by the non-index based algorithms that use binary search (binary search and suffix arrays), or for counting in FM-index. This is due to the use of the M array, which can be used to identify the first and last positions in the sorted array of any character with only two array lookups (see Section 7.2.2) and thus, the locations for any pattern containing just one character.

The number of comparisons for BWT-BM and the decompress-then-search approaches decreases as the pattern length increases. With larger patterns, the probability of a match is reduced, and the shifts proposed by the two heuristics of Boyer-Moore tend to be larger. Thus, more of the text is skipped and the number of comparisons decreases.

The number of comparisons for locating occurrences with the FM-index also decreases with an increasing pattern length, but for a different reason. Because the number of comparisons is highly dependent on the number of occurrences of the pattern, small patterns, which are likely to appear more often in the text, require more comparisons.

Of course, the actual performance of each algorithm is not just dependent on the number of comparisons executed. Search time can vary greatly depending on which arrays are used for indexing and how they are constructed. In the following, we evaluate the performance of the algorithms when locating patterns, and explore reasons for the differences between algorithms. We also discuss the situation where it is necessary only to count the number of times a pattern occurs in the text, without needing to identify the locations of the occurrences. Finally, we explore additional factors that affect search times, such as file size, pattern length and file content.

Locating patterns

Apart from the FM-index, before searching begins, the search algorithms require the compression of the move-to-front coder, run-length coder and arithmetic coder to be reversed, as well as temporary arrays to be constructed in memory. Once created, however, the arrays may be used to execute many searches. Thus, multiple searches during one run of a search program will not take the same amount of time as the equivalent number of searches on separate occasions. Situations where multiple searches may be useful include boolean queries with many terms, or interactive applications where users refine or change their queries. Figure 7.12a shows how the search time increases with the number of patterns being matched. Figure 7.12b shows the same data, but focuses on a smaller range of the results.

Figure 7.12a indicates that binary search and suffix arrays give virtually constant performances regardless of the number of patterns involved. This is because of the small number of comparisons required for a search and means that almost all of the time is used to construct the required arrays before searching begins. From Figure 7.12b, we can see that binary search was a little faster of the two, but there isn't a significant difference between them. The minor difference is largely due to the time taken to construct the different arrays needed by the respective algorithms.

The search times for the decompress-then-search and BWT-BM algorithms increase linearly as the number of patterns increases. For a small number of patterns, the decompress-then-search approach is slower than compressed-domain Boyer-Moore because of the overhead of completely decompressing the text before searching begins. It is the more efficient algorithm, however, when there are more searches to be performed. This is because it has direct access

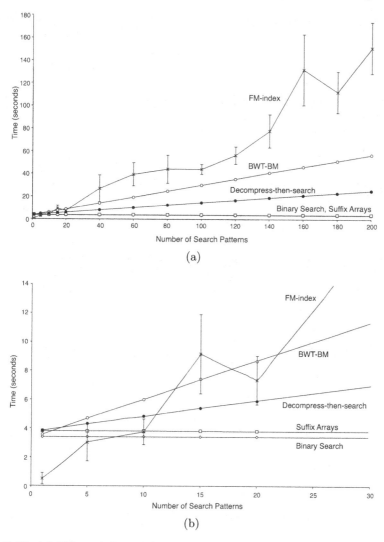

Fig. 7.12. (a) Effect of the number of occurrences (multiple search patterns) on search time; (b) magnified view of the search times

to the text to make comparisons, whereas the compressed-domain version must decompress the required substrings before a comparison can be made, and with more searches, more comparisons are required. Figure 7.12b shows that the overhead of the comparisons outweighs the initial savings of BWT-BM when more than three searches were performed. It also shows that for a small number of patterns, BWT-BM is more efficient than suffix arrays, although it was always slower than binary search. At best, decompress-then-search provided a similar performance to suffix arrays when the number of searches, s, is one.

Finally, we note that the FM-index has the best performance on average until about 10 patterns are involved. For a single search, it takes only 0.5 seconds on average because, unlike the other algorithms, there is no need to construct any indexes before searching begins. Without the indexing information in memory, however, performance deteriorates significantly as the number of patterns increases, and for more than 25 patterns, it has the worst performance on average.

From the error bars in Figure 7.12a, we can see that the performance of the FM-index is highly variable. Variations in the other algorithms are insignificant. The inconsistency of the FM-index is caused by the technique used to locate the positions of matches. If the matching row of the sorted matrix is not marked, the FM-index must iterate backwards through the text until a marked row is found (see Section 7.2.4). When the search pattern appears in the text many times, this inefficient location process is executed often, resulting in a poor performance overall, whereas a pattern that occurs only once will be located quickly. This variation against the number of pattern occurrences is shown explicitly in Figure 7.13.

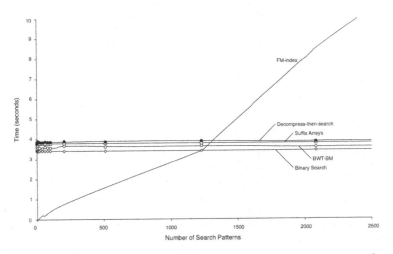

Fig. 7.13. Search times for patterns with various numbers of occurrences (number of search patterns) in the text

Counting occurrences

For some applications, it may be necessary only to determine the number of times that a pattern appears in a text, or perhaps, to determine whether it exists at all. An example of such an application is an Internet search engine

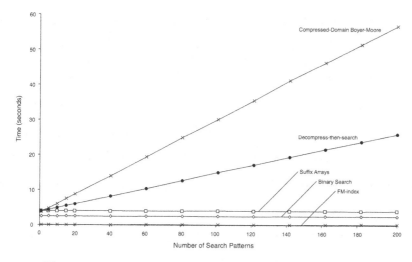

Fig. 7.14. Times for counting occurrences of multiple patterns

that returns a page as long as it contains a specified pattern, possibly ranked by the number of times the pattern appears. Another is a program such as GREP in UNIX (-c option) which locates the directory files that contain a given pattern, and for each file displays the number of lines with the input pattern. Figure 7.14 shows the time taken by each of the methods to count the occurrences of patterns.

Apart from the FM-index and binary search, the algorithms take the same amount of time to count the patterns as they do to locate them — even when match positions are not required, decompress-then-search and compressed-domain Boyer-Moore must still pass through the entire file to count the appearances. Suffix arrays identify the positions of matches using just a single array lookup for each occurrence, so in this case where the positions are not required, they only avoid simple array references and therefore showed no noticeable difference in their performances.

In contrast, FM-index is particularly good at counting occurrences, and it is the location phase that is slow. In fact, it returns the counts almost instantly regardless of the number of patterns because the information is looked up directly without decoding the compressed text. Binary search also saves time by not locating matches because it does not need to construct the R array (which is used to locate the matches). Nevertheless, it is still significantly slower than the FM-index method.

Other factors

The performance reported so far has been for a large file of English text. The performance of many algorithms can vary considerably, however, if a file of a

Algorithm	Search Arrays	Construction Arrays	Memory for Searching	Maximum Memory
Decompress-then-search	T	L, W	n	$6n$
Compressed-domain BM	F, R'	L, W	$5n$	$8n$
Binary Search	R, L, W		$9n$	$9n$
Suffix Arrays	R, T	C, L	$5n$	$6n$
FM-index	1 Bucket		1000	1000

Table 7.5. Memory requirements of the search algorithms, given in bytes

different size is used, or if the file type is altered. In this section we look at the effect of other factors on performance.

File Size. The FM-index method is almost unaffected by file size, since it works with the compressed file and accesses buckets directly. However, the other methods must decode the file at least to get L, as well as some auxiliary arrays, and so the time taken to prepare for any search will increase approximately linearly with the file size. These methods will have problems if the file is too large for memory. The access patterns for BWT processing are not suitable for virtual memory, and so the file will need to be broken up into smaller blocks. In contrast, the FM-index method can work with any size file, since only a small block is decoded at any time.

File type. Files with a very small alphabet (such as E.coli which uses only four characters) can cause slow performance for some compression systems. The binary search and suffix array approaches are resilient to this type of file because they have a logarithmic search time which is not affected significantly by the file content. However, the FM-index method slows down for files with a small alphabet because there is a higher frequency of short patterns, leading to many matches that need to be located individually. The Boyer-Moore based method can also behave poorly if there is a lot of repetition in the input, because the proposed shift will be one if there are many candidate match positions.

Memory Usage. Several of the arrays used by the algorithms are $O(n)$ size, although some space can be saved by using the overwriting technique mentioned in Section 7.2.5. The arrays used by each algorithm are listed in Table 7.5, separating those that are required during searching from those that are needed to construct the search structures, and can then be discarded. The memory size is estimated assuming that arrays storing characters (F, L and T) use 1-byte entries and the remaining arrays store 4-byte integers. We have neglected the small auxiliary arrays M and K, as they contain only one entry for each character in the alphabet and will be very small compared with the other arrays. The FM-index uses just one kilobyte regardless of file size because it loads only one bucket at a time during searching, and the remaining data is stored on disk until it is needed.

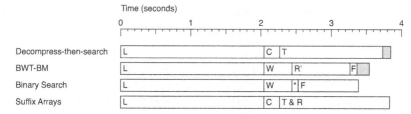

Fig. 7.15. Times for constructing the auxiliary arrays used in BWT searching

7.3.3 Array construction speeds

For most of the methods described there is a considerable overhead in creating the auxiliary arrays before pattern matching can start. Figure 7.15 shows the arrays used by each algorithm and indicates the time required to construct them for the compressed "bible.txt" file. The average time to search for one pattern is indicated in gray, although for some algorithms this search time was insignificant and is not visible on the diagram. As all of these times increase linearly with the file size, the ratios between them will stay fairly constant.

All of the algorithms require L, the Burrows-Wheeler Transform permutation of the file that was compressed. The construction of L involves reading the compressed file from disk, then reversing the arithmetic coding, run-length coding and move-to-front coding that was originally used to compress L. Each algorithm also uses K and M, both of which can be created relatively quickly in comparison to other arrays. They are primarily used in the construction of W or C and have therefore been included in the cost of building those arrays.

Usage of the remaining arrays varies, and is the cause of the difference in performance of the algorithms. In particular, decompress-then-search and suffix arrays both use the decoded text, T. While producing T, however, suffix arrays create R as a by-product. This takes additional time but makes searching considerably more efficient (see Section 7.3.2) so that the first search, and subsequent searches, are performed almost instantly. In contrast, the first search by the decompress-then-search approach takes almost the same amount of time as the construction of R in suffix arrays, so that the time to search for a single pattern is similar for both algorithms. With the availability of R, however, multiple pattern searches were more efficient with suffix arrays. Using the overwriting technique (Section 7.2.5), the cost of creating R' is lower than that of T which means that, even though it also requires F, BWT-BM is more efficient for a single search than decompress-then-search and suffix arrays. The BWT-based binary search is the fastest algorithm because it avoids constructing R' and T. (The asterisk in the binary search time represents the process of copying W).

7.3.4 Comparison with LZ-based compressed-domain pattern matching

With respect to pattern matching, the major focus of this book is on BWT-based methods. However, to place the results in context, this section provides a brief comparison with non-BWT based search methods, especially methods that work with LZ-based compression schemes: GZIP-GREP (compress with GZIP, decompress then search with GREP), GZIP-AGREP (compress with GZIP, decompress then search with AGREP), and LZGREP, a compressed pattern matching program for LZ-compressed files (Navarro and Tarhio, 2005).

The LZ-based methods are generally faster than BWT-based methods for compression, but the major advantage of using BWT over LZ algorithms is the amount of compression achieved. For example, the three files in the Large corpus in the Canterbury corpus give an average compression of 2.33 bits per character (bpc) with GZIP -9, which is one of the best LZ-based compression methods, compared with 1.84 bpc produced by BSMP, or 1.80 bpc for BZIP2.

Figure 7.16 shows the performance of the BWT-based and LZ-based methods in terms of total search time. As usual, this includes the time needed by the BWT algorithms to perform the partial decoding and to compute the auxiliary arrays when needed.

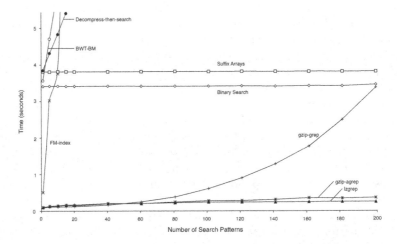

Fig. 7.16. Search times for multiple single-occurrence patterns

The bottleneck for the BWT-based methods is the time required to compute the auxiliary arrays. Table 7.6 shows a break-down of the total time used by the BWT-based search algorithms. The table shows that the actual search time, after these arrays have been constructed, is relatively insignificant. Also, bear in mind that the BSMP method measured is not particularly fast, and the techniques used in the BZIP2 implementation could be used to accelerate it considerably.

Search Method	Auxiliary array Construction Time	Search Time	Total Time
BWT-BM	3.39	53.29	56.68
Binary Search	3.4	0.03	3.43
Suffix Arrays	3.8	0.02	3.82
FM-Index	-	-	151.25
GZIP-GREP	-	-	3.37
GZIP-AGREP	-	-	0.25
LZGREP	-	-	0.36

Table 7.6. Break down of search time (in seconds) measured over a search of 200 patterns

Overall, LZ-based methods will be preferred when speed is more important than compression, while BWT-based methods give better compression, and are also more suited if multiple patterns are to be matched after the overhead of setting up arrays has been done.

7.4 Approximate pattern matching

Until now we have assumed that patterns must match exactly with the text being searched. However, there are many applications where we would prefer to find close matches, rather than require strict identity; and there are other applications where we wish to apply a metric to the difference, and find matches that conform to some specified parameters.

This section is concerned with such situations, which require *inexact* or *approximate* pattern matching. The need to consider approximation may arise in the context of *errors* which might occur in a text file because of inaccuracies in the data stored, or in the pattern being searched for; and it arises in the context of determining how *similar* two strings are.

There are many practical situations where approximate pattern matching algorithms are very useful. The first is searching a text database using keywords where both the text and the keywords could have spelling errors, or are partially specified, or have variants with very similar spelling. The second is to reconstruct a text transmitted via a noisy channel which might have corrupted the text by dropping, inserting or changing characters. Approximate pattern matching algorithms have also been used as powerful tools in the study of genomics and proteomics; in finding genes, regulatory motifs, conserved sequences in DNA, sequence alignment and multiple sequence alignments. The goal of this section is to present a few fundamental algorithms on approximate pattern matching and show how the Burrows-Wheeler Transform can be used to expedite approximate pattern search. There is a huge amount of literature on the subject of approximate pattern matching, and the interested reader is referred to additional references at the end of this chapter to pursue the topic more in-depth.

7.4.1 Edit distance: dynamic programming formulation

Given two strings $S_1 = a_1 a_2 \ldots a_m$ and $S_2 = b_1 b_2 \ldots b_n$, the problem is to determine how similar they are. This can be made more precise by defining an integer parameter k and a *distance function* d and then stating the problem as finding all substrings S of S_2 such that $d(S_1, S) \leq k$. Let us first consider how to compute $d(S_1, S_2)$. A natural way to compare these two strings is to determine their *edit distance* (sometimes called the *Levenshtein* distance), defined as the minimum number of editing operations that will transform one string to the other string. The two simplest such operations are *insertion* and *deletion* of a character, and a cost of 1 is usually associated with each such operation. A third operation is *substitution* or *replacement* of a character of one sequence by another character of the second sequence, as it happens in a mutation of a DNA sequence. The cost for this operation is also usually assumed to be 1, but in text editing operations this can be realized by one delete operation followed immediately by an insert operation in which case the cost should then be 2 for this operation. If two characters match, the cost is assumed to be 0. In general, arbitrary cost values can be defined for these operations depending on the application. The sequence of edit operations to transform S_1 to S_2 is called the *edit transcript*. A dynamic programming formulation to compute the edit distance is as follows: define $d(i,j)$ to be the edit distance between the prefix strings $S_1[1 \ldots i]$ and $S_2[1 \ldots j]$. The "basis" equations are: $d(0,0) = 0$ because no cost is involved in converting a null string to a null string, $d(i,0) = i$ for $1 \leq i \leq m$ signifying that i deletion operations are needed to convert the prefix of S_1 to a null string, and $d(0,j) = j$ for $1 \leq j \leq n$ signifying that j insertion operations are needed to covert a null string to the prefix $S_2[1 \ldots j]$. We can write the recurrence relation as

$$d(i,j) = min\{d(i-1,j) + 1, d(i,j-1) + 1, d(i-1,j-1) + c(i,j)\},$$

where $c(i,j) = 0$ if $a_i = b_j$; otherwise let us assume $c(i,j) = 1$ for the moment. Consider a minimum cost edit transcript for $d(i,j)$. If the last operation of this transcript is an *insertion* operation in S_2, then this corresponds to the term $d(i,j-1) + 1$ and the *alignment* must have been at this point $(-, S_2[j])$ or $\begin{pmatrix} - \\ S_2[j] \end{pmatrix}$ where '-' stands for a gap created in sequence S_1. This is also symbolized by a horizontal arrow in the $m+1$ by $n+1$ matrix $\mathcal{M}$ associated with $d(i,j)$ values, from cell $(i, j-1)$ to cell (i,j) in $\mathcal{M}$. If the last operation of this transcript is a *deletion* operation in S_1, then the corresponding term is $d(i-1,j) + 1$ and the alignment must have been at this point $(S_1[i], -)$ or $\begin{pmatrix} S_1[i] \\ - \end{pmatrix}$. This is also symbolized by a vertical arrow in $\mathcal{M}$ from cell $(i -$

$1, j)$ to cell (i, j) in $\mathcal{M}$. The columns of the alignment having one space are sometimes called *indels*, meaning insertions or deletions. Otherwise, it is either a *match*, or a *substitution* (i.e *replacement*) of $S_2[j]$ by $S_1[i]$. This corresponds to the term $d(i - 1, j - 1) + c(i, j)$ in the expression for $d(i, j)$. Both match and replacement operations are symbolized by a diagonal arrow from cell $(i - 1, j - 1)$ to cell (i, j) in $\mathcal{M}$ or in the alignment diagram as $\begin{pmatrix} S_1[j] \\ S_2[j] \end{pmatrix}$. Recursively, we have assumed that $d(i-1, j)$, $d(i, j-1)$ and $d(i-1, j-1)$ are all minimum values of edit distances up to those points in the computation. Then $d(i, j)$ has to be optimal if we take the minimum cost path from one of these three neighboring points. Note that this path may not be unique, as we will see in our example below.

We have described the recursive procedure as a top-down approach. However, in practical implementations, it can cause an exponential number of calls, and it turns out that a bottom-up tabular computation is more efficient. To compute the value at any point (i, j) in the matrix $\mathcal{M}$ associated with $d(i, j)$ values, it is sufficient if we know the minimum edit distances of its north, north-west and west neighbors, and the pair of characters from the two sequences under consideration. We know how to compute the 0th row and the 0th column of the matrix (the minimum edit distance is simply the index of the row or column), and so we can compute the rest of the matrix one row at a time consecutively with increasing row indexes, or one column at a time consecutively with increasing column indexes. The edit distance of the two strings S_1 and S_2 is given by $d(m, n)$. The time complexity of the algorithm is $O(mn)$ since a matrix of size $(m + 1)(n + 1)$ has to be computed and each entry takes a constant amount of work (three additions, one comparison and a minimum operation). The space complexity is also $O(mn)$, however, this can be reduced to $O(\min\{n, m\})$, since we only need to keep information about the last column or last row in order to perform the required computation at any point.

An example illustrating this algorithm is shown in Figure 7.17 using the sequences S_1=abccdab and S_2=babcabc. Two possible alignments (corresponding to the squares enclosed by heavy lines and arrows indicating insert, delete or match operations) are also shown with the edit transcripts. During construction of the table, back pointers to neighboring cells can be kept to trace the paths taken by the minimum edit distance computation. The forward pointers are drawn to show the operations performed. Since the maximum path length cannot exceed $m + n$, the edit transcript can be obtained in $O(m + n)$ time.

Several variations of the general edit distance problem have been investigated in the literature. In the context of biological applications, scientists are more interested in finding *similarities* than the difference between two sequences. This can be cast into another dynamic programming formulation by defining a *score* or *value* to each of the edit operations, giving the match operation a high score and giving other edit operations an appropriate low or

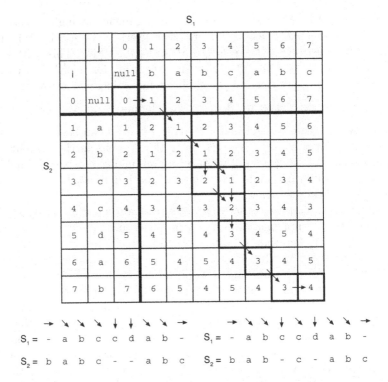

Fig. 7.17. Computation of edit distances

negative score. The problem then is to compute the *maximum* score $v(i, j)$ between the two prefixes of S_1 and S_2. The similarity of the two strings is then expressed by the value $v(m, n)$. Other variations give arbitrary weight to the operations and/or provide a table of weights for pairs of characters in Σ for these operations, or give a penalty for long runs of insert or delete operations; for example, see Gusfield (1997).

7.4.2 Edit graphs

Another way of understanding the alignment of two sequences is to interpret it as a directed *path* in a grid called an *edit graph*. Here, a series of horizontal (thin) lines marked by the symbols of the sequence S_1 (including the empty prefix ϵ) and a series of vertical (thin) lines marked by the symbols of the sequence S_2 (including the empty prefix ϵ) define cells or vertices of the graph, as shown in Figure 7.18.

A typical cell is connected to its east neighbor by a (solid) directed edge representing an insert of a symbol of S_2 corresponding to the vertical line passing through it, and to its south neighbor by a (solid) directed edge representing a delete of a symbol of S_1 corresponding to the horizontal line passing

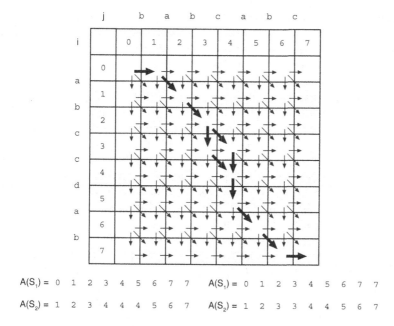

Fig. 7.18. The edit graph

through it. A solid diagonal directed edge connects to its south east neighbor via the point of intersection of a horizontal and a vertical line representing the symbols from S_1 and S_2, respectively, participating in the match or replacement operation. If the edges are weighted by the weights of the indels, match or replacement operations, then it is easy to see that the minimum edit distance alignment corresponds to a directed path from the upper left cell called the *source* vertex at location $(0,0)$ to the lower right cell called the *sink* at location (m, n) in the grid. This lowest cost path can be obtained by a dynamic programming algorithm as discussed before. Two such alignments discussed in the previous subsection are represented by a thick solid directed path on the edit graph.

An interesting way to describe this path is to specify the two-dimensional addresses of the vertices of the path as follows: the sequences -abccdab- and babc--abc can be depicted as 012345677 and 123444567 showing the number of symbols in S_1 and S_2, respectively, up to the positions in the sequences. If we align these two sequences in two rows, as shown in Figure 7.18, the sequence of pairs of integers in the columns of this alignment gives the sequence of addresses in the grid graph, depicted as $A(S_1)$ and $A(S_2)$.

7.4.3 Local similarity

An important variant of similarity search is *local alignment* or *local similarity*. Suppose we have two long DNA sequences in which there is a particularly interesting subsequence representing a gene that is common between the sequences. Doing a global alignment or similarity search will not be able to identify this because there may be a lot of dissimilarities in the rest of the sequence which yield a low value for similarity and a large edit distance, neither of which say anything about this interesting region. If the regions of highly similar local alignment are small, they can get lost in the context of global alignment. An obvious exhaustive algorithm is to enumerate all the substrings of S_1 and S_2 and execute a dynamic programming algorithm on each pair. For one string, a substring is defined by two positions in the string which can be chosen in $O(m^2)$ and $O(n^2)$ ways for S_1 and S_2, respectively. There are $O(m^2 n^2)$ such pairs. For each pair, dynamic programming takes $O(mn)$ time. Thus, the complexity of this simple approach is $O(m^3 n^3)$. Surprisingly, there is an $O(mn)$ algorithm to find the optimal local similarity (Smith and Waterman, 1981), which works as follows.

Consider first a related problem called the *local suffix similarity* problem, which is to find a suffix s_1 (possibly null) of the prefix $S_1[1 \ldots i]$, and a suffix s_2 (possibly null) of the prefix $S_2[1 \ldots j]$, $(i \leq m, j \leq n)$ such that the similarity value $v(i, j)$ between s_1 and s_2 is maximal among all such pairs of suffixes. We will assign a negative or zero value to both the insert and delete operations, a high positive value to matching, and a negative value to the substitution operation. Since we allow empty strings, the maximum similarity value can never be negative. It can be easily proved that the optimal local similarity value $v^*(i, j) = \max\{v(i, j) : i \leq m, j \leq n\}$. This is because for any (i, j), if we find the optimal local suffix similarity value V, then $v^*(i, j) \geq V$. Conversely, if there exist substrings of S_1 and S_2 ending at positions i^* and j^*, respectively, giving an optimal similarity value, then this optimal value is a solution of the suffix similarity problem for the prefixes $S_1[1 \ldots i^*]$ and $S_2[1 \ldots j^*]$. It will be then sufficient if we can show that we can determine $v(m, n)$ in $O(mn)$ time. The dynamic programming equations are very similar to the edit distance computation and $v(i, j)$ is given as:

$$v(i, j) = \max\{\ 0,$$
$$v(i - 1, j) + v(S_1[i], -),$$
$$v(i, j - 1) + v(-, S_2[j]),$$
$$v(i - 1, j - 1) + v(S_1[i], S_2[j])\}$$

where $v(S_1[i], -), v(-, S_2[j])$ and $v(S_1[i], S_2[j])$ are the values assigned to the insertion, deletion and substitution operations, respectively. An example is shown in Figure 7.19. Note that the local similarity alignments are located inside the solid box starting with the maximum alignment value (a match has a score of $+2$, a mismatch or a space are given a score of -1) of $V[6, 6]=5$ to the nearest 0 entry in the alignment path(s) indicated by the bold integers in the matrix. Two such maximum similarity alignments are also shown in Figure 7.19.

It might be intuitively easier to understand the local similarity solution using an interpretation using the edit graph. If we add in the edit graph, edges

		0	1	2	3	4	5	6
		null	a	a	a	b	c	d
0	null	0	0	0	0	0	0	0
1	e	0	0	0	0	0	0	0
2	f	0	0	0	0	0	0	0
3	b	0	0	0	0	2	1	0
4	a	0	2	2	2	1	1	0
5	c	0	1	1	1	1	3	2
6	d	0	0	0	0	0	2	5
7	a	0	2	2	2	1	1	4

Two Local Similarity Alignments

S_1 b a c d S_1 a - c d
S_2 b - c d S_2 a b c d

Fig. 7.19. Local similarity computation

of weight 0 from the source vertex (0,0) to every other vertex in the graph, this will initiate similarity computation starting from any location in the longer string to whatever maximum value it will lead to by a directed path. This is because the source vertex (0,0) becomes a predecessor of every vertex in the graph. This also explains the first entry 0 in the dynamic programming equation as stated above. The local similarity alignments will be located inside the subgraph starting with the maximum alignment value to the nearest source vertex having similarity value of 0. This is illustrated also in the matrix shown in Figure 7.19. The 5×5 submatrix with the maximum value of 5 in the lower right hand cell corresponds to the maximum similarity solutions. There are two possible alignment paths depicted by bold entries.

7.4.4 The longest common subsequence problem

Another important variant of the similarity search problem is the problem of determining the *longest common subsequence* between two sequences S_1 and S_2. Given a string S of length n, a subsequence is a string $S[i_1]S[i_2]\ldots S[i_k]$ such that $1 \leq i_1 \leq i_2 \ldots \leq i_k$ for some $k \leq n$. A substring is a subset of characters from S which is located contiguously, but in a subsequence the characters are not necessarily contiguous, just in the same order from left to right. Thus a substring is a subsequence but the converse is not true. The *longest common subsequence* (LCS) of two strings S_1 and S_2 is the longest subsequence common between S_1 and S_2. As an example, there are two LCS's for the pair of strings (abba, abab), which are abb and aba. Since aba can be derived from abba in two different ways, this gives three distinct solutions. If we assume that the cost of substitution is 2 (one delete followed by an insert, with both insert and delete having a cost of 1), then the edit distance d and the length of the LCS, l, are related by the equation $d = m + n - 2l$. This is because we can convert string S_1 to string S_2 by first deleting all $m - l$ characters from S_1 that are not part of the LCS and then inserting back into it all $n - l$ characters of S_2 that are not part of the LCS. For example, the edit distance of (abba, abab) is 2 ($= 4 + 4 - 2 \times 3$) since we can drop the last a from the first sequence abba to obtain abb and insert the second a from the second string after ab in abb to obtain abab. However, a direct computation of the LCS using dynamic programming is more efficient than going through the edit distance computation first, although the asymptotic complexity of $O(mn)$ remains the same. The formulation is as shown below.

$$l(0,0) = 0$$
$$l(i,0) = 0$$
$$l(0,j) = 0$$
$$l(i,j) = 1 + l(i-1, j-1) \; if \; S_1[i] = S_2[j]$$
$$l(i,j) = max[l(i, j-1), l(i-1, j)] \; if \; S_1[i] \neq S_2[j]$$

An example is shown in Figure 7.20. Note that since $l = 5$, the edit distance has to be $d = 6 + 8 - 2.5 = 4$, which can be verified separately for each entry in the LCS matrix. The LCS matrix also has some interesting properties: the entries in any row or in any column are monotonically increasing, and between any two consecutive entries in any row or column the difference is either 0 or 1. This has important hardware and software implications.

Since the LCS is simpler and is a special case of the edit distance problem, one might wonder whether algorithms with better than $O(mn)$ worst case complexity can be found to solve this problem. Indeed, Hunt and Szymanski (1977) defined a 2-dimensional grid G with $m + 1$ horizontal lines and $n + 1$ vertical lines, and marked the point of intersection of the i-th horizontal line and the j-th vertical line with a 1 if $a_i = b_j$, and 0 otherwise. They showed how to obtain the LCS by drawing a strictly monotonically decreasing line through the points marked 1 in G. If there are r points in the line, their algorithm takes $(r + n) \log n$ time, assuming that n is very large compared to m. When two huge files with small differences are compared, r is of the order of n and this leads to a practical $O(n \log n)$ algorithm. Myers (1986) and Ukkonen (1985a) independently used this idea to come up with a minimum cost path determination problem in the grid where the path takes a diagonal line from $(i-1, j-1)$ to (i,j) if $a_i = b_j$ with cost 0, and takes a horizontal or vertical line with a cost of 1 corresponding to insert or delete operations.

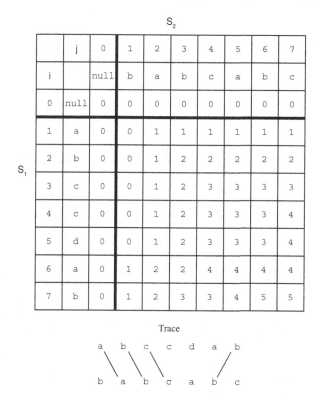

S_2

j	0	1	2	3	4	5	6	7
i		null	b	a	b	c	a	b	c
0	null	0	0	0	0	0	0	0	0
1	a	0	0	1	1	1	1	1	1
2	b	0	0	1	2	2	2	2	2
3	c	0	0	1	2	3	3	3	3
4	c	0	0	1	2	3	3	3	4
5	d	0	0	1	2	3	3	3	4
6	a	0	1	2	2	4	4	4	4
7	b	0	1	2	3	3	4	5	5

S_1

Trace

Fig. 7.20. Longest common subsequence with a trace

These two approaches can be easily visualized with the aid of an edit graph as shown in Figure 7.21 for the sequences abba and abab. The end points of the diagonals then define a LCS. This formulation was then implemented using the classic shortest path algorithm of Dijkstra (1959). Several other improvements of this basic idea have been proposed by Masek and Paterson (1980) and others.

Another interesting formulation of the LCS problem is in terms of the longest increasing subsequence problem, described in Gusfield (1997). Let π be a set of n integers, not necessarily distinct. An *increasing subsequence*, IS of π is a subsequence of values strictly increasing from left to right. For example, if $\pi=(5,3,4,4,9,6,2,1,8,7,10)$ then $IS=(3,4,6,8,10)$, $(5,9,10)$ and so on. A *longest increasing subsequence* (LIS) of π is an IS of maximum length. A *decreasing subsequence* (DS) is a non-increasing subsequence of π, such as $DS=(5,4,4,2,1)$ for the previous example. A *cover* (C) is a set of disjoint DS's of π that cover or contain all elements of π. The *size of the cover* (c) is the number of DS's in the cover. If $\pi=(5,3,4,9,6,2,1,8,7)$ then $C=\{(5,3,2,1),(4),(9,6),(8,7)\}$ and $c=4$. A *smallest cover* (SC) is a cover with

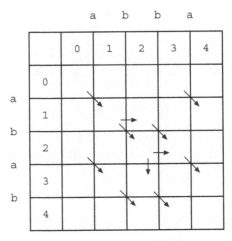

Fig. 7.21. Longest common subsequence on an edit graph

a minimum value of c. Any increasing sequence cannot have more than two elements from a decreasing sequence. This means that no increasing subsequence can have a size greater than the size of *any* cover. Thus, the size $|LIS|$ cannot exceed c, the size of the smallest cover. The converse of this statement is also true. If there exists $c' < c$ and if we derive IS from C, then it must contain more than one element from one of the decreasing sequences of C', which is not possible. This proves an important property: if an increasing sequence IS of π has a length equal to the size of a cover, then IS is an LIS and C is a smallest cover of size c.

A greedy algorithm can be used to derive a cover as follows. Starting from the left of π, examine each successive number in π. Append the current number at the left-most subsequence derived so far if it is possible to do that maintaining the decreasing sequence property. If not, start a new decreasing subsequence beginning with the current element. Proceed until π is exhausted. For example, if $\pi = (5,3,4,9,6,2,1,8,7,10)$ then it has four decreasing sequences: $D_1 = (5,3,2,1), D_2 = (4), D_3 = (9,6), D_4 = (8,7), D_5 = (10)$. The greedy algorithm has $O(n^2)$ complexity. We will now look at a more efficient $O(n \log n)$ algorithm, which is given in Algorithm 7.13.

The algorithm uses two data structures: the decreasing sequence list D_i for the shortest cover, and a list L of items (x, j) to keep the running minimum value x in the decreasing sequence j. Searching the x-field in L takes $O(\log n)$ time. At any time in the execution of the algorithm, the list L is sorted in increasing order with respect to the x-values, as well as with respect to the identifier value i. Since a total of n elements are inserted, the time complexity of the algorithm is $O(n \log n)$. For example, if $\pi = (5,3,4,9,6,2,1,8,7,10)$, then initially, $L = [(5,1)]$ and $D_1 = (5)$. After inserting 3, 4 and 9 the lists become $L = [(3,1),(4,2),(9,3)]$, $D_1 = (5,3)$, $D_2 = (4)$ and $D_3 = (9)$. After inserting

---

DECREASING-SEQUENCE(π)
/* $\pi = (x_1, x_2, \ldots x_n)$ is the list of input numbers */
$i \leftarrow 1$
$D_i \leftarrow x_1$
$L \leftarrow [(x_1, i)]$
$j \leftarrow 1$
for $i \leftarrow 2$ **to** n **do**
  Search the x-field of L using binary search to find the first
    x-value such that $x_i < x$
  if such a value exists **then**
    insert x at the end of the list D_i and $x_i \leftarrow x$ in L
  else
    $j \leftarrow j + 1$
    insert in L a new element (x, j) and start a new $D_j \leftarrow (x)$
  end if
end for

Algorithm 7.13: Decreasing sequence computation

the last element 10, the final lists are: $L=[(1,1),(4,2),(6,3),(7,4),(10,5)]$ and $D_1=(5,3,2,1)$, $D_2=(4)$, $D_3=(9,6)$, $D_4=(8,7)$ and $D_5=(10)$. Now we will show how to map the LCS problem to an LIS problem.

Given sequences S_1 and S_2, let r_i be the number of occurrences of the i-th character of S_1 in S_2. For example, if $S_1 = abacx$ and $S_2 = baabca$, then, $r_1=3$, $r_2=2$, $r_3=3$, $r_4=1$, and $r_5=0$. Define for each character σ in S_1, a $List(\sigma)$ to be the position of σ in S_2 in decreasing order. In the example, $List(a)=(6,3,2)$, $List(b)=(4,1)$, $List(c)=(5)$ and $List(x) = \epsilon$ (the empty sequence). Let $\Pi(S_1, S_2)$ be a sequence obtained by concatenating the set of $List(s_i)$ for $i = 1, 2, \ldots m$, where m is the length of S_1 and s_i is the i-th character of S_1. In the example, $\Pi(S_1, S_2)=(6,3,2,4,1,6,3,2,5)$. One can prove the following theorem:

Theorem: Every increasing sequence I of $\Pi(S_1, S_2)$ specifies an equal length common subsequence of S_1 and S_2 and vice versa. Thus a longest common subsequence LCS of S_1 and S_2 corresponds to a longest increasing sequence of $\Pi(S_1, S_2)$.

For our example $\Pi(S_1, S_2)= (6,3,2,4,1,6,3,2,5)$, the possible longest increasing sequences and the corresponding LCS's are: $(1,2,5)= bac$, $(2,3,5)=aac$, and $(3,4,6)= aba$. Note that the indexes in the LIS's are used to access characters from S_2. An informal justification of the above theorem is that the sequence Π guarantees that the groups of sequences correspond to the sequences of characters in S_1 in left to right order, and the increasing indexes makes sure that the characters from S_2 are also accessed in left to right order, and finally the 'longest' IS guarantees that the common sequence derived by the process is indeed an LCS. With $r = \sum_i r_i = |\Pi(S_1, S_2)|$, the LIS approach solves the LCS problem in $O(r \log n)$ time (where $m \leq n$). Note that $r \leq mn$, although in general, $r \ll mn$. Thus, when $r \approx nm$, the time complexity will be worse than that of using edit-distance.

7.4.5 String matching with k differences

In this subsection we will consider a few important variants of the general edit distance problem. The *k-mismatch problem* finds all positions in T where pattern P occurs with *at most* k mismatches. The *approximate string matching problem with k differences* is to find *all* occurrences of P in T such that $d(P, x) \leq k$ where x is a substring of T. The *k-difference global alignment* problem is to find the best global alignment, if one exists, of strings S_1 and S_2 with at most k mismatches and spaces (insertions and deletions). These problems have applications in situations where one wants to find nearly exact matches of P with T. The dynamic programming formulation with a time complexity of $O(mn)$ can be adapted to solve these problems. But, being special cases, more efficient algorithms have been developed for each of these problems. In this section we will briefly describe some of them and give a brief review for others.

The k-mismatch problem

The *k-mismatch problem* can also be stated in terms of the *Hamming distance*. The Hamming distance between two strings of *equal length* is the number of positions where the characters in the strings mismatch. Thus, the *k-mismatch problem* is to find all positions i in T where pattern P and $T[i, i+1, \ldots i+m-1]$ have a maximum Hamming distance of k. The dynamic programming formulation of local similarity is applicable to this problem, but being a special case it can be solved using running time better than $O(mn)$. Landau and Vishkin (1985) developed an $O(k(m \log m + n))$ algorithm for this problem with a pattern preprocessing time of $O(k(m \log m))$. The algorithm creates a table for shifting the pattern so that certain comparisons can be avoided, as is done in the KMP algorithm, as long as the number of errors do not exceed k. Improvements to this algorithm have been proposed by Galil and Giancarlo (1988), Grossi and Luccio (1989), Tarhio and Ukkonen (1993) and Baeza-Yates and Perleberg (1992, 1996). Baeza-Yates and Gonnet (1992) extended their shift-and algorithm to handle the k-mismatch problem. Wu and Manber (1992a,b) developed the software AGREP incorporating Baeza-Yates and Gonnet's idea.

Recall the definition of a binary matrix M with m rows and n columns such that $M[i, j] = 1$ if and only if the prefix of the pattern $P[1 \ldots i]$ equals the suffix in the text at the j-th position, that is, $T[j - i + 1 \ldots j]$ (see Section 7.1.5). Let M^k be a generalization of M such that $M^k[i, j] = 1$ if and only if at least $i - k$ characters of the pattern $P[1 \ldots i]$ match with the suffix in the text at the j-th position, that is, with $T[j - i + 1 \ldots j]$. The matrix $M^0 = M$. The algorithm computes for any text location j the matrix $M^l[j]$ from the matrix $M^{l-1}[j]$ by the relation

$$M^l[j] = M^{l-1}[j] \cup (Bitshift(M^l[j-1] \cap U[T[j]]) \cup M^{l-1}[j-1])$$

where U is a binary vector of length m, such that, for each symbol $\sigma \in \Sigma$, $U[\sigma] = 1$ for the positions in P where the symbol σ appears.

Thus, $M^l[j]$ is set to 1 under three conditions:

1. The first i characters of P match a substring of the text T ending at location j of T;
2. The first $i-1$ characters of P match a substring of T ending at location $j-1$ of T with at most l mismatches, and that the next pair of characters of P and T match;
3. The first $i-1$ characters of P match a substring of T ending at location $j-1$ with at most $l-1$ mismatches.

Thus, for each value of l, $l = 0, 1, \ldots, k$, and for $n - m$ positions in the text the columns have to be computed leading to a worst case time complexity of $O(kmn)$. Fortunately, like in the computation of M^0, only two columns have to be kept in main memory during the computation. For small k and with a pattern length that fits into a computer word, AGREP is quite fast and efficient. The reader is referred to the text books by Stephen (1994), Gusfield (1997), and Smyth (2003) for further information.

We will conclude this subsection by describing a *suffix tree method* which uses the concept of *longest common extension (lce)* of two strings. The *lce* of two strings S_1 and S_2 for a given pair of indexes (i, j), is the longest substring of S_1 beginning at position i that matches a substring of S_2 beginning at position j. With $O(n + m)$ preprocessing to construct a *generalized suffix tree* and with the help of a constant time *lowest common ancestor* algorithm (Harel and Tarjan, 1984; Gusfield, 1997), a constant time complexity algorithm for determining the length l of the longest common extension can be obtained. Using this result, the k-mismatch algorithm is described in Algorithm 7.14.

Since the while loop can execute a maximum of k times and the *lce* algorithm takes constant time, and j can range from 1 to $n - m$, the total time complexity is $O(nk)$ for the k-mismatch problem, which is an improvement over the $O(mn)$ algorithm, particularly when k is small.

Approximate string matching with k differences

As defined earlier, the *approximate string matching problem with k differences* is to find *all* occurrences of P in T such that $d(P, x) \leq k$ where x is a substring of T. The situation is comparable to the local similarity problem except that we slide the pattern P (recognized as the smaller string S_1) over the text T (identified as string S_2), so that P is aligned with each position in the text, and compute the distance between P and the next m characters in the text. If this distance has a value less than k, we include the text position in

---

K-MISMATCH-SUFFIX-TREE(l, T, P)
  /* l is the longest common extension of strings T and P */
  $i \leftarrow 1$ /* index to pattern P */
  $j \leftarrow 1$ /* index to text T */
  $count \leftarrow 0$ /* mismatch count */
  while ($count \leq k$) **do**
    if $i + l = m + 1$ **then**
      /* a solution has been found with $count$ number of mismatches, since
        $count \leq k$) */
      stop
    else
      $count \leftarrow count + 1$
      $j \leftarrow j + l + 1$
      $i \leftarrow i + l + 1$
    end if
  end while
  if $count = k + 1$ **then** a k-mismatch of P not found in T starting position j

---

Algorithm 7.14: Suffix tree method: Determining the k-mismatch using the longest common extension

our solution. In the context of dynamic programming formulation, this can be achieved by initializing the $(m + 1) \times (n + 1)$ distance matrix $\mathcal{M}$ with $d(0,0) = 0$, $d(i,0) = i$ for $1 \leq i \leq m$ and $d(0,j) = 0$ for $1 \leq j \leq n$. Interpreting this on the edit graph means that we let every node in the first row of the grid to have its predecessor as the source node $(0,0)$. If we now examine the last row of computed edit distance values in $\mathcal{M}$, every entry with a value up to k will represent an approximate string matching solution with k differences. By choosing different definitions of the distance function, we can obtain variants of the solution. For example, we can choose the distance function as the Hamming distance in which case the solution will stand for the approximate k-mismatch solution. We can even extend this to approximate similarity computation by assigning positive values to the distance function in a prescribed way and choosing only those as solutions whose values are greater than or equal to a minimum threshold value. A final variation of the problem will be to initialize $\mathcal{M}$ with conditions $d(0,0) = d(i,0) = d(j,0) = 0$ for all i and j. This will be analogous to the local similarity problem and produce solutions that will compare substrings of S_1 with substrings of S_2 and identify as solutions those pairs whose distance function is less than or equal to k or whose similarity function is greater than or equal to a threshold. A comprehensive survey on approximate pattern matching can be found in Navarro (2001).

The k-difference global alignment problem

A similar approach is applicable to the k-*difference global alignment* problem, where we want to find the best global alignment, if one exists, of strings S_1 and S_2 with at most k insertions and deletions. The dynamic programming formulation presented earlier can again be applied. At the conclusion of the computation of the edit distance matrix, some approximate occurrences of the pattern in the text with up to k differences can be found by identifying an entry in the last row of the matrix having a value less than or equal to k. If this entry is in column j, then the edit distance between P and $T[1, 2, \ldots, j]$ is less than or equal to k. Being a special case, we can expect a running time better than $O(mn)$. Consider the main diagonal cells $[i, i]$ in the dynamic programming matrix $\mathcal{M}$ $(i \leq m \leq n)$. A path specifying a global alignment begins at the cell $[0, 0]$ and ends at the cell $[m, n]$ or to the right of cell $[m, n]$. An insert or delete operation will push the path off the main diagonal by one square and it cannot do this more than k times if the path is to be a k-difference solution. This also means that $n - m \leq k$ must be true to get any k-difference solution. If there is a substitution operation, the path moves diagonally but adds 1 (or some specified number) to the edit distance. It will thus suffice if rather than computing the whole matrix $\mathcal{M}$, a strip of cells of length $2k + 1$ off the main diagonal is computed. The recurrence relations have to be altered slightly at the border cells of this strip to ignore the values of cells that do not fall in the strip. Because of this, the value in the cell $[m, n]$ may not be the actual edit distance, but if it is greater than k, we can conclude that there is no k difference match between strings S_1 and S_2. If there is a k-difference match, the edit distance in the cell $[m, n]$ will be correctly set and it will be less than or equal to k. The total number of cells in the strip is $O(km)$ which is also $O(kn)$ since $n - m \leq k$ and k is a constant. An example is shown in Figure 7.22. The diagonal strip of width 3 for $k=1$ shows that there is no 1-difference global alignment — for this particular example, the smallest value of k for which there is a k-difference global solution is 4.

If the value of k is not specified, we can determine k by successive application of the algorithm by beginning with $k=1$ and doubling the value to 2, 4, 8 . . . until the desired value of k is obtained.

7.4.6 The k-mismatch problem using the BWT

In this section we will describe an efficient algorithm to solve the k-mismatch problem based on the Burrows-Wheeler Transform. The approach described here works on the transformed text, so we assume that L is available, and also the index a which gives the position in L corresponding to the last character of T (from where decoding the text backwards can begin). As we have seen in the earlier chapters, we can reconstruct the original text T, the array F and a list of sorted suffixes of the text from (L, a). In the context of compressed text

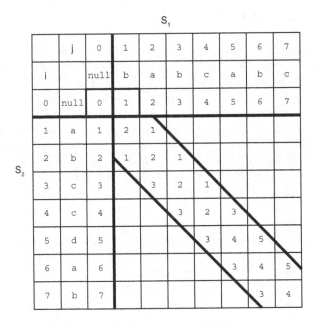

Fig. 7.22. Diagonal strip for $k = 1$

using BWT, we will have $|L| = |T| = n$. We can then perform the k-mismatch or k-approximate pattern matching directly on this data.

The approximate matching techniques are based on using the BWT information to generate q-*grams*, which are simply substrings of a text, where the length of the substring is q. For example, the set of 5-grams for the text mississippi is { missi, issis, ssiss, sissi, issip, ssipp, sippi }. For *exact* pattern matching, we could construct all m length q-grams (the m-grams) of the pattern and the text, and find the intersection of these two sets to produce the set of matches. If instead we wish to perform *approximate* matching, we use smaller q-grams ($q \leq m$), based on the allowable distance between the pattern and a matching string.

There is just one m-gram for the pattern P, which is simply the pattern itself. Construction of the required m-grams of a text from the F and R' BWT arrays is also straightforward and can be performed in $O(n)$ time as follows:

$$\forall i : 1 \leq i \leq n - q + 1, Q_q^T[i] = F[R'[i]] \ldots F[R'[i + q - 1]]$$

where $Q_q^T[i]$ denotes the i-th array of q-gram from T. Although this definition does not list the q-grams in sorted order, sorting can be performed efficiently by reordering them according to the values in the R auxiliary array. For example, the text mississippi has $R = \{11, 8, 5, 2, 1, 10, 9, 7, 4, 6, 3\}$. Thus, for $q = 5$, the sorted q-grams are $\{Q_5^T[5], Q_5^T[2], Q_5^T[1], Q_5^T[7], Q_5^T[4], Q_5^T[6], Q_5^T[3]\}$, with 8, 9, 10 and 11 being ignored because they are greater than $n - q + 1$.

Generating q-grams from the BWT V array output

Algorithm 7.15 generates the sorted set of q-grams given F, L, V and q, in $O(qn)$ rather than $O(n^2)$ time. In this algorithm the sorted x-grams are denoted as $F(x\text{-}gram)$ which is a vector of length $n = |T|$ of x-tuples of characters. We will allow the q-grams to rotate at the end of the text, but this could be avoided later by ignoring the q-grams that correspond to the last $q - 1$ starting positions in the text. Obviously, $F = F(1\text{-}gram)$ and the lexicographically sorted matrix of all cyclic rotations of T is $F(n\text{-}gram)$. We assume $x \leq n$. The character '*' denotes concatenation of character strings.

GRAM(F, L, V, q)
  $F(1\text{-gram}) = F$
  for $x = 2$ to q **do**
    for $i = 1$ to u **do**
      $F(x\text{-gram})[V[i]] \leftarrow L[i] * F((x - 1)\text{-gram})[i]$
    end for
  end for

Algorithm 7.15: Algorithm for generating q-grams using V

For example, if this algorithm is used with $q = 2$, the result will be the sorted bi-grams. The series of 11 2-grams generated with $T = \texttt{mississippi}$ are shown in Table 7.7a. This will place them in sorted order in the vector $F(2\text{-gram})$; Table 7.7b shows the same values in the vector, but with the index ranging from 1 to 11. The sorted matrix A_s (which is not actually stored) is also shown for comparison; the q-grams are simply the first q characters of each line of A_s. Because the algorithm has wrapped the text around to the beginning, the 2-gram starting at the last position of T should not really be used. It happens to be in $F(2\text{-grams})[1]$ in the example, and in practice it would be ignored during pattern matching.

The algorithm to generate the q-grams is $O(qn)$ in the worst case, but in practice q will be a small and constant value, in which case the complexity is $O(n)$.

From the above algorithm we get a set of q-grams that represents all the q-length segments of text, and the q-grams are sorted. This property gives us the advantage of being able to apply binary search on the arrays, in a similar way to the technique for exact matching in Algorithm 7.9.

We need to introduce the idea of a *permissible q-gram*, which is simply a q-gram that is totally contained in T, that is, it doesn't include rotations from the start to the end of T. For example, for $T = \texttt{abac}$, the permissible bi-grams are $\{\texttt{ab}, \texttt{ba}, \texttt{ac}\}$, but not $\texttt{ca}$.

i	$F(\text{2-gram})[V[i]] = L[i] * F(\text{1-gram})[i]$
1	$F(\text{2-gram})[6] = \text{p} * \text{i}$
2	$F(\text{2-gram})[8] = \text{s} * \text{i}$
3	$F(\text{2-gram})[9] = \text{s} * \text{i}$
4	$F(\text{2-gram})[5] = \text{m} * \text{i}$
5	$F(\text{2-gram})[1] = \text{i} * \text{m}$
6	$F(\text{2-gram})[7] = \text{p} * \text{p}$
7	$F(\text{2-gram})[2] = \text{i} * \text{p}$
8	$F(\text{2-gram})[10] = \text{s} * \text{s}$
9	$F(\text{2-gram})[11] = \text{s} * \text{s}$
10	$F(\text{2-gram})[3] = \text{i} * \text{s}$
11	$F(\text{2-gram})[4] = \text{i} * \text{s}$

(a)

$F(\text{2-gram})[i] = \text{2-gram}$	$A_s[i]$
$F(\text{2-gram})[1] = \text{im}$	imississipp
$F(\text{2-gram})[2] = \text{ip}$	ippimississ
$F(\text{2-gram})[3] = \text{is}$	issippimiss
$F(\text{2-gram})[4] = \text{is}$	ississippim
$F(\text{2-gram})[5] = \text{mi}$	mississippi
$F(\text{2-gram})[6] = \text{pi}$	pimississip
$F(\text{2-gram})[7] = \text{pp}$	ppimississi
$F(\text{2-gram})[8] = \text{si}$	sippimissis
$F(\text{2-gram})[9] = \text{si}$	sissippimis
$F(\text{2-gram})[10] = \text{ss}$	ssippimissi
$F(\text{2-gram})[11] = \text{ss}$	ssissippimi

(b)

Table 7.7. (a) The 2-grams in the order generated by Algorithm 7.15 on the text mississippi; (b) the final array $F(\text{2-gram})$

Using the BWT for the k-mismatch problem

This section describes a k-mismatch algorithm based on q-gram matching using the BWT auxiliary arrays. Here, the q-grams are not generated all in advance, but are obtained incrementally by generating the BWT arrays as they are needed. This can be seen in the code in Algorithm 7.16 under the nested **for** loop. It performs a binary search on the sorted q-grams one character of P at a time. The algorithm starts by finding the first character of the pattern in the first column of the matrix, F. All the matches are located contiguously in the sorted matrix and it identifies a suffix block or a segment in A_s that begins with the first character. The binary search then proceeds to the next character of the segment matching the corresponding character of the pattern. When the match is found, the segment is further narrowed. The procedure is continued until the pattern is found in the final segment or there is a mismatch. The average search time is $O(m + \log(n/|\Sigma|))$ and is $O(m\log(n/|\Sigma|))$ in the worst case.

We know that the A_s matrix contains the sorted suffixes of the text. The occurrences of suffixes with the same prefix will be in consecutive segments. For exact matching, there will be only one segment matching the whole pattern. But when k mismatches are allowed, there could be more than one segment that will satisfy the k mismatch criterion. For each segment, the rows have a common prefix with length l of the q-grams in the segment, where l is the position of the last character of P that matches the q-gram or they will have the same number of allowable mismatches. We use a *triplet* $(st, ed, count)$ to store the start and end positions of the segment in F and the number of mismatches between the common prefix of q-grams of T and $P(1 \ldots l)$, respectively. Only the segments with *count* less than or equal to k are considered valid in any step and stored together in a set *Candidate*. Each element of *Candidate* is a valid *triplet* storing the possible matching segment information. In practical implementations, the vector F can be stored in an array of character counts $M = c_1, c_2, \ldots c_{|\Sigma|}$ where Σ is the alphabet with an ordered index for each character. For a given index c, $1 \leq i \leq |\Sigma|$, $M[i]$ stores the beginning index of the segment having σ_i in the first column. For example, with $\Sigma = \{a, b, c, d\}$ and $T = abdaca$, $M[1] = 1, M[2] = 4, M[3] = 5, M[4] = 6$ at the start of the algorithm. The algorithm is given in Algorithm 7.16.

Note that we do not actually create the j-gram for each row in the q-gram matrix during binary search. Instead, given the row index *pos* of a q-gram in F, the j-th character s of the q-gram can be accessed in constant time as: $s = F[R'[R[pos] + j]]$.

An example to illustrate the algorithm is shown in Figure 7.23, with $T =$ mississippi, $P =$ ssis, and $k = 2$. Initially there is one triple set up for each character in the alphabet (in the first column of the Figure 7.23). The left most column gives the index to the rows of the sorted BWT matrix. The column numbers (1,12,123 and 1234) are marked on top for the $1, 2, 3, \ldots, q$-grams being generated by successive iterations of the algorithm along with the character $P[q]$ of the pattern being compared with the last character of the q-gram. For each block of identical q-grams, the associated triplet indicating the start and end indexes of the block and the number of mismatches accumulated so far for each block is appended to the right beside the braces or a left arrow (for a single element block). Triplets are kept as long as the number of mismatches does not exceed k which for our example has a value of 2. If the number of mismatches exceeds 2, the triplet is discarded from the set *Candidate*. This is indicated by the symbol 'x' in the diagram.

The main loop starts with $j = 2$, which is matching the second character of P. For each of the existing triplets, an extension of one character is evaluated for each character σ_c in the alphabet. If that character matches then a new triplet is created that indicates the subrange of A_s that still matches — in the example, extending the triple $(8,11,0)$ with an s does this for the range from 10 to 11, and so the triple $(10,11,0)$ is recorded. If the character doesn't match, then the count of mismatches is incremented for that triple. If the increment makes it greater than k, then we have too many mismatches — in the example

---

BWT-K-MISMATCH(F, P, M, R', R, k)
  Initialize *Candidates* to have no triplets
  for each distinct character $\sigma_c \in \Sigma$, the c-th character in
      Σ, that appears in F **do**
  create a triplet (st, ed, $count$) with
      $st \leftarrow M[c]$ /* start a segment */
      $ed \leftarrow M[c+1] - 1$ if $c < |\Sigma|$ **else** $ed = u$ /* end of a segment */
      if $\sigma_c = P[1]$ **then** $count \leftarrow 0$ **else** $count \leftarrow 1$
  if $count \leq k$ append the triplet to *Candidates*
  end for

  for $j \leftarrow 2$ to m **do**
    for each triplet in *Candidates* **do**
      Remove the triplet ($st, ed, count$) from *Candidates*
      for each distinct character σ_c that appears in F **do**
        locate the start and end positions st' and ed' in F between st and
            ed using binary search with the j-th character of the q-grams
        if $\sigma_c = P[j]$ **then**
          add triplet ($st', ed', count$) into *Candidates*
          /* Since it is a match with $P(j)$, there is no change to $count$ */
        else if $count + 1 \leq k$ **then**
          add triplet ($st', ed', count + 1$) to *Candidates*
          /* Since a mismatch occurred, $count$ is incremented by one */
        end if
      end for
    end for
  end for

  Read the list *Candidates* to report all the k-mismatch results between
      st and ed in each element of *Candidates*.
  /* The position in F can be converted to the position in T using R */

Algorithm 7.16: Determining the k-mismatch based on q-grams

this happens when the triple (2,2,2) in the second column is extended with
a **p**, taking the count from 2 to 3 mismatches. In this case no corresponding
triple is added to the list; this also happens in the few cases where the match
has reached the end of the text, which happens for the character **i** in the
first row of Figure 7.23. If the incremented value is within the bound set by
k then a new triple can be created, such as extending (8,11,0) with the letter
i, giving (8,9,1), a mismatch of 1 character. Once all m characters in P have
been used to extend the triples, the remaining set of triples gives the range
(in A_s) of the matches, and the count gives the size of the mismatch. In the
example, the last column shows 3 matches, at positions 9 (2 mismatches), 10
(1 mismatch), and 11 (exact match).

	P[1] = s	P[2] = s	P[3] = i	P[4] = s
	1	12	123	1234
1	i	x		
2	i ⎫ (1, 4, 1)	ip ← (2, 2, 2)	ipp x	
3	i	is ⎤ (3, 4, 1)	iss ⎤ (3, 4, 2)	issi x
4	i ⎭	is ⎦	iss ⎦	issi x
5	m ← (5, 5, 1)	mi ← (5, 5, 2)	mis x	
6	p ⎤ (6, 7, 1)	pi ← (6, 6, 2)	x	
7	p ⎦	pp ← (7, 7, 2)	ppi x	
8	s ⎤	si ⎤ (8, 9, 1)	sip ← (7, 7, 2)	sipp x
9	s ⎥ (8, 11, 0)	si ⎦	sis ← (9, 9, 2)	siss ← (9, 9, 2)
10	s ⎥	ss ⎤ (10, 11, 0)	ssi ⎤ (10, 11, 0)	ssip ← (10, 10, 1)
11	s ⎦	ss ⎦	ssi ⎦	ssis ← (11, 11, 0)

Fig. 7.23. Example of the q-gram based k-mismatch algorithm, for $T =$ mississippi, $P =$ ssis, and $k = 2$; the symbol × indicates a row that has been exhausted, and thus no further match is required

For this k-mismatch algorithm, the preprocessing time to construct the auxiliary arrays is $O(n)$. For each loop, we have to use binary searches to locate all the segments with the same q-gram. At most n groups will be generated which is really a theoretical worst case scenario. The worst case search time for the whole pattern is $O(mn \log n)$. In practice, for English language most often the groups will be resolved after 4 or 5 refinements of the segments. The average case is $O((\frac{nm}{k}) \log n)$.

Zhang et al. (2003) compared the qgram method for k-mismatches based on the BWT with the suffix tree based method presented in Algorithm 7.14 (described in Gusfield (1997)). They found that the BWT-based method consistently outperforms the suffix tree based method. With $q = 3$, the number of triplets generated initially increases with each iteration, but generally peaks around the fourth iteration because the first few characters play a role in breaking the segments into many sub-segments, but only a few of them actually survive for a given k as the candidate list loses valid triplets.

7.4.7 k-approximate matching using the BWT

In the previous section, we utilized the ease of deriving the q-grams once a text has been transformed by the Burrows-Wheeler Transform to obtain an efficient implementation of the k-mismatch problem. In a similar fashion, it is possible to use the q-grams to expedite the k-approximate pattern matching problem.

One approach is to use two phases. In the first phase, we locate areas in the text that contain potential matches by performing some filtering operations using appropriate q-grams. In the second phase, we verify the results that are suggested by the filtering operations. The verification stage could use any of k-approximate pattern matching algorithms that have been reported in the literature, such as Ukkonen (1985b); Chang and Lawler (1994); Myers (1994); Landau and Vishkin (1986). This means that the overall performance depends critically on the number of suggestions generated. The first phase is based on a known fact in approximate pattern matching due to Baeza-Yates and Perleberg (1992, 1996):

Lemma : *Given a text T, a pattern P with length m, and the parameter k, for a k-approximate match of P to occur in T, there must exist at least one r-length block of characters in P that form an* **exact** **match** *to some r-length substring in T, where $r = \lfloor \frac{m}{k+1} \rfloor$.*

This is trivially the case for exact pattern matching, in which $k = 0$, and hence $r = m$. With this lemma, we can perform the filtering phase in three steps:

1. Compute r, the minimum block size for the q-grams;
2. Generate $\mathcal{Q}_r^T$ and $\mathcal{Q}_r^P$, the permissible r-grams from the text T, and the pattern P, respectively; and
3. Perform q-gram based exact matching of $\mathcal{Q}_r^T$ and $\mathcal{Q}_r^P$ using a Burrows-Wheeler Transform based search algorithm described earlier in Algorithm 7.9.

Let $\mathcal{MQ}_k = \mathcal{Q}_r^P \cap \mathcal{Q}_r^T$, and $\eta_h = |\mathcal{MQ}_k|$. Let $\mathcal{MQ}_k^i$ be the i-th matching q-gram. Let $\mathcal{MQ}_k^i[j]$ be the j-th character in $\mathcal{MQ}_k^i$, $j = 1, 2, \ldots r$. Further, let i_F be the index of the first character of $\mathcal{MQ}_k^i$ in the array of first characters, F. That is, $i_F = x$, if $F[x] = \mathcal{MQ}_k^i[1]$. We call $\mathcal{MQ}_k$ the *matching q-grams at k*. Its size, η_h is an important parameter for the next phase of verifying the matches.

In the second phase we need to verify if the r-grams that were hypothesized in the first phase are true matches. We perform the verification in two steps: (1) Using R' and F determine the potential matching neighborhood in T for each r-gram in $\mathcal{MQ}_k$. The maximum size of the neighborhood will be $m + 2k$; and (2) verify if there is a k-approximate match within this neighborhood.

Let $\mathcal{N}_i$ be the neighborhood in T for $\mathcal{MQ}_k^i$, the i-th matching q-gram. Let t be the position in T where $\mathcal{MQ}_k^i$ starts. That is, $t = R'[i_F]$. The neighborhood is defined by the left and right limits: t_{left} and t_{right} viz:

$$
t_{left} = \begin{cases} t - (m - r) - k & : \quad \text{if } t - k \geq 1, \\ 1 & : \quad \text{otherwise} \end{cases}
$$

$$
t_{right} = \begin{cases} t + m + k & : \quad \text{if } t + m + k \leq n, \\ n & : \quad \text{otherwise} \end{cases}
$$

Hence, the i-th matching neighborhood in T is given by:

$$
\mathcal{N}_i = T[t_{left} \ldots t \ldots t_{right}].
$$

Thus, $|\mathcal{N}_i| \leq 2(m+k)-r, \forall i, i = 1, 2, \ldots \eta_h$. We then obtain a set of matching neighborhoods $\mathcal{S}_{\mathcal{MQ}} = \{\mathcal{N}_1, \mathcal{N}_2, \ldots \mathcal{N}_{\eta_h}\}$, and then verify a match within any given $\mathcal{N}_i$ using a k-approximate pattern matching algorithm such as Ukkonen's. The cost of the first step in the verification will be in $O(\eta_h)$. The cost of the second step will be $O(\eta_h k(m + 2k)) \leq O(\eta_h k(3m)) \approx O(\eta_h km)$.

For example, if $T = abraca$, $P = brace$ and $k = 1$, then $r = 2$, and the permissible q-grams will be $\mathcal{Q}_2^P = \{ac, br, ce, ra\}$, $\mathcal{Q}_2^T = \{ab, ac, br, ca, ra\}$, yielding $\mathcal{MQ}_1 = \{ac, br, ra\}$, and $\mathcal{N}_1 = [3 \ldots 6]; \mathcal{N}_2 = [1, \ldots, 6]; \mathcal{N}_3 = [2, \ldots, 6]$. Matches will be found in $\mathcal{N}_1$ and $\mathcal{N}_2$ at positions 1 and 2 in T, respectively.

There are cases when overlaps between the neighborhood sets may occur. If there is an exact match in the text T, there will be at least $m - r$ such neighborhoods overlapping for the same region in T matching P of length m. Thus we can merge these neighborhoods into a single one covering all of them as stated in the following lemma:

Lemma : *Given strings $S_1 = s_1, \ldots s_i$, and $S_2 = s_j, \ldots s_n$ where $i \leq n$ and $j \geq 1$, the merge of the two string S_1 and S_2, $S = s_1 s_2, \ldots s_n$, will include all the possible k-approximate matches in S_1 and S_2.*

Sometimes the merging overhead is larger than the cost of searching all the neighborhoods directly, as it is possible to have a lot of neighbors scattered over the text. To merge a neighborhood with the current neighborhoods, we may need to search for the right position to merge, incurring an overhead of $O(w)$, where w is the number of distinct neighborhoods in the text T.

7.5 Hardware algorithms for pattern matching

This section gives a brief introduction to the field of hardware algorithms for pattern matching. Interested readers should look at the references for more information.

There is an unwritten theorem understood by hardware designers that whatever can be done in software can also be done in hardware, but the converse is not true. The software that is used to control a robot arm or a nuclear power plant or a space ship can be encoded in hardware microcode and the systems will function autonomously. The problem with this approach is that the hardware is fixed and can not be changed if the system needs to adapt to new or slightly altered design specifications. Special purpose hardware has been used since the early days of computers — for example, the floating point processor has been used as a standard hardware "component" in most computers. With the advent of LSI (large scale integration), which led to the microprocessor revolution in the early seventies, and the development of VLSI (very large scale integration) in the eighties, which led to the advent of very powerful general purpose processors, the special purpose processors faced tough competition. The advantage of the general purpose processor is that it provides programmability and can be used in almost any application (except for time-critical applications where "embedded" processors have an advantage). In fact, high speed general purpose processors have been used in many special purpose applications such as the graphics cards with microcoded graphics applications. Nevertheless, a large number of researchers worldwide continued with a substantial amount of research on the development of hardware algorithms, as is evidenced by the publications of hundreds of papers and the proliferation of journals and conferences on VLSI design and application-specific VLSI architectures.

The area of parallel and "systolic" algorithms and architectures received special attention by many, although by the end of the decade no significant hardware was built that received general acceptance. In the area of string processing, several hardware algorithms have been developed (see later in the section). Two other projects on biosequence analysis are worth mentioning — one led by the California Institute of Technology, and a "Bioscan" chip developed by a group at North Carolina University at Chapel Hill in the early nineties. The whole field of special purpose architectures (systolic algorithms and so on) and massively parallel machines took a hit and more or less collapsed due to the advent of the very powerful chips such as the Pentium and its successors. This led to the development of multi-processor systems (4 to 6 processors on a single motherboard), multi-threaded VLIW (Very Large Instruction Word) architectures with extensive pipelining, and grid architectures. In the early nineties a new technology arrived on the horizon: the FPGA (Field Programmable Gate Arrays). The FPGA was developed in the eighties, but they were not competitive in speed and performance. This is now turning around. The FPGA has become very fast, dense and competitive in performance and speed with general purpose processors, and maintains its inherent programmability and reconfigurability. This coupled with the availability of very high speed DNA sequencing machines which are being used today for accumulating massive amounts of genome and protein sequencing data, plus the need to analyze, search and mine this data, might cause a resurgence in the hardware algorithms field.

7.5.1 An equivalent hardware algorithm

We begin by describing a simple hardware method for pattern matching that was discovered in the late seventies by one of the authors of this book Mukhopadhyay (1979)[7] which used the same basic principle used in the *shift-and* method of Baeza-Yates and Gonnet (1992). The algorithm will be presented at a high functional level so that the reader can understand the basic idea without delving into low-level hardware details. The basic *cell* (*module*, or *block*) used is a two-input one-output functional block (see Figure 7.24). The horizontal input coming from left is binary and is called the *anchor*; the other input coming from the vertical direction is a single character (typically 8 binary signals representing an ASCII code).

---

[7] This paper is also known as Mukherjee, 1979.

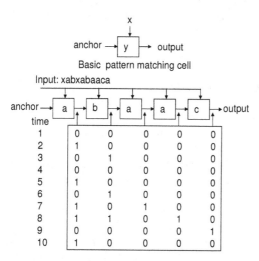

The ith row of matrix M is same as ith column of this matrix

Fig. 7.24. Hardware pattern matching

The cell holds a single character in a buffer and has logic to perform a comparison operation between the incoming character and the resident character. The operation of the cell is as follows: If at time t (coinciding with a *clock pulse*), the *anchor* input is '1' and the incoming character equals the resident character, then the output becomes '1' at time $t + 1$; otherwise, if the *anchor* is '0' or the characters do not match, the output is '0' at time $t + 1$. To perform an exact pattern matching operation with a pattern of length m, m such functional blocks are cascaded together, connecting the output of the i-th block to the anchor input of the $(i + 1)$-th block $1 \le i \le m - 1$. The inputs are all connected in "parallel" via a "bus" so that the same character is input to all cells at the same time. The *anchor* input of the first block is connected to a clock throughout the operation.

The important output to observe is the output of the last cell. The text is applied sequentially, one character at a time, to all cells simultaneously. If at any time $t = k$, the output of the cascade shows a '1' output, the pattern appears in the text beginning at the $(t - m + 1)$-th position. For our example, given the example from Section 7.1.5 with text T =xabxabaaca and a pattern P =abaac, the cascade will have 5 functional blocks holding the pattern and the output will become '1' at time $t = 9$, indicating the pattern appears in the text beginning at the 5-th position. Also note that if we observe the outputs in time sequence from the i-th block in the cascade, it yields a bit string that is exactly equal to the bit string in the i-th row (from left to right order) in the matrix M of the Baeza-Yates-Gonnet method. The role of the "anchor" input is to enable the pattern matching operation starting from any position in the text. This also performs the equivalent operation of shifting downward the column of the bit matrix M by 1 bit with an appended '1' as the first bit in the Baeza-Yates-Gonnet scheme.

7.5.2 A brief review of other hardware algorithms

This subsection discusses several improvements of the basic scheme described above, and a brief overview of other hardware algorithms for pattern matching.

Rather than broadcasting the pattern characters to all the cells in parallel, which might slow down the hardware due to excessive "loading" in the bus, another scheme has been proposed in which the text characters are moved serially from the first to the last stage at half the speed of the propagation of the match signals. Furthermore, in both the schemes the pattern may have $FLDC$ or $VLDC$ characters for fixed- or variable-length don't-cares. To handle these cases, each cell needs only two bits of storage and a few logic gates. In a 1-bit storage device $\mathcal{F}$, the bit is set to 1, simulating a don't-care character. This bit is used to bypass the comparison hardware, and the output signal is set to 1 to enable the next cell. Another 1-bit storage device $\mathcal{V}$ is set to 1 if the character should correspond to a $VLDC$. In this case, the output is set to 1 independent of the success or failure of the comparison operation, but at the same time the storage bit $\mathcal{V}$ enables a feedback path within a cell which circulates the match signal through the cell so that its output is set to 1 again in the next cycle. This action simulates a non-null variable length don't-care by sustaining an enable output to the next cell forever, simulating a match with an arbitrary length string.

Foster and Kung (1980) proposed a similar scheme in which the pattern and the text string enter the array from opposite ends at each clock cycle. The pattern must, however, be recirculated twice through the array. Each cell at every clock cycle encounters two characters entering the cell, compares them for match or mismatch, and accumulates a result that is sent to the output along with the last character of the text. The method does not handle any $FLDC$ or $VLDC$ characters, and this is also true for parallel comparator-based pattern matching proposed earlier by Mead et al. (1976) and Stellhorn (1974).

For matching with a small bit length pattern, associative memories have been used extensively in the context of memory control hardware for high speed table look-up, such as in the management of cached memories and paging schemes. Bird et al. (1977) and Burkowski (1982) proposed similar associative memory based hardware for pattern matching, but these schemes also do not handle don't-care characters. The finite-state automaton based pattern matching schemes proposed by Roberts (1978) and Hollaar and Roberts (1978) can handle both $FLDC$ and $VLDC$, although a large memory overhead is needed to store the transition tables.

Hardware schemes for approximate pattern matching and the computation of the longest common subsequence have been developed by Mukherjee (1989), Mukherjee and Acharya (1995) and Lipton and Lopresti (1985). In particular, Mukherjee and Acharya (1995) describes a hardware scheme to perform compressed-domain pattern matching for the Huffman code.

A collection of classic papers on VLSI algorithms and architectures can be found in Ranganathan (1993). Special purpose VLSI architectures with application to BWT have been presented in Mukherjee et al. (2001) and Martinez et al. (2005). In view of the advent of genomic and proteomic databases, developing hardware support for rapid search of biological sequence patterns and approximate patterns will become a challenge for both algorithm designers and hardware architects, and there is a growing literature on hardware algorithms for pattern matching and biosequence analysis. Some of these are Hunkerpiller et al. (1990), Dettloff et al. (1991), White et al. (1991), Lopresti (1991), Hughey (1991), Yu et al. (2003) and Li et al. (2007).

7.6 Conclusion

In this chapter we have reviewed a range of algorithms for exact and approximate pattern matching, starting with classic methods for the uncompressed domain, and then focusing on ways to exploit the structures in the Burrows-Wheeler transformed text to achieve fast searching.

The first search on an uncompressed file can be faster with conventional pattern matching, because no decoding at all is needed. But conventional pattern matching has no access to structures that can accelerate subsequent searches, and the uncompressed files will be larger, which requires both more storage, and more time to read their contents.

For exact pattern matching, there are three general categories of methods with different performance characteristics:

1. A simple approach is a compressed-domain implementation of a conventional pattern matching algorithm such as the Boyer-Moore algorithm. This involves decoding the entire text each time a pattern match is made, which means that although it is fairly fast for a single search, it will be slow for multiple searches.
2. Another possibility is to take advantage of the sorted information held in the BWT transformed arrays to do a binary search or to use the information as a suffix array. These methods require that the post-transform compression stages be reversed, imposing an overhead before any searching can be done, but after that the logarithmic access times mean that the time taken by each search of the file is negligible. Thus these methods are well suited when multiple pattern matches must be made.
3. The FM-index approach stores a little extra information with the compressed file which saves having to decompress much of it when searching.

This means that the time taken for a single search is very low, and unlike the previous two approaches, very little memory is required because the BWT arrays are not decoded into memory. It is particularly fast at returning the number of matches for a pattern in the compressed text, and is an obvious candidate if one requires only a count of the matches, and not their locations. The main disadvantages are that the size of the compressed file is a little more than normal BWT-compressed files because of the auxiliary information, and individual searches are slower than the binary search type methods, so it is less suitable if multiple pattern matches are to be made for one file.

Approximate pattern matching, which allows for a small difference between the pattern and the matching text, comes in a number of forms depending on the nature of the approximation that is acceptable. We have described several ways that BWT-based methods can be exploited for approximate matching, either by providing fast access to q-grams in the text (substrings of length q that reveal candidate match positions), or by traversing the implicit sorted array available through the BWT structures, but allowing for an acceptable number of mismatches. The possibility of using hardware for pattern matching was explored at the end of the chapter, and although it is not widely applied to general purpose pattern matching at present, there is the potential for it to become important as the demand grows for pattern matching on very long strings. Hardware implementations that are based on the Burrows-Wheeler Transform have begun to emerge, with some initial work reported by Martinez et al. (2005) and Mukherjee et al. (2001).

There is a very rich and growing literature on pattern matching in general, compression-based pattern matching, and approximate pattern matching. The "further reading" section provides more information.

7.7 Further reading

For further details and complete descriptions of the standard pattern matching algorithms such as Knuth-Morris-Pratt, Boyer-Moore and Karp-Rabin, the reader is referred to Baeza-Yates (1989), Gusfield (1997) and Smyth (2003).

The shift-and method was by Baeza-Yates and Gonnet (1992). The basic mechanism of the principle of operation of this algorithm was discovered much earlier by Dömölki (1968) in the context of recognizing symbols in a compiler, and by Mukhopadhyay (1979) in the context of developing hardware algorithms for pattern matching.

Aho and Corasick's multiple pattern matching algorithm is reported in Aho and Corasick (1975). Tao and Mukherjee (2005) developed a pattern matching algorithm in LZW compressed files using the Aho-Corasick algorithm. A similar approach for a single pattern was originally developed by Knuth et al. (1977) following a theorem by Cook (1972). The keyword (digital) tree is presented, for example, in Gusfield (1997). Improvements of the

KMP, Boyer-Moore and Aho-Corasick algorithms have been reported in the literature, including the results reported by Cole (1994), Galil (1978), Hume and Sunday (1991), Sunday (1990), Baeza-Yates and Gonnet (1992), and Crochemore and Rytter (1994). A number of good review articles have also been published and many text books on algorithms describe some of these methods.

Fenwick (2001a) developed a new algorithm for *intensive* pattern matching where a single block of text needs to be searched repeatedly. This occurs in the context of the LZ77 compression algorithm in which successive phrases of the input text are replaced by references to earlier occurrences of such phrases in a window of the most recent characters. A major motivation of developing such an approach comes from the observation by Gutmann (Fenwick, 1995a) that the use of simple data structures which are easy to generate and maintain often perform much more efficiently in practice compared to the use of complex and theoretically efficient data structures. The method creates a hash table linking the text to bigrams (pairs of characters), searching on the least frequent bigrams, which are used as filters to select parts of the text for full pattern matching. Test results on alphabetic data showed that this reduces the number of character comparisons by two orders of magnitude compared to the KMP algorithm, with a small amount of initial overhead.

The *digital trie* is a data structure that is particularly relevant for pattern matching. Knuth (1973) describes tries (also known as digital search trees) in some detail.

A good survey of compressed full-text indexing in general is given by Navarro and Mäkinen (2007). Gupta et al. (2007) provides a recent investigation into compressed indexing. A website devoted to compressed searching methods, and testing them, can be found at the two mirror sites,

`http://pizzachili.dcc.uchile.cl/` and
`http://pizzachili.di.unipi.it/`.

The BWT suffix array approach is due to Sadakane and Imai (1999). Suffix arrays were first developed by Manber (Manber and Myers, 1993). Algorithm 7.10 that constructs R during decoding is due to Sadakane and Imai (1999). The case-insensitive suffix array search is due to Sadakane (1999). Binary search on BWT text and BWT-BM are due to Bell et al. (2002).

The FM-index approach was proposed by Ferragina and Manzini (2000, 2005). The original version was difficult to implement on conventional machines, but a more practical implementation has been described by Ferragina and Manzini (2001b) and evaluation can be found in Ferragina and Manzini (2001a). An extensive analysis of FM-index and variations can be found in Ferragina and Manzini (2005). Experiments to determine good bucket sizes for the FM-index method are reported in Ferragina and Manzini (2001b), who performed extensive experiments with the FM-index and came up with the sizes of 16 kilobyte for superbuckets and 1 kilobyte for buckets. An extension of the FM-index to arbitrary alphabets is reported by Ferragina et al. (2007).

A modification to the FM-index method is given in Firth et al. (2005), which avoids the multiple random disk access by reading all of the data (including L) into memory. This is a little slower to start up, but saves time during pattern matching. It also gives slightly better compression because L is decompressed when read into memory, so coding does not need to restart at each bucket. Obviously it can consume large amounts of memory, depending on the size of L, and it pays off only if the number of pattern matches to be made is in the thousands.

Approximate pattern matching for uncompressed texts is surveyed by Gusfield (1997), including the k-difference global alignment problem. Another improvement over the dynamic programming approach presented in this chapter was suggested by Ukkonen (1985b), who observed that in a diagonal of the matrix the values are non-decreasing, which means that computation for a particular diagonal can be stopped as soon as a value of $k + 1$ is obtained. It has been proved by Chang and Lampe (1992) that this optimization improves the expected performance of the algorithm to $O(kn)$. Another approach was also suggested by Ukkonen (1993), in which a finite state automaton is defined that accepts all strings that differ from the pattern string by a distance of at most k. The text is then applied to this automaton and substrings are recognized when the automaton is in an accepting state. The *diagonalwise monotonicity* property has been used to develop several algorithms (Stephen, 1994).

The method for searching for don't-care characters when the number is not a constant was proposed by Pinter (1985). For the case where both the pattern and the text contain don't-care characters, Fischer and Paterson (1974) reduced the problem to the multiplication of an m-bit number by an n-bit number. The multiplication can then be done using the Schönhage-Strassen method (Schönhage and Strassen, 1971). The method for don't-care matching based on sorted head and tail arrays is an unpublished algorithm by Amar Mukherjee. Other relevant references for pattern matching with don't care characters can be found in Wu and Manber (1992b); Baeza-Yates and Gonnet (1992); Abrahamson (1987). The use of q-grams for exact and inexact pattern matching is described in Adjeroh et al. (2002), Zhang et al. (2003) and Zhang (2005).

The Canterbury corpus, which was used for evaluations in this chapter, was described by Arnold and Bell (1997). The files are available from http://corpus.canterbury.ac.nz. Most of the empirical results reported in this section are from Firth et al. (2005). Firth (2002) reports extensive experiments that evaluate a range of factors for BWT-based pattern matching methods.

Recent papers on applications of BWT and related approaches to searching can be found in the November 2007 *Theoretical Computer Science* special issue on the BWT: Gupta et al. (2007), Mäkinen and Navarro (2007), and Golynski (2007).

Fenwick (2001b) notes that performance analysis of pattern matching algorithms does not always reflect reality; for example, it is traditional to count comparisons, but counting array references may be better, not to mention issues with caching that mean that we can't assume that memory accesses take a constant time.

8

Other applications of the Burrows-Wheeler Transform

Traditionally the major application of the Burrows-Wheeler Transform has been for data compression and efficient storage, and earlier chapters in this book have provided a detailed consideration of the BWT from this viewpoint, analyzing its performance for data compression. However, recent research on the Burrows-Wheeler Transform has shown the versatility of the BWT, and hence efforts are shifting from its traditional application in data compression to other areas of study. In Chapter 7 we showed how the BWT provides an effective mechanism for rapid pattern matching. In this chapter we expand more on its many uses, focusing on new and emerging applications. Some of the applications discussed in this chapter also relate to new data compression applications; given that the original purpose of the Burrows-Wheeler Transform was for text compression, it is no surprise that the method could be used for compression of other types of data. The data compression applications discussed in this chapter exploit the specific nature of the data under consideration in combination with relevant properties of the BWT to provide effective compaction of the data. We discuss the applicability of the BWT to the compression of specialized data sets, including compression of test patterns used in automatic testing in chip manufacturing, image compression, and compression of biological sequences.

Other applications described in this chapter are somewhat different from data compression, but make use of some of the special characteristics of the BWT, such as its clustering property. Examples here include its use in shape analysis in computer vision, and in machine translation. We also discuss recent reports of the application of the BWT in bioinformatics and computational biology, full-text compressed indexes, prediction and entropy estimation, and recent approaches in joint-source channel coding.

The major objective in this chapter is to show the myriad virtues of the BWT, and hopefully motivate others to think of how the BWT could be used to effectively address some important problems that at first glance may seem to be unrelated to the transform.

8.1 Compressed suffix trees and compressed suffix arrays

Given the space required during the construction of the suffix tree, and also during the later stage of searching with the suffix tree, there has been increasing interest in reducing the space requirement for this important data structure. For instance, as discussed in Section 4.3, using Ukkonen's algorithm, even after a careful consideration, we could still need more than $28n$ bytes of storage at the time of construction, and more than $20n$ bytes of storage during searching, if we do not need the suffix links, where n is the length of the sequence. Farach's algorithm requires even more space at the time of construction. Thus for applications such as whole genome sequence analysis involving sequences with potentially billions of symbols (see discussions later in this chapter), the required space could be way beyond the current capabilities of standard computers. The same space problem, though to a smaller extent, also applies to suffix arrays. Compression of the suffix tree and suffix array data structures is one way to deal with the problem of expanding demands on memory space.

Without compression, these data structures generally require space of $O(n \log n)$ bits (since it can be assumed that any number in the range $1, 2, 3, \ldots, n$ can be represented with at most $\log n$ bits), and can support certain operations, such as counting the number of occurrences of a given pattern of length m in $O(m)$ time using the suffix tree, or $O(m \log n)$ time using the suffix array, or $O(m + \log n)$ time using the suffix array with the LCP-array at an additional cost of $O(n \log n)$ bits of space. The challenge in compressing suffix trees and suffix arrays is to reduce the required space, for instance from $O(n \log n)$ bits to say $O(n \log |\Sigma|)$ bits, or even $O(n)$ bits, while maintaining similar time complexities for performing corresponding operations on the compressed representations. In practice, compression could also be used to reduce the space needed in practice to store the suffix tree or suffix array (for instance, by reducing the constants in the complexity figures) without necessarily reducing the theoretical space complexity. This is often easier to achieve and could even have more benefits in practice.

In this section we focus mainly on how suffix trees and suffix arrays can be represented in a compressed form, and how such compressed data structures can be constructed. We consider the use of compressed suffix trees and compressed suffix arrays (in terms of the operations they should support) as an application in full-text indexing and retrieval, which is treated in another section.

Before continuing, we note that the material in this section could easily be placed in Chapter 4. However, from one point of view, compressed suffix arrays (CSA) and compressed suffix trees (CST) can be viewed as another important application of the BWT. For instance, the FM-index (introduced in Chapter 7) can be seen as an example of a compressed suffix array. Furthermore, given that the major applications of compressed suffix arrays and compressed suffix trees are mainly in (or related to) full-text indexing, it makes it more appropriate to cover them in this chapter on applications of the BWT. The discussion on the use of BWT in full-text indexing then follows naturally from that of compressed suffix arrays and trees. Though motivated by the practical need of various applications, compressed suffix trees and suffix arrays and full-text indexing represent an important new direction in both theoretical research and empirical studies on the Burrows-Wheeler Transform.

8.1.1 Compressed suffix trees

One approach to reducing the space required for suffix trees is by exploiting the repeating structures in the suffix tree. For instance, in a suffix tree, we can observe repeated smaller subtrees within the suffix tree. Directed acyclic word graphs (DAWGs) are variations of the suffix tree that exploit this observed isomorphism between subtrees in a suffix tree to construct directed graphs, rather than trees, which can be used to support the functionalities of a suffix tree, such as pattern matching. Details on DAWG data structures can be found in Smyth (2003) and Crochemore and Vérin (1997). Mäkinen (2003) used a similar idea to propose the *compact suffix array*, which uses reduced space compared with the usual suffix arrays. Here we consider more direct approaches that treat the suffix tree as a tree, rather than a graph. Our discussion on compressed suffix trees mainly follows the approach of suffix tree representation using a sequence of parentheses (Munro et al., 1998, 2001).

Parenthesis representation for suffix trees. A rooted tree such as a suffix tree can be represented as a nested string of balanced parentheses. Each node in the tree is represented as a pair of open and closed parentheses, "$(\ldots)$". Thus, for an n-node suffix tree, we need $2n$ parentheses. The procedure performs an inorder traversal starting from the root node of the suffix tree, as follows:

1. If the current node is a leaf, simply output the node's label;
2. For internal nodes, whenever a node is first visited, write an open parenthesis, and visit the subtree rooted at the node;
3. When we finish traversing the subtree rooted at the node, write a closing parenthesis.

We can assume that the suffix tree is constructed such that at each non-leaf node, the edges emanating from the node are sorted in lexicographic order based on their first symbols. The traversal at each node can also follow this ordering. Thus, a listing of the leaf nodes in the order they are visited using this preorder traversal will produce the suffix array of the original text. Figure 8.1 shows an example of the parenthesis representation using the sequence $T = \texttt{mississippi}$. From the properties of a suffix tree (see Section 4.1.1), we know that the suffix tree for an n-length sequence (with the end of sequence symbol \$) has at most n internal nodes, and $n + 1$ leaf nodes. Thus, with the above parenthesis representation, we require at most $4n$ bits to store the topology of the suffix tree, and an additional $n \log n$ bits to store the index for the leaf nodes, plus at most $n \log n$ bits to store the text itself. This is a significant improvement over the $20n$ bytes required to store the suffix tree without the suffix link.

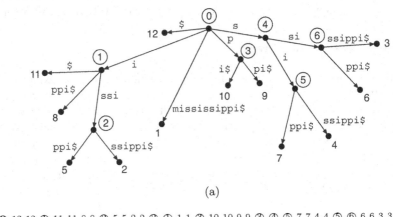

(a)

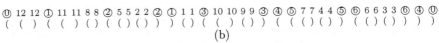

(b)

Fig. 8.1. Example parenthesis representation, using the suffix tree for $T =$ mississippi$: (a) suffix tree with internal nodes labeled; (b) parenthesis representation — the first row indicates the order in which the nodes (both internal nodes and leaf nodes) are visited

A key question then is how operations such as searching and pattern matching can be performed on this compressed representation, and the complexity of such operations. By convention, each node is represented by its corresponding left parenthesis. For the suffix tree of a binary sequence, Munro et al. (2001) showed that using extra space of $o(n)$ bits, basic operations on a given node, such as finding the left child, the right child, the parent, or the size of the subtree rooted at the node, can each be performed in constant time. Two other popular operations on the parenthesis representation (more generally, on binary sequences) are the *rank* and *select* operations defined as follows:

- *rank*(k): returns the number of **1**'s up to and including position k in the binary sequence
- *select*(k): returns the position of the k-th **1** in the sequence

Again, these operations can be performed in constant time (Jacobson, 1989; Munro et al., 1998, 2001). Using an additional $o(n)$ bits of storage, Munro et al. (2001) then generalized these two basic operations to define two more constant time operations, namely,

- $rank_p(k)$: returns the number of occurrences of a binary string pattern p of length m up to and including position k in the given binary sequence. The occurrences could be overlapping.
- $select_p(k)$: returns the position of the k-th occurrence of pattern p in the binary sequence.

Based on these operations, they introduced other operations to aid navigation of the compressed suffix tree, each of which can also be performed in constant time. These include $leafrank(k)$: returns the number of leaves to the left (in the preorder number) of node k; $leafsize(k)$: returns the number of leaves in the subtree rooted at node k; $leftmost(k)$: returns the leftmost leaf in the subtree rooted at node k; $rightmost(k)$: returns the rightmost leaf in the subtree rooted at node k.

For a more general alphabet, each symbol, including the end of sequence marker (\$) is first converted into a binary representation. The suffix tree for the resulting binary sequence is then encoded using the parenthesis representation, and the operations described above can be used to navigate the tree. We describe how pattern matching is performed on this structure in Section 8.2 on full-text indexing.

Various improvements have been made on the above basic representation. For instance, Munro et al. (2001) described how the suffix array can be used to reduce the actual space required to store the suffix tree encoded using the parenthesis representation. The basic idea is to recursively decompose the suffix array. At each level, the current suffix array is divided into $\log^2 n$ partitions, and for each partition, the suffix tree is constructed for every suffix starting at the first position in the partition. With three levels of decomposition, the result is a structure with $n\lceil \log n\rceil + O(\frac{n}{\log\log n})$ bits of storage, plus the space for the original sequence. Details of this scheme and how it can be used to search for patterns on the suffix tree can be found in Munro et al. (2001). Sadakane (2002, 2007) introduces new operations on the basic structure, such as for retrieving the depth of a node, the suffix links, and for answering LCA queries. Efficient methods for supporting $rank$ and $select$ operations on large alphabets were studied by Grossi et al. (2003) and Golynski et al. (2006), along with techniques to use them in full-text indexing. Kim and Park (2005) introduced a method for suffix tree compression different from the parenthesis representation, based on the notions of LCP-intervals, and an LCP-interval tree, which can be constructed based on the LCP-array. Another method for suffix array-based representation of compressed suffix trees is discussed below in Section 8.1.2 on compressed suffix arrays.

One major problem with the above approaches for compressed suffix trees is the very initial step. The methods all require that the suffix tree be constructed first, presumably using standard approaches such as Ukkonen's algorithm. Thus, they will still have to deal with the huge space needed for suffix tree construction. Lam et al. (2002) provide ideas toward a direct construction of compressed suffix arrays (and hence suffix trees), without initial construction of the uncompressed versions. There is also the question of whether the $O(\log n)$ bit factor for the space requirement can be reduced to, say, $O(\log \log n)$, or even to $O(1)$ space. Optimal representations of balanced parentheses are considered in Geary et al. (2006), where they present a method that requires $2n + o(n)$ bits of storage, and still supports the navigational operations in constant time.

8.1.2 Compressed suffix arrays

While the space requirement for storing suffix arrays is generally smaller than that of suffix trees, it may still be too high for certain applications that require huge volumes of data. Compressing the suffix array provides one method to reduce the space requirement without an undue cost to the time of query operations, as compared with performing the same operations on an uncompressed suffix array. Grossi and Vitter (2000, 2005) introduced the problem of compressing suffix arrays, and showed how compressed suffix trees (CSTs) can be constructed via their compressed suffix arrays (CSAs). Their work has generated a lot of attention, and different variations and improvements have been proposed. Our discussion on compressed suffix arrays follows their description.

Without compression, the suffix array is represented simply as a permutation of a list of n integers, in the range 1 to n. This thus requires $n \log n$ bits of storage, since each integer can be stored in $\log n$ bits. The text sequence itself can be stored using $\log |\Sigma|$ bits. This disparity provides a basis for potential compression of a suffix array. The motivation for possible compression is the observation that for a given n-length sequence, T, the elements in its suffix array form a one-to-one correspondence with the symbols in T. Since there are a maximum of $|\Sigma|^n$ different n-length sequences over a given alphabet Σ, we should have at most $|\Sigma|^n$ suffix arrays. Assuming each of these permutations is equally probable, we should require $n \log |\Sigma|$ (rather than $n \log n$) bits to represent each suffix array. A direct implication of this argument is that not all the potential $n!$ permutations of n numbers in a given suffix array represent valid suffix arrays. In fact, we can even do better: given that the uniform distribution represents the worst compression, it could be possible to reduce the size to a value that is proportional to the entropy of the sequence, that is, to $nH(T)$, where $H(T) \leq \log |\Sigma|$ is the entropy of the text, T. The above information-theoretic argument, however, only indicates the *existence* of a possible succinct representation. The challenge is in *how* such data structures can be constructed.

Grossi and Vitter (2005) addressed this problem by viewing the suffix array as an abstract data type, with two basic operations, namely *compress* and *lookup*. The two operations are defined as follows for a given text T and its suffix array $\mathcal{A}$:

- *compress*$(T, \mathcal{A})$: compress $\mathcal{A}$ to obtain the compressed suffix array, CSA. Retain T and the CSA. The suffix array $\mathcal{A}$ can be discarded.

- $lookup(k)$: Given the CSA, return $\mathcal{A}[k]$, the index position in the suffix array, of the k-th lexicographically smallest suffix in T. That is, the index position of the suffix $T_{\mathcal{A}[k]} = T[\mathcal{A}[k] \ldots n]$.

For the uncompressed suffix array, the *lookup* operation can be performed in constant time, requiring $O(n \log n)$ bits of storage. Thus, the problem of compressed suffix arrays is to develop succinct representations for the suffix array using $O(n \log |\Sigma|) + o(n)$ bits of storage, or even $O(nH(T)) + o(n)$ bits, while supporting standard query operations in time bounds comparable to those obtained with the uncompressed suffix array. Constructing the compressed suffix array is performed using a recursive divide and conquer approach, similar in spirit to the recursive construction of suffix trees (see Chapter 4). A given suffix array (which is a permutation of numbers) is divided into smaller permutations, which are further divided. At each level, certain information is stored to aid later reconstruction of the suffix array.

Suffix array decomposition. We assume that n, the number of entries in the suffix array, is a power of 2. The decomposition is performed recursively as follows. At level $k = 0$, let $\mathcal{A}_0 = \mathcal{A}$, with $n_0 = n$. At level k, $k \geq 0$, we have $\mathcal{A}_k$, the suffix array at the k-level of length $n_k = n/2^k$. Thus, $\mathcal{A}_k$ will be a permutation of numbers in the set $\{1, 2, \ldots n_k\}$. Essentially, the permutation is what we obtain if we sort the suffixes of T whose position indexes in the suffix array are multiples of 2^k. Transforming $\mathcal{A}_k$ into its corresponding compressed representation is then performed in four major steps:

1. **Bit vector:** Compute a bit vector B_k of length n_k using $\mathcal{A}_k$ as follows:

$$B_k[i] = \begin{cases} 1, & : & \text{if } \mathcal{A}_k[i] \text{ is even;} \\ 0, & : & \text{otherwise} \end{cases}$$

2. **Mapping function:** Compute the CSA mapping function:

$$\Psi_k(i) = \begin{cases} j, & : & \text{if } \mathcal{A}_k[i] \text{ is odd and } \mathcal{A}_k[j] = \mathcal{A}_k[i] + 1; \\ i, & : & \text{otherwise} \end{cases}$$

Thus $\Psi_k(i) = j$ implies that $B_k[i] = 0$ and $B_k[j] = 1$.

3. **Rank operation:** Count the number of **1**'s for each prefix of B_k. This can be performed using the function $rank_k(j)$, similar to the rank function introduced earlier in this section. $rank_k(j)$ returns the number of **1**'s in $B_k[1, 2, \ldots j]$, the first j entries in B_k.

4. **Computing $\mathcal{A}_{k+1}$:** Sequentially, pick out the even values in $\mathcal{A}_k[i]$, and divide each by 2. The result is a new (reduced) suffix array $\mathcal{A}_{k+1}$, a permutation of the numbers in the set $\{1, 2, \ldots, n_{k+1}\}$, where $n_{k+1} = n/2^{k+1} = n_k/2$. Store $\mathcal{A}_{k+1}$, the reduced suffix array. Discard $\mathcal{A}_k$, the old suffix array.

An example of the above decomposition for our running example $T = $ mississippi\$, with suffix array $\mathcal{A} = [12, 11, 8, 5, 2, 1, 10, 9, 7, 4, 6, 3]$ is shown in Figure 8.2 for three levels of decomposition.

Remarkably, this recursive decomposition preserves all the information in the original suffix array. That is, $\mathcal{A}_k$ can be completely recovered using $\mathcal{A}_{k+1}$ and the other auxiliary arrays. This is supported by an important lemma proved in Grossi and Vitter (2005): Let the $rank_k$ function, $B_k, \Psi_k, \mathcal{A}_{k+1}$, the resulting vectors after the k-th level of decomposition be given. Then $\mathcal{A}_k$, the suffix array at the previous level of decomposition, can be reconstructed from $\mathcal{A}_{k+1}$, using the relation:

for $1 \le i \le n_k$

$$\mathcal{A}_k[i] = 2.\mathcal{A}_{k+1}[rank_k(\Psi_k(i))] + (B_k[i] - 1) \tag{8.1}$$

For example, using the decomposition in Figure 8.2, we can recover $\mathcal{A}_1[1]$ and $\mathcal{A}_1[2]$ as follows:

$$\mathcal{A}_1[1] = 2.\mathcal{A}_2[rank_1(\Psi_1(1))] + (B_1[1] - 1) = 2.\mathcal{A}_2[rank_1(1)] + (1 - 1) = 6$$

$$\mathcal{A}_1[2] = 2.\mathcal{A}_2[rank_1(\Psi_1(2))] + (B_1[2] - 1) = 2.\mathcal{A}_2[rank_1(2)] + (1 - 1) = 4$$

We can also observe that for the positions with $B_k[i] = 0$, the $\Psi_k(i)$ values in any given σ-partition form an increasing subsequence. See for example, the cases with $\sigma = \texttt{i}$, and $\sigma = \texttt{s}$. This is the key to compressing the decomposed

$k = 0, n_0 = 12:$

ID	1	2	3	4	5	6	7	8	9	10	11	12
$T =$	m	i	s	s	i	s	s	i	p	p	i	\$
$\mathcal{A}_0$	12	11	8	5	2	1	10	9	7	4	6	3
B_0	1	0	1	0	1	0	1	0	0	1	1	0
$rank_0$	1	1	2	2	3	3	4	4	4	5	6	6
Ψ_0	1	1	3	11	5	5	7	7	3	10	11	10

$k = 1, n_1 = 6:$

ID	1	2	3	4	5	6
$\mathcal{A}_1$	6	4	1	5	2	3
B_1	1	1	0	0	1	0
$rank_1$	1	2	2	2	3	3
Ψ_1	1	2	5	1	5	2

$k = 2, n_2 = 3:$

ID	1	2	3
$\mathcal{A}_2$	3	2	1
B_2	0	1	0
$rank_2$	0	1	1
Ψ_2	1	2	2

Fig. 8.2. Recursive decomposition of the Ψ function, using the suffix array for $T = \texttt{mississippi\$}$

suffix array. The result of the *compress* operation is a representation of the information from all the k-levels of decomposition, with $k = 0, 1, \ldots, l$ for a given choice of l. This representation forms the compressed suffix array of the original suffix array.

At level $k, 0 \leq k < l$, we store only the vectors B_k, Ψ_k and $rank_k$. The suffix array $\mathcal{A}_k$ is not stored. Also the arrays Ψ_k and $rank_k$ are not stored directly, but in a compressed form, based on the observed nature of these arrays. At the last level $k = l$, the suffix array $\mathcal{A}_l$ is stored directly since it is typically very small, and can be represented in $O(n)$ bits. Thus, the other vectors (B_l, Ψ_l and $rank_l$) are not needed at this level.

The operation $lookup(i)$ to return the value at $\mathcal{A}[i]$ can then be performed recursively, using Equation 8.1, for instance, using a recursively defined function:

$$\mathcal{A}_k[i] = \begin{cases} \mathcal{A}_l[i], & : \text{ if } l = k; \\ 2.\mathcal{A}_{k+1}[rank_k(\Psi_k(i))] + (B_k[i] - 1), & : \text{ otherwise} \end{cases}$$

That is, at the last level, $k = l$, it simply uses direct lookup in the array $\mathcal{A}_l[i]$. For levels less than l, it then returns the value in $\mathcal{A}_k[i]$ using Equation 8.1. Grossi and Vitter (2005) suggested a choice of $l = \Theta(\log \log n)$. However, a number of authors have suggested a much simpler form, using only one level of decomposition (i.e. with just $k = 0$, $l = 1$). Our further discussion on CSAs will assume this one-level decomposition, hence we can drop the subscript on the Ψ function, and simply use Ψ in place of Ψ_0.

Compressing the resulting vectors. Given the above decomposition, the next question is how compression is achieved. Compression of the arrays is based on key observations about the nature of these arrays. The major concern is the mapping vector Ψ_k, since the arrays B_k and $rank_k$ can easily be represented succinctly for constant time access (see for example, Jacobson (1989)). Consider, say, Ψ_0. An important characteristic of this mapping vector is that for positions $i, 1 \leq i \leq n$ with $B_0[i] = \mathbf{0}$ and having the same first symbol in their corresponding suffixes (that is, $T_{\mathcal{A}[i]}$), the corresponding values in Ψ_0 form an increasing subsequence.

Thus, for each $\sigma \in \Sigma$, we can form a σ-list, which contains the subsequence in the σ-partition of Ψ_0. Since each list is an increasing subsequence, we can use simple compression schemes such as using gap encoding (Witten et al., 1999) or Elias codes for the integers (see Sections 3.1, 5.5.2) on the difference between adjacent numbers in each list. The resulting differences will typically be much smaller than n, and hence this can achieve significant compression. Grossi and Vitter (2005) described various ways to perform the compression with tradeoffs between space and time complexities. Overall, for the simplest of the schemes, it was shown that for a sequence of length n over a binary alphabet, the CSA can be built using $\frac{1}{2} \log \log n + 6n + O(\frac{n}{\log \log n})$ bits, and $O(n)$ processing time such that the $lookup$ operation can be performed in $O(\log \log n)$ time. For a general alphabet, Σ, with $|\Sigma| > 2$, the CSA can be constructed in $O(n \log_{|\Sigma|} n)$ processing time and stored in $(1 + \frac{1}{2} \log \log_{|\Sigma|} n +$

$5n + O(\frac{n}{\log\log n})$)) bits, such that each *lookup* operation can be performed in $O(\log\log_{|\Sigma|} n)$ time.

From suffix trees to suffix arrays and back. Originally suffix arrays were constructed from a suffix tree, using a linear time traversal of the suffix tree. More recent results have shown that the compressed suffix array can be used for more compact representation of the suffix tree. The basic idea is as follows: represent information about the tree topology using the parenthesis approach; use the CSA (either Ψ or the L to F mapping function, which are the BWT W and V arrays respectively) to deduce information about the suffix links; use the LCP-array to deduce information about the edge labels and leaf nodes; the text itself can now be compressed independently, or compressed via the BWT L array. It could also be recovered from the compressed CSA, using array C of BWT and Ψ, or LF mapping. Thus, given the new results on linear time worst case direct suffix sorting without first building a suffix tree, and the fact that this construction circumvents the huge storage requirement for the suffix tree construction, it appears that one way to construct the compressed suffix tree will be to first build the suffix array (requiring smaller memory space), construct the compressed suffix array, then build the compressed suffix tree based on the compressed suffix array. We have then gone a full cycle — from suffix trees to suffix arrays and back!

Connection with the BWT. An interesting issue is the relationship between the BWT and the Ψ function used in compressed suffix arrays and compressed suffix trees. Consider a variation of the Ψ mapping function which is given as follows (Grossi and Vitter, 2005):

$$\Psi_k(i) = \begin{cases} j & : \quad \text{if } \mathcal{A}_k[i] \neq n_k \text{ and } \mathcal{A}_k[j] = \mathcal{A}_k[i] + 1; \\ 1 & : \quad \text{otherwise} \end{cases} \qquad (8.2)$$

Assume just one level of decomposition, $\Psi_0 = \Psi$. With the above variation, we can see that with i as the position in $\mathcal{A}$ of the suffix starting at position $\mathcal{A}[i]$ in T, that is, the suffix $T_{\mathcal{A}[i]} = T[\mathcal{A}[i]\dots n]$. Then the value returned by $\Psi(i)$ is simply the position in $\mathcal{A}$ of the next suffix in T, which is the suffix starting at position $\mathcal{A}[i] + 1$ in T, or equivalently, the suffix $T_{\mathcal{A}[i]+1} = T[\mathcal{A}[i]+1\dots n]$. Thus, Ψ can be viewed as the suffix link for positions in the suffix array, $\mathcal{A}$. We can also observe that, except for the case when $\Psi(i) = 1$, in general we have $\Psi(i) = \tilde{\mathcal{A}}[\mathcal{A}[i] + 1]$, where $\tilde{\mathcal{A}}$ is the inverse of $\mathcal{A}$.

Figure 8.3 shows the values for Ψ, and the corresponding suffix array, using the example string $T = \texttt{mississippi}$. For each given symbol partition, we can see the increasing subsequence formed by the Ψ values.

The major connection between Ψ and the BWT is that the Ψ function in Equation 8.2 is simply the inverse of the BWT transform vector, V, that maps symbols in the BWT output L to their corresponding positions in F, the array of first characters. This vector V is the LF (last-to-first) mapping function, which is the basis of the FM-index. (The FM-index was discussed in some detail in Section 7.2.4). Therefore the Ψ function corresponds to our array W, which is defined as the inverse of V (see Section 2.6). This relationship becomes clearer when we compare Figure 8.3 with Figure 2.7 (page 28), in Chapter 2. This important relationship therefore implies that we can derive the Ψ function directly from the BWT output, L, by simply computing the V array, and then computing W, its inverse, all in linear time.

Although the original motivation was different, Ferragina and Manzini (2005) have shown that the FM-index based on the LF-mapping (the V array) can indeed be viewed as a variant of the compressed suffix array, supporting analogous *compress* and *lookup* operations, in a manner similar to Grossi and Vitter's CSA, which is based on the Ψ mapping function (the W array). While the FM-index based CSA performs *backward search* (that is, the pattern is matched in reverse (right to left) from the last to the first symbol), the Ψ-based CSA supports *forward search* (that is, matching left to right), in a manner similar to standard uncompressed suffix arrays. Ferragina and Manzini (2005) showed that a variant of FM-index based CSA can support enumerative queries in $O(m + \eta_{occ} \log^{1+\epsilon} n)$ time, for some fixed constant $0 < \epsilon < 1$, using storage space of $5nH_k(T) + o(n)$ bits, where $H_k(T)$ is the k-th order empirical entropy of T. Hon et al. (2003b) showed how the Ψ function could be augmented to support backward search.

8.2 Compressed full-text indexing

In Chapter 7 we provided a detailed discussion of the problems of general pattern matching and how the BWT can be used in such problems. In this section the focus is on the use of the BWT and related data structures in full-text indexing. The pattern matching methods discussed in Chapter 7 are mainly geared toward applications where the text, the pattern, and the accompanying data structures required for pattern matching (if any) can all fit

Position ID	Sorted Rotations (A_s matrix)	Suffix Array	F L	Ψ (= W)	LF-map (= V)
1	$mississippi	12	$ i	1	11
2	i$mississipp	11	i p	1	7
3	ippi$mississ	8	i s	8	9
4	issippi$miss	5	i s	11	10
5	ississippi$m	2	i m	12	6
6	mississippi$	1	m $	5	1
7	pi$mississip	10	p p	2	8
8	ppi$mississi	9	p i	7	3
9	sippi$missis	7	s s	3	11
10	sissippi$mis	4	s s	5	12
11	ssippi$missi	6	s i	9	4
12	ssissippi$mi	3	s i	10	5

Fig. 8.3. Relationship between Ψ and the BWT; the Ψ function is simply the BWT transformation vector W, which is the inverse of the BWT vector, V

in main memory, or where the text is changing so frequently that storing indexes for later matching doesn't make sense, since it may have to be rebuilt many times. For some applications, however, for instance, in natural language processing, or in whole-genome sequence analysis, the data may be relatively static for a reasonable time, or could be too large to fit into memory, and thus it may be beneficial to construct some indexes for searching on the data. For these applications, constructing such indexes without compression could actually exacerbate the problem of space — for instance, the suffix tree could expand the required space 20-fold over that needed for the original text.

Traditionally text indexing is performed using the inverted index. This is a list of important terms and keywords in the text. For each keyword there is a corresponding list of the positions where it occurred in the text. For huge multi-page documents or web pages, the positions could simply be the page numbers or web page ID where the keyword occurred. In such systems, the choice of keyword(s) is a critical issue, as it would affect space considerations, indexing time, time for query support, and retrieval effectiveness. Compressed inverted indexes have been studied as a way to further reduce the space requirement (Ziviani et al., 2000; Zobel and Moffat, 2006). Witten et al. (1999) provide a detailed study on issues in text indexing using inverted files, for both compressed and uncompressed formats. While this may be appropriate for some natural languages where there are clear word boundaries, text indexing using inverted indexes may not be applicable in other applications such as genomic sequence analysis, where there are no clear-cut boundaries between tokens. The subjectivity of determining keywords is also another issue.

Rather than indexing based on a selected subset of the keywords in the text, full-text indexing aims at indexing *every* substring of the text. A basic problem with this approach is the amount of space that is required, and the solution is compressed full-text indexing, whereby the text is indexed while it is being compressed. A variation is the concept of *self-indexing*, whereby the compressed index not only supports search and retrieval, but can also be used to recover the original text without error. This means that the self-index can in fact replace the text. Depending on the nature of the input text, the size of the compressed index (even for some self-indexes) can be significantly smaller than the original text.

8.2.1 Full-text indexing using CSTs and CSAs

As pointed out by Grossi and Vitter (2005), a full-text indexing system is expected to be able to support three basic types of queries, namely, *existential query*: returns a binary value (true or false) indicating whether a pattern, P occurs in the text, T; *counting query*: returns η_{occ}, $(0 \leq \eta_{occ} \leq n)$, the number of occurrences of P in T; and *enumerative query*: returns η_{occ} numbers, each indicating the starting position in T, of an occurrence of P.

The suffix tree and suffix array are two data structures that are used in full-text indexing. But these are not compressed, and usually take a significant amount of extra space, beyond that of the original text. A recent trend has been to use the compressed suffix tree and/or compressed suffix array in full-text indexing. Sadakane (2007) listed different functionalities that are needed for the compressed suffix tree to support the different types of query. In addition to the operations on compressed suffix trees discussed in Section 8.1, the functionalities include $child(u, s)$: returns node v that is a child of u and the edge (u, v) that starts with s as the first symbol; $edge(u, k)$: returns the k-th symbol of the edge label of an edge pointing to u; $depth(u)$: returns the string depth of node u — simply $|L(u)|$, the length of its path label; $lca(u, v)$: returns $\mathrm{LCA}(u, v)$, the lowest common ancestor of nodes u and v; $sl(u)$: returns the node v pointed to by the suffix link from u.

8.2.2 Searching on compressed suffix trees

Searching and retrieval of a pattern using a compressed suffix tree can be performed by using the navigational operations on the suffix tree. Consider the example in Figure 8.1 for the sequence $T = $ mississippi. Let $P = $ iss be the search pattern. Given that the edges emanating from each node are sorted by their first characters, searching for a pattern in the parenthesis representation can be performed in a manner similar to the method described for exact pattern matching using the BWT in Section 7.2. Searching for a pattern starts at the root node, which corresponds to the first open parenthesis. At each internal node we first determine the leftmost and rightmost leaf nodes in the subtree rooted at the node. These are done in constant time using the $leftmost(k)$ and $rightmost(k)$ operations, respectively. Start comparing the text starting at these positions until there is a mismatch. This can be done using binary search on the leaf nodes in the range of the leftmost and rightmost leaves. For the example, at step 1, we have $P[1] = $ i. Recall that the text T is stored as part of the suffix tree. The first step is to perform a binary search between the leftmost and rightmost leaf nodes emanating from the root (that is, nodes 12 and 3 respectively). This will point to the leaf node 10. Since $P[1] = $ i $< T[10] = $ p, another binary search is performed (between leaf nodes 12 and 1). Finally, binary search reports leaf node 2, where we determine that P[1] matches T[2]. Matching is then continued on the i-edge from the root, which leads to the internal node labeled ①. The above procedure is repeated at this node, finding the leftmost and rightmost leaf nodes rooted at this internal node ① (that is, leaf nodes 2 and 11). This will show that $P[2]$ matches $T[3]$. We continue in this vein until a mismatch is found or the pattern is exhausted.

If a mismatch occurs before we reach the end of the pattern (that is, at some step $i \leq m$), then the pattern P does not occur in T. Otherwise P is exhausted, and thus must occur in T. If the pattern matching ended at an internal node, then the number of occurrences η_{occ} is given by the size of the subtree rooted at that node. If the pattern matching ended between two nodes (on an edge), η_{occ} will be given by the size of the subtree rooted at the immediate node moving down the edge. The size of the subtree can be returned in constant time using the *leafsize(k)* operation. Reporting the actual positions of occurrences will require $O(\eta_{occ})$ extra time, by listing all the leaves rooted under the subtree. If the pattern matching ended at a leaf node, then there is only one occurrence, and the position of occurrence in T is given simply by the leaf identifier. The overall time will be in $O(m \log |\Sigma|)$ to determine if p occurs in T, and to count all the occurrences (if any), and in $O(m \log |\Sigma| + \eta_{occ})$ to find and report all the η_{occ} occurrences of P in T. Using the LCP-array and an additional $O(n \log |\Sigma|)$ bits of storage, the time can be reduced to $O(m + \log |\Sigma|)$ to answer existential and counting queries, and $O(m + \log |\Sigma| + \eta_{occ})$ to answer enumerative queries.

8.2.3 Searching on compressed suffix arrays.

For a full-text index based on the compressed suffix array, searching and text retrieval can be performed in a manner similar to binary search using standard non-compressed suffix arrays, or using BWT-based arrays as described in Section 7.2. The matching requires comparing a prefix of some suffix in T, say suffix $T_{\mathcal{A}[j]}$, with the pattern, P. The symbols making up such a prefix can be recovered recursively, using the Ψ mapping function: $j, \Psi[j], \Psi^2[j], \Psi^3[j], \ldots$, where, for example, $\Psi^3[j] = \Psi[\Psi[\Psi[j]]]$. These will thus point to the sequence of symbols $T[\mathcal{A}[j]], T[\mathcal{A}[j]+1], T[\mathcal{A}[j]+2], \ldots$. For each $i = j, \Psi[j], \Psi^2[j], \Psi^3[j], \ldots$ we can use the *lookup(i)* function defined for the CSA to recover the corresponding symbol. With some extra space of $n + o(n)$ bits, each *lookup()* operation can be supported in constant time. The overall time for existential and counting queries will thus be in $O(m \log n)$, while enumerative queries will be in $O(m \log n + \eta_{occ})$ time. Again, this is similar to the time bound on pattern matching on standard suffix arrays, or for BWT-based exact pattern matching. With extra space of $O(n \log |\Sigma|)$ bits for storing the compressed LCP-table, the above complexities can be reduced to $O(m + \log n)$ and $O(m + \log n + \eta_{occ})$ for counting and existential queries, respectively.

8.3 Bioinformatics and computational biology

Given the availability of complete genomes of various organisms, a major challenge is how to make some sense out of the growing mass of data. Computational methods have been brought to bear on this problem, and different algorithms have been proposed for various problems. One major characteristic of problems in this area is the huge size of data often involved. The human genome, for instance, contains about 3 billion symbols, and there are organisms with genomes that are orders of magnitude larger. A suffix array would require 12 gigabytes of storage for the human genome, while the suffix tree may take as much as 5 times this amount. This will dwarf the storage capabilities in terms of the main memory available in present-day standard computers. Developing efficient search algorithms for patterns of various forms in the genomic sequence thus represents an important problem. It is easy to see that given the problem of data sizes, the suffix array or the suffix tree may not be used directly for this problem, and hence, another approach is needed to perform compression.

Another important characteristic of genomic sequences is the relatively large amount of repetition often observed in such data, which can cause poor behavior in some compression and searching algorithms. Identification, grouping and effective exploitation of the various types of repetition found in biological sequences is another challenge. Currently, most applications of the BWT in bioinformatics and computational biology mainly exploit the context clustering ability of the BWT, which leads to logarithmic time for most search operations. Given the background material on BWT-based pattern matching (Chapter 7), and BWT-based compressed full-text indexing (Sections 8.1 and 8.2), the discussion in this section will be brief. The objective will be mainly to relate the biological problem being solved to one or more problems with a known effective solution based on the BWT, for instance pattern matching or full-text indexing.

8.3.1 DNA sequence compression

Given the large data sizes involved in biological sequences, one way to deal with the increasing data sizes is by compressing the sequence. Yet most compression algorithms (such as GZIP or traditional BWT) will expand the size of a DNA sequence rather than compress it. The major problem is that these algorithms deal with the data as merely a sequence of symbols, without exploiting the special nature of such sequences. In Adjeroh et al. (2002), two off-line dictionary-oriented methods were proposed for DNA sequence compression, based on the BWT. The basic idea was to exploit the different repetition structures observed in DNA sequences in order to compress them. Thus, repetition analysis was performed on the sequence based on the relationship between the BWT and suffix trees and suffix arrays. They proposed two vocabulary parsing schemes which use a repetition code for repeat types, to parse the input sequence. Here, vocabulary refers to the ensemble of repeat structures without reference to their specific locations in the sequence. In one scheme, each repeated substring is removed from the input sequence, and moved to an external dictionary. The positions in the sequence where each repetition occurred, along with the corresponding repetition code, is recorded in the dictionary. Thus there is no reference or pointer information in the original sequence.

The suggested repetition analysis could be performed at different stages in the BWT-compression pipeline, for instance, before the BWT, between the BWT and LGT, or a combination of these. The compression performance will depend on factors such as the size of the pointers and the way they are coded; the type of referencing used (absolute or relative); the type of dictionary used (on-line or off-line); the size of the dictionary (the number of distinct repetition structures); the type of referencing used in the dictionary (if any), especially for offline dictionaries; and the encoding method adopted for the dictionary and the remaining parsed sequence. Results in the paper showed that the introduction of repetition analysis and parsing in the BWT compression pipeline generally improves the compression result. In essence, the analysis and parsing stage further exposed the hidden regularities in the DNA sequence (such as reverse complements), which typically will not be discovered by traditional compression algorithms such as the BZIP2 or GZIP. This was the case whether the repetition analysis was done before or after the BWT. However, it was also observed that repetition analysis and parsing before the BWT generally produced a better result than after. One reason for this is that the replacement of various types of repetition typically disrupts the original nature of the BWT output, and hence could make the results less suitable for MTF transformation. Thus, an analysis of the nature of the resulting sequence after the replacement of repeats will be important in matching the subsequent stages of the BWT compression pipeline to the parse results, and hence will be a key to further compression.

While the overall result on DNA sequences was better than those obtained using general compression schemes, the performance could still be improved, for instance, by considering the more recent context-partitioning view of the Burrows-Wheeler Transform. In a related work on biological sequence compression, Adjeroh and Nan (2006) proposed a method for compressing protein sequences based on long-range correlations in the sequence. In this work, the BWT was not used directly for compression; rather, its clustering property was used as the basis for identifying long range correlations in protein sequences, which were then exploited for improved compression of the sequences.

8.3.2 Analysis of repetition structures

Repetition structures represent an important characteristic of genomic sequences. Long runs of tandem repeats and of randomly interspersed repeats are prominent features of DNA sequences. The family of ALU repeats (usually about 300 bases in length) is typical of short interspersed repeat sequences, referred to as SINEs — short interspersed nuclear elements. These have been estimated to make up about 9% of the human genome, thus out-numbering the proportion of protein coding regions (Herzel et al., 1994). There are also the long interspersed repeat sequences (LINEs — long interspersed nuclear elements) which are usually more than 6000 bases in length. In the human genome, the L1 family is the most common LINEs, with about 60,000 to 100,000 occurrences. There are also short repeats (sometimes called "random repeats"), attributed to the fact that typical sequences and genomes are orders of magnitude larger than the alphabet size (4 in this case).

Although the precise biological function of these repetition structures is still a topic of intensive debate, it is well known that the redundancy due to the repetition structures provides some form of stability for the genome. Tandem repeats in particular play a major role in various regulation mechanisms in the genome, such as in protein binding (Richards et al., 1993). Repetition structures have been implicated in various diseases and genetic disorders. For instance, the triplet repeats $(CTG)_n/(CAG)_n$ have been associated with Huntington's disease, while the hairpins formed in $(CGG)_n/(CCG)_n$ repeats have been linked to the Fragile-X mental retardation syndrome (Bat et al., 1997). Sinden et al. (2002) identified fourteen such genetic diseases that are linked with triplet repeats. An important observation for computational analysis of such repetition structures is that, in every single case listed, the susceptibility to (or incidence of) the disease critically depends on the number of copies (that is, the copy exponents in the repeat), and how many times the triple repeat occurs with a given exponent.

Obviously, given the strong relationship between the BWT and data structures such as suffix trees and suffix arrays, it can be expected that the BWT can be used in the identification and analysis of repetitions. Again, finding repeats can be viewed as a variant of the pattern matching problem. Identification of interspersed repeats, for instance, is simply the same as locating all the occurrences of a given pattern. The difficult problems in repetition arise in dealing with tandem repeats, in its various forms. This can be performed as a pattern matching (or search retrieval) problem, with a later stage of post-processing. Abouelhoda et al. (2005) provide a detailed treatment on how the suffix array, enhanced with the LCP-array, can be combined with the BWT for various applications, including repetition finding. They gave specific algorithms for locating maximal unique matches (MUMs), supermaximal repeats, and maximal tandem repeats. Adjeroh and Feng (2004) used the BWT as a basis for analyzing tandem repeat families in DNA sequences.

8.3.3 Whole-genome comparisons

Despite the significant space reduction provided by compressed suffix arrays and compressed suffix trees, their use in applications such as bioinformatics and computational biology is still hampered by the space needed for their initial construction. The problem is due to the typically large amounts of data often involved in these applications. Thus, there is an interest in space-efficient methods that are practical and can support data-intensive problems in biology. Lippert (2005); Lippert et al. (2005) adapted the space-efficient construction of CSAs originally proposed in Lam et al. (2002) for the specific purpose of DNA sequences, suitable for genome-scale comparison of mammalian genomes. First, the DNA sequence was converted into a binary representation, using a unary encoding of each symbol in the DNA alphabet. The motivation for the unary encoding (rather than simply using 2 bits per symbol) is that with unary codes, the boundaries between symbols are easily identified (for instance, by a **0**), and that the encoding maintains the lexicographic ordering between the symbols. The BWT is then applied on this binary sequence, based on which the CSA is constructed. Their implementation resulted in a reduced space requirement, from about 10 bits per symbol during CSA construction to about 5 bits, and from about 5 bits per symbol for storage to about 2.5 bits per symbol.

Using the above, pattern matching and searching on the genome sequence can then be performed on the CSA of this binary representation using an equivalent encoding of the patterns, using search methods such as those described in Section 8.2. Thus, Lippert (2005); Lippert et al. (2005) performed whole-genome comparisons using human and mouse genomes by finding all the unique q-mers (that is q-grams) that are common to both genomes. More specifically, they used exact matching 20-mers between the two genomes (with size of 2.84GB and 2.74GB respectively) and reported a total time of 14 hours 22 minutes on a Macintosh G5 with 1.5GHz and 1.8GB of RAM. They showed that their result was better than those obtained using other data structures used in comparative genomics.

8.3.4 Genome annotation

Another issue in the analysis of genomic sequences is determining changes in the copy number of certain important repeating elements over time, perhaps in response to a drug or environmental changes. A special case of this problem is in detecting changes in the gene copy number between a normal genome and a mutant genome (Lucito et al., 2003). For such analysis, substrings in the genome sequence can be viewed as a word, and the major problem becomes that of performing a word count over the genome. When the word length is small (for instance ≤ 15), or we have only one or two words, the problem is easy and could be solved using direct methods. However, with increasing word lengths, or an increasing number of words, improved data structures and algorithms are needed. Again, given the problem of data sizes, the suffix array or the suffix tree can not be used directly for this problem. Using the BWT and related data structures, Healy et al. (2003) developed a method for genome-wide annotation using exact word counts. Thus, the problem is turned into that of simply reporting counting queries for each word or pattern, for instance using either BWT-based compressed-domain pattern matching methods discussed in Chapter 7, or using BWT-based full-text indexing methods, described earlier in this chapter.

At each position along the genome, annotation is performed in terms of the number of occurrences of the q-mer at this position in both the forward and the reverse directions, for different values of q. The result is a visualization of the annotation "terrain" along the entire genome, which provides a quick view of the structure of repeats within a localized region along the genome. Healy et al. (2003) also describe how this terrain could be used in addressing other challenging problems in computational biology, such as identifying chromosome-specific repeats, in probe design for oligonucleotides, and in monitoring genome assemblage.

8.3.5 Distance measure between sequences and phylogeny

In Section 6.3 we described the extended BWT proposed by Mantaci et al. (2005, 2007). In the same set of papers they showed how the extended BWT can be used to define a distance measure between sequences. Such a distance measure can thus be used to cluster species based on their similarity with respect to this measure. This is based on the nature of the resulting output from the extended BWT. The basic premise is that, given two input sequences, say S and T, the number of segments shared by S and T could be used as a measure of their similarity over evolution. Given the extended BWT, the extent to which the two sequences share some segments can be captured by considering the extent of mixing between symbols from the two sequences in the output array after the transformation. Thus, even when large but similar segments of two genomes are shuffled within each genome, the distance measure can still capture their potential relatedness. This is important in other applications such as in the analysis of genome rearrangements in computational biology.

Using the above, a distance measure is defined based on the extent of mixing between conjugates from the two sequences in the final transform output. The distance measure is therefore simply given by the number of alternations between symbols from each sequence in the output of the extended BWT. Using a marking scheme on the symbols in the L array, the transform output, it is easy to compute the distance between two sequences. Each conjugate is assigned a color or mark, based on its originating sequence. Let γ_i be the marker for sequence S_i. Suppose we use $\gamma = \{\gamma_1, \gamma_2, \gamma_3, \ldots\} = \{A, B, C, \ldots\}$. Then, the marker sequence between two strings u and v can be represented as $A_\gamma(u, v) = A^{n_1} B^{n_2} A^{n_3} \ldots B^{n_k}$, where the n_i's are the exponents. Then, the distance measure between u and v is defined as:

$$\delta(u, v) = \sum_{\substack{i=1 \\ n_i \neq 0}}^{k} (n_i - 1) = \sum_{\substack{i=1 \\ n_i \neq 0}}^{k} n_i - k.$$

Figure 8.4 shows an example of this marking scheme using the same multiset of sequences

$$T = \{S_1, S_2, S_3, S_4\} = \{\mathtt{ab}, \mathtt{aba}, \mathtt{cbac}, \mathtt{bac}\}$$

used in Section 6.3. Using the example, we obtain the sequence of markers $A_\gamma(S_1, S_2, S_3, S_4) = BBADCBADCDCC = B^2 ADCBADCDC^2$. For pairwise distances, we just use only the markers from the pair of interest. Thus, we have, for example: $A_\gamma(S_1, S_2) = B^2 ABA$, $A_\gamma(S_2, S_3) = B^2 CBCC^2$, $A_\gamma(S_2, S_4) = B^2 DBDD$, $A_\gamma(S_3, S_4) = DCDCDC^2$, with the respective distances: $\delta(S_1, S_2) =$

$1, \delta(S_2, S_3) = 3, \delta(S_2, S_4) = 2, \delta(S_3, S_4) = 1$. The distances show S_3 should be closer to S_4, than to S_2.

This scheme can easily be extended to computing pair-wise distances between multiple sequences in the input multiset. Based on this measure, Mantaci et al. (2007) constructed phylogenic trees between different species based on their mitochondria DNA. It's easy to see that this distance measure is not a metric, since it does not obey the triangular inequality. Also, it could be significantly affected by a simple difference in sequence lengths. In a sense, the distance measure could be related to general methods in alignment-free sequence comparison (Vinga and Almeida, 2003), and hence could help to reduce the time required in multiple sequence alignments. BWT-based methods for DNA sequence alignment have been studied in Lam et al. (2007).

Conjugates, A	Index	A_s	F	L	A_γ
ab	1	aab	a	b	B
ba	2	aba	a	a	B
aba	3	ab	a	b	A
baa	4	acb	a	b	D
aab	5	accb	a	b	C
cbac	6	baa	b	a	B
bacc	7	ba	b	a	A
accb	8	bac	b	c	D
ccba	9	bacc	b	c	C
bac	10	cba	c	a	D
acb	11	cbac	c	c	C
cba	12	ccba	c	a	C

Fig. 8.4. Measuring distance between sequences using the extended BWT. Results are for the multiset of strings, $T = \{\text{ab}, \text{aba}, \text{cbac}, \text{bac}\}$. The last column is the marker sequence needed to compute the distance

8.4 Test data compression

Test data compression is an important problem in the design and development of high performance chips, such as application-specific integrated circuits (ASICs) and core-based system-on-chips (SoCs). For instance, SoC designs are usually made up of various reusable intellectual property (IP) cores (potentially from different manufacturers) which are integrated on a single die to provide a wide range of functionality. With the growing complexity of the cores, each core must be rigorously tested using a set of test patterns. These test vectors could be random patterns or deterministic patterns, designed to exercise the cores for specific faults. For effective testing of the IP cores, however, a huge volume of test data is required, and this poses critical problems.

One approach is to use *built-in-self-test* (BIST) which allows the use of pre-computed test sequences or pseudo-random test patterns that will be generated by hardware included as part of the chip. The major motivation is to reduce both the complexity of testing, and avoid reliance on expensive external automatic testing equipment. Not all IP cores, however, have the capability for BIST. Furthermore, given hardware limitations, BIST may not be able to provide enough test patterns for complete testing of the device.

An alternative approach is to use an external *automatic test equipment* (ATE) to perform the required testing of the chip. Typically with the ATE, pre-computed test sets are stored on an external workstation. During testing, test patterns are then downloaded from the workstation to an interface workstation attached to the ATE, as needed for the particular test required. The test data is then later transferred from the ATE interface workstation to the main pattern memory using a dedicated high-speed bus.

The testing time under such scenarios will depend critically on the volume of test data required to be downloaded, the rate at which the data is being downloaded, and the rate of data transfer from the ATE interface workstation to the main pattern memory. Data compression is useful in such a situation as it reduces the overall amount of data to be downloaded, and consequently the download time, and therefore the overall testing time and idle time of the expensive ATE. Compression in such ATE environments requires that the compression be lossless, and that decompression be as simple and as fast as possible. We can compress the data off-line (at the workstation), but decompression must be on-the-fly, and simple enough to be implemented in hardware.

Various methods have thus been proposed for compression of test data (Chandra and Chakrabarty, 2001; Yamaguchi et al., 2002; Karimi et al., 2002). The asymmetry between the decoding and encoding time of the BWT makes it particularly suited for compression under the ATE environment, where very fast and simple decompression is needed, but encoding is only done once, and can be done on a fast system. Given this asymmetry and the specific nature of test data sequences, Yamaguchi et al. (2002) presented a BWT-based method for compressing test data sequences.

8.4.1 Nature of test data

A test pattern is generally a collection of binary sequences. During testing, each pin of the device under test is subjected to a sequence of test patterns. For compression, an important characteristic of test data sets is that for a given pin, the sequence of test patterns subjected to the pin are usually highly correlated; but the patterns applied to different pins are relatively weakly correlated. Another observation (Yamaguchi et al., 2002) is that a block of test sequences is usually directed to test a few modules of the IC at a time, while the other modules are kept in a relatively constant state. Thus, for the module, only a subset of the input pins will be subjected to varying test patterns, while the test patterns to the other pins will be held relatively constant. Therefore, for given input lines (to a given pin), there will be stretches of relative inactivity, where the test patterns will have relatively constant values. A final observation made by Yamaguchi et al. (2002) is that, for large industrial test suites, the test sequences to an active input pin usually contain repeating test patterns (or cycles). Based on the above, each pin in the chip can be characterized by the *activity* on its test sequence, defined simply as the number of transitions on the test sequence applied to the pin.

8.4.2 BWT-based test data compression

Given the correlated nature of the test patterns to the same input pin, and the observed cycles in the sequences, the clustering property of the BWT can be exploited to bring such similar test patterns together in the BWT output. Thus, after applying the BWT to sequences, run-length encoding could become an effective means to exploit the exposed redundancies. Further, given that the decoding stage of the BWT is straightforward, with a relatively more time consuming encoding stage (given the suffix sorting process), the BWT provides a good tool for the compression of test patterns for use in automatic test equipment. The decoding can also be implemented in hardware for more speed, even if the encoding stage may be more difficult to be implemented in hardware (see Section 7.5 for hardware considerations in the Burrows-Wheeler Transform).

Let $D = D[1 \ldots n, 1 \ldots m]$ be an $n \times m$ matrix representing a given test dataset. Typically, m corresponds to the number of pins in the device under test. Thus, each column in D represents the sequence of test patterns applied to a particular pin. The number of rows, n, indicates the extent of the test. Given that n could be very large, to compress the test data using the BWT, Yamaguchi et al. (2002) divided D into smaller submatrices, D_i, each with m columns: $D = [D_1, D_2, \ldots, D_k]$. The BWT is then applied independently to each column of D_i, rather than the submatrix D_i, and run-length encoding is then used on the output sequence. The problem is that even though the BWT will cluster symbols with similar contexts in the BWT output, it does not guarantee that the resulting output will have less activity than the original input sequence. Thus, before applying RLE, the BWT output is checked for its level of activity. More specifically, let $\alpha(S)$ be the activity computed for sequence S, that is, the number of transitions in S. Let d_k be the k-th column of the submatrix D_i, and let L_k^* be the corresponding BWT output for d_k. Given the input D_i, the output submatrix $E_i = [e_1 e_2 \ldots e_m]$ that is passed to the RLE stage is defined as follows:

$$
e_k = \begin{cases} L_k^*, & : \quad \text{if } \alpha(L_k^*) < \alpha(d_k) \text{ and } \alpha(L_k^*) < \tau \\ d_k & : \quad \text{otherwise} \end{cases}
$$

where τ is a threshold.

Thus, the matrix E_i includes the data from the BWT transformed sequence only if the activity in the sequence is below a threshold, and not worse than the activity in the original sequence. Run-length encoding is then applied only to columns in E_i with activity less than the same threshold. This guarantees that the RLE always does better on E_i compared with D_i, apart from the minor issue of having to encode whether or not the BWT coding has been applied to each d_k. Avoiding the use of the BWT on high activity sequences also saves decompression time, which is a critical parameter in compression for ATEs.

Applying the BWT to the individual columns rather than to the entire data set exploits the observed characteristics of test sequences applied to the same pin. It also implies less time to compress the entire data, since the time-consuming sorting stage will now be applied only to smaller-sized blocks. This is akin to the blocking used in the earlier days of the BWT to make the transform practical. Although the partitioning is not strictly necessary for the BWT to work in this scenario, applying the BWT to each column of a smaller partition makes it possible to use parallel hardware for faster processing, especially at the decoder. Furthermore, for some activity values on a given column of the D_i's, we do not gain any compression improvement by applying the BWT (for instance, when the activity is 0). Thus we can save some time in both decoding and encoding by avoiding the use of the BWT in such cases. Results in Yamaguchi et al. (2002) showed that the BWT-based method performed better than six other popular methods of test data compression on standard test data sets, including those for a disk controller, RISC microcontroller, and CD-ROM controller.

8.5 Image compression, computer vision and machine translation

In this section we look at some of the more creative applications that the Burrows-Wheeler Transform has been used for. The BWT was designed for lossless compression, but it can be useful for compressing images, even though they normally require a lossy approach. The BWT has also found applications in computer vision, where matching shapes can be formulated as a pattern matching problem. Finally, we will look at applications in machine translation, where it can be used to recognize language patterns.

8.5.1 Image compression

Image compression methods are generally classified as *lossless* or *lossy*. Lossless methods enable the original image to be recovered exactly, and are important for general purpose situations, particularly medical and legal applications where small changes in the image can have significant consequences. In contrast, lossy image compression allows some deterioration in the original image. Usually the level of deterioration is near-imperceptible, yet considerable compression improvement can be achieved because the system is not storing unnecessary detail. Many lossy image compression methods include a lossless compression scheme as a sub-component. For example, an image compression system might transform the image to a frequency domain, and then encode only the lower frequency components using a lossless compression algorithm. Thus techniques for lossless compression can be of relevance to lossy systems, such as image and video compression systems.

Figure 8.5 shows a general model for image compression. The data transformation stage transforms the input data into some form that will expose the redundancies or repetitions in the data. This stage can also be used to reduce other forms of redundancy in an image. For instance, pixel prediction is often used as an initial transformation stage, since neighboring pixels in an image are likely to have similar pixel values unless there is an edge boundary between them. The encoding stage (also called the coding stage) codes the data to remove the exposed redundancies. The quantization stage is used to reduce some other forms of redundancy in the image (for instance, detail that is beyond the limitations of the human eye), at the expense of accuracy in the data representation.

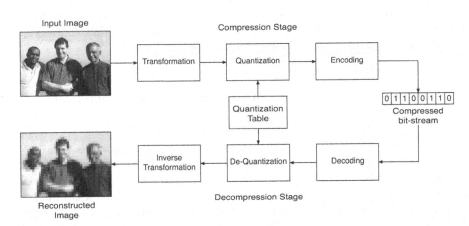

Fig. 8.5. General model for image compression

Decompression involves doing the reverse operations: decoding, inverse quantization and inverse transformation. The operations before and after the quantization stage are generally reversible and hence do not introduce any loss or artifacts in the compression. Quantization, however, is not reversible and thus introduces some errors in the compression process. In effect, from the viewpoint of compression models, the major difference between lossless and lossy image compression is the quantization stage: lossless image compression does not involve any quantization. The quantization stage also accounts for the huge compression ratios often achievable in lossy image compression.

The BWT in lossless image compression. As might be expected, given its performance in text compression, there have been various attempts to use the BWT in lossless compression of images and other digital signals such as video, audio, and electrocardiogram signals. In general, however, the BWT (especially with the MTF as the second stage) does not produce competitive results for natural images. This may be related to the difficulty in defining contexts in images in a way that is similar to contexts as encountered in natural languages and other text documents.

Since nearby samples in most digital signals are similar (for example, neighboring pixels at a given position typically have similar pixel values), an initial step in their compression is often a prediction stage, whereby the current sample is predicted based on its neighboring samples that have already been encoded. The difference between the actual value and predicted value is the prediction error. For natural images, the sequence of prediction errors has more well-defined characteristics, and hence is generally more compressible than the original sequence of pixels. The final step is the entropy encoding of the prediction errors, using schemes such as arithmetic coding or Huffman codes.

Motivated by the context-sorting method of the BWT, Ciavarella and Moffat (2004) proposed a permutation method that re-orders the prediction errors based on the nature of their conditioning contexts. In a sense, this is similar to the BWT that reorders the symbols in text based on their forward contexts. Thus, after the reordering, nearby prediction error values in the reordered list are expected to be similar, and should have similar contexts. Symbol ranking schemes such as the MTF that exploit the local clustering of similar contexts can then be used for effective compression of the re-ordered list. On a test set of 12 standard 8-bit images, the approach resulted in an average compression rate of 4.59 bits per pixel (bpp) using the MTF followed by an adaptive arithmetic coder, and 4.41 bpp without the MTF. Using a special scanning order with pixel reordering, as opposed to prediction error reordering (that is, without prediction), they achieved 4.52 bpp with BZIP2. Without reordering, BZIP2 produced 4.62 bpp. These results can be compared with the results of 4.63 bpp and 4.42bpp for LOCO-I (the JPEG-LS standard) and CALIC respectively, which are among the best performing lossless compression algorithms with comparable space and time complexity.

The performance of the BWT and its variants such as a low-order sort transform, or Arnavut's linear order transform, has been evaluated on electrocardiogram (EEG) signals by Arnavut (2007b). Using the MTF as the second stage, he showed that block sorting provides an effective way to compress such signals, after the initial stage of sample prediction. Here, sample prediction was performed using a simple auto-regressive model. In Arnavut (2007a), a similar study was conducted using the BWT, but with inversion ranks, rather than MTF as the second stage. The results showed that the BWT-based methods are competitive, if not better than, the state-of-the-art compression schemes specially designed for EEG signals. A similar experiment on using the BWT for compression of volume data was reported in Komma et al. (2007), where it was found that BZIP2 produced the best result when compared with other general-purpose compression schemes. BWT-based methods for lossless compression of DNA microarray images were reported in Lonardi and Luo (2004). The BWT produced the best result for general purpose compression schemes. Although not as good, the results can be compared with those for special purpose DNA microarray compression algorithms (see Adjeroh et al. (2006) for example).

The BWT in lossy image compression. Lossy image and video compression schemes such as JPEG[1] and MPEG[2] typically include a lossless entropy encoding stage. Thus, lossless compression schemes such as the BWT often find applications in lossy image compression.

For lossy image compression, after initial pixel prediction, the transformation stage is often based on linear transforms, such as the FFT (Fast Fourier Transform), DCT (Discrete Cosine Transform, used in JPEG and MPEG), or DWT (Discrete Wavelet Transform, used in JPEG2000). The applicability of the BWT in lossy image compression is motivated by the nature of the quantized coefficients, after the linear transformation stage. After application of a zig-zag scan of the two-dimensional array of coefficients, the quantized coefficients' values in a given block of the DCT or DWT usually contain runs of repeating zeros, or other symbols with generally small values. Thus, an immediate way to exploit the properties of the BWT is to apply the BWT directly on the quantized coefficients, and then code the resulting BWT output as for conventional BWT-based compression (using RLE and entropy encoding), or using standard entropy encoding that is used in image compression. The latter approach was taken in Baik et al. (1999b), where they observed mixed results using JPEG compression: some images resulted in improved compression using the BWT, while compression deteriorated in others.

A better approach would be to apply the BWT selectively, based on some measure of the degree of repetitiveness in the quantized coefficients. Baik et al. (1999a) defined the degree of repetitiveness using the frequency of given substrings in the quantized DCT block, and the length of substrings. Then, the BWT is applied to the quantized block only if the degree of repetitiveness is more than a predefined threshold. As reported, on average, this improved scheme resulted in an 18.19% improvement in compression on a test set of 30 images, compared with the standard JPEG compression. One can observe the similarity with the problem of activity in test data compression in Section 8.4. Thus, one form of improvement could be to use activity (as defined in Section 8.4) as the degree of repetitiveness, and to make the decision on

---

[1] Joint Photographic Experts Group.

[2] Motion Picture Experts Group.

whether to use the BWT output *after* (rather than *before*) the application of the BWT. In other words, as with the case of test data compression, we can compare the activity of the quantized coefficients before and after the BWT, and then select the BWT results only if they pass a threshold. There three variations are depicted in Figure 8.6.

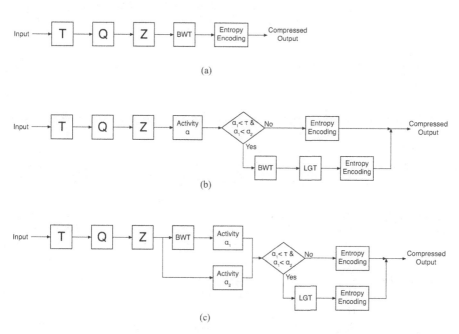

(a)

(b)

(c)

Fig. 8.6. Three approaches to BWT-based lossy image compression: (a) basic BWT-based method; (b) improved approach proposed in Baik et al. (1999a); (c) suggested modification (see text); the abbreviations T, Q, and Z in the figures denote transformation, quantization, and zig-zag scan, respectively

More recently, Wiseman (2006) suggested a slight modification to the BWT-based lossy image compression scheme described above. Rather than feeding the quantized coefficients directly to the BWT, a run-length encoder is used, and the RLE results are used as the input to the BWT. Subsequently the BWT outputs are encoded as in usual BWT-based compression (via MTF, RLE, and entropy encoding). The general BWT-based approach to lossy image compression can equally be applied for improved JPEG2000 compression, even though the underlying transformation is different from that used in JPEG. In fact, similar modifications were suggested for wavelet-based image compression by Guo and Burrus (1997).

Perhaps with the exception of the work of Ciavarella and Moffat (2004), most other research on BWT-based compression of digital signals, be it lossy or lossless compression, have treated the BWT as a black box, using the prediction residues as the input. While improved compression is observed in some cases, these methods fail to exploit the important properties of the BWT in compressing these signals. This may explain the widely held belief that in general, the BWT (with MTF) does not produce competitive results in compressing natural images. However, the results in Ciavarella and Moffat (2004) have shown that improved performance is possible by a careful consideration of the data at hand, and relating it to one or more of the processing steps in BWT-based compression. This represents a promising direction for future work in BWT-based compression of digital signals.

8.5.2 Shape matching

Shape matching and the analysis of object shapes are well-known object recognition problems in computer vision and in general pattern recognition. Applications range from motion planning in robotics to content-based image retrieval in multimedia databases (where images are retrieved based on automatically extracted information in the image, rather than manually entered keywords). Given an input query shape, the problem of shape matching is to produce a list (or ranking) of object shapes in a database of shapes that are similar to the query shape. To match one m-length query shape segment against one n-length shape in a database, existing methods require $O(nmk^2)$ time for open shapes, or $O(nm^2k^2)$ for closed shapes, where m is the number of segments in the query shape, n is the number of segments in the database shape, and k is an error parameter (number of segments), used to model the merging and splitting required for scale invariance, and for robustness against noise. With N shapes in the database, and an average of n segments per database shape, this would mean an average cost of $O(nm^2k^3N)$ for matching closed shapes, for example. Thus, scalability in terms of database size, and in terms of the number of shape segments, will become a major problem for such algorithms. This is important, especially given that shape databases with millions of shape objects, each with potentially hundreds or thousands of segments, are becoming common. These sizes occur, for example, in the analysis of protein structure in bioinformatics, or for a large database of mechanical parts, such as for an airplane.

Using the context clustering property of the BWT, Adjeroh et al. (2007) proposed a method to perform efficient shape matching for boundary-based shape representations. Given a shape boundary, they decompose it into primitive shape segments that capture the salient aspects of object parts, and perform matching based on the primitives. Motivated by the sorted contexts of the Burrows-Wheeler Transform, they developed an algorithm for efficient shape matching, suitable for large-scale shape databases, where the shape boundaries are represented as a sequence of shape primitives. Their approach is related in principle to the method of shape contexts used in shape representation and shape matching (Belongie et al., 2002; Mori et al., 2001). For a given point on a shape, the shape context is captured in terms of the relative position of all the remaining points on the shape, using both boundary points and internal points on the shape. However, rather than shape contexts as described above, they used the concept of sorted shape contexts, as induced by the BWT. Conceptually, when the BWT is applied to a database of shape sequences, shapes with similar contexts will be clustered together in the transformed sequence, making it easier to identify similar shapes to a query. Thus, unlike with shape contexts, the contexts are sorted, and the method depends primarily on boundary-based information, since no information from the internal shape regions is used.

The basic idea is as follows: Decompose each shape segment into a sequence of primitive shapes, namely *line, concave,* or *convex* segments (see Figure 8.7). Given that the important determinants of the saliency of an object's part include its size, protrusion, curvature, and the turning angle between adjacent parts (Hoffman and Singh, 1997), three different string sequences are used to capture these important features. These are: (i) the string of primitive shape types, (ii) the string of primitive shape lengths, and (iii) the string of transition angles. These three shape primitives capture an object's curvature and protrusion. Their lengths are a measure of a part's size, while the transition angle between the primitives provides information about the turning angle. These are thus represented using symbols from three shape alphabets.

Consider the example in Figure 8.7c. The three symbols for the basic segments are C, V, L for concave curves, convex curves, and line segments, respectively. Angles are represented using 16 symbols ($\Sigma_A = \{a, b, c, \ldots, p\}$). The segments and angles have been marked with their corresponding symbols (d for $90°$, h for $180°$). The lengths have been left out for this example. The resulting strings will be $LLCVL$ for the segments, and $dddhd$ for the transition angles. Using the three string sequences, shape comparison can then be performed using methods of string pattern matching, as described in Chapter 7.

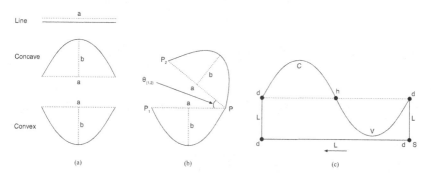

Fig. 8.7. Shape representation using shape strings: (a) primitive shape segments; (b) transition angle; (c) example shape representation. S denotes the starting point, and the arrow indicates the scanning direction. The parameters a and b capture the size of the primitives, while θ is the transition angle

For instance, Adjeroh et al. (2007) described a two-phase shape matching algorithm, using BWT-based methods for k-approximate matching (see Section 7.4.7). At the *hypothesis phase*, the algorithm locates the areas in the database sequence that contain potential matches to the query shape. This is done by filtering the database sequence using carefully chosen q-gram sizes. At the *verification phase*, the algorithm confirms the results proposed at the hypothesis phase. The verification stage is generally slow, but usually, it will be performed on only a small proportion of the database sequence. Thus, the performance of the algorithm depends critically on the efficiency of the filtering stage — in terms of computational time and also the number of hypotheses generated.

As an example, consider the two sample shapes in Figure 8.8. Assume the first shape to be the database sequence, with $T = CLVLLL.CLVLLL$, and the query shape to be the second, $P = CLVCL.CLVCL$ (Shapes are represented using the original concatenated to itself to eliminate the problem of knowing the starting point). For ease of illustration, we ignore the respective symbols from the angle and length alphabets. Assume $k = 1$. Here, $m = 5$, and hence, hypothesis generation will be performed using exact matching on shape segments of length 2. After shape q-gram generation, the 2-grams from T will be: CL, LV, VL, LL, LL, LC. Similarly, from the query shape P we get the 2-grams: CL, LV, VC, CL, LC. These will produce the matching 2-grams CL, LC, LV, with potential match neighborhoods in T given by $\mathcal{N}_1 = [1 \ldots 6]; \mathcal{N}_2 = [2 \ldots 6]; \mathcal{N}_3 = [6 \ldots 12]$. These will then be verified. The correct matches will be found in $\mathcal{N}_1$ and $\mathcal{N}_3$, starting at positions 1 and 6 respectively in the database sequence (The last match required wrapping around the database shape). The matching segments are shown in Figure 8.8c and 8.8d. The segments are quite similar in terms of the segment primitives. Using the angle and length primitives will improve the accuracy of the matching.

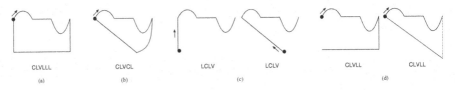

| CLVLLL | CLVCL | LCLV | LCLV | CLVLL | CLVLL |
| (a) | (b) | (c) | | (d) | |

Fig. 8.8. Example of shape matching using sorted shape contexts: (a) database shape; (b) query shape; (c) and (d) two sets of matching segments, at $k = 1$

8.5.3 Machine translation

The problem of machine translation can be stated as follows: Given a stream of text or speech from one originating natural language, develop an automated system to translate the source text or speech to a given target natural language. In its simplest form, machine translation can be performed by substituting words in the source language with corresponding words in the target language, for instance using a lookup table, or a dictionary. However, improved quality in translation calls for more sophisticated methods that can account for issues such as linguistic typology, phrase recognition, idiomatic expressions, word-sense disambiguation, recognition of named entities, and identification and handling of anomalies (Hutchins and Somers, 1992). Such sophisticated methods therefore face the core challenge of first understanding the original text, and then expressing this understanding in the target language, in a way that will sound natural (that is, similar to what a skilled human would have done). This decoding and re-encoding process is the key challenge in machine translation.

Example-based machine translation (EBMT) is one popular approach to machine translation and involves the use of a large bilingual corpus for training at the time of translation. Translation is then performed by analogy based on examples extracted from the training corpus. Thus, a primary component of such a system is an effective index of the training instances. Most existing systems use traditional indexing methods such as the inverted file. Brown (2004) showed how the BWT clustering property and BWT-based compressed indexes can be used to provide improved quality in machine translation. The basic observation is that the BWT provides a clustering of all occurrences of a given q-gram, and thus can be used to extract the most frequent q-grams in the corpus. In principle there is no restriction on the q-gram — it could be a word, substring, phrase, or even a complete sentence. The key idea then is to pre-compute the translation for these frequent q-grams, and store the translations for later use. The result is an order-of-magnitude speedup in processing time. The side effect of this improved processing speed is that the system now has enough time to perform more detailed analysis of the resulting initial translation, leading to an overall improved quality of the translation.

For ambiguous lookups involving equivalence classes or sets of terms, the matching is split into different steps. At each step (corresponding to some word position in the input text), an extension of the match is attempted for each active partial match using each alternative term in the set. If an extension results in a match, the process is applied recursively on the resulting matches. Otherwise the extension is discontinued and matching terminates for the particular word. This is therefore very similar to the BWT-based k-mismatch algorithm, described in Section 7.4.6. The corpus was represented using FM-index style compressed full-text indexes, with self-indexing supported. Therefore, the actual matching referred to above is performed using backward search using the compressed V array. Thus, the original source language is not stored explicitly, as it can be recovered from the compressed representation of V.

8.6 Joint source-channel coding

For certain applications the major problem is data storage, and hence efficient compression of the data from a given information source is all that is needed. So far, we have seen that the BWT provides an effective mechanism for compressing the data. For some other applications (such as in wireless communications), data compaction is not enough: we still need mechanisms for efficient and reliable transmission of the compressed data, even in the presence of errors in the transmission channel.

Figure 8.9 shows a general communication system. Data from an information source is passed to a source encoder which performs compression to remove redundancy in the original sequence. The information source here could be a human, a sensor, a computer, or something else. The compressed sequence is then passed to a channel encoder which systematically introduces controlled redundancy in order to protect the data from potential errors in the communication channel. Thus, while source coding involves the removal of redundancy from the data, channel coding essentially introduces redundancy in the compressed sequence.

In his ground breaking work in information theory, Shannon (1948) showed that, in fact, as long as the transmission rate is below the capacity of the channel, it is possible to transmit information with near-zero error (or with the error made as small as we may wish), with appropriate encoding (for both the source coding and channel coding). Various methods exist for channel coding. A simple example is *repetition codes*, whereby the data is simply repeated, typically an odd number of times. Channel decoding is then performed by a simple majority rule. Other methods include cyclic-redundancy-codes, low-density parity check codes (LDPC), convolutional codes, and turbo codes. The book by Lin and Costello Jr. (2004) provides a detailed treatment of channel coding and error protection.

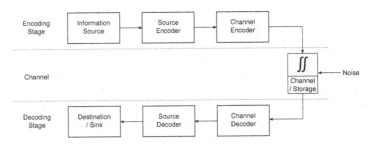

Fig. 8.9. Basic communication system

8.6.1 General source coding via channel coding

Figure 8.9 suggests that source coding and channel coding need to be treated separately and sequentially in order to achieve Shannon's results. This, however, requires asymptotically long sequences for its realization, which may not be the case in most practical applications. This has led to the idea of *joint source-channel coding*, whereby source encoding can make use of some knowledge of the channel and/or the channel encoding algorithm, and conversely, the channel encoding process can exploit known characteristics of the information source, the source coding algorithm, and the channel.

In linear error correction codes, such as parity check codes or LDPC, the channel encoder is characterized by a parity check matrix $\mathbf{H}$. Given a source sequence, say $\mathbf{s}$, channel encoding is then a simple matter of matrix multiplication using $\mathbf{s}$ and $\mathbf{H}$. The result will be an *error syndrome*. That is, given the result, we can see immediately whether there is an error or not, since every valid codeword will result in a zero vector for the product. Any nonzero vector implies that there is an error, and the syndrome can be used to determine the location of the error. Similarly, a linear fixed-length n-to-m compression scheme can be viewed as a mapping of n-length source symbols to m-length codewords. Thus, the compression process can be described using an $m \times n$ matrix $\mathbf{H}$, such that for a given n-length input $\mathbf{s}$, the corresponding m-length output will be the matrix product $\mathbf{Hs}$. At the decoder, we can use a maximum-likelihood decoder which selects some source vector, say u, such that $\mathbf{Hu} = \mathbf{Hs}$, as the decoded message. The encoder can determine whether decoding will be possible by a simple check, given its knowledge of both the decoder and the message being transmitted. This shows that source coding and channel coding are closely related, and both can be performed using essentially the same basic framework.

The key idea in using channel coding for compression (i.e. source coding) is that the encoder has access to all information that is available to the decoder. Therefore, it can check to determine whether the decoder can correctly decode the output without error. This is depicted in Figure 8.10. The channel encoder can iteratively modify its parameters, and at each iteration it can check the integrity of the encoded outputs to determine if the decoder will be able to decode it without error, or possibly the amount of compression achieved. The effectiveness of lossless data compression (in terms of both lossless decoding and achieved compression) therefore critically depends on how this parameter modification is performed.

Caire et al. (2004, 2006) proposed methods for source encoding using low-density parity-check codes (LDPC). They used an ensemble of LDPCs, which is maintained at both the encoder and at the decoder. Parameter modification then involves the selection of an appropriate matrix. The label of the selected matrix is sent to the encoder, based on which of the encoded data can be decoded. Caire et al. (2004) also described a modification of the basic idea whereby coding is performed using an erasure channel encoder. Here, parameter modification is performed by intelligently discarding part of the resulting encoded output.

Dütsch et al (Dütsch and Hagenauer, 2004; Dütsch et al., 2006) adopted the same basic approach for source coding via channel codes, but used turbo codes rather than linear block codes. To achieve compression, coded bits are *punctured* in a rate-compatible manner — puncturing here simply means deleting some specific bits in the encoder output. The choice of specific bits to be deleted is defined in a *puncturing matrix*. The final encoded sequence is thus composed of the surviving non-punctured bits, and the additional side information required for lossless recovery. Here, parameter adjustment is in the form of modification to the puncturing rate. Essentially, the puncturing rate is increased (reduced redundancy) if the integrity test is successful, and decreased (increased redundancy) whenever there is a failure. This is performed in an iterative loop until a desired level of compression (or data redundancy) is reached. The surviving coded bits that resulted in a successful decoding are then stored as the compressed data.

8.6.2 BWT-based joint source-channel coding

The major advantage of joint source-channel coding is that sequences compressed using a channel code are usually more resilient to channel errors during transmission, when compared with traditional compression schemes, even for the same overall compression rate. This is important for low capacity devices, such as cell phones, or sensors in a wireless sensor network. However, as discussed in Caire et al. (2004),Dütsch and Hagenauer (2004) and Dütsch et al. (2006), the above general scheme for compression via channel coding works only for independent and identically distributed (i.i.d.) sources, and it breaks down for sources with memory, such as Markov sources. The problem is the difficulty of designing an optimal decoder using the non-memoryless source statistics.

To address the problem of memory, and thus extend the method to sources with memory, the Burrows-Wheeler Transform can be used. This exploits the context partitioning property of the BWT and the statistical properties of the BWT output, as discussed in Chapter 5. Recall that for very long sequences, the output distribution of the BWT is piece-wise i.i.d., with the

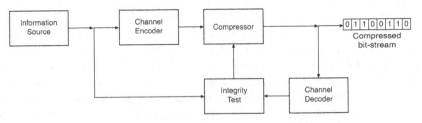

Fig. 8.10. General source coding via channel coding

length and distribution of the i.i.d. segments being determined by the statistics of the input sequence. Thus, to solve the problem of memory in the general scheme for compression via channel codes, the source sequence can first be passed through the BWT. Subsequently, each context partition in the BWT output (which now is i.i.d.) is passed through the scheme described above, which works for memoryless sources. Figure 8.11 shows a modified version of Figure 8.10, incorporating the BWT stages. At the decoder, after decoding, the different segments are arranged back into their correct order, and the inverse BWT is performed to recover the original data. The context partition boundaries need to be transmitted to the decoder for correct decoding.

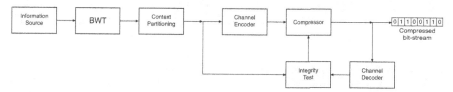

Fig. 8.11. BWT-based joint source-channel coding

Observe that the compressibility of BWT transformed sequences is not the issue here, and hence was not really exploited in this application. Also, the use of the BWT does not depend on the specific channel coding method adopted. For instance, both Caire et al. (2004) and Dütsch and Hagenauer (2004) used the BWT as a way to extend their respective methods to sources with memory, but using different underlying channel coding methods. The results in both cases showed that the use of the BWT in joint source-channel coding led to a significant improvement over traditional source coding followed by independent channel coding, for instance, using BZIP2 and rate-compatible punctured turbo codes. Extending the method to universal source coding mainly requires the encoder to send the model parameters for each context partition, in addition to information on the block boundaries. This is also related to the issue of prediction and entropy estimation — see the next section.

8.7 Prediction and entropy estimation

The problem of entropy estimation is very closely related to universal coding in data compression. In compression, there is the decoding stage that must be able to recover the input sequence given the compressed data stream. Both compression and entropy estimation can be based on the same basic information, namely, an estimate of the probability of each symbol generated by the source. For compression this estimate of probabilities is passed to a subsequent entropy encoder, such as an arithmetic coder. For entropy estimation, however, there is no decoding stage, and the objective is to predict as close as possible, what the true entropy of the source is. Thus, the estimated probabilities can be used to directly compute an estimate of the source entropy. Actual compression need not be performed. The important role of entropy in information theory makes it important to study methods for estimating the entropy of a source. Entropy estimation has been used in various applications, such as sequence classification, identification of tree sources, performance measurement between compression algorithms, phylogenic tree construction in computational biology (Lanctot et al., 2000; Schmitt and Herzel, 1997), language modeling, analysis of neural spike trains in neuroscience (Strong et al., 1998) and so on.

The use of the BWT in entropy estimation and tree source identification have been studied in (Baron and Bresler, 2004, 2000; Cai et al., 2004). The basis is the fact that the BWT output distribution for a tree source can be modeled as being piecewise constant i.i.d. Thus, based on the context-partitions of the BWT output, entropy estimation can be performed by estimating the parameters for each partition and averaging over all the partitions. In Chapter 5, we defined entropy, empirical entropy, and entropy rate of a source. For a finite memory Markov source, the entropy rate can also be expressed as follows:

$$H(p) = \sum_{c \in C} p(c) \sum_{\sigma \in \Sigma} p(\alpha|c) \log \frac{1}{p(\alpha|c)} \qquad (8.3)$$

where p denotes a probability measure on the source, $c \in C$ is a state in the Markov model, and $\sigma \in \Sigma$ is a symbol emitted by the source. Thus, if the source is known to be i.i.d. or piecewise i.i.d. (that is, we know the states, and the parameters of the model), entropy estimation will be easy, since all we need to do is to plug in the numbers in the formula, based on the context partitions in the BWT. Here, each unique context will correspond to a state in the model. The real challenge is that the source is typically unknown, and thus we need to estimate its parameters – the states and the symbol distribution at each state.

Building on the context partitioning induced by the clustering property of the BWT, Cai et al. (2004) outlined the following procedure to estimate the empirical conditional distributions, based on which the estimated entropy can be computed.

1. Compute the BWT of the reversed sequence. The inverse BWT is not needed.
2. Divide L, the BWT output into b segments. Segment lengths could, but need not, be equal.
3. Estimate the first-order probability distribution for each segment, using the count of each symbol σ within the segment. Compute the empirical entropy of each segment, using Equation 5.3.

4. Compute the overall entropy estimate by taking the average of all the segment entropies computed in step 3 above. This implements Equation 8.3 above.

Therefore, the main problem is in Step 2: segmentation of the BWT output. Since we do not know the Markov order of the source, we cannot rely on k-order contexts for performing segmentation. Thus, Cai et al. (2004) proposed two methods to perform the segmentation, and hence determine the length of each segment. The first method simply used a uniform length for each partition. For a sequence of length n, they suggested $w(n) = O(\sqrt{n})$ for the length of each sequence for a total of $b(n) = \frac{n}{w(n)}$ segments. With this scheme, $b(n)$ the number of segments could grow without bounds, as $n \to \infty$. Thus, they suggested a second approach which is based on an adaptive segmentation. The method starts out with a uniform length for each segment, assuming a fixed number of segments. Then, each segment is considered for potential merging or splitting based on a metric that depends on the statistics of its neighboring segments. Surprisingly, the simple partitioning scheme using the same length for each segment also resulted in an entropy estimate that converges to the true entropy, with probability 1, for stationary ergodic sources. For the specific case of finite memory sources, they showed that estimates produced by the uniform length scheme approaches the true entropy at a convergence rate in $O(\frac{\log^2 n}{n})$. Simulation results showed that the method produces a better entropy estimate (with respect to the mean-square error) than published LZ-based and PPM-based estimation schemes. These rather theoretical results can be contrasted with the empirical compression results reported in (Wirth, 2001), where it was shown that a uniform segmentation of the BWT output does not lead to good practical compression performance.

8.8 Further reading

In this chapter we have tried to discuss some of the observed and promising applications of the Burrows-Wheeler Transform. Apart from the sections on compressed suffix trees and suffix arrays, and compressed full-text indexing, the descriptions have been at a relatively high level, without going into all the details, and in most cases we have provided pointers to related work within the specific sections. In this section we simply provide further information that may be helpful in following the many applications of the BWT.

A detailed treatment of text indexing and document retrieval is presented in the book by Witten et al. (1999). Baeza-Yates and Ribeiro-Neto (1999) discuss various issues in modern information retrieval, for both text and non-text information. Zobel and Moffat (2006) provide a survey of recent advances in text indexing using inverted indexes. Ferragina and Venturini (2007) adapt existing compressed indexing systems (including the BWT) to implement the "permuterm" index in a space-efficient manner.

Compressed suffix arrays, compressed suffix trees, and full-text indexing are active and exciting areas of research very closely related to the BWT. The original work by Grossi and Vitter (2000, 2005) and by Ferragina and Manzini (2000, 2001b) laid the foundation for work in this area, and has no doubt motivated various researchers to study different problems in compressed indexing and compressed pattern matching. The recent survey by Navarro and Mäkinen (2007) provides a thorough review of work in this field, especially for compressed suffix arrays and full-text indexing. Firth et al. (2005) provide a comparison of various algorithms for BWT-based pattern matching.

Methods for dynamic update have been proposed for compressed suffix arrays (Hon et al., 2007), and for compressed suffix trees (Chan et al., 2005). The use of the LCP-array in compressed suffix arrays and in compressed suffix trees was mentioned, but without much detail. Details on these approaches can be found in Sadakane (2007, 2002) and Kim and Park (2005). Further methods for compressed indexing with different forms of compression are reported in Foschini et al. (2006); Golynski et al. (2007) and Gonzalez and Navarro (2006). Välimäki et al. (2007) present a practical implementation of Sadakane's CST that was reported in Sadakane (2007). The relationship between BWT-based compressed indexes and LZ-based compressed index structures (Kärkkäinen and Sutinen, 1998) was discussed in Ferragina and Manzini (2005).

In general, image compression using the BWT still represents a major challenge, as is the compression of other multidimensional data, such as video, or some types of medical images. One major problem is how to define contexts in two or more dimensions. Given that the BWT is context-based, this can have a definite impact on its performance on such data. Although the BWT has shown promising results in image compression (for both lossy and lossless compression), so far most of the methods use a simple application of the BWT to an image — simply using the BWT as a black box. A better matching of some of the established properties of the BWT with the image compression problem should lead to improved results. The work by Ciavarella and Moffat (2004) provides an initial indication of the potential of this approach. But more work is needed to modify one or more steps of the BWT compression pipeline to take advantage of specific image characteristics, or the specific nature of images for a given application. A similar comment applies to using the BWT in compressing general digital signals. General discussions on the relationship between image compression and text compression, and on searching compressed text and images can be found in Bell et al. (2001).

Cover and Thomas (1991, 2006) is the classic reference that provides an excellent theoretical background on source coding. Channel coding is treated in great detail in another classic text by Lin and Costello Jr. (2004). This contains detailed material on linear block codes, such as parity check codes and LDPC, and non-linear codes such as convolutional codes and turbo codes. The LDPC was introduced by Gallager (1962). Further details on LDPC and the belief propagation mechanism that it uses can be found in Richardson and Urbanke (2001). Punctured convolutional codes were introduced by Hagenauer (1988). The effect of the BWT in energy savings for energy-constrained devices is explored in Sadler and Martonosi (2006). They showed that for general compressed data, the BWT can result in significant savings in transmission energy, especially for long-range radio transmissions. Fenwick (2007) also mentioned the possible connection between lossless compression and error-correction codes, though in a manner different from those described in this chapter.

9

Conclusion

The story of the Burrows-Wheeler Transform is a valuable case study in the process of research and discovery. The idea was conceived in 1978, but it didn't see the light of day until published through a collaboration that led to the seminal technical report number 124 at Digital Equipment Corporation, published in 1994. Despite this being Burrows and Wheeler's only publication relating to the idea, a few people recognized its value, picked it up, evaluated it, and gave it enough exposure that it grew a large community that brought it to a level of maturity where it could be used in a general purpose compression utility. In the following dozen or so years, literally hundreds of papers had been published by scores of researchers based on the single technical report. The most visible application coming out of the BWT is the BZIP2 compression program, which will have saved many terabytes of disk space and weeks of download time. And with the number of papers produced that are built on the method, no doubt many careers have been greatly helped by the fertile research ground that it provided.

Through this book we have covered many of the directions that the BWT has led people in: new algorithms and data structures for performing the transform, fine-tuning the coding that can be done with the transformed file, new ways to sort the strings for the transform, a better understanding of other compression methods by relating them to the BWT, using the BWT data structures to aid searching and pattern matching, and applying its algorithms and data structures in contexts ranging from image analysis to computational biology. Yet there is a strong sense that we are only just beginning to understand the transform and its potential, as new variants and applications continue to be published regularly. The BWT is a powerful idea, and in the process of decoding generates a collection of useful arrays (R, V, W and so on) which can be used to provide a variety of indexes and views of the original text. The transform process thus provides us with data structures that have opened up novel possibilities, and may yet hold more opportunities for future applications.

As a compression system, the BWT is quite mature, having experiments done on it with that purpose in mind for over 10 years. It has been related to a broad range of the main lossless compression methods, including Ziv-Lempel methods, PPM, and DMC; the obvious relationship is that they all are using longest matches in some sense as part of their processing, but the literature has also established more subtle relationships where these apparently different methods gain their compression power by exploiting variable size contexts. The BWT has forced the issue of considering forward and backwards contexts, and has led us through a different path to the suffix array as a structure for identifying contexts, performing longest matches, and supporting compressed full-text indexing.

The promising theory underpinning the BWT for compression is backed up by practice. Seward's free open source system, BZIP2, is one of the best general purpose compression systems implemented, and is available for Linux, Windows and Macintosh systems. In contrast to the maturity of work relating to compression with the BWT, for other applications, especially pattern matching and text indexing, important new ideas are still being published, and we are only now starting to understand how to exploit it.

Even in the area of compression new developments are being made; for example, it has only recently come to light that the MTF list may not be necessary despite having been very closely associated with the BWT since its first publication. These developments (like most in lossless compression) are generally to do with the tradeoff between compression and speed. Squeezing extra compression out of existing systems seems to have hit very firm limits, and only small gains are made by applying even large amounts of computing power. However, researchers are still finding faster data structures and coding techniques that are not so demanding, which provide more options for applications where a balance must be struck between computing effort and compression.

Another issue that has serious implications for the future of the BWT is how it interacts with real computer hardware, particularly cache memory systems that may not be able to work well given the random nature of the transform's accesses to the large block of data that is being processed in memory. Other general-purpose compression methods (such as the widely used derivatives of Ziv-Lempel coding) appear to work better with cached systems because of the repeated use of a smaller section of memory, and potentially this may give them an advantage over BWT methods in the future, if speed is the issue. Balanced against this are two important trends in hardware: larger caches, and parallelization. In general the BWT benefits from having as large a block size as possible, but there are diminishing returns on this, and it is possible that caches will grow to the size that the BWT is able to exploit them and yet still give some of its best compression performance. Perhaps more significantly, multiprocessor systems with a large amount of memory parallelism have the potential to, for example, process different parts of a BWT decoding at the same time, which offers significant speed improvements.

In addition to applying parallel systems to existing BWT-based methods, variants of the BWT may develop that are more amenable to working in a parallel environment, or with whatever architectures develop in the future. There is also a growing body of work on hardware-based BWT implementations which are specifically designed for this kind of processing. Again, there is considerable potential here for improvement.

Because this area is such an active area of research, we have included in Appendix B a list of web sites that have up-to-date information about the Burrows-Wheeler Transform, and its connection with compression, suffix arrays and pattern matching.

We look forward to a promising future for this transform as it goes through its second decade; it is being applied in an environment of new data structures, more powerful computers with new models of computation, increasing amounts of data to be processed for storage, indexing and pattern matching, and new theory to help us better understand how we can exploit a powerful technique that is based on simply muddling up the contents of a file.

A

Notation

This appendix summarizes the main notation used in the book.

Where possible the notation that we use is the same as the main literature; however, unfortunately there is a conflict between the main notation used in the BWT literature and the pattern matching literature, and of course, this book uses both. The key problem is that the original Burrows-Wheeler paper, and many others about the Burrows-Wheeler Transform, use S for the input string, and T for the decoding array for the transform. The pattern matching literature generally uses T for the input string. We have chosen to use the latter, and hence some of the BWT terminology is non-standard.

Inputs	
T	The input text or string, i.e. the original document that is being transformed or searched. It is an array of characters $T[1 \ldots n]$.
n	The number of characters in T, i.e. $n = |T|$.
P	The pattern (or key) being matched in the search of T. It is an array of characters $P[1 \ldots m]$ (Section 7.1).
m	The number of characters in P, i.e. $m = |P|$.
Σ	The alphabet on which T and P draw their symbols. There are $|\Sigma|$ characters, and $\Sigma = \{\sigma_1, \sigma_2, \ldots \sigma_{|\Sigma|}\}$. Σ is assumed to be indexed and ordered.
σ_i	The i-th character of the alphabet Σ.
Σ^*	Set of all finite strings in Σ, including the empty string ϵ. $\Sigma^* = \Sigma^+ \cup \epsilon$, where Σ^+ is the set of all possible finite concatenations of symbols from Σ.

BWT arrays and values	
F	The first column of the sorted block A_s, which is all n characters of the text in sorted order (Section 1.1).

L The last column of the sorted block A_s, which is the n-character output of the Burrows-Wheeler Transform. Also referred to as $BWT(T)$ (Section 2.1).

$BWT(T)$ See L (this notation is used in Chapter 5).

a The position in L of the first character that should be decoded, which is the last character in T, since the text is usually decoded from right to left (Section 2.1).

A The n by n matrix constructed by listing all n rotations of T. This array is not normally constructed in practice (Section 2.1).

A_s The sorted version of A, in which the first and last columns are F and L respectively. This array is not normally constructed in practice, but is represented by R (Section 2.1).

R An array of n entries used to store the sorted order of the rotated substrings. $T[R[i]\ldots]$ is the i-th substring in sorted order (i.e. the i-th row in A_s). This array is used during encoding instead of A_s, since it contains the same information, but is much more compact. It is also sometimes reconstructed by the decoder as it provides a one-to-one mapping between F and T, which can assist with pattern matching ($T[R[i]] = F[i]$) (Section 2.1 and 2.2).

R' The reverse mapping of R; $R'[R[i]] = i$, $F[R'[i]] = T[i]$ (Section 2.2).

V One-to-one mapping between L and F, used in the decoder to map the transform to the original text. $V[j]$ identifies which character in L is *previous* to the one at $L[j]$, hence it can be traversed to generate T in reverse. V is sometimes referred to as the *LF* mapping. $F[V[j]] = L[j]$ (Section 2.2).

W The inverse of V, so renders the output in forward order. $W[j]$ identifies which character in L comes *after* the one at $L[j]$, hence it can be traversed to generate T in the original order. W is sometimes referred to as the *FL* mapping. $L[W[j]] = F[j]$, $W[V[i]] = i$, $V[W[i]] = i$ (Section 2.2).

Q The decoded file, output from the BWT decompressor, which will be the same as T (Section 2.2).

$C[i]$ Number of occurrences of character $L[i]$ in $L[1\ldots i-1]$ (Section 2.2).

$K[c]$ Number of occurrences of character c in L, which is the same as the number of times that c occurs in T (Section 2.2).

$M[c]$ Cumulative count of the values in K, used to index the starting position of c in F; if the first character in the alphabet is represented as zero and the first element of F is $F[1]$ then $M[0] = 1$, $M[c] = M[c-1] + K[c-1]$ (Section 2.2). M also has other meanings in the text; in Sections 7.1.5 and 7.5.1 it is used as a bit-map for the shift-and pattern matching method.

Other notation

ϵ	The empty string.
T_i	The i-th suffix of T, that is, $T[i \ldots n]$ (Section 4.1.1).
T^i	The i-th prefix of T, that is, $T[1 \ldots i]$ (Section 4.1.1).
$\hat{T}$	Reverse of the string T.
$\mathcal{A}_T$	The suffix array of the text T (Section 5.1).
$\tilde{\mathcal{A}}_T$	Inverse of $\mathcal{A}_T$.
η_{occ}	The number of times that pattern P occurs in the text T (Section 7.1.7).
$\mathrm{LCP}(\alpha, \beta)$	The longest common prefix between two strings α and β (Section 4.1.5).
$\mathrm{LCA}(u, v)$	The lowest common ancestor of nodes u and v in a tree; the node furthest from the root that has both u and v as a descendant (Section 4.1.5).
$L(u)$	In a tree, the label of the path from the root node to u (Section 4.1.1).
$\mathcal{J}_T$	The suffix *trie* of the string T (Section 4.1.3).
$\mathcal{J}_T^i$	The suffix *trie* in phase i of Ukkonen's construction algorithm (Section 4.1.3).
$\mathcal{T}_{S'}$	The suffix *tree* for the mapped sequence S' (Section 4.1.5).
$\alpha \prec \beta$	Denotes that the string α lexicographically precedes the string β (Section 4.2).
$\alpha \prec_k \beta$	Denotes that the string α lexicographically precedes the string β in an order-k sorting (i.e. comparing the first k characters) (Section 4.2).
$\mathcal{C}$	The set of partitions of the BWT input based on having the same context (Section 5.3.1 and 5.5.2).
$\mathcal{Q}(c)$	The set of symbols in t_1^n with the same context, c (Section 5.3.1).
$P_e(T)$	Estimated probability of the string T (Section 5.3.2).
$P_a(T)$	Actual probability of the string T (Section 5.3.2).
$H(Y)$	Entropy of the random variable Y (Section 5.5).
$H(Y^k)$	k-th order entropy of the random variable Y (Section 5.5).
$\tilde{H}(Y)$	Empirical entropy of a random variable Y (Section 5.5).
$H_\theta(T)$	The entropy of T using the probability distribution defined by the model parameter θ (Section 5.5.2).
ℓ_n	Average code length per symbol, for an n-length sequence (Section 5.5).
$f_i(x)$	Code length function for the family of C_i codes. (Section 5.5.2).
$n_{\sigma, T}$	Number of times that the symbol σ occurred in the prefix $T[1 \ldots i]$.
$D(p \| q)$	The relative entropy (*Kullback-Leibler distance*) between two distributions $p(y)$ and $q(y)$ (Section 5.5.2).

$\rho_n(\theta, T)$ The coding redundancy of the sequence T of length n using the probability distribution defined by the model parameter θ (Section 5.5.2).

B_i Boundary points for context partitions (Section 5.5.2).

ϕ The fixed-length don't-care character (FLDC) (Section 7.1.7).

θ The variable-length don't care character (VLDC) (Section 7.1.7).

B

Ongoing work on the Burrows-Wheeler Transform

There is an active body of continuing research relating to the Burrows-Wheeler transform. This appendix lists some websites that will help the reader to access "live" material on the BWT, and also a list of related Ph.D. theses that have been published.

B.1 BWT-related web sites

This section provides links to websites that report on useful background and ongoing work relating to the BWT. These links are also available from the book's web page, at `http://www.cosc.canterbury.ac.nz/tim.bell/bwt/`.

`http://www.hpl.hp.com/techreports/Compaq-DEC/SRC-RR-124.html`
  The original Burrows and Wheeler technical report, stored online at HP labs (originally DEC).

`ftp://ftp.cl.cam.ac.uk/users/djw3/`
  Wheeler's experimental programs ("bred" and "bexp" for block-reduction and expansion respectively).

`http://citeseer.ist.psu.edu/76182.html`
  Citeseer page for the original Burrows and Wheeler report, listing hundreds of papers that cite it.

`http://en.wikipedia.org/wiki/Burrows-Wheeler_transform`
  Wikipedia entry for BWT.

`http://pizzachili.di.unipi.it/`, `http://pizzachili.dcc.uchile.cl/`
  Web site on compressed indexes and testing.

`http://datacompression.info/BWT.shtml`
  List of projects working with BWT.

`http://www.data-compression.info/Algorithms/BWT/`
  More information and references about the BWT.

`http://www.cs.auckland.ac.nz/~peter-f/`
  Peter Fenwick's papers about the BWT, published between 1995 and 2007

`http://www.dogma.net/markn/FAQ.html#Q5`
Mark Nelson's FAQ about the BWT and links to his articles about compression, including his 1996 article about the BWT.

`http://en.wikipedia.org/wiki/Comparison_of_file_archivers`
A comparison of file archiving software, including BWT-based systems (BZIP).

`http://corpus.canterbury.ac.nz/`
The Canterbury corpus, which provides test files and compares compression methods, including BWT variants.

`http://www.nist.gov/dads/HTML/burrowsWheelerTransform.html`
NIST dictionary of algorithms entry for the BWT.

`http://dimacs.rutgers.edu/Workshops/BWT/`
Site for the 10th anniversary conference on the BWT (2004).

`http://www.bzip.org/`
The BZIP2 home page (Seward's implementation).

`http://www.compressconsult.com/szip/`
The SZIP home page (Schindler's implementation).

`http://www.frozenether.com/?s=bwt`
Online tutorial on the BWT.

`http://james.fabpedigree.com/bwt.htm`
An extensive example of the BWT with source code of an implementation.

`http://www-math.mit.edu/~lippert/software/bbbwt/`
Implementations of the BWT by Ross Lippert.

B.2 Ph.D. theses relating to the Burrows-Wheeler Transform

Larsson, N.J. 1999. Structures of String Matching and Data Compression. PhD thesis, Department of Computer Science, Lund University, Sweden.

Sadakane, K 2000. Unifying Text Search And Compression -Suffix Sorting, Block Sorting and Suffix Arrays. PhD thesis, Graduate School of Information Science, University of Tokyo, Japan.

Deorowicz, S. 2000. Universal lossless data compression algorithms, PhD thesis, Silesian University of Technology.

Chapin, B. 2001. Higher Compression from the Burrows-Wheeler Transform with New Algorithms for the List Update Problem, PhD dissertation, Dept. of Computer Science, Univ. of North Texas.

Mäkinen, V. 2003. Parameterized approximate string matching and local-similarity-based point-pattern matching. Department of Computer Science, University of Helsinki.

Baron, D. 2003. Fast Parallel Algorithms for Universal Lossless Source Coding, Ph.D. dissertation, Electrical and Computer Engineering Department, University of Illinois at Urbana-Champaign.

Hon, W-K. 2004. On Construction and Application of Compressed Text Indexes. Doctoral thesis, University of Hong Kong.

Zhang, N. 2005. Transform based and search aware text compression schemes and compressed domain text retrieval, PhD dissertation, School of Computer Science, University of Central Florida.

Tao, T. 2005. Compressed Pattern Matching For Text and Images, PhD dissertation, School of Computer Science, University of Central Florida.

Abouelhoda, M. I. 2005. Algorithms and a Software System for Comparative Genome Analysis, PhD Thesis, University of Ulm, Germany.

References

Abel, J. (2005). A fast and efficient post BWT-stage for the Burrows-Wheeler compression algorithm. In Storer and Cohn (2005), page 449.

Abel, J. (2007a). Incremental frequency count — a post BWT-stage for the Burrows-Wheeler compression algorithm. *Software—Practice and Experience*, 37(3):247–265.

Abel, J. (2007b). Post BWT stages of the Burrows-Wheeler compression algorithm. *Unpublished manuscript, private communication.*

Abel, J. and Teahan, W. J. (2005). Universal text preprocessing for data compression. *IEEE Trans. Computers*, 54(5):497–507.

Abouelhoda, M. I., Kurtz, S., and Ohlebusch, E. (2005). Enhanced suffix arrays and applications. In Aluru, S., editor, *Handbook of Computational Molecular Biology*, pages 7-1 – 7-27. Chapman and Hall/CRC Computer and Information Science Series. Chapter 7.

Abrahamson, K. (1987). Generalized string matching. *SIAM Journal on Computing*, 16(6):1039–1051.

Adjeroh, D. and Nan, F. (2008). Suffix sorting via Shannon-Fano-Elias codes. In *DCC*, page to appear. IEEE Computer Society.

Adjeroh, D., Zhang, Y., Mukherjee, A., Powell, M., and Bell, T. (2002). DNA sequence compression using the Burrows-Wheeler transform. In *IEEE Computer Society Bioinformatics Conference*, pages 303–313.

Adjeroh, D. A. and Feng, J. (2004). Locating all tandem repeat families in a sequence. In Markstein (2004), pages 676–681.

Adjeroh, D. A., Kandaswamy, U., Zhang, N., Mukherjee, A., Brown, M. T., and Bell, T. (2007). BWT-based efficient shape matching. In Cho, Y., Wainwright, R. L., Haddad, H., Shin, S. Y., and Koo, Y. W., editors, *SAC*, pages 1079–1085. ACM.

Adjeroh, D. A. and Nan, F. (2006). On compressibility of protein sequences. In Storer and Cohn (2006), pages 422–434.

Adjeroh, D. A., Zhang, Y., and Parthe, R. (2006). On denoising and compression of DNA microarray images. *Pattern Recognition*, 39(12):2478–2493.

Aho, A. V. and Corasick, M. (1975). Efficient string matching: an aid to bibliographic search. *Communications of the ACM*, 18(6):333–340.

Andersson, A., Larsson, N. J., and Swanson, K. (1999). Suffix trees on words. *Algorithmica*, 23(3):246–260.

Andersson, A. and Nilsson, S. (1995). Efficient implementation of suffix trees. *Softw., Pract. Exper.*, 25(2):129–141.

Apostolico, A. (1985). The myriad virtues of suffix trees. In Apostolico, A. and Galil, Z., editors, *Combinatorial Algorithms on Words*, volume 12 of *NATO Advanced Science Institutes, Series F*, pages 85–96. Springer-Verlag, Berlin.

Apostolico, A., Crochemore, M., and Park, K., editors (2005). *Combinatorial Pattern Matching, 16th Annual Symposium, CPM 2005, Jeju Island, Korea, June 19-22, 2005, Proceedings*, volume 3537 of *Lecture Notes in Computer Science*. Springer.

Arimura, M. and Yamamoto, H. (1998). Asymptotic optimality of block sorting data compression algorithm. *IEICE Trans. Fundamentals*, E81-A(10):2117–2122.

Arnavut, Z. (2002). Generalization of the BWT transformation and inversion ranks. In Storer and Cohn (2002), page 447.

Arnavut, Z. (2007a). ECG signal compression based on Burrows-Wheeler transformation and inversion ranks of linear prediction. *IEEE Transactions on Biomedical Engineering*, 54(3):410–418.

Arnavut, Z. (2007b). Lossless and near-lossless compression of ECG signals with block-sorting techniques. *International Journal of High Performance Computing Applications*, 21(1):50–58.

Arnavut, Z. and Arnavut, M. (2004). Investigation of block-sorting of multiset permutations. *International Journal of Computer Mathematics*, 81(10):1213–1222.

Arnavut, Z. and Magliveras, S. S. (1997a). Block sorting and compression. In Storer and Cohn (1997), pages 181–190.

Arnavut, Z. and Magliveras, S. S. (1997b). Lexical permutation sorting algorithm. *Computer Journal*, 40(5):292–295.

Arnold, R. and Bell, T. C. (1997). A corpus for the evaluation of lossless compression algorithms. In Storer and Cohn (1997), pages 201–210.

Atallah, M. J., Génin, Y., and Szpankowski, W. (1999). Pattern matching image compression: Algorithmic and empirical results. *IEEE Trans. Pattern Anal. Mach. Intell.*, 21(7):614–627.

Awan, F. S. and Mukherjee, A. (2001). LIPT: A lossless text transform to improve compression. In *ITCC*, pages 452–460. IEEE Computer Society.

Awan, F. S., Zhang, N., Motgi, N., Iqbal, R. T., and Mukherjee, A. (2001). LIPT: A reversible lossless text transform to improve compression performance. In *Data Compression Conference*, page 481.

Bachrach, R. and El-Yaniv, R. (1997). Online list accessing algorithms and their applications: Recent empirical evidence. In *SODA*, pages 53–62.

Baeza-Yates, R. and Gonnet, G. (1992). A new approach to text searching. *Communications of the ACM*, 35(10):74–82.

Baeza-Yates, R. and Ribeiro-Neto, B. (1999). *Modern Information Retrieval.* ACP Press/Addison-Wesley.

Baeza-Yates, R. A. (1989). Algorithms for string searching: A survey. *SIGIR Forum*, 23(3-4):34–58.

Baeza-Yates, R. A., Chávez, E., and Crochemore, M., editors (2003). *Combinatorial Pattern Matching, 14th Annual Symposium, CPM 2003, Morelia, Michocán, Mexico, June 25-27, 2003, Proceedings*, volume 2676 of *Lecture Notes in Computer Science*. Springer.

Baeza-Yates, R. A. and Perleberg, C. H. (1992). Fast and practical approximate string matching. In Apostolico, A., Crochemore, M., Galil, Z., and Manber, U., editors, *CPM*, volume 644 of *Lecture Notes in Computer Science*, pages 185–192. Springer.

Baeza-Yates, R. A. and Perleberg, C. H. (1996). Fast and practical approximate string matching. *Information Processing Letters*, 59(1):21–27.

Baik, H., Ha, D. S., Yook, H.-G., Shin, S.-C., and Park, M.-S. (1999a). Selective application of Burrows-Wheeler transformation for enhancement of JPEG entropy coding. In *Proc. 2nd International Conference on Information Communications and Signal Processing (ICICS'99), Singapore*.

Baik, H., Yook, H., Shin, S., Park, M., and Ha, D. (October 1999b). A new method to improve the performance of JPEG entropy encoding using Burrows-Wheeler transformation. In *Proceedings of International Symposium on Computer and Information Sciences*, pages 502–509.

Balkenhol, B. and Kurtz, S. (1998). Universal data compression based on the Burrows-Wheeler transformation: Theory and practice. Technical Report TR98-069, University of Bielefeld, Germany.

Balkenhol, B. and Kurtz, S. (2000). Universal data compression based on the Burrows-Wheeler transformation: Theory and practice. *IEEE Trans. Computers*, 49(10):1043–1053.

Balkenhol, B., Kurtz, S., and Shtarkov, Y. M. (1999). Modifications of the Burrows and Wheeler data compression algorithm. In Storer and Cohn (1999), pages 188–197.

Baron, D. and Bresler, Y. (2000). Tree source identification with the Burrows Wheeler transform. *Conference in Information Sciences and Systems*.

Baron, D. and Bresler, Y. (2004). An $O(N)$ semipredictive universal encoder via the BWT. *IEEE Transactions on Information Theory*, 50(5):928–937.

Bat, O., Kimmel, M., and Axelrod, D. (1997). Computer simulation of expansions of DNA triplet repeats in the fragile X syndrome and Huntington's disease. *Journal of Theoretical Biology*, 188(1):53–67.

Bell, T. (1986). Better OPM/L text compression. *IEEE Transactions on Communications*, COM-34:1176–1182.

Bell, T. (1987). *A Unifying Theory and Improvements for Existing Approaches to Text Compression.* PhD thesis, University of Canterbury, Christchurch, New Zealand.

Bell, T., Adjeroh, D., and Mukherjee, A. (2001). Survey of techniques for pattern matching in compressed or reduced texts. Technical report, Department of Computer Science, University of Canterbury, Christchurch, NZ.

Bell, T., Powell, M., Mukherjee, A., and Adjeroh, D. A. (2002). Searching BWT compressed text with the Boyer-Moore algorithm and binary search. In Storer and Cohn (2002), pages 112–121.

Bell, T. C., Cleary, J. G., and Witten, I. H. (1990). *Text Compression.* Prentice-Hall, Englewood Cliffs, New Jersey.

Bell, T. C. and Moffat, A. (1989). A note on the DMC data compression scheme. *Computer Journal*, 32(1):16–20.

Bell, T. C. and Witten, I. H. (1994). The relationship between greedy parsing and symbolwise text compression. *Journal of the ACM*, 41(4):708–724.

Belongie, S., Malik, J., and Puzicha, J. (2002). Shape matching and object recognition using shape contexts. *IEEE Trans. Pattern Anal. Mach. Intell.*, 24(4):509–522.

Bender, M. A. and Farach-Colton, M. (2000). The LCA problem revisited. In Gonnet, G. H., Panario, D., and Viola, A., editors, *LATIN*, volume 1776 of *Lecture Notes in Computer Science*, pages 88–94. Springer.

Bentley, J. L. and McIlroy, M. D. (1993). Engineering a sort function. *Software—Practice and Experience*, 23(11):1249–1265.

Bentley, J. L. and Sedgewick, R. (1997). Fast algorithms for sorting and searching strings. In *Symposium on Discrete Algorithms (SODA)*, pages 360–369.

Bentley, J. L., Sleator, D. D., Tarjan, R. E., and Wei, V. K. (1986). A locally adaptive data compression scheme. *Communications of the ACM*, 29(4):320–330.

Bieganski, P., Riedl, J., Carlis, J. V., and Retzel, E. F. (1994). Generalized suffix trees for biological sequence data: Applications and implementation. In *HICSS (5)*, pages 35–44.

Bird, R. M., Tu, J. C., and Worthy, R. M. (1977). Associative/parallel processors for searching very large textual data bases. *SIGMOD Record*, 9(2):8–16.

Boyer, R. and Moore, J. (1977). A fast string searching algorithm. *Communications of the ACM*, 20(10):62–72.

Brown, R. D. (2004). A modified Burrows-Wheeler Transform for highly scalable example-based translation. In Frederking, R. E. and Taylor, K., editors, *AMTA*, volume 3265 of *Lecture Notes in Computer Science*, pages 27–36. Springer.

Bunton, S. (1997). Semantically motivated improvements for PPM variants. *Computer Journal*, 40(2/3):76–93.

Burkowski, F. J. (1982). A hardware hashing scheme in the design of a multiterm string comparator. *IEEE Trans. Computers*, 31(9):825–834.

Burrows, M. and Wheeler, D. J. (1994). A block-sorting lossless data compression algorithm. Technical Report 124, Digital Equipment Corporation, Palo Alto, California.

Cai, H., Kulkarni, S. R., and Verdu, S. (2004). Universal entropy estimation via block sorting. *IEEE Transactions on Information Theory*, 50(7):1551–1561.

Caire, G., Shamai, S., and Verdu, S. (2004). Noiseless data compression with low-density parity-check codes. In Gupta, P., Kramer, G., and Wijngaarden, A. J. V., editors, *Advances In Network Information Theory: DIMACS Workshop on Network Information Theory, March 17-19, 2003, Piscataway, New Jersey (DIMACS Series in Discrete Mathematics and Theoretical Computer Science)*, Boston, MA, USA. American Mathematical Society.

Caire, G., Shamai, S., and Verdu, S. (2006). Feedback and belief propagation. In *4th Int. Symp. on Turbo Codes and Related Topics - 6th Int. ITG-Conf. on Source and Channel Coding*.

Chan, H.-L., Hon, W.-K., Lam, T. W., and Sadakane, K. (2005). Dynamic dictionary matching and compressed suffix trees. In *Symposium on Discrete Algorithms (SODA)*, pages 13–22. SIAM.

Chan, W.-H. and Nong, G. (2005). Generalizing the Burrows-Wheeler Transform. Technical report, Department of Mathematics, Hong Kong Baptist University, Hong Kong.

Chandra, A. and Chakrabarty, K. (2001). System-on-a-chip test-data compression and decompression architectures based on Golomb codes. *IEEE Trans. on CAD of Integrated Circuits and Systems*, 20(3):355–368.

Chang, W. I. and Lampe, J. (1992). Theoretical and empirical analysis of approximate string matching algorithms. *Proceedings, Combinatorial Pattern Matching, LNCS 644*, pages 175–184.

Chang, W. I. and Lawler, E. L. (1994). Sublinear approximate string matching and biological applications. *Algorithmica*, 12(4/5):327–344.

Chapin, B. (2000). Switching between two on-line list update algorithms for higher compression of Burrows-Wheeler Transformed data. In *Data Compression Conference*, pages 183–192.

Chen, X., Li, M., Ma, B., and Tromp, J. (2002). DNACompress: fast and effective DNA sequence compression. *Bioinformatics*, 18(12):1696–1698.

Cheung, C.-F., Yu, J. X., and Lu, H. (2005). Constructing suffix tree for gigabyte sequences with megabyte memory. *IEEE Transactions on Knowledge and Data Engineering*, 17(1):90–105.

Ciavarella, M. and Moffat, A. (2004). Lossless image compression using pixel reordering. In Estivill-Castro, V., editor, *ACSC*, volume 26 of *CRPIT*, pages 125–132. Australian Computer Society.

Clark, D. R. and Munro, J. I. (1996). Efficient suffix trees on secondary storage (extended abstract). In *Symposium on Discrete Algorithms (SODA)*, pages 383–391.

Cleary, J. G. and Teahan, W. J. (1997). Unbounded length contexts for PPM. *Computer Journal*, 40(2/3):67–75.

Cleary, J. G., Teahan, W. J., and Witten, I. H. (1995). Unbounded length contexts for PPM. In Storer and Cohn (1995), pages 52–61.

Cleary, J. G. and Witten, I. H. (1984). Data compression using adaptive coding and partial string matching. *IEEE Transactions on Communications*, COM-32:396–402.

Cole, R. (1994). Tight bounds on the complexity of the Boyer-Moore string matching algorithm. *SIAM Journal on Computing*, 23(5):1075–1091.

Cook, G. (2007). Untangling the mystery of the Inca. *Wired*, 15(1).

Cook, S. (1972). Linear time simulation of deterministic two-way pushdown automata. *Information Processing*, 71:75–80.

Cormack, G. V. and Horspool, R. N. (1987). Data compression using Dynamic Markov Modelling. *Computer Journal*, 30(6):541–550.

Cover, T. and King, R. (1978). A convergent gambling estimate of the entropy of English. *IEEE Transactions on Information Theory*, IT-24(4).

Cover, T. M. and Thomas, J. A. (1991). *Elements of Information Theory*. Wiley Series in Telecommunications. John Wiley & Sons, New York, NY, USA.

Cover, T. M. and Thomas, J. A. (2006). *Elements of Information Theory*. Wiley Series in Telecommunications and Signal Processing. John Wiley & Sons, New York, NY, USA.

Crauser, A. and Ferragina, P. (2002). A theoretical and experimental study on the construction of suffix arrays in external memory. *Algorithmica*, 32(1):1–35.

Crochemore, M., Désarménien, J., and Perrin, D. (2005). A note on the Burrows-Wheeler transformation. *Theoretical Computer Science*, 332(1-3):567–572.

Crochemore, M. and Rytter, W. (1994). *Text Algorithms*. Oxford University Press.

Crochemore, M. and Vérin, R. (1997). Direct construction of compact directed acyclic word graphs. In Apostolico, A. and Hein, J., editors, *CPM*, volume 1264 of *Lecture Notes in Computer Science*, pages 116–129. Springer.

de Moura, E. S., Navarro, G., Ziviani, N., and Baeza-Yates, R. A. (2000). Fast and flexible word searching on compressed text. *ACM Trans. Inf. Syst.*, 18(2):113–139.

Delcher, A., Kasif, S., Fleischmann, R., Peterson, J., White, O., and Salzberg, S. (1999). Alignment of whole genomes. *Nucleic Acids Research*, 11(27):2369–2376.

Deorowicz, S. (2002). Second step algorithms in the Burrows-Wheeler compression algorithm. *Software—Practice and Experience*, 32(2):99–111.

Deorowicz, S. (2005). Context exhumation after the Burrows-Wheeler transform. *Information Processing Letters*, 95(1):313–320.

Dettloff, W., Singh, R., White, C., and Erickson, B. (1991). A 50mhz 1.5m transistor ASIC for biosequence analysis. In *1991 IEEE International Solid-State Circuits Conference. Digest of Technical Papers. 38th ISSCC*, pages 40–285.

Dijkstra, E. W. (1959). A note on two problems in connexion with graphs. *Numerische Mathematik*, 1(1):269–271.

Dömölki, B. (1968). A universal compiler system based on production rules. *BIT Numerical Mathematics*, 8(4):262–275.

Dütsch, N., Graf, S., Garcia-Frias, J., and Hagenauer, J. (2006). Source model aided lossless turbo source coding. In *4th International Symposium on Turbo Codes and Related Topics, Munich, Germany*.

Dütsch, N. and Hagenauer, J. (2004). Combined incremental and decremental redundancy in joint source-channel coding. *International Symposium on Information Theory and its Applications, ISITA2004, October 10–13, Parma, Italy*.

Effros, M. (1999). Universal lossless source coding with the Burrows Wheeler transform. In Storer and Cohn (1999), pages 178–187.

Effros, M. (2000). PPM performance with BWT complexity: A fast and effective data compression algorithm. *Proceedings of the IEEE*, 88(11):1703–1712.

Effros, M., Visweswariah, K., Kulkarni, S. R., and Verdu, S. (2002). Universal lossless source coding with the Burrows Wheeler transform. *IEEE Transactions on Information Theory*, 48(5):1061–1081.

Elias, P. (1975). Universal codeword sets and representations of the integers. *IEEE Transactions on Information Theory*, 21(2):194–203.

Elias, P. (1987). Interval and recency rank source coding: Two on-line adaptive variable-length schemes. *IEEE Transcation on Information Theory*, IT-33(1):3–10.

Farach, M. (1997). Optimal suffix tree construction with large alphabets. In *38th Annual Symposium on Foundations of Computer Science, FOCS '97, Miami Beach, Florida, USA, October 19-22*, pages 137–143.

Farach, M. and Muthukrishnan, S. (1996). Optimal logarithmic time randomized suffix tree construction. In auf der Heide, F. M. and Monien, B., editors, *ICALP*, volume 1099 of *Lecture Notes in Computer Science*, pages 550–561. Springer.

Farach-Colton, M., Ferragina, P., and Muthukrishnan, S. (2000). On the sorting-complexity of suffix tree construction. *Journal of the ACM*, 47(6):987–1011.

Fenwick, P. M. (1995a). Differential Ziv-Lempel text compression. *Journal of Universal Computer Science*, 1(8):587–598.

Fenwick, P. M. (1995b). Experiments with a block sorting text compression algorithm. Technical Report 111, The University of Auckland, Department of Computer Science.

Fenwick, P. M. (1995c). Improvements to the block sorting text compression algorithm. Technical Report 120, The University of Auckland, Department of Computer Science.

Fenwick, P. M. (1996a). Block sorting text compression — final report. Technical Report 130, The University of Auckland, Department of Computer Science.

Fenwick, P. M. (1996b). The Burrows-Wheeler Transform for block sorting text compression: Principles and improvements. *Computer Journal*, 39(9):731–740.

Fenwick, P. M. (1997a). A fast, constant-order, symbol ranking text compressor. Technical Report 145, The University of Auckland, Department of Computer Science.

Fenwick, P. M. (1997b). Symbol ranking text compression with Shannon recodings. *Journal of Universal Computer Science*, 3(2):70–85.

Fenwick, P. M. (1998). Symbol ranking text compressors: Review and implementation. *Software—Practice and Experience*, 28(5):547–559.

Fenwick, P. M. (2001a). Fast string matching for multiple searches. *Software—Practice and Experience*, 31(9):815–833.

Fenwick, P. M. (2001b). Some perils of performance prediction: a case study on pattern matching. *Software—Practice and Experience*, 31(9):835–843.

Fenwick, P. M. (2002a). Burrows-Wheeler compression with variable length integer codes. *Software—Practice and Experience*, 32(13):1307–1316.

Fenwick, P. M. (2002b). Variable-length integer codes based on the Goldbach conjecture, and other additive codes. *IEEE Transactions on Information Theory*, 48(8):2412–2417.

Fenwick, P. M. (2003a). Burrows Wheeler compression. In Sayood (2003), pages 169–194.

Fenwick, P. M. (2003b). Symbol ranking and ACB compression. In Sayood (2003), pages 195–206.

Fenwick, P. M. (2003c). Universal codes. In Sayood (2003), pages 55–78.

Fenwick, P. M. (2007). Burrows-Wheeler compression: Principles and reflections. *Theoretical Computer Science*, 317(3):200–219.

Ferragina, P. (2005). String search in external memory: algorithms and data structures. In Aluru, S., editor, *Handbook of Computational Molecular Biology*, chapter 35. Chapman and Hall/CRC Computer and Information Science Series.

Ferragina, P. (2007). String algorithms and data structures. *Unpublished manuscript, private communication*.

Ferragina, P., Giancarlo, R., and Manzini, G. (2006a). The engineering of a compression boosting library: Theory vs practice in BWT compression. In Azar, Y. and Erlebach, T., editors, *ESA*, volume 4168 of *Lecture Notes in Computer Science*, pages 756–767. Springer.

Ferragina, P., Giancarlo, R., and Manzini, G. (2006b). The myriad virtues of wavelet trees. In Bugliesi, M., Preneel, B., Sassone, V., and Wegener, I., editors, *ICALP (1)*, volume 4051 of *Lecture Notes in Computer Science*, pages 560–571. Springer.

Ferragina, P., Giancarlo, R., Manzini, G., and Sciortino, M. (2005a). Boosting textual compression in optimal linear time. *Journal of the ACM*, 52(4):688–713.

Ferragina, P., Luccio, F., Manzini, G., and Muthukrishnan, S. (2005b). Structuring labeled trees for optimal succinctness, and beyond. In *46th Annual*

IEEE Symposium on Foundations of Computer Science (FOCS 2005), 23-25 October 2005, Pittsburgh, PA, USA, pages 184–196. IEEE Computer Society.

Ferragina, P., Luccio, F., Manzini, G., and Muthukrishnan, S. (2006c). Compressing and searching XML data via two zips. In Carr, L., Roure, D. D., Iyengar, A., Goble, C. A., and Dahlin, M., editors, *Proceedings of the 15th international conference on World Wide Web, WWW 2006, Edinburgh, Scotland, UK, May 23-26, 2006*, pages 751–760. ACM.

Ferragina, P. and Manzini, G. (2000). Opportunistic data structures with applications. In *41st IEEE Symposium on Foundations of Computer Science, FOCS*, pages 390–398.

Ferragina, P. and Manzini, G. (2001a). An experimental study of a compressed index. *Inf. Sci.*, 135(1-2):13–28.

Ferragina, P. and Manzini, G. (2001b). An experimental study of an opportunistic index. In *12th ACM-SIAM Symposium on Discrete Algorithms, SODA*, pages 269–278.

Ferragina, P. and Manzini, G. (2004). Compression boosting in optimal linear time using the Burrows-Wheeler Transform. In Munro, J. I., editor, *Proceedings of the Fifteenth Annual ACM-SIAM Symposium on Discrete Algorithms, SODA 2004, New Orleans, Louisiana, USA, January 11-14*, pages 655–663. SIAM.

Ferragina, P. and Manzini, G. (2005). Indexing compressed text. *Journal of the ACM*, 52(4):552–581.

Ferragina, P., Manzini, G., Mäkinen, V., and Navarro, G. (2007). Compressed representations of sequences and full-text indexes. *ACM Transactions on Algorithms*, 3(2).

Ferragina, P. and Venturini, R. (2007). Compressed permuterm index. In Kraaij, W., de Vries, A. P., Clarke, C. L. A., Fuhr, N., and Kando, N., editors, *SIGIR '07: Proceedings of the 30th annual international ACM SIGIR conference on research and development in information retrieval*, pages 535–542. ACM.

Firth, A. (2002). A comparison of BWT approaches to compressed-domain pattern matching. Technical Report HONS05/02, Department of Computer Science, University of Canterbury, Christchurch, NZ.

Firth, A. E., Bell, T., Mukherjee, A., and Adjeroh, D. A. (2005). A comparison of BWT approaches to string pattern matching. *Software—Practice and Experience*, 35(13):1217–1258.

Fischer, M. and Paterson, M. (1974). String matching and other products. In Karp, R., editor, *Complexity of Computation*, volume 7, pages 113–125. SIAM-AMS Proceedings, Amer. Mathematical Soc., Providence, RI.

Foschini, L., Grossi, R., Gupta, A., and Vitter, J. S. (2004). Fast compression with a static model in high-order entropy. In Storer, J. and Cohn, M., editors, *Data Compression Conference*, pages 62–71. IEEE Computer Society.

Foschini, L., Grossi, R., Gupta, A., and Vitter, J. S. (2006). When index-ing equals compression: Experiments with compressing suffix arrays and applications. *ACM Transactions on Algorithms*, 2(4):611–639.

Foster, M. and Kung, H. (1980). The design of special-purpose VLSI chips. *Computer*, 13(1):26–40.

Franceschini, G. and Muthukrishnan, S. (2007). In-place suffix sorting. In Arge, L., Cachin, C., Jurdzinski, T., and Tarlecki, A., editors, *ICALP*, vol-ume 4596 of *Lecture Notes in Computer Science*, pages 533–545. Springer.

Franek, F. and Smyth, W. F. (2006). Reconstructing a suffix array. *Interna-tional Journal of Foundations of Computer Science*, 17(6):1281–1296.

Gagie, T. and Manzini, G. (2007). Move-to-front, distance coding, and inver-sion frequencies revisited. In Ma and Zhang (2007), pages 71–82.

Galil, Z. (1978). On improving the worst case running time of the Boyer-Moore string matching algorithm. In Ausiello, G. and Böhm, C., editors, *ICALP*, volume 62 of *Lecture Notes in Computer Science*, pages 241–250. Springer.

Galil, Z. and Giancarlo, R. (1988). Data structures and algorithms for ap-proximate string matching. *J. Complexity*, 4(1):33–72.

Gallager, R. (1962). Low-density parity-check codes. *IEEE Transactions on Information Theory*, 8(1):21–28.

Geary, R. F., Rahman, N., Raman, R., and Raman, V. (2006). A simple opti-mal representation for balanced parentheses. *Theoretical Computer Science*, 368(3):231–246.

Gessel, I. M. and Reutenauer, C. (1993). Counting permutations with given cycle structure and descent set. *Journal of Combinatorial Theory, Ser. A*, 64(2):189–215.

Giancarlo, R. (1995). A generalization of the suffix tree to square matrices, with applications. *SIAM J. Comput.*, 24(3):520–562.

Giancarlo, R., Restivo, A., and Sciortino, M. (2007). From first principles to the Burrows and Wheeler transform and beyond, via combinatorial opti-mization. *Theoretical Computer Science*, 317(3):236–248.

Giancarlo, R. and Sciortino, M. (2003). Optimal partitions of strings: A new class of Burrows-Wheeler compression algorithms. In Baeza-Yates et al. (2003), pages 129–143.

Giegerich, R. and Kurtz, S. (1997). From Ukkonen to McCreight and Weiner: A unifying view of linear-time suffix tree construction. *Algorithmica*, 19(3):331–353.

Golynski, A. (2007). Optimal lower bounds for rank and select indexes. *The-oretical Computer Science*, 317(3):348–359.

Golynski, A., Grossi, R., Gupta, A., Raman, R., and Rao, S. S. (2007). On the size of succinct indices. In Arge, L., Hoffmann, M., and Welzl, E., editors, *ESA*, volume 4698 of *Lecture Notes in Computer Science*, pages 371–382. Springer.

Golynski, A., Munro, J. I., and Rao, S. S. (2006). Rank/select operations on large alphabets: a tool for text indexing. In *Symposium on Discrete Algorithms (SODA)*, pages 368–373. ACM Press.

Gonnet, G. H., Baeza-Yates, R. A., and Snider, T. (1992). New indices for text: Pat trees and pat arrays. In Frakes, W. and Baeza-Yates, R., editors, *Information Retrieval: Data Structures and Algorithms*, pages 66–82. Prentice Hall, New Jersey, USA.

Gonzalez, R. and Navarro, G. (2006). Statistical encoding of succinct data structures. In Lewenstein and Valiente (2006), pages 294–305.

Grabowski, S. (1999). Text preprocessing for Burrows-Wheeler block-sorting compression. In *Proc. VII Konferencja Sieci i Systemy Informatyczne-Teoria, Projekty, Wdrożenia*. IEEE Computer Society.

Grossi, R., Gupta, A., and Vitter, J. S. (2003). High-order entropy-compressed text indexes. In *Symposium on Discrete Algorithms (SODA)*, pages 841–850.

Grossi, R. and Luccio, F. (1989). Simple and efficient string matching with k mismatches. *Information Processing Letters*, 33(3):113–120.

Grossi, R. and Vitter, J. S. (2000). Compressed suffix arrays and suffix trees with applications to text indexing and string matching. In *STOC*, pages 397–406.

Grossi, R. and Vitter, J. S. (2005). Compressed suffix arrays and suffix trees with applications to text indexing and string matching. *SIAM Journal on Computing*, 35(2):378–407.

Guo, H. and Burrus, C. S. (1997). Waveform and image compression using the Burrows Wheeler transform and the wavelet transform. In *Proceedings of the International Conference on Image Processing*, volume 1, pages 65–68.

Gupta, A., Hon, W.-K., Shah, R., and Vitter, J. S. (2007). Compressed data structures: Dictionaries and data-aware measures. *Theoretical Computer Science*, 317(3):313–331.

Gusfield, D. (1997). *Algorithms on Strings, Trees and Sequences: Computer Science and Computational Biology*. Cambridge University Press.

Hagenauer, J. (1988). Rate-compatible punctured convolutional codes (RCPC codes) and their applications. *IEEE Transactions on Communications*, 36(4):389–400.

Harel, D. and Tarjan, R. E. (1984). Fast algorithms for finding nearest common ancestors. *SIAM J. Comput.*, 13(2):338–355.

Healy, J., Thomas, E. E., Schwartz, J. T., and Wigler, M. (2003). Annotating large genomes with exact word matches. *Genome Res*, 13:2306–2315.

Herzel, H., Ebeling, W., and Schmitt, A. O. (1994). Entropies of biosequences: The role of repeats. *Phys. Rev. E*, 50(6):5061–5071.

Hoang, D. T., Long, P. M., and Vitter, J. S. (1995). Multiple-dictionary coding using partial matching. In Storer and Cohn (1995), pages 272–281.

Hoang, D. T., Long, P. M., and Vitter, J. S. (1999). Dictionary selection using partial matching. *Inf. Sci.*, 119(1-2):57–72.

Hoffman, D. D. and Singh, M. (1997). Salience of visual parts. *Cognition*, 63(1):29–78.

Hollaar, L. A. and Roberts, D. C. (1978). Current research into specialized processors for text information retrieval. In Yao, S. B., editor, *VLDB*, pages 270–279. IEEE Computer Society.

Hon, W.-K., Lam, T. W., Sadakane, K., and Sung, W.-K. (2003a). Constructing compressed suffix arrays with large alphabets. In Ibaraki, T., Katoh, N., and Ono, H., editors, *ISAAC*, volume 2906 of *Lecture Notes in Computer Science*, pages 240–249. Springer.

Hon, W.-K., Lam, T. W., Sadakane, K., Sung, W.-K., and Yiu, S.-M. (2007). A space and time efficient algorithm for constructing compressed suffix arrays. *Algorithmica*, 48(1):23–36.

Hon, W.-K., Sadakane, K., and Sung, W.-K. (2003b). Breaking a time-and-space barrier in constructing full-text indices. In *FOCS*, pages 251–260. IEEE Computer Society.

Howard, P. G. and Vitter, J. S. (1993). Design and analysis of fast text compression based on quasi-arithmetic coding. In Storer, J. and Cohn, M., editors, *DCC*, pages 98–107. IEEE Computer Society.

Huffman, D. A. (1952). A method for the construction of minimum-redundancy codes. *Proceedings of the IRE*, 40(9):1098–1101.

Hughey, R. P. (1991). Programmable systolic arrays. Technical report, Brown University, Providence, RI, USA.

Hume, A. and Sunday, D. (1991). Fast string searching. *Software—Practice and Experience*, 21(11):1221–1248.

Hunkerpiller, T., Waterman, M., Jones, R., Eggert, M., Chow, E., Peterson, J., and Hood, L. (1990). Special purpose VLSI-based system for the analysis of genetic sequences. Technical report, Human Genome: 1989-90 Program Report, U.S. Department of Energy, Washington D.C.

Hunt, E., Atkinson, M. P., and Irving, R. W. (2001). A database index to large biological sequences. In Apers, P. M. G., Atzeni, P., Ceri, S., Paraboschi, S., Ramamohanarao, K., and Snodgrass, R. T., editors, *VLDB*, pages 139–148. Morgan Kaufmann.

Hunt, J. W. and Szymanski, T. G. (1977). A fast algorithm for computing longest subsequences. *Commun. ACM*, 20(5):350–353.

Hutchins, W. J. and Somers, H. L. (1992). *An Introduction to Machine Translation*. Academic Press.

Isal, R. Y. K. and Moffat, A. (2001a). Parsing strategies for BWT compression. In Storer and Cohn (2001), pages 429–438.

Isal, R. Y. K. and Moffat, A. (2001b). Word-based block-sorting text compression. In *ACSC*, pages 92–99. IEEE Computer Society.

Isal, R. Y. K., Moffat, A., and Ngai, A. C. H. (2002). Enhanced word-based block-sorting text compression. In Oudshoorn, M. J., editor, *ACSC*, volume 4 of *CRPIT*, pages 129–137. Australian Computer Society.

Itoh, H. and Tanaka, H. (1999). An efficient method for in memory construction of suffix arrays. In *SPIRE/CRIWG*, pages 81–88.

Jacobson, G. (1989). Space-efficient static trees and graphs. In *FOCS*, pages 549–554. IEEE.

Kaplan, H., Landau, S., and Verbin, E. (2006). A simpler analysis of Burrows-Wheeler based compression. In Lewenstein and Valiente (2006), pages 282–293.

Kaplan, H., Landau, S., and Verbin, E. (2007). A simpler analysis of Burrows-Wheeler-based compression. *Theoretical Computer Science*, 317(3):220–235.

Kaplan, H. and Verbin, E. (2007). Most Burrows-Wheeler based compressors are not optimal. In Ma and Zhang (2007), pages 107–118.

Karimi, F., Meleis, W., Navabi, Z., and Lombardi, F. (2002). Data compression for system-on-chip testing using ATE. In *DFT*, pages 166–176. IEEE Computer Society.

Kärkkäinen, J. (2007). Fast BWT in small space by blockwise suffix sorting. *Theoretical Computer Science*, 317(3):249–257.

Kärkkäinen, J. and Sanders, P. (2003). Simple linear work suffix array construction. In Baeten, J. C. M., Lenstra, J. K., Parrow, J., and Woeginger, G. J., editors, *ICALP*, volume 2719 of *Lecture Notes in Computer Science*, pages 943–955. Springer.

Kärkkäinen, J., Sanders, P., and Burkhardt, S. (2006). Linear work suffix array construction. *Journal of the ACM*, 53(6):918–936.

Kärkkäinen, J. and Sutinen, E. (1998). Lempel-Ziv index for q-grams. *Algorithmica*, 21(1):137–154.

Karlin, S., Ghandour, G., Ost, F., Tavare, S., and Korn, L. J. (1983). New approaches for computer analysis of nucleic acid sequences. *Proceedings, National Academy of Sciences*, 80(18):5660–5664.

Karp, R. and Rabin, M. (1987). Efficient randomized pattern-matching algorithms. *IBM Journal of Research and Development*, 31(2):249–260.

Karp, R. M., Miller, R. E., and Rosenberg, A. L. (1972). Rapid identification of repeated patterns in strings, trees and arrays. In *STOC*, pages 125–136. ACM.

Kim, D. K. and Park, H. (2005). A new compressed suffix tree supporting fast search and its construction algorithm using optimal working space. In Apostolico et al. (2005), pages 33–44.

Kim, D. K., Sim, J. S., Park, H., and Park, K. (2003). Linear-time construction of suffix arrays. In Baeza-Yates et al. (2003), pages 186–199.

Kim, D. K., Sim, J. S., Park, H., and Park, K. (2005). Constructing suffix arrays in linear time. *J. Discrete Algorithms*, 3(2-4):126–142.

Knuth, D., Morris, J., and Pratt, V. (1977). Fast pattern matching in strings. *SIAM Journal on Computing*, 6(2):323–350.

Knuth, D. E. (1973). *The Art of Computer Programming, Volume III: Sorting and Searching*. Addison-Wesley.

Ko, P. and Aluru, S. (2003). Space efficient linear time construction of suffix arrays. In Baeza-Yates et al. (2003), pages 200–210.

Ko, P. and Aluru, S. (2005). Space efficient linear time construction of suffix arrays. *J. Discrete Algorithms*, 3(2-4):143–156.

Komma, P., Fischer, J., Duffner, F., and Bartz, D. (2007). Lossless volume data compression schemes. In Schulze, T., Preim, B., and Schumann, H., editors, *SimVis*, pages 169–182. SCS Publishing House e.V.

Kopylov, P. and Fränti, P. (2005). Compression of map images by multilayer context tree modeling. *IEEE Transactions on Image Processing*, 14(1):1–11.

Krichevsky, R. E. and Trofimov, V. K. (1981). The performance of universal encoding. *IEEE Transactions on Information Theory*, 27(2):199–206.

Kruse, H. and Mukherjee, A. (1998). Preprocessing text to improve compression ratios. In *Data Compression Conference*, page 556.

Kruse, H. and Mukherjee, A. (1999). Improving text compression ratios with the Burrows-Wheeler Transform. In *Data Compression Conference*, page 536.

Kurtz, S. (1999). Reducing the space requirement of suffix trees. *Software—Practice and Experience*, 29(13):1149–1171.

Kurtz, S. and Balkenhol, B. (2000). Space efficient linear time computation of the Burrows and Wheeler transformation. In *Numbers, Information and Complexity*, pages 375–383. Kluwer Academic Publishers.

Kurtz, S., Phillippy, A., Delcher, A., Smoot, M., Shumway, M., Antonescu, C., and Salzberg, S. (2004). Versatile and open software for comparing large genomes. *Genome Biology*, 5(2):R12.1–R12.9.

Lam, T. W., Sadakane, K., Sung, W.-K., and Yiu, S.-M. (2002). A space and time efficient algorithm for constructing compressed suffix arrays. In Ibarra, O. H. and Zhang, L., editors, *COCOON*, volume 2387 of *Lecture Notes in Computer Science*, pages 401–410. Springer.

Lam, T. W., Sung, W.-K., Tam, S.-L., Wong, C.-K., and Yiu, S.-M. (2007). An experimental study of compressed indexing and local alignments of DNA. In Dress, A. W. M., Xu, Y., and Zhu, B., editors, *COCOA*, volume 4616 of *Lecture Notes in Computer Science*, pages 242–254. Springer.

Lanctot, J. K., Li, M., and Yang, E.-H. (2000). Estimating DNA sequence entropy. In *Symposium on Discrete Algorithms (SODA)*, pages 409–418.

Landau, G. M. and Vishkin, U. (1985). Efficient string matching in the presence of errors. In *Proceedings of the 26th Annual IEEE Symposium on Foundations of Computer Science*, pages 126–136. IEEE.

Landau, G. M. and Vishkin, U. (1986). Efficient string matching with k mismatches. *Theoretical Computer Science*, 43:239–249.

Langdon Jr., G. G. (1983). A note on the Ziv-Lempel model for compressing individual sequences. *IEEE Transactions on Information Theory*, 29(2):284–.

Larsson, N. J. (1998). The context trees of block sorting compression. In Storer and Cohn (1998), pages 189–198.

Larsson, N. J. and Sadakane, K. (1999). Faster suffix sorting. Technical Report LU-CS-TR:99-214 [LUNFD6/(NFCS-3140)/1-20/(1999)], Dept of Computer Science, Lund University, Sweden.

Larsson, N. J. and Sadakane, K. (2007). Faster suffix sorting. *Theoretical Computer Science*, 317(3):258–272.

Lewenstein, M. and Valiente, G., editors (2006). *Combinatorial Pattern Matching, 17th Annual Symposium, CPM 2006, Barcelona, Spain, July 5-7, 2006, Proceedings*, volume 4009 of *Lecture Notes in Computer Science*. Springer.

Li, I., Shum, W., and Truong, K. (2007). 160-fold acceleration of the smith-waterman algorithm using a field programmable gate array (FPGA). *BMC Bioinformatics*, 8(1):185.

Lin, S. and Costello Jr., D. J. (2004). *Error Control Coding*. Prentice-Hall, Upper Saddle River, NJ. TUB-HH 2413-469 3.

Lippert, R. (2005). Space-efficient whole genome comparisons with Burrows-Wheeler transforms. *Journal of Computational Biology*, 12(4):407–415.

Lippert, R. A., Mobarry, C. M., and Walenz, B. P. (2005). A space-efficient construction of the Burrows-Wheeler Transform for genomic data. *Journal of Computational Biology*, 12(7):943–951.

Lipton, R. and Lopresti, D. (1985). A systolic array for rapid string comparison. In *Proceedings of the 1985 Chapel Hill Conference on Very Large Scale Integration*, pages 363–76. Computer Science Press, Rockville, MD.

Lonardi, S. and Luo, Y. (2004). Gridding and compression of microarray images. In Markstein (2004), pages 122–130.

Lopresti, D. P. (1991). Rapid implementation of a genetic sequence comparator using field-programmable logic arrays. In *Proceedings of the 1991 University of California/Santa Cruz conference on Advanced research in VLSI*, pages 138–152, Cambridge, MA, USA. MIT Press.

Lucito, R., Healy, J., Alexander, J., Reiner, A., Esposito, D., Chi, M., Rodgers, L., Brady, A., Sebat, J., Troge, J., West, J. A., Rostan, S., Nguyen, K. C., Powers, S., Ye, K. Q., Olshen, A., Venkatraman, E., Norton, L., and Wigler, M. (2003). Representational oligonucleotide microarray analysis: a high-resolution method to detect genome copy number variation. *Genome Research*, 13(10):2291–2305.

Ma, B. and Zhang, K., editors (2007). *Combinatorial Pattern Matching, 18th Annual Symposium, CPM 2007, London, Canada, July 9-11, 2007, Proceedings*, volume 4580 of *Lecture Notes in Computer Science*. Springer.

Mäkinen, V. (2003). Compact suffix array – a space-efficient full-text index. *Fundam. Inform.*, 56(1-2):191–210.

Mäkinen, V. and Navarro, G. (2007). Rank and select revisited and extended. *Theoretical Computer Science*, 317(3):332–347.

Manber, U. and Myers, E. W. (1993). Suffix arrays: A new method for on-line string searches. *SIAM Journal on Computing*, 22(5):935–948.

Manber, U. and Myers, G. (1990). Suffix arrays: A new method for on-line string searches. In *Symposium on Discrete Algorithms (SODA)*, pages 319–327.

Maniscalco, M. A. and Puglisi, S. J. (2006). Faster lightweight suffix array construction. In Ryan, J. and Dafik, editors, *17th Australasian Workshop on Combinatorial Algorithms (AWOCA'06)*, pages 16–29.

Mantaci, S., Restivo, A., Rosone, G., and Sciortino, M. (2005). An extension of the Burrows Wheeler transform and applications to sequence comparison and data compression. In Apostolico et al. (2005), pages 178–189.

Mantaci, S., Restivo, A., Rosone, G., and Sciortino, M. (2007). An extension of the Burrows-Wheeler transform. *Theoretical Computer Science*, 317(3):298–312.

Mantaci, S., Restivo, A., and Sciortino, M. (2003). Burrows-Wheeler transform and Sturmian words. *Information Processing Letters*, 86(5):241–246.

Manzini, G. (1999). An analysis of the Burrows-Wheeler transform. In *Symposium on Discrete Algorithms (SODA)*, pages 669–677.

Manzini, G. (2001). An analysis of the Burrows-Wheeler transform. *Journal of the ACM*, 48(3):407–430.

Manzini, G. and Ferragina, P. (2004). Engineering a lightweight suffix array construction algorithm. *Algorithmica*, 40(1):33–50.

Markstein, V., editor (2004). *3rd International IEEE Computer Society Computational Systems Bioinformatics Conference (CSB 2004), 16-19 August 2004, Stanford, CA, USA*. IEEE Computer Society.

Martinez, J., Cumplido, R., and Feregrino, C. (2005). An FPGA-based parallel sorting architecture for the Burrows Wheeler Transform. In *IEEE International Conf on Reconfigurable Computing and FPGAs*, page 17.

Masek, W. and Paterson, M. (1980). A faster algorithm for computing string-edit distances. *Journal of Computer and System Sciences*, 20(1):18–31.

McCreight, E. M. (1976). A space-economical suffix tree construction algorithm. *Journal of the ACM*, 23(2):262–272.

McIlroy, P. M., Bostic, K., and McIlroy, M. D. (1993). Engineering radix sort. *Computing Systems*, 6(1):5–27.

Mead, C. A., Pashley, R. D., Britton, L. D., Daimon, Y. T., and Sando, S. F. (1976). 128-bit multicomparator. *IEEE Journal of Solid-State Circuits*, 5(11):692–695.

Merhav, N. (1993). On the minimum description length principle for sources with piecewise constant parameters. *IEEE Transactions on Information Theory*, 39(6):1962–.

Moffat, A. (1990). Implementing the PPM data compression scheme. *IEEE Transactions on Communications*, 38(11):1917–1921.

Moffat, A., Neal, R. M., and Witten, I. H. (1995). Arithmetic coding revisited. In Storer and Cohn (1995), pages 202–211.

Moffat, A., Neal, R. M., and Witten, I. H. (1998). Arithmetic coding revisited. *ACM Trans. Inf. Syst.*, 16(3):256–294.

Moffat, A. and Turpin, A. (2002). *Compression and Coding Algorithms*. Kluwer.

Mori, G., Belongie, S., and Malik, J. (2001). Shape contexts enable efficient retrieval of similar shapes. In *CVPR (1)*, pages 723–730. IEEE Computer Society.

Morrison, D. (1968). PATRICIA—Practical algorithm to retrieve information coded in alphanumeric. *Journal of the ACM*, 15(4):514–534.

Mukherjee, A. (1989). Hardware algorithm for determining similarities between two strings. *IEEE Transactions on Computers*, 38(4):600–607. Included in the IEEE Computer Society collection of reprints VLSI Algorithms and Architectures (Ed. N. Ranganathan,1993).

Mukherjee, A. and Acharya, T. (1995). VLSI algorithms for compressed pattern search using tree based codes. In *ASAP*, pages 133–136. IEEE Computer Society.

Mukherjee, A. and Awan, F. (2003). Text compression. In Sayood (2003), pages 227–246.

Mukherjee, A., Motgi, N., Becker, J., Friebe, A., Habermann, C., and Glesner, M. (2001). Prototyping of efficient hardware algorithms for data compression in future communication systems. In *IEEE 12th International Workshop on Rapid System Prototyping*, pages 58–63. IEEE Computer Society.

Mukhopadhyay, A. (1979). Hardware algorithms for non-numeric computation. *IEEE Transactions on Computers*, C-28(6):384–94.

Munro, J. I., Raman, V., and Rao, S. S. (1998). Space efficient suffix trees. In Arvind, V. and Ramanujam, R., editors, *FSTTCS*, volume 1530 of *Lecture Notes in Computer Science*, pages 186–196. Springer.

Munro, J. I., Raman, V., and Rao, S. S. (2001). Space efficient suffix trees. *J. Algorithms*, 39(2):205–222.

Myers, E. W. (1986). An $O(ND)$ difference algorithm and its variations. *Algorithmica*, 1(2):251–266.

Myers, E. W. (1994). A sublinear algorithm for approximate keyword searching. *Algorithmica*, 12(4/5):345–374.

Na, J. C. (2005). Linear-time construction of compressed suffix arrays using o(n log n)-bit working space for large alphabets. In Apostolico et al. (2005), pages 57–67.

Navarro, G. (2001). A guided tour to approximate string matching. *ACM Computing Surveys*, 33(1):31–88.

Navarro, G., de Moura, E. S., Neubert, M. S., Ziviani, N., and Baeza-Yates, R. A. (2000). Adding compression to block addressing inverted indexes. *Information Retrieval*, 3(1):49–77.

Navarro, G. and Mäkinen, V. (2007). Compressed full-text indexes. *ACM Computing Surveys*, 39(1).

Navarro, G. and Tarhio, J. (2005). LZgrep: a Boyer-Moore string matching tool for Ziv-Lempel compressed text. *Software—Practice and Experience*, 35(12):1107–1130.

Nelson, M. and Gailly, J.-L. (1995). *The data compression book (2nd ed.)*. MIS:Press, New York, NY, USA.

Nelson, M. R. (1996). Data compression with the Burrows Wheeler transform. *Dr. Dobb's Journal of Software Tools*, 21(9):46–50.

Nong, G. and Zhang, S. (2006). Unifying the Burrows-Wheeler and the Schindler transforms. In Storer and Cohn (2006), page 464.

Nong, G. and Zhang, S. (2007a). Efficient algorithms for the inverse sort transform. *IEEE Trans. Computers*, 56(11):1564–1574.

Nong, G. and Zhang, S. (2007b). Efficient algorithms for the inverse sort transform. *IEEE Trans. Computers*, 56(11):1564–1574.

Pascoe, R. (1976). *Source coding algorithms for fast data compression.* PhD thesis, Stanford University, Stanford Univ., Stanford, CA.

Pinter, R. (1985). Efficient string matching with don't-care patterns. In Apostolico, A. and Galil, Z., editors, *Combinatorial Algorithms on Words.* Springer, Berlin.

Puglisi, S. J., Smyth, W. F., and Turpin, A. (2005). The performance of linear time suffix sorting algorithms. In Storer and Cohn (2005), pages 358–367.

Puglisi, S. J., Smyth, W. F., and Turpin, A. (2007). A taxonomy of suffix array construction algorithms. *ACM Computing Surveys*, 39(2).

Ranganathan, N. (1993). *VLSI Algorithms and Architecture (2 volumes).* IEEE Computer Society Press.

Richards, R. I., Holman, K., Yu, S., and R, S. G. (1993). Fragile X syndrome unstable element, p(CCG)n, and other simple tandem repeat sequences are binding sites for specific nuclear proteins. *Human Molecular Genetics*, 2(9):1429–1435.

Richardson, T. J. and Urbanke, R. L. (2001). The capacity of low-density parity-check codes under message-passing decoding. *IEEE Transactions on Information Theory*, 47(2):599–618.

Rissanen, J. (1976). Generalised Kraft inequality and arithmetic coding. *IBM Journal of Research and Development*, 20:198–203.

Rissanen, J. (1986). Complexity of strings in the class of Markov sources. *IEEE Transactions on Information Theory*, IT-32(4):526–532.

Rissanen, J. and Langdon, G. G. (1979). Arithmetic coding. *IBM Journal of Research and Development*, 23(2):149–162.

Roberts, D. C. (1978). A specialized computer architecture for text retrieval. *SIGMOD Record*, 10(1):51–59.

Sadakane, K. (1998). On optimality of variants of the block sorting compression. In Storer and Cohn (1998), page 570.

Sadakane, K. (1999). A modified Burrows-Wheeler transformation for case-insensitive search with application to suffix array compression. In Storer and Cohn (1999), page 548.

Sadakane, K. (2002). Succinct representations of lcp information and improvements in the compressed suffix arrays. In *Symposium on Discrete Algorithms (SODA)*, pages 225–232.

Sadakane, K. (2007). Compressed suffix trees with full functionality. *Theory of Computing Systems*, 41(4):589–607.

Sadakane, K. and Imai, H. (1999). Text retrieval by using k-word proximity search. In *DANTE*, pages 183–188. IEEE Computer Society.

Sadler, C. M. and Martonosi, M. (2006). Data compression algorithms for energy-constrained devices in delay tolerant networks. In Campbell, A. T., Bonnet, P., and Heidemann, J. S., editors, *SenSys*, pages 265–278. ACM.

Salomon, D. (2004). *Data Compression: The Complete Reference, 3rd Edition.* Springer, New York, 3rd edition edition.

Sayood, K. (2000). *Introduction to Data Compression*. Morgan Kaufmann Publishers, San Francisco, CA, USA, second edition.

Sayood, K., editor (2003). *Lossless compression handbook*. Academic Press.

Schieber, B. and Vishkin, U. (1988). On finding lowest common ancestors: Simplification and parallelization. *SIAM J. Comput.*, 17(6):1253–1262.

Schindler, M. (1997a). A fast block-sorting algorithm for lossless data compression. In Storer and Cohn (1997), page 469.

Schindler, M. (1997b). A fast block-sorting algorithm for lossless data compression (extended abstract). http://www.compressconsult.com/st/, Full version of DCC 97 poster.

Schindler, M. (2001). Method and apparatus for sorting data blocks. US Patent 6,199,064.

Schmitt, A. O. and Herzel, H. (1997). Estimating the entropy of DNA sequences. *Journal of Theoretical Biology*, 188(3):369–377.

Schönhage, A. and Strassen, V. (1971). Schnelle multiplikation großer zahlen. *Computing*, 7:281–292.

Schürmann, K.-B. and Stoye, J. (2005). An incomplex algorithm for fast suffix array construction. In Demetrescu, C., Sedgewick, R., and Tamassia, R., editors, *ALENEX/ANALCO*, pages 78–85. SIAM.

Schürmann, K.-B. and Stoye, J. (2007). An incomplex algorithm for fast suffix array construction. *Software—Practice and Experience*, 37(3):309–329.

Seward, J. (2000). On the performance of BWT sorting algorithms. In Storer, J. and Cohn, M., editors, *DCC*, pages 173–182. IEEE Computer Society.

Shamir, G. I. and Merhav, N. (1999). Low-complexity sequential lossless coding for piecewise-stationary memoryless sources. *IEEE Transactions on Information Theory*, 45(5):1498–1519.

Shannon, C. E. (1948). A mathematical theory of communication. *Bell System Technical Journal*, 27:379–423.

Shannon, C. E. (1951). Prediction and entropy of printed English. *Bell System Technical Journal*, pages 50–64.

Shannon, C. E. and Weaver, W. (1949). *The Mathematical Theory of Communication*. University of Illinois Press, Urbana, Illinois.

Sinden, R. R., Potaman, V. N., Oussatcheva, E. A., Pearson, C. E., Lyubchenko, Y. L., and Shlyakhtenko, L. S. (2002). Triplet repeat DNA structures and human genetic disease: dynamic mutations from dynamic DNA. *Journal of Biosciences*, 24(1):53–65.

Smith, T. F. and Waterman, M. S. (1981). Identification of common molecular subsequences. *Journal of Molecular Biology*, 147:195–197.

Smyth, W. (2003). *Computing Patterns in Strings*. Addison-Wesley.

Stellhorn, W. H. (1974). A processor for direct scanning of text. *Proc. 1st Workshop on Computer Architecture for Non-numeric Processing*.

Stephen, G. A. (1994). *String Searching Algorithms*, volume 3 of *Lecture Notes Series on Computing*. World Scientific.

Storer, J. and Cohn, M., editors (1995). *1995 Data Compression Conference (DCC 1995), 28-30 March, 1995, Snowbird, UT, USA*. IEEE Computer Society.

Storer, J. and Cohn, M., editors (1997). *1997 Data Compression Conference (DCC 1997), 25-27 March, 1997, Snowbird, UT, USA*. IEEE Computer Society.

Storer, J. and Cohn, M., editors (1998). *1998 Data Compression Conference (DCC 1998), 30 March - 1 April, 1998, Snowbird, UT, USA*. IEEE Computer Society.

Storer, J. and Cohn, M., editors (1999). *1999 Data Compression Conference (DCC 1999), 29-31 March, 1999, Snowbird, UT, USA*. IEEE Computer Society.

Storer, J. and Cohn, M., editors (2001). *2001 Data Compression Conference (DCC 2001), 27-29 March, 2001, Snowbird, UT, USA*. IEEE Computer Society.

Storer, J. and Cohn, M., editors (2002). *2002 Data Compression Conference (DCC 2002), 2-4 April, 2002, Snowbird, UT, USA*. IEEE Computer Society.

Storer, J. and Cohn, M., editors (2003). *2003 Data Compression Conference (DCC 2003), 25-27 March 2003, Snowbird, UT, USA*. IEEE Computer Society.

Storer, J. and Cohn, M., editors (2005). *2005 Data Compression Conference (DCC 2005), 29-31 March 2005, Snowbird, UT, USA*. IEEE Computer Society.

Storer, J. and Cohn, M., editors (2006). *2006 Data Compression Conference (DCC 2006), 28-30 March 2006, Snowbird, UT, USA*. IEEE Computer Society.

Storer, J. A. (1988). *Data Compression: Methods and Theory*. Computer Science Press.

Strassen, V. (1969). Gaussian elimination is not optimal. *Numer. Math.*, 13:354–356.

Strong, S. P., Koberle, R., de Ruyter van Steveninck, R. R., and Bialek, W. (1998). Entropy and information in neural spike trains. *Phys. Rev. Lett.*, 80(1):197–200.

Sun, W., Zhang, N., and Mukherjee, A. (2003a). Dictionary-based fast transform for text compression. In *ITCC*, pages 176–182. IEEE Computer Society.

Sun, W., Zhang, N., and Mukherjee, A. (2003b). A dictionary-based multi-corpora text compression system. In Storer and Cohn (2003), page 448.

Sunday, D. (1990). A very fast substring search algorithm. *Commun. ACM*, 33(8):132–142.

Szpankowski, W. (1993a). Asympotic properties of data compression and suffix trees. *IEEE Transactions on Information Theory*, 39(5):1647–1659.

Szpankowski, W. (1993b). A generalized suffix tree and its (un)expected asymptotic behaviors. *SIAM Journal of Computing*, 26(6):176–1198.

Tao, T. and Mukherjee, A. (2005). Pattern matching in lzw compressed files. *IEEE Trans. Comput.*, 54(8):929–938.

Tarhio, J. and Ukkonen, E. (1993). Approximate Boyer-Moore string matching. *SIAM Journal on Computing*, 22(2):243–260.

Tjalkens, T. J., Volf, P., and Willems, F. (1997). A context-tree weighting method for text-generating sources. In Storer and Cohn (1997), page 472.

Ukkonen, E. (1985a). Algorithms for approximate string matching. *Information and Control*, 64(1-3):100–118.

Ukkonen, E. (1985b). Finding approximate patterns in strings. *J. Algorithms*, 6(1):132–137.

Ukkonen, E. (1993). Approximate string-matching over suffix trees. In Apostolico, A., Crochemore, M., Galil, Z., and Manber, U., editors, *CPM*, volume 684 of *Lecture Notes in Computer Science*, pages 228–242. Springer.

Ukkonen, E. (1995). On-line construction of suffix trees. *Algorithmica*, 14(3):249–260.

Välimäki, N., Gerlach, W., Dixit, K., and Mäkinen, V. (2007). Engineering a compressed suffix tree implementation. In Demetrescu, C., editor, *WEA*, volume 4525 of *Lecture Notes in Computer Science*, pages 217–228. Springer.

Vinga, S. and Almeida, J. S. (2003). Alignment-free sequence comparison — a review. *Bioinformatics*, 19(4):513–523.

Visweswariah, K., Kulkarni, S., and Verdu, S. (2000). Output distribution of the Burrows-Wheeler transform. *ISIT*, 2(4):611–639.

Volf, P. (1997). Context-tree weighting for text-sources. In *Proceedings, IEEE International Symposium on Information Theory*, page 64. IEEE.

Volfovsky, N., Haas, B. J., and Salzberg, S. L. (2001). A clustering method for repeat analysis in DNA sequences. *Genome Biology*, 8(2):research0027.1–0027.11.

Weiner, P. (1973). Linear pattern matching algorithm. *Proceedings, 14th IEEE Symposium on Switching and Automata Theory*, 21:1–11.

Welch, T. A. (1984). A technique for high-performance data compression. *IEEE Computer*, 17(6):8–19.

Wheeler, D. (1997). Upgrading bred with multiple tables. ftp://ftp.cl.cam.ac.uk/users/djw3/bred3.ps.

White, C. T., Singh, R. K., Reintjes, P. B., Lampe, J., Erickson, B. W., Dettloff, W. D., Chi, V. L., and Altschul, S. F. (1991). BioSCAN: A VLSI-based system for biosequence analysis. In *ICCD*, pages 504–509. IEEE Computer Society.

Willems, F. M. J. (1996). Coding for a binary independent piecewise-identically-distributed source. *IEEE Transactions on Information Theory*, 42(6):2210–2217.

Willems, F. M. J. (1998). The context-tree weighting method : Extensions. *IEEE Transactions on Information Theory*, 44(2):792–798.

Willems, F. M. J., Shtarkov, Y. M., and Tjalkens, T. J. (1995). The context-tree weighting method: Basic properties. *IEEE Transactions on Information Theory*, 41(3):653–664.

Willems, F. M. J., Shtarkov, Y. M., and Tjalkens, T. J. (1996). Context weighting for general finite-context sources. *IEEE Transactions on Information Theory*, 42(5):1514–1520.

Williams, R. N. (1991). *Adaptive Data Compression*. Kluwer Academic, Norwell, Massachusetts.

Wirth, A. (2001). Symbol-driven compression of Burrows Wheeler transformed text. Master's thesis, The University of Melbourne.

Wirth, A. I. and Moffat, A. (2001). Can we do without ranks in Burrows Wheeler transform compression? In Storer and Cohn (2001), pages 419–428.

Wiseman, Y. (2006). Burrows-Wheeler based JPEG. *Data Science Journal*, 6:19–27.

Witten, I. H. and Bell, T. C. (1991). The zero-frequency problem: Estimating the probabilities of novel events in adaptive text compression. *IEEE Transactions on Information Theory*, 37(4):1085–1094.

Witten, I. H., Moffat, A., and Bell, T. C. (1999). *Managing Gigabytes: Compressing and Indexing Documents and Images, Second Edition*. Morgan Kaufmann.

Wu, S. and Manber, U. (1992a). agrep — a fast approximate pattern matching tool. In *Proceedings of the Winter 1992 USENIX Conference*, pages 153–62. USENIX Association, Berkeley, CA.

Wu, S. and Manber, U. (1992b). Fast text searching allowing errors. *Communications of the ACM*, 35(10):83–91.

Yamaguchi, T. J., Ha, D. S., Ishida, M., and Ohmi, T. (2002). A method for compressing test data based on Burrows-Wheeler transformation. *IEEE Trans. Computers*, 51(5):486–497.

Yokoo, H. (1996). An adaptive data compression method based on context sorting. In Storer, J. and Cohn, M., editors, *DCC*, pages 160–169. IEEE Computer Society.

Yokoo, H. (1997). Data compression using a sort-based context similarity measure. *The Computer Journal*, 40(2/3):95–102.

Yokoo, H. (1999). A dynamic data structure for reverse lexicographically sorted prefixes. In Crochemore, M. and Paterson, M., editors, *CPM*, volume 1645 of *Lecture Notes in Computer Science*, pages 150–162. Springer.

Yu, C. W., Kwong, K. H., Lee, K.-H., and Leong, P. H. W. (2003). A smith-waterman systolic cell. In Cheung, P. Y. K., Constantinides, G. A., and de Sousa, J. T., editors, *FPL*, volume 2778 of *Lecture Notes in Computer Science*, pages 375–384. Springer.

Zhang, N. (2005). *Transform based and search aware text compression schemes and compressed domain text retrieval*. PhD thesis, University of Central Florida, Orlando, Florida.

Zhang, N., Mukherjee, A., Adjeroh, D. A., and Bell, T. (2003). Approximate pattern matching using the Burrows-Wheeler Transform. In Storer and Cohn (2003), page 458.

Zipf, G. K. (1949). Human behaviour and the principle of least-effort. *Addison-Wesley, Cambridge MA.*

Ziv, J. and Lempel, A. (1977). A universal algorithm for sequential data compression. *IEEE Transactions on Information Theory*, 23(3):337–343.

Ziv, J. and Lempel, A. (1978). Compression of individual sequences via variable-rate coding. *IEEE Transactions on Information Theory*, 24(5):530–536.

Ziviani, N., de Moura, E. S., Navarro, G., and Baeza-Yates, R. (2000). Compression: A key for next generation text retrieval systems. *IEEE Computer*, 33(11):37–44.

Zobel, J. and Moffat, A. (2006). Inverted files for text search engines. *ACM Computing Surveys*, 38(2):1–56.

Index

Bibliography index

Abel and Teahan (2005), 185, 317
Abel (2005), 50, 317
Abel (2007a), 50, 317
Abel (2007b), 49, 50, 317
Abouelhoda et al. (2005), 281, 317
Abrahamson (1987), 262, 317
Adjeroh and Feng (2004), 281, 317
Adjeroh and Nan (2006), 280, 317
Adjeroh and Nan (2008), 89, 317
Adjeroh et al. (2002), 262, 279, 317
Adjeroh et al. (2006), 290, 317
Adjeroh et al. (2007), 292, 294, 317
Aho and Corasick (1975), 200, 260, 317
Andersson and Nilsson (1995), 75, 89, 318
Andersson et al. (1999), 88, 318
Apostolico et al. (2005), 318, 329, 332, 333
Apostolico (1985), 52, 88, 318
Arimura and Yamamoto (1998), 123, 127, 150, 318
Arnavut and Arnavut (2004), 163, 318
Arnavut and Magliveras (1997a), 49, 129, 163, 165, 167, 185, 318
Arnavut and Magliveras (1997b), 163, 165, 167, 185, 318
Arnavut (2002), 50, 129, 185, 318
Arnavut (2007a), 289, 318
Arnavut (2007b), 289, 318
Arnold and Bell (1997), 262, 318
Atallah et al. (1999), 52, 318
Awan and Mukherjee (2001), 186, 318

Awan et al. (2001), 186, 318
Bachrach and El-Yaniv (1997), 49, 318
Baeza-Yates and Gonnet (1992), 189, 199, 244, 256, 260–262, 318
Baeza-Yates and Perleberg (1992), 244, 254, 319
Baeza-Yates and Perleberg (1996), 244, 254, 319
Baeza-Yates and Ribeiro-Neto (1999), 301, 319
Baeza-Yates et al. (2003), 319, 326, 329
Baeza-Yates (1989), 260, 319
Baik et al. (1999a), 290, 291, 319
Baik et al. (1999b), 290, 319
Balkenhol and Kurtz (1998), 104, 150, 319
Balkenhol and Kurtz (2000), 49, 92, 102, 104, 123, 150, 319
Balkenhol et al. (1999), 49, 319
Baron and Bresler (2000), 300, 319
Baron and Bresler (2004), 300, 319
Bat et al. (1997), 281, 319
Bell and Moffat (1989), 147, 320
Bell and Witten (1994), 135, 320
Bell et al. (1990), 17, 135–138, 150, 320
Bell et al. (2001), 302, 319
Bell et al. (2002), 208, 212, 261, 320
Bell (1986), 145, 175, 319
Bell (1987), 135, 146, 319
Belongie et al. (2002), 292, 320
Bender and Farach-Colton (2000), 67, 71, 320

Bentley and McIlroy (1993), 76, 86, 87, 320
Bentley and Sedgewick (1997), 77, 81, 86, 87, 320
Bentley et al. (1986), 17, 49, 123, 125, 128, 150, 153, 183, 184, 208, 320
Bieganski et al. (1994), 51, 89, 320
Bird et al. (1977), 258, 320
Boyer and Moore (1977), 189, 320
Brown (2004), 295, 320
Bunton (1997), 139, 320
Burkowski (1982), 258, 320
Burrows and Wheeler (1994), 6, 16, 31, 49, 51, 88, 93, 123, 320
Cai et al. (2004), 300, 301, 320
Caire et al. (2004), 297–299, 321
Caire et al. (2006), 297, 321
Chan and Nong (2005), 157, 158, 185, 321
Chan et al. (2005), 302, 321
Chandra and Chakrabarty (2001), 285, 321
Chang and Lampe (1992), 262, 321
Chang and Lawler (1994), 254, 321
Chapin (2000), 49, 321
Chen et al. (2002), 143, 321
Cheung et al. (2005), 89, 321
Ciavarella and Moffat (2004), 289, 291, 292, 302, 321
Clark and Munro (1996), 89, 321
Cleary and Teahan (1997), 137–140, 150, 321
Cleary and Witten (1984), 6, 17, 136, 137, 150, 321
Cleary et al. (1995), 140, 321
Cole (1994), 261, 322
Cook (1972), 200, 260, 322
Cook (2007), 52, 322
Cormack and Horspool (1987), 147, 150, 322
Cover and King (1978), 151, 322
Cover and Thomas (1991), 302, 322
Cover and Thomas (2006), 120, 123, 126, 127, 129, 302, 322
Crauser and Ferragina (2002), 89, 322
Crochemore and Rytter (1994), 261, 322
Crochemore and Vérin (1997), 267, 322
Crochemore et al. (2005), 50, 185, 322

de Moura et al. (2000), 182, 184, 322
Delcher et al. (1999), 51, 322
Deorowicz (2002), 49, 50, 93, 105, 322
Deorowicz (2005), 50, 322
Dettloff et al. (1991), 259, 322
Dijkstra (1959), 241, 322
Dömölki (1968), 260, 322
Dütsch and Hagenauer (2004), 298, 299, 323
Dütsch et al. (2006), 298, 323
Effros et al. (2002), 104, 123, 127, 129, 132, 150, 323
Effros (1999), 150, 323
Effros (2000), 140, 150, 323
Elias (1975), 37, 49, 123, 124, 323
Elias (1987), 49, 123, 125, 128, 323
Farach and Muthukrishnan (1996), 66, 82, 323
Farach-Colton et al. (2000), 66, 82, 88, 89, 96, 323
Farach (1997), 66, 82, 88, 96, 323
Fenwick (1995a), 261, 323
Fenwick (1995b), 6, 16, 31, 153, 323
Fenwick (1995c), 6, 16, 31, 153, 323
Fenwick (1996a), 6, 16, 31, 49, 93, 105, 106, 153, 323
Fenwick (1996b), 7, 16, 31, 49, 93, 129, 153, 323
Fenwick (1997a), 148, 324
Fenwick (1997b), 92, 93, 105, 129, 148, 324
Fenwick (1998), 148, 150, 324
Fenwick (2001a), 261, 324
Fenwick (2001b), 262, 324
Fenwick (2002a), 49, 96, 129, 324
Fenwick (2002b), 123, 324
Fenwick (2003a), 17, 324
Fenwick (2003b), 148, 185, 324
Fenwick (2003c), 49, 324
Fenwick (2007), 17, 31, 49, 138, 150, 303, 324
Ferragina and Manzini (2000), 215, 261, 302, 325
Ferragina and Manzini (2001a), 261, 325
Ferragina and Manzini (2001b), 215, 220, 261, 302, 325
Ferragina and Manzini (2004), 50, 325

Ferragina and Manzini (2005), 215, 261, 275, 302, 325
Ferragina and Venturini (2007), 301, 325
Ferragina et al. (2005a), 50, 91, 129, 135, 149, 150, 324
Ferragina et al. (2005b), 186, 324
Ferragina et al. (2006a), 38, 39, 49, 50, 105, 106, 324
Ferragina et al. (2006b), 49, 50, 324
Ferragina et al. (2006c), 186, 325
Ferragina et al. (2007), 261, 325
Ferragina (2005), 89, 324
Ferragina (2007), 184, 324
Firth et al. (2005), 262, 302, 325
Firth (2002), 262, 325
Fischer and Paterson (1974), 205, 262, 325
Foschini et al. (2004), 49, 50, 325
Foschini et al. (2006), 302, 325
Foster and Kung (1980), 258, 326
Franceschini and Muthukrishnan (2007), 89, 326
Franek and Smyth (2006), 185, 326
Gagie and Manzini (2007), 49, 50, 326
Galil and Giancarlo (1988), 244, 326
Galil (1978), 261, 326
Gallager (1962), 302, 326
Geary et al. (2006), 270, 326
Gessel and Reutenauer (1993), 172, 185, 326
Giancarlo and Sciortino (2003), 129, 135, 150, 326
Giancarlo et al. (2007), 17, 326
Giancarlo (1995), 52, 326
Giegerich and Kurtz (1997), 88, 150, 326
Golynski et al. (2006), 269, 326
Golynski et al. (2007), 302, 326
Golynski (2007), 262, 326
Gonnet et al. (1992), 51, 54, 88, 327
Gonzalez and Navarro (2006), 302, 327
Grabowski (1999), 185, 327
Grossi and Luccio (1989), 244, 327
Grossi and Vitter (2000), 89, 270, 302, 327
Grossi and Vitter (2005), 52, 88, 89, 270, 272–274, 276, 302, 327
Grossi et al. (2003), 50, 269, 327

Guo and Burrus (1997), 291, 327
Gupta et al. (2007), 261, 262, 327
Gusfield (1997), 52, 57, 62, 73, 88, 189, 236, 241, 245, 253, 260, 262, 327
Hagenauer (1988), 302, 327
Harel and Tarjan (1984), 67, 71, 245, 327
Healy et al. (2003), 282, 327
Herzel et al. (1994), 280, 327
Hoang et al. (1995), 135, 327
Hoang et al. (1999), 135, 327
Hoffman and Singh (1997), 293, 327
Hollaar and Roberts (1978), 258, 328
Hon et al. (2003a), 89, 328
Hon et al. (2003b), 275, 328
Hon et al. (2007), 302, 328
Howard and Vitter (1993), 133, 328
Huffman (1952), 6, 17, 328
Hughey (1991), 259, 328
Hume and Sunday (1991), 261, 328
Hunkerpiller et al. (1990), 259, 328
Hunt and Szymanski (1977), 240, 328
Hunt et al. (2001), 89, 328
Hutchins and Somers (1992), 295, 328
Isal and Moffat (2001a), 181, 185, 328
Isal and Moffat (2001b), 181, 185, 328
Isal et al. (2002), 181, 184, 185, 328
Itoh and Tanaka (1999), 84, 86, 88, 96, 328
Jacobson (1989), 268, 273, 328
Kaplan and Verbin (2007), 150, 329
Kaplan et al. (2006), 135, 150, 329
Kaplan et al. (2007), 17, 135, 329
Karimi et al. (2002), 285, 329
Kärkkäinen and Sanders (2003), 81, 88, 96, 329
Kärkkäinen and Sutinen (1998), 302, 329
Kärkkäinen et al. (2006), 66, 81, 88, 89, 96, 329
Kärkkäinen (2007), 88, 95, 149, 329
Karlin et al. (1983), 80, 329
Karp and Rabin (1987), 189, 197, 329
Karp et al. (1972), 78, 329
Kim and Park (2005), 89, 269, 302, 329
Kim et al. (2003), 89, 329
Kim et al. (2005), 66, 81, 89, 329
Knuth et al. (1977), 189, 260, 329
Knuth (1973), 51, 88, 185, 261, 329

Ko and Aluru (2003), 88, 96, 329
Ko and Aluru (2005), 81, 84, 89, 96, 329
Komma et al. (2007), 290, 329
Kopylov and Fränti (2005), 143, 330
Krichevsky and Trofimov (1981), 101, 131, 150, 330
Kruse and Mukherjee (1998), 186, 330
Kruse and Mukherjee (1999), 186, 330
Kurtz and Balkenhol (2000), 96, 149, 330
Kurtz et al. (2004), 51, 330
Kurtz (1999), 75, 89, 330
Lam et al. (2002), 269, 281, 330
Lam et al. (2007), 284, 330
Lanctot et al. (2000), 300, 330
Landau and Vishkin (1985), 244, 330
Landau and Vishkin (1986), 254, 330
Langdon Jr. (1983), 135, 146, 330
Larsson and Sadakane (1999), 81, 88, 330
Larsson and Sadakane (2007), 81, 86, 88, 96, 330
Larsson (1998), 88, 140, 150, 330
Lewenstein and Valiente (2006), 327, 329, 330
Li et al. (2007), 259, 331
Lin and Costello Jr. (2004), 296, 302, 331
Lippert et al. (2005), 281, 282, 331
Lippert (2005), 281, 282, 331
Lipton and Lopresti (1985), 259, 331
Lonardi and Luo (2004), 290, 331
Lopresti (1991), 259, 331
Lucito et al. (2003), 282, 331
Mäkinen and Navarro (2007), 262, 331
Mäkinen (2003), 267, 331
Ma and Zhang (2007), 326, 329, 331
Manber and Myers (1990), 76, 78, 88, 331
Manber and Myers (1993), 75, 76, 78, 80, 85, 88, 96, 261, 331
Maniscalco and Puglisi (2006), 88, 331
Mantaci et al. (2003), 185, 332
Mantaci et al. (2005), 168, 169, 185, 283, 331
Mantaci et al. (2007), 168, 169, 185, 283, 284, 332
Manzini and Ferragina (2004), 85, 87, 96, 332

Manzini (1999), 105, 133, 150, 332
Manzini (2001), 105, 123, 133, 150, 332
Markstein (2004), 317, 331, 332
Martinez et al. (2005), 259, 260, 332
Masek and Paterson (1980), 241, 332
McCreight (1976), 52, 57, 75, 88, 96, 332
McIlroy et al. (1993), 86, 332
Mead et al. (1976), 258, 332
Merhav (1993), 104, 332
Moffat and Turpin (2002), 17, 48, 332
Moffat et al. (1995), 48, 332
Moffat et al. (1998), 48, 332
Moffat (1990), 96, 136–138, 150, 332
Mori et al. (2001), 292, 332
Morrison (1968), 88, 332
Mukherjee and Acharya (1995), 259, 333
Mukherjee and Awan (2003), 186, 333
Mukherjee et al. (2001), 259, 260, 333
Mukherjee (1989), 259, 332
Mukhopadhyay (1979), 256, 260, 333
Munro et al. (1998), 267, 268, 333
Munro et al. (2001), 89, 267–269, 333
Myers (1986), 240, 333
Myers (1994), 254, 333
Navarro and Mäkinen (2007), 215, 261, 302, 333
Navarro and Tarhio (2005), 232, 333
Navarro et al. (2000), 184, 333
Navarro (2001), 246, 333
Na (2005), 89, 333
Nelson and Gailly (1995), 17, 333
Nelson (1996), 7, 17, 333
Nong and Zhang (2006), 157, 158, 333
Nong and Zhang (2007a), 157, 158, 333
Nong and Zhang (2007b), 185, 333
Pascoe (1976), 17, 334
Pinter (1985), 205, 262, 334
Puglisi et al. (2005), 150, 334
Puglisi et al. (2007), 76, 85, 89, 150, 334
Ranganathan (1993), 259, 334
Richards et al. (1993), 281, 334
Richardson and Urbanke (2001), 302, 334
Rissanen and Langdon (1979), 6, 17, 334
Rissanen (1976), 17, 334
Rissanen (1986), 132, 334

Roberts (1978), 258, 334
Sadakane and Imai (1999), 261, 334
Sadakane (1998), 150, 334
Sadakane (1999), 261, 334
Sadakane (2002), 269, 302, 334
Sadakane (2007), 269, 277, 302, 334
Sadler and Martonosi (2006), 303, 334
Salomon (2004), 17, 180, 185, 334
Sayood (2000), 17, 334
Sayood (2003), 17, 49, 324, 333, 335
Schönhage and Strassen (1971), 205,
    262, 335
Schürmann and Stoye (2005), 96, 335
Schürmann and Stoye (2007), 88, 335
Schieber and Vishkin (1988), 67, 71, 335
Schindler (1997a), 49, 50, 154, 155, 157,
    185, 335
Schindler (1997b), 49, 154, 155, 157,
    185, 335
Schindler (2001), 154, 157, 335
Schmitt and Herzel (1997), 300, 335
Seward (2000), 86–88, 96, 335
Shamir and Merhav (1999), 132, 335
Shannon and Weaver (1949), 17, 335
Shannon (1948), 6, 17, 34, 296, 335
Shannon (1951), 148, 151, 335
Sinden et al. (2002), 281, 335
Smith and Waterman (1981), 238, 335
Smyth (2003), 169, 196, 245, 260, 267,
    335
Stellhorn (1974), 258, 335
Stephen (1994), 245, 262, 335
Storer and Cohn (1995), 321, 327, 332,
    335
Storer and Cohn (1997), 318, 335–337
Storer and Cohn (1998), 330, 334, 336
Storer and Cohn (1999), 319, 323, 334,
    336
Storer and Cohn (2001), 328, 336, 338
Storer and Cohn (2002), 318, 320, 336
Storer and Cohn (2003), 336, 339
Storer and Cohn (2005), 317, 334, 336
Storer and Cohn (2006), 317, 333, 336
Storer (1988), 17, 336
Strassen (1969), 205, 336
Strong et al. (1998), 300, 336
Sun et al. (2003a), 186, 336
Sun et al. (2003b), 186, 336
Sunday (1990), 261, 336

Szpankowski (1993a), 88, 150, 336
Szpankowski (1993b), 88, 336
Tao and Mukherjee (2005), 260, 336
Tarhio and Ukkonen (1993), 244, 337
Tjalkens et al. (1997), 143, 337
Ukkonen (1985a), 240, 337
Ukkonen (1985b), 254, 262, 337
Ukkonen (1993), 51, 262, 337
Ukkonen (1995), 52, 57, 88, 96, 337
Välimäki et al. (2007), 302, 337
Vinga and Almeida (2003), 284, 337
Visweswariah et al. (2000), 104, 150,
    337
Volfovsky et al. (2001), 51, 337
Volf (1997), 143, 337
Weiner (1973), 52, 57, 88, 96, 337
Welch (1984), 150, 337
Wheeler (1997), 209, 219, 337
White et al. (1991), 259, 337
Willems et al. (1995), 141, 142, 150, 337
Willems et al. (1996), 142, 338
Willems (1996), 104, 132, 337
Willems (1998), 142, 337
Williams (1991), 17, 338
Wirth and Moffat (2001), 50, 129, 185,
    338
Wirth (2001), 49, 50, 185, 301, 338
Wiseman (2006), 291, 338
Witten and Bell (1991), 137, 138, 338
Witten et al. (1999), 17, 49, 137, 150,
    223, 273, 276, 301, 338
Wu and Manber (1992a), 244, 338
Wu and Manber (1992b), 244, 262, 338
Yamaguchi et al. (2002), 285–287, 338
Yokoo (1996), 173, 338
Yokoo (1997), 135, 145, 150, 173, 175,
    180, 185, 338
Yokoo (1999), 175, 178, 180, 185, 338
Yu et al. (2003), 259, 338
Zhang et al. (2003), 253, 262, 338
Zhang (2005), 262, 338
Zipf (1949), 109, 339
Ziv and Lempel (1977), 6, 17, 144, 150,
    339
Ziv and Lempel (1978), 6, 17, 144, 150,
    339
Ziviani et al. (2000), 276, 339
Zobel and Moffat (2006), 276, 301, 339

Main index

A (rotated string array), 310
A_s (sorted rotated string array), 310
ACB (Associative Coder of Buyonoski),
    180, 185
active point (in Ukkonen's algorithm),
    62
adaptive BWT, 173
adaptive coding, 35
Aho and Corasick algorithm, 200
alpha (α) code, 36, 49
alphabet, 19
    English words, 181
    extended, 127
anagrams, 1, 11, 17
applications of the BWT, 265
    bioinformatics, 278
    computational biology, 278
    distance between sequences, 283
    DNA sequence compression, 279
    entropy estimation, 299
    entropy prediction, 299
    full-text indexing, 275
    genome annotation, 282
    genome comparison, 281
    image compression, 287
    joint source-channel coding, 298
    lossless image compression, 289
    lossy image compression, 290
    machine translation, 294
    microarray compression, 290
    phylogenic trees, 283
    protein sequence compression, 279
    repetition structures, 280
    sequence alignment, 283
    shape matching, 292
    test data compression, 284
approximate pattern matching, 262
arithmetic coding, 6, 34, 48
    FAST adaptation, 105
automatic test equipment (ATE), 285

banana
    Schindler's transform, 156
Bell Labs, 7
bexp (block expand), 8, 313
bible, 8, 106, 222
bigram, 107, 155, 261

bioinformatics, 278
block size, 47
block sorting, 2
boosting, 46, 50
boundary path, 59
    suffix trie, 59
Boyer-Moore, 260
branching node, 54
bred (block reduce), 8, 313
built-in-self-test (BIST), 285
Burrows, Michael, 7
BWT
    applications, 265
    computational complexity, 95
    context trees, 103
    relation with PPM, 139
    relation with suffix trees, 93
BZIP, 7, 8, 16, 48, 161, 180, 222, 314
    alpha (α) code, 37
    entropy coding, 42
BZIP2, 305, 306, 314

cache
    BWT interaction with, 22, 48, 306
    LRU, 12
    pattern matching, 258
    suffix trees, 221
Calgary corpus, 180
Cambridge Ring, 7
Canterbury corpus, 106, 180, 221, 262
Cartesian form (permutation), 164
channel coding, 296
circular shift permutation, 11
code
    alpha (α), 36, 49
    arithmetic, 6, 34, 48
    channel, 296
    delta (δ), 37, 49, 124
    Elias, 37, 49, 123, 124
    gamma (γ), 37, 49, 124
    Huffman, 6, 34, 48
    Shannon-Fano, 6
    source, 296
    universal, 37, 49
    Ziv-Lempel, 6
coding redundancy, 122, 132, 312
compressed domain searching, 261
compressed full-text indexing, 261, 275
compressed suffix array, 266, 270, 274

compressed suffix tree, 266, 267, 274
compression boosting, 46, 50
compression, relationship with pattern
    matching, 13, 187
computational biology, 278
conjugate strings, 168
context
    exhumation, 50
    preceding (left), 97
    succeeding (right/forward), 97
context similarity measurement
    ranking, 173
    sorted-based, 173
context tree weighting, 140
COPY suffix sorting algorithm, 86
coupled-depth-first traversal, 71

D (relative entropy), 311
DAWG, 267
delta (δ) code, 37, 49, 124
derived sorting, 86
digital trie
    keyword tree, 201
direct suffix sorting, 66, 78, 81
directed acyclic word graphs (DAWGs),
    267
distance coding, 44, 49, 50
DNA sequence compression, 279
don't-care characters, 262

ϵ (empty string), 311
E.coli, 106, 222
edge-label compression, 54, 60
edit graph, 236
EDSAC, 7
Elias codes, 37, 49, 123, 124
empirical entropy, 121
encryption, 11
    Tiny Encryption Algorithm (TEA), 7
end of string character (sentinel), 3, 20,
    22, 31, 52, 158
end point (in Ukkonen's algorithm), 62
entropy, 120, 311
    estimated, 113
    relative, 104, 122, 311
entropy coding, 33
entropy estimation, 299
    DNA sequence, 300
    language modeling, 300

neural spike train, 300
phylogenic tree, 300
entropy rate, 121
ergodic information source, 100, 121
estimated entropy, 113
Euler's phi function, 166
even tree, 67
    merging with odd tree, 71
exhumation, context, 50
explicit node, 60
extended BWT, 168

F (first column), 4, 24, 31, 309
Farach's suffix tree construction, 66
FAST adaptation, 105
fixed length don't-care character, 204,
    258
FL mapping, 310
FLDC character, 204, 258
FM-index, 215, 261, 266, 275
    as a compressed suffix array, 275
forward BWT, 19
forward context, 97
frequency counting LGT, 42
full-text indexing, 266, 275

gamma (γ) code, 37, 49, 124
generalized suffix trees, 73
genome annotation, 282
genome comparison, 281
GIF, 6, 144
GZIP, 6, 8, 144, 180

H (entropy), 311
Hamlet
    anagram, 17
    BWT, 10, 15, 34
hardware based pattern matching, 255
history of BWT, 5
Huffman coding, 6, 34, 48

image compression, 287
    lossless, 289
implicit node, 60
implicit suffix link, 62
implicit suffix tree, 57, 64
Inca mystery, 52
incremental frequency count (IFC)
    LGT, 43, 50

indels, 235
intensive pattern matching, 261
inversion frequencies (IF), 43, 49, 50
Itoh-Tanaka suffix sorting algorithm, 86

Jensen's inequality, 123, 126
joint source-channel coding, 296
JPEG, 290

Karp-Rabin, 260
keyword tree, 201
KMP, 260
Ko and Aluru algorithm for suffix
    sorting, 84
Krichevsky-Trofimov (K-T) estimator,
    101, 130, 150
Kullback-Leibler distance, 104, 122, 311

L (last column), 4, 20, 24, 31, 154, 231,
    310
L-suffix, 84
LCA (lowest common ancestor), 66, 70,
    71, 269
LCP (longest common prefix), 66, 71
LDPC (low-density parity check codes),
    297
left context, 97
lena, 106
lexical index permutation, 167
lexical permutation sorting, 163
lexical permutation sorting algorithm
    (LPSA), 167
LF mapping, 274, 275, 310
LGT (local to global transform), 33, 92
lightweight suffix array construction, 85
local to global transform, 33, 92
longest common prefix (LCP), 66, 71
lossless image compression, 289
lossy image compression, 290
low-density parity check (LDPC) codes,
    297
lowest common ancestor (LCA), 66, 70,
    71, 269
LPSA (lexical permutation sorting
    algorithm, 167
LRU (least recently used), 12
LZ coding, 6, 144, 306
LZW, 144

machine translation, 294

Manber-Myers suffix sorting algorithm,
    78
memoryless source, 100
merge refinement, 72
merging odd and even trees, 71
microarray compression, 290
mississippi
    Ψ function, 275
    A_s (sorted array), 24
    BWT arrays, 29
    context similarity, 174, 176
    context tree, 99
    decomposition, 272
    estimated probability $P_e(T)$, 103
    extended alphabet, 128
    FM-index, 217
    Itoh-Tanaka algorithm, 87
    LZ77, 144
    LZW, 146
    MTF, 41
    odd and even trees, 68
    partition of L array, 98
    PPM, 137
    PPM*, 139
    prefix list, 177
    prefix tree, 104
    rotations, 20
    sorted prefixes, 177
    sorted suffixes, 210
    sorted suffixes on reverse string, 179
    suffix array, 80
    suffix tree, 65, 66
    suffix tree and suffix array relation-
        ship, 94
    suffix tree parenthesis representation,
        268
    suffix trie, 61
    weighted context tree, 143
move-to-front (MTF), 12, 17, 39, 49, 92,
    96, 123
    analysis, 105, 128
    compared with fast adaptation, 106,
        306
    comparison with related methods, 50
    empirical entropy, 150
    multiple splay trees, 184
MPEG, 290
MSD radix sort, 86
MTF, *see* move to front

multikey quicksort, 86
multiple pattern matching, 73, 200
multiset permutation, 167

node (in suffix tree)
  branching, 54
  explicit, 60
  implicit, 60
  splitting, 63
non-adaptive coding, 35
notation, 31, 309

odd tree, 67
  merging with even tree, 71
online BWT, 173
order-k sorting, 76

ϕ (FLDC character), 204
parallel processing, 306
parenthesis representation for suffix
    trees, 267
parity check codes, 297
pastors, comedian, 1
path-label compression, 54, 60
pattern matching, 13, 187
  approximate, 262
  hardware based, 255
  intensive pattern matching, 261
  relationship with compression, 13,
    187
performance analysis, 263
permutation, 11, 163
  Cartesian form, 164
  circular shift, 11
  encryption, 11
  inverse, 164
  lexical index, 167
  multiset, 167
  sorting, 164
permutations, 46
Ph.D. theses (BWT-related), 314
phylogenic trees, 284
pizzachili (web site), 215, 261, 313
PNG, 6, 144
PPM (Prediction by Partial Matching),
    6, 136, 150, 180
preceding context, 97
prefix
  proper, 52

prefix list, 175
  performance, 180
primitive strings, 168
proper prefix, 52
proper suffix, 52
protein sequence compression, 279

q-grams (for pattern matching), 262
QSUFSORT suffix sorting algorithm, 86
quicksort, 20, 31, 76

R (sorted index), 310
R' (reverse mapping), 310
radix sort, 155
random16, 106
rank operation (on suffix trees), 268
recency, 12
redundancy (coding), 122, 132, 312
refinement node, 72
relative entropy, 104, 122, 311
repetition structures, 280
reverse BWT, 23
right context, 97
RLEAC compression method, 38, 49
Roman numerals, 8
run-length encoding, 38, 49

Σ (alphabet), 309
S-suffix, 84
Sapir–Whorf hypothesis, 9
Schindler's sort transform, 154
  inverse transform, 155
  performance, 159
select operation (on suffix trees), 268
sentinel, 3, 20, 22, 31, 52, 158
Shannon-Fano coding, 6
shape context, 292
shape matching, 292
shift-and pattern matching method,
    199, 260, 310
  hardware version, 256
Smith-Waterman local similarity
    algorithm, 238
sort order, 168
sort transform algorithm, 154
sorted shape context, 293
sorted-based context similarity
    measurement, 173
sorting

lexical permutation, 163
permutations, 164
sorting suffixes, 76
source
    memoryless, 100
    stationary, 102
source coding, 296
    via channel coding, 297
splitting a node (in suffix trees), 63
Squeamish Ossifrage, 17
stationary ergodic source, 100, 121
stationary source, 102
subroutine, 7
succeeding context, 97
successive doubling, 78
suffix
    L-suffix, 84
    proper, 52
    S-suffix, 84
    Type 1, 82
    Type 2, 82
    Type A , 86
    Type B , 86
suffix array, 75
    compressed, 266, 270
    construction from suffix tree, 78
    COPY algorithm, 86
    lightweight construction, 85
    QSUFSORT algorithm, 86
    space, 85
suffix link, 57, 59
    implicit, 62
suffix sorting
    COPY algorithm, 86, 87
    deep-shallow algorithm, 87
    derived, 86
    direct, 66, 78, 81
    Itoh-Tanaka algorithm, 86
    Ko and Aluru algorithm, 84
    KS Algorithm, 81
    Manber-Myers algorithm, 78
    order-k, 76
    QSUFSORT algorithm, 86
    traditional approach, 76
    TWO-STAGE algorithm, 86
suffix tree, 51
    cache interaction, 221
    compressed, 266, 267, 274
    construction, 54

Farach's construction, 66
for multiple pattern matching, 73
from LCA, 70
from suffix array, 274
generalized, 73
implementation issues, 74
implicit, 57, 64
node splitting, 63
parenthesis representation, 267
properties, 53
space, 85
space requirement, 74
suffix link, 57, 59
Ukkonen's algorithm, 57
suffix trie, 58
SZIP, 154, 161, 180, 314

θ (VLDC character), 204
T (input text), 309
tenth anniversary, 17, 314
test data compression, 284
test patterns, 284
Tiny Encryption Algorithm (TEA), 7,
    11
transform, 8
    DCT, 290
    DWT, 290
    Fourier, 9, 10, 290
    Roman numerals, 8
    Schindler's sort, 154
tree
    compressed suffix, 266, 267, 274
    even, 67
    keyword, 201
    odd, 67
    phylogenic, 284
    suffix, 51
    wavelet, 45, 50
tree-source identification, 299
trie, 54
    keyword tree, 201
    suffix, 58
turbo codes, 298
Type 1 suffix, 82
Type 2 suffix, 82
Type A suffix, 86
Type B suffix, 86

Ukkonen's suffix tree algorithm, 57

update rules, 58
unary code, 36, 49
universal code, 37, 49, 123
unmerge, 72

V (L and F mapping), 310
variable length don't-care character
    (VLDC), 204, 258
VLDC (variable length don't-care)
    character, 204, 258

W (inverse L and F mapping), 310
wavelet tree, 45, 50
web sites (BWT-related), 313

weighted frequency count (WFC), 43,
    50
Wheeler, David, 7
whole-genome annotation, 282
whole-genome comparison, 281
wild-card character, 204, 258
word-based BWT, 183
word-based compression, 180, 185
world192, 106, 222

ZIP, 6, 144
Zipf's law, 109, 111
Ziv-Lempel (LZ) coding, 6, 180